Empowerment Skills for Family Workers©
The Comprehensive Curriculum of the
National Family Development Credential Program

A Worker Handbook

Claire Forest, Ph.D.

Topic Editor: Carol West, M.A.

Copy Editor: Robert Kulik

Illustrator: Camille Doucet

Family Development Press

Within each person lies a bone-deep longing for freedom, safety, hope, self-respect, and the chance to make an important contribution to family, community, and the world. To live fully, we each need ways to express this powerful, natural longing.

Without healthy outlets, the desire for freedom turns into lawlessness, and the need for safety and self-respect degenerates into violence. Without avenues to make an important contribution, hopelessness translates into dependency, depression, violence, substance abuse and other forms of self-abuse.

No government program or religious group can help people become self-reliant, contributing members of their communities unless it is built on an understanding of this powerful force inside each human heart.

– Claire Forest, Ph.D.

Empowerment Skills for Family Workers©

A word about copyright

As author of *Empowerment Skills for Family Workers*© and related books, and to protect the integrity of the Family Development Credential (FDC) Program, I own the copyright to *Empowerment Skills for Family Workers*, its accompanying *Instructor Manual* and *Portfolio Advisor Manual, Empowerment Skills for Leaders*, all Family Development Credential exams and protocols, and all forms used in the management of the Family Development Credential Program. Likewise, as National Family Development Credential program director, I own the copyright to the website www.familydevelopmentcredential.org.

What is a copyright, and how does it affect me?
A copyright protects an author (or program developer) from others claiming that original author's work as their own, or from inserting bits and pieces of that work into their own without permission or proper attribution. Thus, the copyright protects the original work from being misrepresented. In the context of the current work, it helps ensure that people who earn the Family Development Credential have studied the genuine and authentic course.

How do I share what I've learned?
Enjoy your FDC class and its accompanying *Empowerment Skills for Family Workers* text book, and learn skillful ways to help families and yourself. I hope you are inspired! If you want to share what you're learning, you have many options; for example, you could:

- Offer a short workshop (e.g., for your co-workers or a community group). If you copy a short hand-out, leave the copyright and source statements intact. Send me a copy. Provide people in your workshop with the Web address of the National FDC Program (www.familydevelopmentcredential.org).

- Write an article, including short quotes from this book, with proper attribution; for example:
  "From Claire Forest, *Empowerment Skills for Family Workers* Ithaca, NY, Family Development Press, distributed by Cornell University Press Services, 2015)."
  When citing quotations, include the relevant page number(s).

- E-mail me with your feedback and experiences. I continue to learn from FDC workers, instructors, portfolio advisors, and state coordinators.

The Core Principles of Family Development

1. All people and all families have strengths.

2. All families need and deserve support. How much and what kind of support varies throughout their lives.

3. Most successful families are not dependent on long-term public support. They maintain a healthy interdependence with extended family, friends, and other people; spiritual, cultural, and community organizations and groups; schools and agencies; and the natural environment.

4. Diversity (race, ethnicity, gender, class, family form, religion, physical and mental ability, age, sexual orientation) is an important and valuable reality in our society. Family workers need to understand oppression in order to learn to work skillfully with families from all cultures.

5. The deficit approach, which requires families to show what is wrong in order to receive services, is counterproductive to helping families move toward self-reliance.

6. Changing from the deficit model to the family development approach requires a whole new way of thinking, not simply more new programs. Individual workers cannot make this shift without corresponding policy changes at agency, state, and federal levels.

7. Families need coordinated services in which all the agencies they work with use a similar approach. Collaboration at the local, state, and federal levels is crucial to effective family development.

8. Families and family development workers are equally important partners in this process, with each contributing important knowledge. Workers learn as much as the families from this process.

9. Families must choose their own goals and methods of achieving them. Family development workers' roles include helping families set reachable goals for their own self-reliance, providing access to services needed to reach these goals, and offering encouragement.

10. Services are provided so families can reach their goals, and are not in themselves measures of success. New methods of evaluating agency effectiveness are needed to measure program outcomes in families and communities, and not just count the number of services provided.

11. For families to move out of dependency, helping systems must shift from a *power over* to a *shared power* paradigm. Human service workers have power (which they may not recognize) because they decide who gets valued resources. Workers can use that power to work with families rather than use power over them.

– Claire Forest, Ph.D.
Empowerment Skills for Family Workers©

Table of Contents

Acknowledgments

To the families whose courage and creativity have shaped the work we call "family development," I offer my deep admiration and thanks. You called for a profound change in our nation's and state's approach families, told us what was needed, and continue to shape this work with generous feedback.

I proudly recognize as esteemed colleagues the thousands of front-line family workers who have earned the Family Development Credential, as well as the dedicated FDC Instructors and Portfolio Advisors who taught and guided you as you studied and applied my course *Empowerment Skills for Family Workers©*. Together with your forward-thinking organizations, you've stood side by side with me and the National FDC program, to reshape the way America treats families. Through your FDC work, you continue to recognize (and often uncover) families' inherent wisdom and drive toward healthier lives. I am heartened by the ways you've effectively used FDC methods to help families set and reach their own goals.

The Introduction of the 2003 edition of *Empowerment Skills for Family Workers* began:

> Twenty-five years ago I realized that the most effective way to help people live healthy, self-reliant lives was to help them reclaim their ability to dream of a better life, then use proven methods to set and reach their own goals.

My colleagues and I spent a quarter of a century practicing and developing the strengths-based methods called family development. In 1994, I wrote the first edition of *Empowerment Skills for Family Workers*, describing those methods in detail. There I thanked those who'd contributed to developing this work, including the New York State Council on Children and Families and the state agencies it convened, especially Evelyn Harris of New York's Department of State, Division of Community Services program. Meryl Jones of New York City's Department of Youth and Community Development has been a dedicated and skillful partner since FDC's inception, coordinating New York City's extensive FDC program, with collaboration of Joan Delaloye (now retired) of City College of New York (CUNY) and, more recently, Deborah Douglass.

In that earlier work, I gratefully acknowledged the remarkable environment Cornell University provided in which to birth and nurture the Family Development Credential through its early years, steeped in the atmosphere of Dr. Urie Bronfenbrenner's direct presence as he developed his Ecology of Human Development theory. I acknowledged Professor Moncrieff Cochran, who developed the initial four core principles of parental empowerment, which I incorporated into FDC's Core Principles (see Chapter 1). I expressed my appreciation for the Cornell FDC team, including Program Manager Joan Padula, staffer Georgia Howe, and later, FDC Sr. Instructor Dr. Katie Palmer-House's remarkable ability to inspire the confidence of FDC Instructors, as well as Department Chairs Professor Stephen Hamilton and Professor John Eckenrode, who both recognized FDC as a model of the land-grant outreach mission and thus accorded me appropriate latitude. I also noted my burgeoning system for training state FDC programs.

I also introduced the concept of FDC as "life coaching":

> The difference between our work and life coaching offered to corporate executives lies not in effectiveness, but in our public service orientation. Corporate coaches guide executives in developing the skills of visioning, goal setting, communication, stress reduction, managing diversity, and effective collaboration. [In FDC] we use our state-of-the-art leadership and educational acumen to bring guidance on similar topics to people trying to leave welfare, rebuild their lives from within homeless shelters, or become more self-reliant against other formidable odds. We also help overworked, underpaid health care and agency workers learn to apply these methods within their organizations and personal lives. Family development is helping to transform health care, human services, and education one person and one agency at a time, while also profoundly influencing state and federal policy. The cornerstone of our work is respect for each person's culture and definition of family.

In 2010, the National FDC Program moved to the University of Connecticut, still under my leadership. Here, Professor Sara Harkness, director of the Center for the Study of Culture, Health, and Human Development (CHHD), together with Co-Director Professor Charles Super and Associate Director Dr. Caroline Mavridis, warmly welcomed National FDC into CHHD's ecologically based translational research contributions. I continue to appreciate their steadfast wisdom. In 2012, the US Trademark Office awarded me the trademark for the name "Family Development Credential," thereby ensuring the integrity of the National FDC Program and protecting it from misrepresentation by others.

My long-standing collaboration with the National Head Start Association blossomed in 2012 into an invitation to lead a series of FDC Instructor Institutes at National Head Start conferences. This, plus collaborations with several universities, resulted in many new FDC state coordinators, as well as a large number of new FDC instructors adding their commitment to teaching FDC. With this solid and growing strength, the National FDC Program is ever better able to fulfill its mission of helping families, communities, states, and our nation become increasingly healthy and self-reliant.

In 2012, long-time FDC Instructor Carol West retired from Cornell Cooperative Extension then joined the National FDC team as senior instructor when Dr. Katie Palmer-House moved on from that role. As one of the first FDC instructors affiliated with Cornell FDC, Carol brought her remarkable breadth and depth of FDC experience, along with extensive background in adult education and consummate program development skills. Carol capably oversees the National FDC's Portfolio Review, co-leads FDC Updates and Instructor Institutes, stays in touch with FDC state coordinators and new FDC instructors, and advises on FDC curriculum updates. Carol is a consummate professional: honorable, knowledgeable, kind, and impeccable. In 2012, Amy Knight joined National FDC as Program Manager, ably serving as hub of the FDC office. Amy's is the pleasant voice greeting callers, eager to help with information, dates, and forms. Amy assists with many aspects of National FDC management, always with integrity and intelligence.

In 2014, National FDC expanded its University of Connecticut association to also include CEHHP (Center for Environmental Health and Health Promotion). I appreciate the warm welcome and collegiality of Pouran D. Faghri MD, FACSM, Professor of Health Promotion Sciences, Department of Allied Health Sciences, and Professor of Community Medicine and Health Care/Public Health, School of Medicine. Dr. Faghri's research on the health benefits of walking adds an important dimension to FDC's focus on health. I also appreciate the support of Dr. Nancy Bull, Interim Department Chair, Department of Allied Health Sciences, and Dean Gregory Weidemann College of Agriculture and Natural Resources. Their deep knowledge of the Land Grant University Outreach Mission enabled them each to grasp why National FDC is an ideal fit.

Many thanks also to Connecticut FDC State Coordinator Gina Beebe for serving so ably as National FDC state coordinator liaison from 2010–13. In 2014 we welcomed New Jersey State Coordinator Julissa Vizcaino into the position, to which she brings her own clarity and unifying energy.

I appreciate Carol West's insightful program edit of this 2015 edition, and Robert Kulik's skillful copy edit and layout. Illustrator Camille Doucet's artistic skill and appreciation of diversity continues to animate *Empowerment Skills for Family Workers* . Growing up in a multicultural society, Camille understood the importance of respectfully portraying people from a wide range of cultures.

With boundless gratitude, I thank my parents and grandparents for living principled, creative, welcoming, frugal lives that honored Mother Nature and each person's unique gifts. I marvel at the spirited family I helped to bring forth from these roots—the beloved ones who make me laugh, protect and help me; the "fleet-foot" who daily defies gravity and fills our home with friends young and mature; and my eldest son who explores the world's rivers in a quest to bring attention to the vital role of clean water in our lives. They call me outside to see the new moon overhead, cook me delicious meals, bring me berries, and humble me with the creative new ways in which they express the wilderness and farm life I shared with them as very young children. I am infinitely proud to be their mother. I give thanks for the remarkable clan of family and friends that surrounds and uplifts me with love, good food, protection, and laughter.

And now, I invite you along on this exciting, life-transforming journey we call the Family Development Credential!. Many thanks, and please keep in touch.

Claire Forest, Ph.D., 2015

Introduction to the 2015 Edition

The hectic pace of modern life poses a threat to our children second only to poverty and unemployment. We are depriving millions of children—and thereby our country—of their birthright … virtues, such as honesty, responsibility, integrity and compassion. The signs of this breakdown are all around us in the ever growing rates of alienation, apathy, rebellion, delinquency and violence among American youth.

It is still possible to avoid that fate. We now know what it takes to enable families to work the magic that only they can perform. The question is, are we willing to make the sacrifices and the investment necessary to enable them to do so?[1]

The responsibilities of the researcher extend beyond pure investigation, especially in a time of national crisis. Scientists in our field must be willing to draw upon their knowledge and imagination in order to contribute to the design of social inventions: policies and strategies that can help to sustain and enhance our most precious human resources—the nation's children.[2]

– Dr. Urie Bronfenbrenner

I was hired by Cornell University in 1981 to translate research from Professor Bronfenbrenner's landmark "ecology of human development" research into policies and practical programs designed to support families as they raised their children. I was blessed with the remarkable privilege of cultivating the Family Development Credential Program within Cornell's College of Human Ecology at a time when the atmosphere was directly steeped in Urie's presence and insights. He had co-designed Head Start a decade earlier and remained its persuasive champion.

Many other scholars and practitioners, trained or influenced by his vision, went on to develop innovative ways to support families and communities. My particular contribution was to develop new methods to train agency workers based on Cornell's research on the ecology of human development and parental empowerment. In 1993, anticipating federal Welfare Reform, the New York State Council on Children and Families asked Cornell for help in formulating family policy based on this research. I recommended establishing an interagency training and credentialing program for family workers and agency leaders. With leadership from Cornell, the New York Department of State, funding from the Robert Wood Johnson Foundation, and others, the Family Development Credential (FDC) program was launched as a means of implementing these theories within state agency practices. The goal was to infuse these state agency policies and practices with this new strengths-based approach.

In 1994, I wrote the first edition of *Empowerment Skills for Family Workers*, describing these methods in detail. I collaborated with New York State (NYS) agencies, as well as with hundreds of local agencies and workers, to create the NYS FDC program administered by Cornell University. As the first FDC classes completed their requirements and were awarded the Family Development Credential, other states approached me for help establishing systems using *Empowerment Skills for Family Workers* and these training and credentialing protocols. The FDC program grew.

In 2003, I updated *Empowerment Skills for Family Workers*, incorporating insights from a decade of practice and a growing body of research on the FDC program (see the General Appendix for an updated research summary). In 2010, because of restructuring at Cornell, the National FDC program moved to the University of Connecticut's Center for the Study of Culture, Health, and Human Development (CHHD). This move was facilitated largely by the CCHD's grounding in Bronfenbrenner's approach and ability to provide a stable, yet forward-thinking future for the FDC Program. I continued as director of the National FDC program and remain so today.

---

[1] Quoted by Jerome Bruner in Moncrieff Cochran and Rebecca Staples New, *Early Childhood Education: A–D* (Westport, CT: Praeger, 2007, p. 88).

[2] Urie Bronfenbrenner, *Making Human Beings Human: Bioecological Perspectives on Human Development* (Thousand Oaks, CA: SAGE, 2004, p. 272).

Bronfenbrenner's ecology of human development theory offered important insights into child development as well as into the adults and communities surrounding them. Today, more than ever, the insights and skills taught by the National FDC program guide adults and communities to develop the healthy relationships and family stability that are so necessary for children's healthy development. Thus, it was once again time to update *Empowerment Skills for Family Workers*. This new edition is informed by feedback from families and workers whose lives have been touched by the FDC, and by the research of many scholars who've studied it. This edition also responds to unprecedented changes in the world in which we live.

Family workers credentialed through the National FDC program at the University of Connecticut (and its official state partners) learn skillful methods of coaching families to envision a better life, then bring their dreams to fruition. This approach is based on "compassionate presence" and specific skills for building mutually respectful relationships that are the cornerstone of both productive worker-family relationships and relationships within families. As such, the National FDC program embraces diversity in its many forms.

The FDC program guides families to build healthier, more self-reliant lives, despite thorny circumstances like unemployment, serious illness, homelessness, or addiction in the family. We also help overworked, underpaid family workers learn to apply these methods within their organizations and personal lives.

Family development is helping to transform health care, human services, and education one person—and one organization—at a time, while also profoundly influencing state and federal policy. *The cornerstone of our work is respect for each person's culture and definition of family.* My recent research demonstrated that the relationship between a family and a worker credentialed by the FDC program (especially their dialog when using the Family Development Plan) engages families in the self-reflection that is so necessary for transformative learning to occur.

Today, as Dr. Bronfenbrenner predicted, not only is it the case that families' lives are hectic and too often fraught with poverty, but also the simple *presence* of a parent's warm cuddle is overshadowed, or even absent, for too many children. Addiction (e.g., to drugs or alcohol, credit card overuse, gambling, overeating unhealthy foods) is robbing millions of children of a healthy youth. The challenges and stressors of parents with limited education and poor job prospects—or increasingly, of middle-class parents newly weighed down by lay-offs, extreme debt, foreclosure, violent media, or, for military families, repeated deployments—show that Bronfenbrenner's concerns about chaos were well founded and almost prophetic.

This edition of *Empowerment Skills for Family Workers* offers strategies based on my own recent research on transformative learning, as well as on hopeful new research from others on positive psychology and neuroplasticity (the ability of the brain to change), and includes a new section on financial literacy and an expanded section on presence. I hope this edition will help family workers skillfully guide families in transforming their lives in the face of society's growing stressors. I invite you along on this transformative journey. Family development makes a difference!

Claire Forest, Ph.D.
2015

What is the Family Development Training and Credentialing Program?

The Family Development Credential (FDC) is a proven professional training and credentialing program in which family workers learn to engage families in self-empowerment. To earn the FDC credential, you are required to take the *Empowerment Skills for Family Workers* course as taught by an FDC instructor certified by the National Family Development Credential Program at the University of Connecticut, work with an FDC portfolio advisor to document your ability to practice the skills learned in the course, and pass the National FDC credentialing exam.

The FDC portfolio has three components:

- Activities to Extend Learning
- Skills Practices
- Family Development Plans

At the end of each chapter of this text, you will find an Activities to Extend Learning section, from which you will choose three activities and answer them in writing. You will then discuss your answers with your portfolio advisor, who may provide feedback in writing or in person.

For each chapter, you are also required to complete one activity from the Skills Practices, which you will develop in partnership with your portfolio advisor. First, you and your advisor will discuss your plan so that it is both meaningful and manageable. After completing your skills practice, you will write a short reflection on the experience. Your portfolio advisor will discuss the experience with you and provide written feedback.

The final component of the portfolio involves completing three Family Development Plans (an initial plan with two follow-up plans) that you will prepare with an agency family or colleague who identifies a goal and steps to achieve it. After the three plans are completed, you will write a one-page reflection on the strengths you recognized in yourself and the family through the experience, the skills and competencies practiced, and ideas for using empowerment-based support in future work with families.

Who are FDC instructors?

A certified FDC instructor is someone from your community who has been trained either directly by the National FDC program at the University of Connecticut, or by a state FDC system appointed by the National FDC program. To verify an instructor's certification, contact the National FDC office at (860) 486-0606, or e-mail nationalfdc@uconn.edu.

Your instructor will have experience helping adults learn new skills and is likely to work in a state, health, or human service agency. Some are faculty members at your local state or community college. Your instructor will:

- Lead activities to help you and the other front-line workers in your class understand *Empowerment Skills for Family Workers*
- Provide opportunities for you to practice your skills during the FDC class
- Help you become more familiar with services offered to families in your community
- Assign you a portfolio advisor
- Administer the FDC exam

Who are FDC portfolio advisors?

FDC portfolio advisors work in agencies or colleges in your community. Your advisor will help you develop an FDC portfolio to document the new skills you will practice over the course of your FDC training. Portfolio advisors are selected by FDC instructors and trained by your state's FDC system. In some cases, the FDC instructor also serves as portfolio advisor.

How do I earn the FDC Credential?

At the conclusion of your FDC course, your instructor and portfolio advisor will review your portfolio to ensure it is complete. You, the FDC instructor, and the portfolio advisor all sign the Application to Receive the

FDC Credential: Portfolio Checklist and Affirmations, verifying that you have satisfactorily completed the requirements to take the FDC Credentialing Exam. Your portfolio will then be sent to your state's designated FDC portfolio reviewer for approval.

Like all FDC applicants nationwide, you will take a multiple-choice exam. You must correctly answer 70 percent of the questions to pass. Results are returned as either "passed" or "not passed." Once your portfolio has been approved by your state's designated portfolio reviewer and you have passed the exam, a notification will be sent to the National FDC Office at the University of Connecticut, which will issue your Family Development Credential. (In some cases, a credential may be issued by a university in your state that has a written agreement with the National FDC program at the University of Connecticut.)

College credit, continuing education, and professional development through the FDC

Workers who earn the Family Development Credential can earn undergraduate college credit or continuing education units for professional development. Many community colleges allow you to apply the FDC toward an associate's degree in human services. Individual colleges determine specific courses and credits awarded as well as any other requirements for students to apply the FDC toward college credit. At this time, Charter Oak State College in New Britain, Connecticut is offering a "special credit registry." For a fee, credits earned from successfully achieving the FDC will be placed on a transcript. Applicants may then request that an official transcript be sent to their college of choice.

Individuals who receive an FDC from the University of Connecticut may also apply for Continuing Education Units (CEUs) through the University of Connecticut's Center for Continuing Studies, Academic Partnerships, and Special Programs. CEUs provide a means of documenting and awarding a record of participation for relevant professional development activities. For details, and the most current information regarding college credit and CEUs, check with your instructor or the National FDC Program office at the University of Connecticut.

For more information on how to earn the FDC, help your organization send instructors to the FDC for training, or establish an FDC system in your state or nation, please contact:

National FDC Program Manager
    University of Connecticut, Unit 2058
    348 Mansfield Road
    Storrs, CT 06269-2058
    Phone: (860) 486-0606
    Fax: (860) 486-0300
    E-mail: NationalFDC@UConn.edu

To order additional copies of *Empowerment Skills for Family Workers,* the accompanying *Instructors'* or *Portfolio Advisors* manuals, or *Empowerment Skills for Leaders,* use the order form available at http://www.familydevelopmentcredential.org/publication-order-form.pdf, contact Cornell University Press Services at http://www.cupserv.org/, or write to

Cornell University Press Services
    PO Box 6525
    750 Cascadilla Street, Ithaca, NY 14851
    Phone: (800) 666-2211 (USA/Canada)/(607) 277-2211 (international)
    Fax: (800) 688-2877 (USA/Canada); (607) 277-6292 (international)
    E-mail: orderbook@cupserv.org
    SAN: 202 1862
    Business hours: 8:30 a.m.–5:00 p.m. Eastern Time (US), Monday–Friday

Chapter 1
Family Development: A Sustainable Route to Healthy Self-Reliance

Objectives

A. Understand how to help families restore their sense of healthy self-reliance.

B. Explain ways the "providing services" orientation limits families and workers.

C. Describe why using the term "family development" is more empowering for families than "case management."

D. Discuss the core principles underlying the family development approach.

E. Explain the seven steps of family development and the seven roles of family development workers.

F. Discuss the differences between using the deficit and family development approaches.

G. Assist families to develop a plan for achieving a major goal of healthy self-reliance using the Family Development Plan.

H. Explore selected research on brain development and how it impacts transformative learning.

I. Recognize the importance of family systems and how poverty and environmental chaos impact health and development, starting in childhood.

J. Focus family development on the "here and now," and offer support based on a commitment to families' goals.

A. A bone-deep longing for freedom and self-respect

Within each person lies a bone-deep longing for freedom, safety, hope, self-respect, and the chance to make an important contribution to family, community, and the world. To live fully, we each need ways to express this powerful, natural longing.

Without healthy outlets, the desire for freedom turns into lawlessness, and the need for safety and self-respect degenerates into violence. Without avenues by which to make important contributions, hopelessness translates into dependency, depression, violence, substance abuse, and other forms of self-abuse.

No government program or religious group can help people become self-reliant, contributing members of their communities unless its approach is built on an understanding of this powerful force inside each human heart.

Replacing the self-sufficiency myth with healthy interdependence

Instead of promoting the myth of self-sufficiency—the idea that families should provide for all their needs without outside help—it is much more realistic to promote healthy interdependence with the rest of the community. Healthy families are interdependent with extended family members, friends, fellow members of spiritual organizations and cultural/social groups, neighbors, co-workers, businesses, organizations, schools, day care and health care providers, and others. Although they may not think much about it, they are also influenced by local, state, national, and international economic, political, environment, and social trends. No family is truly self-sufficient.

All families use some forms of public assistance: public schools, libraries, well baby clinics, Social Security insurance, safe roads, and public health departments are all publicly funded services. The difference between these and public assistance services (e.g., Medicaid, free lunch programs, some job training programs) is that only people of low incomes are eligible for the latter.

Most people do not want to be dependent on public assistance or agencies. The majority of Americans want the benefits of self-reliance: a good job, a nice house in a safe neighborhood, a reliable car, quality care for young children and elders, skillful medical care, feelings of pride and independence, and time to enjoy the "good life" with loved ones. Yet millions of people live every day faced with red tape, intrusions into their privacy, prejudice, and lack of dignity that go hand in hand with dependency on government programs.

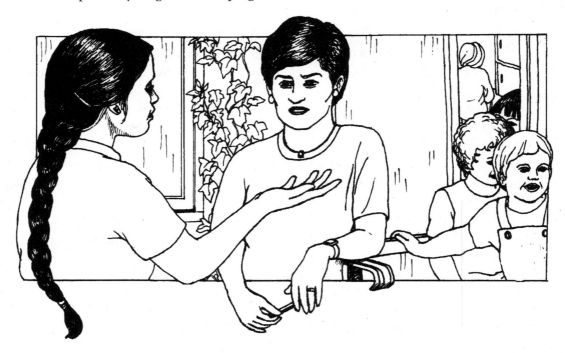

Increasingly, everyone, regardless of financial status, lives with the consequences of this cycle of dependency, including the violence that erupts when people must live without dignity, a poorly prepared work force, unhealthy children and elders living in poverty, and skyrocketing insurance costs. A woman who received public assistance said:

> My husband came down with epilepsy and lost his job because of it. We had to go on public assistance, which is a major killer to your pride, but you have to do it. And to get on PA, which is a huge fight, you call trying to get ahold of your case worker, and the phone is busy all day.

Another said:

> When I go in stores and use food stamps, I try to be the last in line. It's not always the cashiers; it's the other people behind me who look at me. It's embarrassing.

Yet today, in the wake of recent recessions, millions of the unemployed, ill, or laid off have turned to public assistance. Many families who have been on public assistance continually for generations have lost their faith in their ability to care for themselves. Family development is as important for these families as it is for those who are reluctant to accept help, but workers may have a much harder time showing long-term public assistance recipients the benefits of family development. Practical strategies for working skillfully both with families eager for family development help and with those who want to continue to get as many services as possible are included in each of the chapters in *Empowerment Skills for Family Workers*.

Restoring a sense of self-reliance and community

We need a reliable way to restore a sense of self-reliance and community to people who have lost faith in their ability to provide sufficiently for themselves and their families and live the "good life" with health and dignity. *Empowerment Skills for Family Workers* is a practical guide for family development workers to help themselves and the families they serve rekindle a sense of self-reliance and community, and build the skills they need to take good care of themselves and their families. *Empowerment Skills for Family Workers* also teaches family development workers how to collaborate skillfully with others to help communities become more supportive to families.

Front-line family development workers

The terms *family workers* and *family development workers* refer to people from public, private, and voluntary agencies, organizations, and businesses who work directly with families. Family development workers work with individuals, families with young children, teen parents, retired people, people with disabilities, and many other groups. By "families" we mean families at all stages of the human life span and all different family forms.

Although family development workers should have an appreciation for the whole family system and are encouraged to work with an entire family when possible, workers who use the family development approach with individuals are still doing family development work. Whether they serve an elderly person living alone, a developmentally disabled person living in a supervised apartment, or a single person in a homeless shelter, by using the FDC approach, they are doing family development work.

Family workers include:

- case managers
- social workers
- home health aides and direct care workers
- intake and social welfare workers
- community health or nutrition workers
- early intervention staff
- outreach workers
- employment and training counselors
- crisis intervention staff
- home visitors
- volunteers and paid staff in faith-based groups

In recent years, teachers, after-school program staff, utility company customer service advocates, probation and police officers, clergy, hospital staff, and funeral directors have also been earning the family development credential. Many community action agencies (sometimes referred to as "economic opportunity councils") and county departments of social services have trained their entire staff in the FDC.

Family workers are often paraprofessionals from the same neighborhoods as the families they work with. They may have first-hand understanding of the circumstances families face because they have "been there" themselves. And, as the benefits of family development become more widely understood, increasing numbers of professionals are graduating from colleges of social work with knowledge of this strengths-based approach.

As you embark on this journey, what is important in considering yourself a family development worker is to believe in the strengths of the families you work with, and to develop the skills needed to assist a wide range of families through the family development process. Families provide many crucial societal functions: nurturing children and teenagers, finding and keeping a place to live, earning money, obtaining food, cooking, cleaning, caring for elders, and getting along with neighbors. We also recognize that all families benefit from living in a community that supports them and encourages them to make a contribution. Likewise, families vary a great deal in the ways they approach these responsibilities.

B. Beyond "providing services"

The limits of providing services

Most human service programs have been built on the "providing services" approach, yet this approach is increasingly considered obsolete, as more agencies move toward strengths-based practice and outcomes-based evaluation. Still, it is important to understand this "services" approach, since many agencies base their practice on it while adding the expectation of more measurable outcomes.

In the providing services approach, workers assess what a "recipient" needs, determine eligibility and arrangements for the person to receive some of the services their agency offers, make referrals to other appropriate services, and provide incentives or pressures to get the recipient to follow through until those services are no longer needed. This approach sometimes works, assuming that a highly motivated, intelligent recipient is lucky enough to find a highly skilled, dedicated family worker to help piece together services to meet a clear-cut goal.

One example of this approach is a mother of young children using counseling, battered women's shelters, Temporary Assistance to Needy Families (TANF), job training, subsidized child care, Medicaid, Head Start, and subsidized housing to maneuver from an abusive marriage into a good job with medical insurance. Another example is a middle-aged family man who is disabled in a car accident, then able to rebuild his life with help from TANF, job retraining, home health care, and publicly provided adaptive equipment.

Unfortunately, examples of families who haven't made it even though services were provided are much more common, such as cases in which:

- training led to a low-paying job without medical insurance, forcing a return to TANF

- a serious medical need arose and services provided did not adequately meet the need

- a young mother's or a newly disabled person's shaky sense of her/his own strengths was undermined by a welfare system that constantly emphasized an inability to provide for her/his family's needs

- vital support services such as child care, job training, transportation, or home health care were cut off just when a person's efforts to rebuild his/her family's life were beginning to pay off ("success" turning into loss of support)

In addition, many agencies are moving toward measuring success by outcomes and not by number of services provided. When measuring outcomes, counting services provided becomes irrelevant; what matters is how a family's circumstances change as a result of a service. For that reason, the provision-of-services approach is becoming obsolete as an effective model of family support.

Discouragement of workers and families

Workers whose jobs depend on providing these services often feel just as discouraged as the families they work with. Workers watch a third generation of welfare mothers giving birth to children with dim futures. They see neighborhoods taken over by the violence of young men who see no other way to seize their share of the "good life." Workers labor under large caseloads, finding little time to follow up with any of the families they serve.

A program supervisor said:

> I don't think people trust people like they used to. There are so many drugs and killing and shootings, and you know, you're just afraid. A lot of people are afraid to go door to door, or do follow up or case management work. People aren't as cordial as they used to be and I don't blame them. If a stranger knocked at my door, I wouldn't answer it either.

Workers and families alike feel such frustration:

> Some workers, they see you in a certain category, in a certain program, so therefore they think you are a certain kind of person. And they think you are always going to be this way, instead of it being a temporary situation. [a family member]

> The belief that people can change is not always there, on the part of people or systems, due to regulations, hierarchy, personality or burnout. Line workers often have very little opportunity for influence in our own agencies, so I can imagine how the families feel. [a front-line worker]

The providing services approach is based on a set of assumptions, seldom discussed, that can be summed up as follows:

1. If families can't manage on their own, there is something wrong with them.
2. They need professionals to assess what is wrong and to prescribe services.
3. If families don't follow professionals' advice or it doesn't work, it must be the families' fault, and the appropriate professional action would be to withdraw services.
4. Providing services is the goal of human service agencies.

It will always be necessary to provide some services, because there will always be families with emergency needs for the basics of food, shelter, safety. Family development always starts with a family's present situation. If the family is hungry, out on the street, or scared, that need must be attended to first, as compassionately, respectfully, and efficiently as possible. As a family worker, you still need to know how to help families get the services they need. But family development only starts there. Once a family's crisis is stabilized, the process of working through the steps of family development that will lead to lasting positive change can begin.

C. Does case management empower families?

As a front-line family worker, you may collaborate with other agencies and the families you work with around "case management" or "case coordination." This usually means that a worker from one agency coordinates services or a plan of care from several agencies for one person or family. In the family development approach, it can also mean that a person or family manages its own services, sometimes with the help of a family development worker, sometimes on its own.

The term "case management" has a major limitation: referring to a person a "case" to be "managed" (or "coordinated") does not promote healthy self-reliance. It is much more empowering to refer to people by their names, and to the work you (and possibly others) are doing with them as "family development" or simply "work." You might help a person or family "coordinate services," but in doing so you are not really "managing a case."

It is essential that you keep in mind the effects of the labels we use in the empowerment process. Whenever possible, try to use more accurate, empowering words, even if people in other agencies or families you work with use outdated terms. An example of a more empowering term, suggested by Community Health Workers, is "care coordination." You can politely explain what you mean and why you use the words you do. The ultimate goal is to help families find and coordinate the services they need for themselves, so that eventually they will be able to do this work without your help.

These outdated terms are widely used, and in many cases are civil service classifications that will require a major change in perception at the systems level in order to change. Such changes can occur; remember that before "case manager" became widely used, other (not necessarily more empowering) terms were used. Until such changes in perception become widespread enough for "case managers" to be called "family development workers" or another term that recognizes the responsibilities and capabilities families have for their own development, it is important that you understand the effects and limitations of "case management." Be careful not to let your job title influence you to "manage cases" instead of helping family members build on their strengths and become increasingly capable of taking responsibility for managing their own lives within their communities.

Helping a person or family set a goal, decide what services it needs to meet its goals, and make the arrangements for those services are basic to family development. These services comprise a large part of what you will do with families, especially when you first begin to work together. In Chapter 8, you will learn much more about specialized services within your community and how to support families as they use these services to meet their goals.

Families sometimes need help coordinating services so they don't overlap, and so that important services aren't missed. Agencies can use different terms for the same program, which makes it hard for family members to know what is really useful to them. For example, a mother who immigrated to this country after several years in a refugee camp wanted to learn to speak and read English. She also wanted her children to be able to do well in school. Her son's teacher told her about a "family literacy" program at the school. One of her employers told her about adult education classes. Her other employer told her about "literacy volunteers." She knew that "literacy" means reading and writing, and that "education" is about school, but she was having trouble sorting out all these programs. When she went to her children's school for information, they told her about "ESL" classes—all of these terms causing her to be thoroughly confused! Also, her family badly needed dental care, but she had no idea where to go for help. This mother clearly needed someone to help her access and coordinate services for her family.

A worker in a focus group gave an example related to health services:

> A man lived in an area where we don't have very many general practitioners. They're really specialists that people go to. This man had arthritis and heart disease, so any time his arthritis was acting up, he would call the heart specialist because he had nobody else. But if you go to the heart specialist you get charged so much money, and then they run all the tests. And then the heart specialist would say, "Well, you know, I really think you should go see the guy who's a specialist in arthritis." So there we go to another specialist and use the system again. And all he needed was a primary care physician who would listen and say, "Increase your Tylenol dosage and you'll be fine."

Teaching the role of advocate

Sometimes families can find and coordinate the services they need, but run into a roadblock that requires a helpful advocate, or help learning how to advocate for themselves. For example, say that a family has written to their landlord, asking him to get someone to clean up trash left by a neighbor. The landlord, who lives in another state, has not responded to their letter (although their rent check was cashed). The garbage had begun to attract rats, so the family paid $20 to have a garbage hauler take the trash away. The following month, they took the $20 off their rent.

Within two weeks, the family received an eviction notice. Now they have turned to you for help. You had helped them find low-rent housing, and helped the father find a job when he was laid off.

At this point, the family needs an advocate, someone to stand by them to make sure they are treated fairly and spoken up for, if necessary. They may also need a referral to legal aid services. Your first task would be to coach them through advocating for themselves. In this case, they had tried to advocate for themselves by writing a letter to their landlord. Since the landlord didn't respond and then tried to evict them, they are likely to feel that they won't be successful if they write again. Ask them to brainstorm a list of options with you. Their list might look like this:

- Send the landlord another letter, explaining why we paid $20 less rent, and saying that we want to stay and don't think it is fair that he evict us. Give him our phone number and ask him to call us to talk about it.

- Find a new apartment. This one is not so great, anyway.

- Call the landlord and explain what happened.
- Report the landlord to the housing authority.

Advocating for themselves is a vital first step. There are times when advocating for them (e.g., calling or writing the landlord on your agency's letterhead) might be appropriate, but it is seldom the best first step. It is better to teach families how to advocate for themselves and stand by them as they try.

Often, families you work with will complain that another agency, school, or hospital has treated them unfairly by denying them services they believe they are eligible for, or treating them disrespectfully. You may hear similar complaints about a particular agency or agency worker from several families. Again, encourage families to advocate for themselves.

Here's an example from a focus group participant, who advocated for herself:

> I called the Commissioner, I wrote him and (her state Congressman) a letter because for two months in a row I went to get my food stamps and they weren't there. By the second month, I was feeding my kids free peanut butter and crackers for breakfast. We had no cereal, no eggs, nothing. I flipped. I called there; I was told that Mrs. [name] was sick, so she could not get to my work. I said, "I want to speak to the supervisor." I got on the phone with the supervisor: "I'm sorry but Mrs. [name] wasn't able to get you any food stamps." I don't care if that's the problem; I need you to get me into the system. "It's not my problem," she said, "that you don't go to work." "Do you realize what my kids had for breakfast?" I flipped. I wrote three letters. ... I did get a response, a call from the Congressman. He called [name] and [name] called me. He said, "Mrs. [name], you can get your food stamps at six o'clock." I said, "I knew I could."

Fueled by her desperation over her children's hunger, this mother advocated for herself. Your role as a family development worker is to teach people how to find information that will help them advocate for themselves, such as eligibility requirements, and to teach them effective communication skills. If they succeed, they will have learned skills that will help them in many other life situations. Only if their efforts don't work is it time for you to consider calling the worker at the agency at which the family encountered problems.

Playing the role of advocate

Sometimes a family is unable to advocate for itself, requiring you to intervene. When you intervene for a family, use the communication skills you will learn in Chapter 2, especially skillful listening and speaking. Be professional and courteous, even if you are outraged by what the family has told you. It's fine to express your own feelings. For example, you might say,

> I was dismayed to hear that you turned down [name] for food stamps. According to my understanding of the eligibility requirements, I believe this family is eligible. The mother asked for my help, but it is hard to help until I know whether they will have these benefits. I would be very appreciative if you could review this situation, and call me back, so I will understand. Would it be possible for you to call me back this afternoon? Or if you get tied up, I could call you back. Thank you very much for looking into this.

Remember that you will be most useful to more people in the long run if you are able to maintain good relationships and open lines of communication with other agencies.

D. Core principles of family development

Family development is based on the following core principles:[3]

1. All people, and all families, have strengths.
2. All families need and deserve support. How much and what kind of support varies over time.

---

[3] Contributions from earlier principles developed by the Family Matters Project and the Cornell Empowerment Group are gratefully acknowledged.

3. Most successful families are not dependent on long-term public support. They maintain a healthy interdependence with extended family, friends, and others; spiritual organizations, cultural, and community groups; schools and agencies; and the natural environment.

4. Diversity (race, ethnicity, gender, class, family form, religion, physical and mental ability, age, sexual orientation) is an important reality in our society, and is valuable. Family workers need to understand oppression in order to learn to work skillfully with families from all cultures.

5. The "deficit approach," which requires families to show what is wrong in order to receive services, is counterproductive to helping families move toward self-reliance.

6. Changing from the deficit model to the family development approach requires a whole new way of thinking, not simply more new programs. Individual workers cannot make this shift without corresponding policy changes at agency, state, and federal levels.

7. Families need coordinated services in which all the agencies they work with use a similar approach. Collaboration at the local, state, and federal levels is crucial to effective family development.

8. Families and family development workers are equally important partners in this process, with each contributing important knowledge. Workers learn as much from the process as do families.

9. Families must choose their own goals and methods of achieving them. Family development workers' roles include helping families set reachable goals for their own self-reliance, providing access to services needed to reach these goals, and offering encouragement.

10. Services are provided so families can reach their goals but are not themselves measures of success. New methods of evaluating agency effectiveness are needed to measure family and community outcomes, not just the number of services provided.

11. For families to move out of dependency, helping systems must shift from a "power over" to a "shared power" paradigm. Service workers have power (which they may not recognize), because they decide who gets valued resources. Workers can use that power to work with families rather than use power over them.

E. Understanding family development

Seven steps of family development

Family development is an effective way of applying these principles to the practical problems faced by families trying to lead healthy, self-reliant lives. This process, which is empowering for both families and workers, has seven important steps:

1. The family *develops* a *partnership* with a worker.

2. A worker helps the family *assess its needs and strengths* in an ongoing process.

3. The family *sets its own major goal* (e.g., providing care for a disabled family member or getting off welfare) *and smaller goals* that build toward the major goal, then identifies ideas for reaching them.

4. The worker helps the family *make a written plan* for pursuing these goals, with some tasks being family members' responsibility and some the worker's. Accomplishments are celebrated, and the plan is continually updated.

5. The family *learns and practices skills* needed to become self-reliant in an ongoing process.

6. The family *uses services as stepping stones* to reach goals.

7. The family's *sense of responsibility, self-reliance, and strength is restored*. Each family member is likewise affected through the family development process, and thus better able to meet future challenges.

The steps do not always occur in this order. Most families will spiral through several of the steps more than once before reaching and sustaining their major goal.

Families vary in the help they need. Some already have a clear goal and many resources for reaching it, needing only one or two short-term services. For most families seeking help, though, the process of gaining a sense of self-reliance requires much more help.

Their capacity to take good care of their families has been hurt both by their own personal and family experiences and, all too often, by a complicated, bureaucratic human services system that focuses on clients' weaknesses and provides them with fragmented services, without the kind of goal-setting and skill-building help they really need. Workers commented:

> Some people are so damaged they need time for healing. I try to help them figure out the next step, make some order out of the chaos.

> My goal is to find out what the family's goals are. And that's not an easy task because people have been conditioned by a system that traditionally told them what their goals ought to be.

> Some families are system-scared. They have so many people working with them we are tripping over one another. We use the same buzzwords but we don't have the same training, skills, or approach.

> Tremendous barriers are created by having to meet numbers, and by competition for funding. There are too many agencies involved, picking up the pieces due to fragmentation, short-term funding, instead of one agency doing long-term work with the family, picking up all the different angles.

Seven roles of family development workers

Family development workers have seven major roles:

1. To help families restore their sense of *self-respect,* self-reliance, and hope.
2. To help families reclaim their *dreams of a better life.*
3. To help families assess their own *strengths and needs,* reflect critically on how they arrived where they are, and determine what will help them move toward self-reliance.
4. To help families create their own *long- and short-term goals.*
5. To help families gain *access to the services* they need to reach these goals.
6. To encourage families to develop their own *strengths* as they move toward their goals, including developing and practicing *needed skills.*
7. To encourage *communities* to support families.

Empowerment Skills for Family Workers will help you learn practical ways to use the family development approach to help families become more self-reliant.

F. Power and family development

The goal of family development is empowerment of families and the communities they live in, so families will be better able to reach their goals of health and self-reliance. The more you understand power dynamics, the better able you will be to form mutually respectful and productive relationships with a wide range of families.

What does power have to do with family development?

Family development is a dynamic process through which families reach their own goals. No one can truly empower someone else. In order to build their capacity to take good care of themselves, families must first reclaim their ability to envision a better life, then set and reach their own goals. The more you understand power dynamics, the better able you will be to form mutually respectful relationships with a wide range of families, and facilitate this process by helping them successfully navigate toward reaching their goals. This also means helping communities, states, and nations to create the conditions by which families can reach their own goals, which may mean changing human service systems.

Family development is not a one-time goal to be attained, but an ongoing process that feeds itself and the development of others. When one family member becomes more self-reliant, the rest of the family, and its community, also benefit.

Limits of the deficit approach

Family development is the opposite of the deficit approach, which focuses on a family's weaknesses (or "deficits"), with the primary goal of moving people off of public services. This deficit model is currently the most common approach to providing family services in the United States, although not very many agencies or family workers realize that they use this approach. The deficit model originated in the welfare services of the last century, in which churches and other organizations provided food, shelter, and other basic services to society's "unfortunates." The current human service system has also been influenced by the medical system, where expert doctors diagnose problems and prescribe treatment.

The deficit approach forces families to show what is wrong before they can get the services they need. For example, it is hard for parents to get help with child care so they can work to support their families. Yet, if they abuse their children, they are given care to prevent further abuse. Another example is the senior citizen who has to show receipts from her bills and social security checks to prove lack of funds before being given food stamps. She might decide that food stamps are not worth the invasion to her privacy and independence, and choose instead to do without enough food.

Some empowering alternatives to these examples would be to offer child care programs that are available to all families on an affordable, sliding fee scale, and a community lunch for senior citizens at which they can make a donation based on their resources.

Crises usually result from relatively small problems that have been neglected until they fester and become major problems. Yet it is easier and less expensive to resolve a small problem rather than a full-blown crisis. Under the deficit approach, agencies wait until families are in crisis before offering "help," and then require that families accept it. During a crisis, people don't feel very capable or worthwhile, and their ability to make good choices and act resourcefully is limited. Although crisis services are necessary, it is much better for agencies to provide supportive services to families early on and without embarrassing conditions such as the invasion of privacy, so fewer crises will occur.

Family Development versus the deficit approach

The deficit approach assumes that it is a worker's role to find out what is wrong with a family, then decide how best to fix it. It's all too easy to fall into a relationship with families (or "clients") in which we assume it is our job to diagnose their problem(s) and prescribe (and even enforce) a solution. This approach is based on *three faulty assumptions*:

1. The family is providing the worker with all the information relevant to their situation.
2. The worker knows what's best for the family.
3. The family will follow up on whatever treatment plan we create for them.

It is seldom that simple, and it can be frustrating when families do not follow through on plans we make for them. When they don't, we might label them "noncompliant," then take away services. The problem sometimes lies not in the family's noncompliance but with the plan itself. Although the family still needs services, family members may conclude that the particular plan offered does not serve their needs. In that case, taking away services amounts to punishing the family for knowing their own needs better than the worker—as they naturally would, since they have much more access to information about their lives than the worker does.

In the family development approach, we assume family members know best what their strengths and problems are, and that they will be most successful in accomplishing plans they create. The worker's role is to help them recognize their strengths and challenges, and to help them set and reach their own goals. A family development worker is more like a midwife who attends a birth but leaves the mother in charge. Unless there is a life-threatening crisis (requiring intervention), we work best with families when we assume that we are there to support the family in "giving birth" to their new family life—one that works better to meet their needs.

Table 1-1. The Family Development/Deficit Approach

Concept	Family Development	Deficit Approach
Family attitude	"I am responsible for my family's future"	"The system owes it to me"
Family-worker relationship	Family–family development worker partnership; families set their own goals	Professionals decide what families need
Worker philosophy	What is *strong* with this family (and how can we help them build on it)?	What is wrong with this family (and how can we make them fix it)?
Worker focus	Focus on supporting ongoing healthy family development	Focus on current crisis
Power dynamic	Shared power ("power with")	Wielded power ("power over")
Worker view of diversity	Diversity is valuable	People should "fit in"

"Power over" or shared power?

An understanding of power is important for family workers, because power—and the ways people and organizations use (or abuse) it—has a strong influence on whether families stay dependent or become self-sufficient. Simply put, understanding power can help you, the family worker, be more effectively with families.

Power is an uncomfortable idea for many people. Everyone has had bad experiences in which someone else abused power, leaving the abused feeling angry, betrayed, or bewildered. Whether this experience was with a playground bully, a trusted parent, or an institution (like a school or the police), it usually left us with bad feelings regarding power. When most people talk about power, they mean one person or institution having power over others. "Power over" is not the only kind of power, but it is the one most familiar.

People react in different ways to bad experiences they have had with power. Some want to get as much power as they can themselves, so they won't again become victim of its abuse. Some try to avoid the whole issue by focusing on helping others, or by numbing their feelings through addictions or keeping constantly busy. Others resign themselves to not having power. In all of these cases, people preserve a power-over structure in which some wield power and others feel powerless. Within this framework, it is very difficult to establish a trusting relationship that fosters self-reliance.

When families have to turn to agencies for help, they often feel powerless. Even when the family worker at the agency respects family members and wants to help them, those asking for help remember all the people who have used power-over tactics on them, their family, and others in their cultural group. Those memories of past injury cause them to feel suspicious of the worker's intentions.

People seeking help would rather have what they need for their families without having to depend on an agency. Their embarrassment and wounded pride foster defensiveness, another barrier to trust.

A family worker's attitudes and workplace limitations can also interfere with trust building. When the family worker does not respect a family, it is very difficult for a trusting relationship to develop. Unfortunately, it is very common for agency family workers to lack respect for the families they work with. Kathy Castania of the Cornell Migrant Program Diversity Group has written:

> All of us have learned to play roles that perpetuate the power imbalance. These roles seem natural to us because we were born into them and they were taught and reinforced through our families, schools, and other institutions. People in the dominant groups (such as men, able-bodied, white, native-English speakers, adults, Christians, wealthy) assumed roles of superiority.
>
> Much of our learning came in subtle forms and without language, so we often learned from nonverbal communication as well as media images. The lack of positive models left us without guidance about how to think and act toward others and how to think about ourselves. ...

In our dominant roles, we can choose to act on the misinformation we received and become an *agent* of the continued perpetuation of the system of inequality, or we can become an *ally*, working to change the way we think and act. The process of moving from *agent* to *ally* is long. It requires commitment and conscious behavior. It means making mistakes and continuing to act in alliance with people [who belong to groups with less power].[4]

A woman who has been a recipient of services, and is also a family worker, noted:

I have run into a few workers where if we had a mutual client who was a single parent or someone you would consider low income, the worker tended to take an air of superiority, as though they could rule the person's life and make them do things. And that's very disheartening.

Another family member said:

With Ekemini [her worker], I feel a bond. The other workers, they came in with this kind of attitude. There's a big difference there. A lot of people, they come and they tell you to do this or you have to do that. And if you don't do this, this is going to happen. With Ekemini, we're going to do this to benefit Peter [her child]. This is teamwork. We work as a team. And there's a big difference! Because if you come into somebody and you're telling them "Oh, you have to do this," nobody wants to listen to you.

Along with disrespect, a worker's need for control over the family can make it hard to build trust. A family worker may have ideas about helping that a family member doesn't find very helpful. The worker may become disappointed in the family member for not succeeding quickly using the worker's ideas.

Finally, even if an atmosphere of trust exists, and a worker and family agree about the kind of help needed, the family worker may not be able to offer it because the agency doesn't offer that service, or the worker may have too many families to help. For whatever reason, if the worker cannot offer a service, trust is weakened.

Because trust is so difficult to establish in them, *relationships built on the power-over approach almost never help families become self-reliant.* They may lead to meeting some short-term goals of the family or the agency, but they do not create the conditions that lead to the family being able to care for itself in the long term.

The power-over approach is not cost-effective, either, although it might seem to be at first. It costs significantly more for the government to have to keep dealing with a family's problems than it does to work in depth with them for a relatively short time to help them set and reach goals they believe in themselves, and become more self-reliant in solving their future problems.

For example, when a young person is in trouble with the law for the first time, it is much more cost-effective to take the time *then* to build trust with him and his family, help them set goals they believe in, and find ways to reach them, than it is to pay later for residential drug treatment, covering the costs of raising the baby he and his girlfriend might have, convicting him of a crime, sending him to jail, and then supporting him, off and on, for life because he lacks the education and motivation to get a good job.

Why adding another program is not enough

The goal of restoring dignity and self-reliance to families cannot be accomplished by adding another new program to the existing social service structure. Empowering families to take responsible control over their own futures, and urging communities to become more supportive of families, requires an underlying paradigm shift, a whole new way of thinking and working based on strengths rather than only on providing services. This requires not only that individual family workers learn new skills, but also that human service agencies at local, state, and federal levels approach families in an entirely different way.

---

[4] Kathy Castania, *Diversity* (Ithaca, NY: Cornell Cooperative Extension, 1996). Diversity Fact Sheet #1.

Providing services alone has failed to help substantial numbers of families become healthy, self-reliant members of their communities, yet most welfare reform proposals still use variations on this approach. Revisions of this providing-services approach—even major ones—will not move families toward dignity and self-reliance. We cannot expect the tools and methods of that approach to build empowered, self-reliant families, even though on the surface there are some similarities between the two models. In order to promote strong, empowered families who can take care of themselves and create sustainable healthy relationships within their communities, building blocks based on strengths, healthy relationships, and an understanding of empowerment must be used. Tools and methods based on what is wrong with families (their deficits) and on professionals doling out services cannot, in the long term, lead to strong families.

For example, a senior citizen might need help with heating bills during a long, cold winter. Before she can receive help, she must fill out many forms and present overdue fuel bills. The process is very demoralizing to this proud woman, who doesn't want to take "welfare." No one at the agency has time to talk with her about her family, neighbors, and church (who might be willing to help, if they knew of the problem). She leaves the agency without completing the "intake" process and goes home to turn down the thermostat. A month later she is brought to a hospital emergency room by ambulance with severe pneumonia. Her medical bills (paid for by Medicare) are far more expensive than the cost of weatherizing her home or subsidizing her fuel bills during a particularly cold winter. When the hospital calls her relatives and minister, they express dismay that no one had informed them earlier of her need. When the woman's daughter, called by the hospital, inquires about local services to help her mother return home, she ends up talking to the same worker who gave her mother the forms to fill out for heating bill assistance two months earlier. She is told that "Your mother never completed the intake process."

If a family development worker had established a mutually respectful relationship with this elderly woman, found out who among her network might help, and followed through, it would have strengthened the woman's ability to help herself (which she wanted to do), protected her health, and saved the government thousands of dollars. Even if the worker had been successful in finding the woman help with her fuel bills this time, unless the worker used the tools and methods of empowerment (for example, inquiring about family and friends who might be able to help, and getting the house insulated), this elderly woman would be back year after year needing more money for her fuel bills.

Positive response of family workers

Throughout a quarter century of helping families, agency workers, and policy makers shift to the family development approach, we have found many very relieved to hear about it. Many people have said something like this to us:

> This is how I have been trying to work with families, but until now 1 haven't known the words for what I'm trying to do. It has been an uphill battle because my agency (or the regulations that govern my agency) works in the opposite way. It is wonderful to discover that without knowing it, I have been part of a major national movement to transform family services.

Although making this change requires a new way of thinking, most family workers are able to do it quite readily *because it is in harmony with what they feel and believe as people.* Many of the skills you have learned as a friend, family member, and community member will combine well with what you will learn in this training program.

For example, when your friend tells you about a problem she's having, you naturally want to help. After listening to her description of the problem, you tell her about some community resources you know about, and help her brainstorm possible solutions. You don't say, "You must do this, otherwise I'll cut off contact with you"—which you might be required to say to a client in your agency. You reflect your friend's good points back to her, help her explore her options, and keep the door open for the future. *These are the same skills that will help you be a successful family development worker.*

Building partnerships based on shared power

For families to become more self-reliant, family member(s) seeking help and a worker need to create a partnership. *Empowerment Skills for Family Workers* teaches you, as family worker, how to *share power*—and responsibility—with the families you will work with.

The deficit approach teaches us to see the helping relationship as one in which those seeking help bring little to the table, while the helpers bring their training, experience, and knowledge of available resources. The partnership model recognizes that each partner brings important information and abilities to the table. Family members know their own families best, have dreams for their families and ideas about how to reach them, and often have many of the practical skills needed to do so.

Family members are well aware of workers' power. Workers have power over resources that families need, like money, housing, food, education, and jobs. To build the trust that supports self-reliance, we workers need to recognize our own limits, as well as the assets of the family. When family members and family workers share power, there is agreement on the purpose of the partnership, and talk about what each partner brings.

The services-focused approach teaches workers to "diagnose" families' "problems," then "prescribe" solutions. This process seldom builds self-reliance. Instead, it teaches families dependency by conveying the message that they need an outsider to solve their problems. In the shared-power partnership model, workers help family members clarify their own goals, and create and follow a practical plan for reaching them. This way, workers teach family members the skills to manage future problems themselves—the skills of self-reliance.

One of the benefits of the partnership model is that workers can learn as much from the relationship as the family members they are trying to help. A worker in a focus group said:

> When I visit a family, it's usually because something isn't working out. So I say, let's figure out what's not working and how we can facilitate change to make it work. A lot of what I'm doing is really educating and giving people skills to help them manage their lives better, so that we can all manage our lives better. I'm in a partnership with them. I'm helping them develop skills for critical thinking. I think I'm building these skills for myself as well.

It takes courage and confidence to work with people in a shared partnership. You let go of the protective sense of superiority. You reveal your own vulnerability when you admit you don't have all the answers. The reward is the opportunity to grow through your work, and to *really* help people. Another worker commented:

> I developed a partnership with the family. That is an ongoing process. I go into the home weekly and listen to them. Not judge them. Not necessarily give them advice either. I am not a therapist, but listen to their strengths and point them out as we are talking, because sometimes they don't see their strengths.

Choice is essential to shared power, but people who live in poverty or with another ongoing serious problem are often denied the choices others take for granted. A family member in a focus group commented:

> Rich people can decide what they want to do. Poor people are usually told what they have to do.

If you make choices for family members, either directly or indirectly—by presenting only a narrow range of possibilities—you take away the power of choice, sending an unspoken message that you lack confidence in the family's ability to make wise choices. This message chips away at the family's confidence in themselves, which is already shaken by their crisis, setting the stage for dependency.

In contrast, when you offer choices but do not make decisions for family members, you send a message of confidence: "I believe you can do it." One family worker said:

> Some people are so used to people telling them what to do—You have to do this, you have to do that—like a parent with a kid. Instead, we should let people start thinking, well, maybe I have other options instead of staying in this. Maybe I can do this. Then they would feel better about themselves too, because they made their own decision and they got themselves out of their trouble themselves.

When people have reasonable choices, and the power to carry through with their choices, they are much more motivated to bring their own resourcefulness to the hard work of moving their families out of dependency, and to stay committed when faced with obstacles.

G. The Family Development Plan

Workers can use strengths-based tools as part of their efforts to work in partnership with families. The Family Development Plan is a profoundly simple assessment tool, based on the seven basic principles of strengths-based assessment, that gives you and the family *shared responsibility* for assessment.

Families decide what they need and want. Their ideas for reaching their own goals are considered important resources. The family member's own words are used to describe their goals and concerns. You and the family each keep a copy of the Plan, which is updated each time you meet. If used consistently and respectfully, the Family Development Plan can become a powerful tool in promoting family development.

The first time you meet, offer the family a new file folder for their forms, and tell them you'll also keep your copies in a folder. Tell them you'd like them to update the plan with you each time you meet. Each time you meet with the family, bring the copy you and the family member filled out last time, plus blank forms. Be sure to bring pens and carbon paper if you can't use a copy machine. (If your agency keeps records on computer, make a paper copy to give to the family.) These Family Development Plans, completed over time, provide a record of the family's work with you, and make it easy for you and the family to see what progress is being made.

You and the family member agree on what information goes into the record, and you each keep a copy. You both have tasks to do after each meeting, and discussing progress on these tasks forms the basis for the next meeting. Since introducing the Family Development Plan in 1994, we have seen widespread changes in how agencies do assessments. Many agencies have replaced their former assessment forms and procedures with the Family Development Plan, or where that has not been possible, have revised the forms and protocols to more closely reflect Cornell's strengths-based assessment principles. Here is what typical agency workers have said about using the Family Development Plan.

> The Family Development Plan helps a whole lot because in the process of making the goals, accomplishing the goals, they're building self-confidence. They're learning on how to actually walk the walk on their own and by the time the goal is accomplished they've accomplished something and they feel good about it. They feel like, "Okay, I had input in it. I started it and finished it." I think it really helps a whole lot.

> A lot of times, I would just automatically write and now I let them know that this is their plan and their goal, and ask, "Would you like to write or would you like me to?" A lot of people I work with don't have reading or writing skills, or are limited. I'm involving them more in everything. Making sure they know that these papers I have are theirs; that they're confidential. That I'm here to help them accomplish not what I want, but what they want.

> When I first started, I was doing most of the work and doing what they needed to do. I was setting the goals. Five months from now, it will be hard to say "five months ago, you wrote this goal and now you've achieved it" if they didn't write it.

> It's a process for families to set their own goals. It's important for me to step back and not set goals for them. The goals are something they set for themselves. My role is to help empower them and provide the education that they need to achieve the goals. The whole process became a lot clearer when I took FDC training.

A family member stated:

> I am glad that I got hooked up with Mercedes [worker]. We wrote my goals on a Family Development Plan. She doesn't really have to spell out the steps for me that much because I am the type of person where if you tell me one thing I can go and do it myself. Mostly I just need help getting places.

FAMILY DEVELOPMENT PLAN

Instructions to the Family Worker

Please ask the family if they want to fill out the form or want you to write. If you write, be sure to use their words. If the family wants you to do the writing, read aloud what you have written. Ask the family for any corrections, and make the requested corrections on all the sections except those "in the worker's words." Give a copy to the family, and keep a copy in your file. Each of you should review the form before your next meeting, to make sure you've each taken the steps you've agreed on. Begin your next meeting by reviewing the last Plan.

- **Family member's name** (Note any preferred title; e.g., Mr., Mrs., Miss, Ms.)
  _____

- **Address** _____
  _____

- **Phone(s)** (note whether Home, Work, Friends', etc.)
  _____

- **Other family members involved in family development process.** (Let family define who they consider family members. Note ages and gender.)
  _____
  _____
  _____
  _____

- **Today's date**_____ • **Worker's name** _____

- **Goal** (in family member's words)
  _____
  _____
  _____
  _____

Help the family brainstorm possible steps leading to their goals.

  _____
  _____
  _____
  _____

Help family choose steps to take. (Note date each will take place.)

Steps family will take and when   Progress/Obstacle

  _____
  _____
  _____

Steps worker will take and when   Progress/Obstacles

  _____
  _____
  _____

At your next meeting, note progress or obstacles to each step.

- **Family strengths and resources** (in family member's words)

- **Family strengths and resources** (in worker's words)

- **Concerns** (in family member's words)

- **Concerns** (in worker's words)

- **Services available** (include details such as names, addresses, phone numbers hours, etc.)

- **Notes**

- **Family member's signature** and **date**

    _____

- **Worker's signature and date**

    _____

- **Next meeting date, time, place**

    _____

IF YOU CAN'T KEEP THIS APPOINTMENT, PLEASE CALL _____

AT _____ BY _____ .

THANK YOU FOR YOUR COURTESY.

Adapted from Christiann Dean, *Empowerment Skills for Family Workers,* 1996, updated 2003.

Using the Family Development Plan: An example

Ms. Williams, the young mother whose Family Development Plans are described below, said that she needed child care in order to reach her goal of getting a job to support herself and her daughter. She brainstormed possible ideas, and then chose those she thought most likely to lead to her goal. Her series of Family Development Plans reminded her and her worker of her goal, stated what she needed to reach this goal, recorded her ideas for fulfilling this need, and traced her progress in meeting her goals. Her strengths and concerns (from her point of view as well as from the worker's) are noted. Available services are listed.

All of this information is recorded on the same form (updated regularly), with both Ms. Williams and her worker keeping copies. Think of how this form compares, from her perspective, to a standardized assessment in which she would simply check a box saying she needed child care.

The Family Development Plan provides a good balance between completely non-standardized assessment (in which a worker responds to whatever concerns a family brings up, taking whatever notes she feels are needed) and highly standardized assessment (in which a family or a worker checks off needs from a general list at the first "intake" meeting). There is some standardization (the same form and procedure is used with many families), so it is possible for a program, policy maker, funder, or researcher to look at trends across many families, if the families give written permission for their forms to be reviewed by these people.

Let's look at Ms. Williams' Family Development Plans. Ms. Williams, a teenage mother, wanted to get a job so she could support herself and her two-year-old daughter. When Ms. Williams applied at a fast food restaurant, the manager said he would hire her part time at minimum wage. If she wanted health insurance, she'd have to have it deducted from her paycheck. She did some figuring and quickly realized she wouldn't earn enough to pay the rent and other expenses, no matter how thrifty she was. But, she said that, before she dropped out of school when her baby was born, she was enrolled in a computer course at BOCES, which she enjoyed. She thought she could make better money if she finished this course.

This goal is concrete, specific, and measurable. When completing the Family Development Plan, it is important to encourage families to be specific about their goals and the steps needed to reach them. In this situation, "further my education" would be too broad a goal. "Finish computer course so I can get a job that will support myself and my daughter" is specific enough for you and her to know if the goal has been reached. Write it on the Plan and ask her if it is accurate (or she can write it herself).

Before you work together on the steps leading to their goal, and what steps each of you might take, it helps to brainstorm all the possible steps that could be taken. You can teach the family the rules of brainstorming: all ideas are written down; no judgment until the list is finished; and the goal is to get as many ideas as possible, even if some seem crazy. Once you have a list, you can talk about how practical each item is, and then choose those you want to write on the Family Development Plan. One worker said:

> I find brainstorming particularly useful and an integral part of any problem solving process. It is freeing in that it allows a flow of creativity, and can help a person become "unstuck." A side benefit is that it frees the mind by getting it all down on paper, and helps the person make an informed choice.

Next, ask the family member what strengths and resources she can bring to her goals. Then add your own observations. Ms. Williams might have said, "I liked computers when I took it before, and I was pretty good at it." She might have added, "Maybe my mom would take care of Alicia while I go back to school, or maybe my sister would." (You might have to ask, "Is there anyone who could help you with child care?")

Ask the family member you're working with whether she would like to record the items or she would prefer you to do so. If you do it, ask her if what you've written is accurate. You can tell her the strengths you observe as well, such as, "I noticed you were on time for our appointment. That will help you in school, and will help you keep a job once you've finished the word processing course, too. And I appreciate it." In this situation, you might write, "Mother or sister might help with child care; was on time for appointment" under the section on strengths and resources worker's words. Ask her whether these items are accurate.

Ask her about her concerns, too. At the first meeting, she might tell you she is worried about her car breaking down. Note that on the Plan, and ask if it is accurate (or she can write it in).

Later on, when trust has been built, she might tell you that she is concerned about her daughter growing up as an only child, and wonders if she should get pregnant again. She has a boyfriend now, and thinks it would be great to have a baby with him. You could ask her if she would like information about birth control while she is sorting out how another baby would affect her job goals. At that point, you can ask her if she wants to enter that under "concerns" on that week's plan. She might feel it is too personal to put in writing, a feeling you need to honor. Once more trust has been built, you could revisit these issues.

At the next meeting, you and Ms. Williams will discuss the progress you've each made, and fill out the Plan anew. Perhaps you have found that the local vocational center has an adult word processing course starting in three weeks. Classes take place downtown, from 8 a.m. to 2:30 p.m. Monday through Friday, and last twelve weeks. People who finish the course successfully receive a certificate and referrals to jobs. The cost is $850.

You found out Ms. Williams is eligible for $150 per week for child care subsidy while in class, while she looks for work, and for the first six months of a new job. You brought the forms she needs to fill out, and the name, address, and phone number of the office. Ask whether she wants to fill out the child care subsidy forms now with you or fill them out later herself.

Ask Ms. Williams for her ideas on paying for the word processing course, and tell her whether she is eligible for job training funds. She tells you her car has been breaking done a lot, and she's worried about getting to class. She's also worried about good clothes to wear to the course. You ask if she has any resources for dealing with these concerns. She doesn't have any ideas. You tell her that students in the auto mechanics course will sometimes work inexpensively on people's cars. She says she'll call them back and find out about it. You tell her about a free-clothes closet at the Women's Building, where women can get clothes for job interviews or to start new jobs. You offer to find out whether she can use this service to get back-to-school clothes. Note that as she takes "ownership" of her own family development process, her list is growing longer than yours.

Ask Ms. Williams whether she wants to fill out the form or wants you to do so. If you write, use her words. If she wants you to do the writing, read aloud what you have written. Ask her for any corrections, and make the corrections she requests on all the sections except those "in the worker's words." If you are entering your notes on the laptop computer provided by your agency, ask her if she has a computer and e-mail address, and if so, whether she would prefer a written copy or one that you send her via e-mail. Keep an additional copy on file. Both of you should review the form before your next meeting, to make sure you've each taken the steps you've agreed on.

At the close of your next meeting, Ms. Williams' Family Development Plan might look like this:

FAMILY DEVELOPMENT PLAN

HOW TO USE THE FAMILY DEVELOPMENT PLAN: Family worker, please ask the family if they want to fill out the form or want you to write. If you write, be sure to use their words. If the family member wants you to do the writing, read out loud what you have written. Ask the family member for any corrections, and make the corrections they request on all the sections except "in the worker's words." Give a copy to the family member, and keep a copy in your file. Each of you should review the form before your next meeting, to make sure you've each taken the steps you agreed on. Begin your next meeting by reviewing the last Plan.

- **Family member's name** Ms. Cassandra Williams
  (Note what s/he likes to be called—Mr., Mrs., Miss, Ms, etc.)
- **Address** 1475 South Ave. (apt. 14c), Buffalo, NY 14000
- **Phone(s)** (note if home, work, or friends' phone) 223-1234
- **Other family members involved in family development process** (Let family define who they consider family members.) Note ages and male or female.

  Alicia   2 yr. old daughter

- **Today's date** 8/12/96   • **Worker's name** Ms. Fiola Cummings
- **Major goal** (in family member's words)

  finish word processing course so I can get a job to support Alicia and myself

- **Steps leading to this goal** (note date each will take place.)

Steps family will take & when	Progress/Obstacles
—Apply for job training $ to pay for BOCES course (by 8/12 meeting)	
— Register for BOCES word pro course (by 8/19)	
— Apply for child care subsidy (by 8/19)	
— Get clothes for first day at BOCES (by 9/5)	
— ~~can~~ Find someone to take care of Alicia (probably Mom) (by 8/19)	

Steps worker will take & when	Progress/Obstacles
If BOCES won't let Ms. Williams register without $650, write letter saying she is eligible for Job Training funds, has applied, worker says BOCES will get check by 9/4.	

(At your next meeting, note progress or obstacles to each step.)

• **Family strengths and resources** (in family member's words)

—I was good at word processing in high school.

— Mom will probably take care of Alicia while I go to course.

• **Family strengths and resources** (in worker's words)

— Ms. Williams has kept appointments promptly.

— She seems highly motivated to learn marketable job skills.

— Her mother is supportive and probably available for childcare

• **Concerns** (in family member's words)

Car keeps breaking down - how will I get to course?

need good clothes to wear to course

• **Concerns** (in worker's words)

_____

_____

_____

• **Services available** (include details such as names, addresses, phone numbers hours, etc.)

BOCES word processing course starts 9/6 (classes Mon.-Fri. 8:00-2:30 at center city BOCES, 2600 Washington Ave. Call Mrs. Whitebird to confirm, 222-3344. $650 cost might be covered by Job Training, call Mr. Alexandro at 536-8800 to discuss application process.

• **Notes**

— $75/week child care subsidy available. Apply at JOB Center, 2680 Washington Ave. (Ms. Johnson). FILL OUT FORMS.

— Women's Bldg (23 Center St. - good clothes, free, for job interviews etc.)

• **Family member's signature & date** _Alexandra Williams 8/12/96_

• **Worker's signature & date** _Ms. Fiola Cummings_ 8-12-96

• **Next meeting date, time, place** Aug. 19 2:00 pm Ms. William's apartment

IF YOU CAN'T KEEP THIS APPOINTMENT, PLEASE CALL _Ms. Fiola Cummings_ AT _225-1123_ BY _Wed. Aug 18 noon_. THANK YOU FOR YOUR COURTESY.

Source: Christiann Dean, <u>Empowerment Skills for Family Workers</u>, 1996.

Source: Claire Forest, *Empowerment Skills for Family Workers*, 1996/2003/2015.

Setting and reaching goals

Using the Family Development Plan can offer hope to families who have lost faith in the possibility of ever providing a good life for themselves. *Although basic services are needed to help families facing hard times, helping them develop their ability to set and reach goals, and to build confidence, skills, and hope, is much more important in the long run.*

Family development is not a "quick fix." Helping families set and reach their own goals is a crucial part of this process, but people who have lost faith in their own capabilities usually have also lost some of their natural ability to envision a better life for their families, and to set the goals needed to make that life a reality.

The more aware you are of these feelings in yourself and these stages in your own family's ongoing development, the more effective you will be as a family development worker. You do not need to share your own family's entire story with the families you work with. In fact, later in *Empowerment Skills for Family Workers* you will learn guidelines to help you know when sharing your own story is helpful, and when it interferes with another family's development.

It is essential, however, that you realize that you and your own family are also in a continual process of development. Applying the skills of continual reassessment, goal setting, and skill building in your own life will help you grow comfortable with the family development process. Life will inevitably offer you opportunities to practice family development in your own life. Recognizing these opportunities will make you a more humble, empathetic, courageous, and skillful family development worker.

H. Your mind and your brain

Until recently, scientists believed our brains were "hard wired," through the genes we were born with. Many body functions certainly are hard wired, creating automatic messages from the brain that keeping vital functions operating without us having to do anything.

Over the past three decades, thanks to the availability of new equipment (especially the "functional" MRI) and research methods, discoveries from the field of neuroscience (the study of how the brain and mind work) and the neuroscience specialty known as neuroplasticity (the study of the brain's ability to change) have shown that:

- people's brains continue to grow throughout life

- a person's brain is shaped by thoughts, stress, and repeated action

- repeated actions can cause new neural pathways to open in the brain, or expand the neural pathways

    "*Neuroplasticity* describes the ability of the brain to change—literally to rewire itself in response to experience."

    – National Institute for the Clinical Application of Behavioral Medicine.

Although family workers certainly do not need to become neuroscientists, the neuroscience specialty Neuroplasticity offers great potential as we encourage families to set and reach their own goals for a better life. In his ground-breaking book *Mindsight: The New Science of Personal Transformation*, Daniel J. Siegel, M.D., (2011) wrote:

    One of the key practical lessons of modern neuroscience is that the power to direct our attention has within it the power to shape our brain's firing patterns, as well as the power to shape the architecture of the brain itself. (p. 39)

A family development worker credentialed by the National FDC program at University of Connecticut (or its recognized affiliates) uses the Family Development Plan to help clients set their own goals plus methods and steps for reaching them. This is followed by regularly scheduled meetings in which the credentialed worker and client together direct their attention to those steps.

This work is consistent with the conditions modern neuroscience considers necessary for reshaping the brain's functioning. But first, let's learn some basic brain science facts, terms, and basic neuroscience theory.

Our brains are highly specialized communication networks that communicate between the body and emotions, through communication among neurons. A *neuron* is a specialized cell that transmits nerve impulses; in other words, a nerve cell. Neurons communicate information to other specialized neurons, to keep the brain and body functioning well.

Neurons communicate via neural pathways. For example, when you see delicious food, neurons that oversee the complex ability to see communicate with many neurons that govern your hand's ability to reach out, with neurons that oversee your saliva glands, and neurons governing your digestive system, work together. *Neural pathways* are the highways and byways nerves use to connect to each other throughout the body and brain. Main pathways, along with interconnecting byways, connect approximately 10 billion nerves throughout the body and brain. Neural pathways are shaped by thoughts, stress, repeated action, exercise, and what we eat.

In 1949, Donald Hebb wrote, "Neurons that fire together, wire together." This became known as Hebbian Theory, a basic theory of neuroscience. Dr. Hebb explained,

> The general idea is an old one, that any two cells or systems of cells that are repeatedly active at the same time will tend to become "associated," so that activity in one facilitates activity in the other. (p. 70)

> When one cell repeatedly assists in firing another, the axon of the first cell develops synaptic knobs (or enlarges them if they already exist) in contact with the soma of the second cell. (p. 63)

Although it is not necessary for a family development worker to learn about brain physiology and functions, if you are interested, there are several resources available that describe these brain sections and functions in terms understandable to a layperson. I find the "Minding the Brain" chapter of Dr. Siegal's *Mindsight* presents this information in an easy-to-understand manner, because Dr. Siegal uses the image of a human hand to teach the location and function of important brain sections, including the limbic regions (amygdala, hippocampus), cerebral cortex, prefrontal cortex, brain stem, and spinal cord.

In *The Buddha's Brain: The Practical Neuroscience of Happiness, Love, and Wisdom*, Rick Hanson and Richard Mendius (2009) suggest:

> If you change your brain, you can change your life. Great teachers like the Buddha, Jesus, Moses, Mohammed, and Gandhi were all born with brains built essentially like anyone else's—and then they changed their brains in ways that changed the world. Science is now revealing how the flow of thoughts actually sculpts the brain, and more and more, we are learning that it's possible to strengthen positive brain states. (p. 252)

There are thousands of research studies in the field of neuroscience. Here, I'll present highlights from three well-known studies, to give you a better understanding of how this field can be useful to family workers:

- Paul Bach y Rita (1987) was among first to design practical applications based on neuroplasticity principles.

- The University of Toronto's Norman Doidge showed that in some cases the brain can repair itself from traumatic brain damage. Repetition is key.

- University of California neuroscience researcher Jeffrey M. Schwartz taught people with obsessive-compulsive disorder to notice when obsession is taking hold, and to replace it with healthier action.

Paul Bach-y-Rita (1987) had been a neuroscientist for many years when his father suffered a stroke which damaged the intricate system of the inner ear that controls balance. The elder Bach-y-Rita, Pedro, came to live with his son Paul. Paul believed that healthy brain regions could take over functions of brain regions damaged by stroke. He developed exercises which enabled his father to make a nearly full recovery of language and physical impairments. This encouraged others to develop practical exercises designed to restore or change the brains' functioning.

University of California neuroscience researchers Schwartz and Begley (2002) distinguished between the physical brain and the mind. Schwartz suggested that the mind affects and is affected by the physical brain. His research found that in some cases the people could use their minds to help their brain reorganize and modify itself. He went on to suggest that the parts of the brain that correspond to the parts of the body used most, tend to grow larger and more complex.

Schwartz wondered if people diagnosed with obsessive-compulsive disorder (OCD), could re-train their brain to function normally. OCD is a psychiatric condition in which people feel compelled to repeat an action (such as washing their hands), even after they know it is unnecessary. His research found that in people with this condition, an abnormal brain pathway hindered healthy neurological responses, prompting compulsive behavior. In his study, he taught people diagnosed with OCD to notice each time their compulsive behavior started to take hold and instead replace it with a different action.

Although it took time, effort, and attention, most participants were able to redirect their compulsive tendencies. Essentially, Schwartz was teaching his patients' mindfulness practice: to bring moment-to-moment awareness to their lives, catch obsessive behaviors before they took over, and replace them with healthier actions.

These studies indicate that with awareness and effort, it is possible to rewire the brain. Schwartz suggested that mindful attention to an action may be part of the reason the brain rewires itself. Business coach and trainer David Rock (2006) interviewed Schwartz, asking him "Why is change hard?" Schwartz replied that brains are designed to

> detect change in the environment and send out strong signals to alert us to anything unusual. Error detection signals are generated by a part of the brain called the orbital cortex ... which is very closely connected to the brain's fear circuitry in a structure called the amygdala. These two areas compete with and direct brain resources away from the prefrontal region, which is known to promote and support higher intellectual functions. This pushes us to act more emotionally and more impulsively: our animal instincts start to take over ... trying to change a routine behavior sends out strong messages in our brain that something's not right. These messages are designed to distract our attention, and they can readily overpower our rational thoughts. It takes a strong will to push past such mental activity. (p. 42)

Rock then asked Schwartz about the area of the brain used for new learning. Schwartz explained that the brain is organized so that habitual tasks, once learned, are stored in the basal ganglia of the brain and require little energy to access. New learning, however, takes place in the frontal cortex, which has limited energy and tires more quickly. Schwartz explained: "routine habits get pushed down into the automatic pilot parts of the brain, to free up cognitive resources" (Rock, 2006, p. 43)

This brief introduction to key aspects of brain development helps us see why coaching by credentialed family development workers shows promise in helping people remodel their brains in more positive ways. Credentialed coaches use tools such as the Family Development Plan to help families set their own goals, which worker and client repeatedly revisit. This can help new learning become routine, and thus move into the easier-to-access part of the brain and become habitual.

Transformative learning—It's a process

Transformative learning, or the ability to reflect on and change certain behaviors, can be facilitated by family development workers serving as coaches. Initially, there must be awareness of or concern for the issue. That is why ordering someone to change or do something they don't feel is important usually doesn't work. Instead, they tend to push back and dig in their heels or simply not follow through. However, a crisis or a significant challenge that is being faced by a family often opens the door for transformative learning.

Columbia University researcher Jack Mezirow (1978b) used an image borrowed from mythology (Camus, 1955), of Sisyphus struggling to push a heavy boulder up a mountainside, only to watch it repeatedly come crashing down, to illustrate his new concept of "transformative learning." Only after a person becomes aware of his/her situation can he/she begin to reflect. Reflection can be encouraged by family development workers, using tools such as the Family Development Plan and the Family Circles Assessment (introduced in Chapter 4). Identifying potential strengths, supports, consequences and desired outcomes are all part of self-reflection. Writing these down makes them even more concrete. Coaches can assist by posing questions and perhaps offering information and resources. What they shouldn't do is give advice, as difficult as that might be. Researchers tell us that internal reflection engages a part of our brain that makes links across the whole brain, again setting the stage for transformative learning.

The term "illumination" refers to that "aha!" moment when we figure out how to go about something or are successful at implementing a new strategy. The Family Development Plan breaks down goals into small, more achievable steps. When these are accomplished, families begin to see what the possibilities are, gaining insight. The illumination phase brings a rush of energy, with new pathways being created in our brain. Family development workers, as coaches, encourage, discuss, provide reminders, and point out what families are learning along the way. With repetition, new behaviors move to the "automatic pilot" part of the brain, making them easier. The neuroplasticity of the brain allows this to happen.

Neuroscience has helped us to better understand transformative learning and why coaching works. If we want people to change unhealthy behaviors, they need to come up with that idea themselves to give their brain the best chance of creating a new map. A credentialed coach encourages mindfulness, paying attention to solutions, providing follow-up and practice works the best. In this way, skilled family workers can facilitate the process of transformative learning.

I. The importance of family context

People are deeply influenced by their families—both their current families and, for adults, the families they grew up in. Actions and decisions of one family member affect all the others, for better or worse. Families develop patterns that work for them, even though outsiders can see ways they think would work better. Until one or more family members decide these patterns don't work or are too painful, they will maintain them.

For example, neighbors might think it is impractical for a rural woman to depend on a family member to drive her everywhere she and the children need to go. But until she decides for herself that she needs a driver's license and is willing to face the changes this decision will create in her family's balance of power, nothing the worker can do will change the situation.

Families give their members both stress and support, sometimes more of one, sometimes more of the other. It is usually more productive to work with people in the context of their families than as individuals. This does not mean that family development workers need to meet with the whole family each time (or ever), but that it is best to think of individuals as members of families, and to consider the family supports, stresses, and current and past influences they bring to their goals. For example, an individual with an alcohol abuse problem can be referred for evaluation and treatment, but unless the family is also brought into treatment, the alcoholic is very likely to slide back into old behavior patterns.

Within most families, there are at least three subsystems:

- partner system
- parent-child system
- sibling (brothers and sisters) system

In addition, in many cultures, extended family members are vital members of a family system. Mothers, fathers, and extended family all play an important role in children's lives. Each contributes something unique.

The "father factor"

According to the U.S. Census Bureau, 24 million children in America—one out of every three—live in homes in which their biological father is absent. Consequently, there is a "father factor" in many of the social issues facing families today and a growing recognition of the important role fathers play in children's development and in a family's economic stability. There are significant data showing the negative impacts of an absent father on poverty, maternal and child health, crime, teen pregnancy, child abuse, drug and alcohol use, childhood obesity, and education levels. Consequently, there is a growing movement and focus in the human services and education fields to implement programs that promote greater father involvement. One example is the National Head Start Program's initiative.

An excellent source of the latest statistics regarding fatherhood is the National Fatherhood Initiative (http://www.fatherhood.org). The Fatherhood Resource Center also has an extensive listing of websites for Fatherhood Initiatives and Resources. Articles on fatherhood and links for many of these websites can be found at http://www.cyfernet.org.

The healthiest families are those in which messages can be communicated effectively to all family members who need that information. Although different cultures exhibit varying patterns of healthy communication, all cultures have established healthy ways of communicating among the members.

In healthy families, every member's opinions and feelings are respected, and they work toward helping each person's goals to be met, as well as developing and meeting family goals. There is a healthy balance of power among its members, with adults making big decisions with input from the children, and children making decisions appropriate to their ages. In less healthy families, one or more members rule the others through violence, intimidation, or passive-aggressive techniques such as guilt or psychosomatic illnesses.

Family development workers need to maintain clear communication with all the family members they work with, and to encourage clear, direct communication between all family members, while respecting the communication patterns of that family's culture. For example, you may work with a family of a cultural background where women usually make all decisions about childcare and child rearing. In this case, it may be inappropriate for you to initiate discussion about child care options with the father, although you can respectfully raise the topic either with the mother or when all family members are present, saying, "Here is a booklet about the school's free preschool program, which you might decide would be great for Elena. I know you'll want to talk this over among yourselves. Let me know if you have questions." Out of respect for the communication patterns and roles of this family's culture, you might hand the booklet to the mother.

Unless abuse or neglect is occurring, it is not the family development worker's job to get families to change the ways their family system functions. It is your role to help families develop and pursue wise goals for their future. This work may involve helping them understand what supports and what hinders their goals (including their own family system). Keeping the focus on family goals for self-reliance prevents family workers from becoming overinvolved in unhealthy family systems.

Families in communities

Families are profoundly affected by the communities in which they live. An increasing number of communities are filled with violence, drugs, unhealthy housing, and many other problems, what sociologist James Garbarino calls "toxic" social environment.[5] Individual families' best attempts at

---

[5] James Garbarino, *Raising children in a socially toxic environment* (San Francisco: Jossey-Bass, 1999).

creating a better life for their children are undermined by communities in which many influences are working against positive family development.

Poverty and chaos impact development

A number of researchers have also studied the connections between poverty, chaotic living environments, and child development. They found significant interconnections and impacts on families, including brain development. Specifically, children's personalities and learning are negatively affected from a very young age by chaos in the home and neighborhood. These negative effects are cumulative; that is, the more kinds of chaos and the longer it lasts, the more harmful its effects.

Poverty's detrimental effects on children's physical and psychological development and school success are well established. Cornell University Professor Gary Evans, who worked closely with Urie Bronfenbrenner, has focused his research on the role of chaos in development. Evans and his colleagues have shown that children living in poverty are exposed to significantly more noise (Evans, Brauchie, et al., 2007), crowding in their living environments (Evans, Eckenrode, & Marcynyszyn, 2007), more frequent moves and school changes (Evans, Brauchie, et al., 2007), and disrupted adult relationships (Evans, 2004) than are middle-class children.

Evans also found that parents raising children in poverty are less likely to have predictable mealtime and bedtime routines than middle-class children, leading to lower school achievement. Chaotic living conditions adversely affect children's cognitive, socio-emotional, and physical well-being.

Evans and Lepore (1993) found that chronic noise in a child's environment, whether from traffic, nearby overhead airplanes, or loud noises within the home (such as a television, personal music device, or computer), can damage not only the child's hearing but also cause the child and adults to become less responsive to each other, promoting adverse effects on auditory health (hearing), parent-child relationships, and delays in reading ability and cognitive development. Evans and Lepore found that sudden or ongoing noise can negatively affect a child's long-term memory. This appears to happen when children "tune out" chronic noise as a coping mechanism, which, unfortunately, also causes children to ignore people speaking to them. Their studies also showed that teachers in noisy schools are less patient than teachers in quieter schools.

Evans and his colleagues recently conducted studies to determine whether growing up in poverty leads to differences in brain structure and function in adulthood. Some of these studies use functional magnetic resonance (fMRI) and psychological and physical tests to examine three brain regions—the hippocampus, prefrontal cortex, and amygdala—which may be impacted by childhood poverty. This growing body of research is providing preliminary evidence that high levels of chaos, often found in low-income households, contributes to psychological distress, learned helplessness, and self-regulatory behavior that extends to adulthood. (Evans, Brauchie, et al., 2007).

Professor Evans also studied how other aspects of the physical environment, particularly overcrowding, affected mental health, motivation, and health. He found that family density (number of people per room) was more significant than family size. He found that children aged 10–12 years tended to withdraw in crowded settings, perhaps as a way of coping with too much stimulus. He also found that parents in crowded homes paid less attention to young children and were more likely to use punitive discipline, which tended to make the children more stressed.

School-age children living in crowded homes show higher stress levels and more behavior problems in school. These problems were found to be more intense among children 8–10 years old whose home life was chaotic. Overcrowding also reduced children's motivation to perform tasks. Regardless of family income, children 6–12 years old, particularly girls, came to believe they had no control over their lives and therefore made no efforts to improve their situations, despite actually having the means to do so. This result is consistent with the notion of learned helplessness.

Although children at all income levels are negatively affected by overcrowding and noise, children living in poverty are more likely to be exposed to them repeatedly. Parents and teachers therefore have a responsibility to try to reduce children's exposure to noise and crowding.

Professor Evans' research showed that natural settings are therapeutic because they give children room to exercise and interact socially with others. More immediately, natural settings also mitigate some of the negative effects of stress. Therefore, it's important that caregiving adults take the time to check the volume control on music devices and computers, and turn them down, if necessary. If children become hardened to noise and begin to ignore others, it's important to take action. Likewise, caregivers should spend time outdoors with their children or students in peaceful quiet settings, and engage in quiet indoor activities such as reading books.

It's also important for caregivers to reflect on the excess noise they might be creating or allowing in their children's lives. Do they turn up the TV? Do their children eat near noisy electronic devices? Do they give children headphones to "keep them quiet" (not realizing that this might be harming the child's hearing)? Could they unclutter their home somewhat? Although they might not be able to control the noise and crowding in their neighborhood, they may have more control than they realize over the noise and crowding in their own home.

It is also important that families understand the important role they play in their community and the influence they can have on their world. As a front-line worker in a focus group put it,

> I help families strengthen connections they already have within the immediate family, the extended family, their neighborhoods, connections with schools, and then make connections to other parts of the community that can be of help.

> [I want to] help families see the very important role that they play in the whole big picture. I don't think a lot of families see themselves as having an impact on the big picture. They only see how the world affects them, not how they affect the world.

Families can influence their own lives and their communities for the better, both in formal ways (like urging their local transportation service to operate wheelchair-accessible vans, or becoming involved in a neighborhood watch association) and in informal ways (like sharing child care with friends). It is good to encourage families to contribute to their communities in ways that are meaningful to them. A family member shared her story:

> I hear a lot of people say that this is a tough neighborhood. I don't. These people here, they are living their lives. If you are respectful, they don't care about what they do. It is between them and the police. And I am not the police. I respect them when I pass. If I can say hello, I say hello. And they don't bother me and I don't bother them. Same as when I met you on the street today, I didn't know that you were the person going to interview me, but you treated me respectfully. I treated you respectfully.

It takes time, confidence, and in some cases money (for gas, phone calls, child care), to be a community volunteer or to help out friends and neighbors. The families you work with will probably rely more on formally organized services at first and then, as their lives become more stabilized, may be able to help others more.

J. Putting it all together as a family development worker

Start with the here and now

It is important to start with the here and now, rather than the past. Unlike a conventional social work approach to families, in which the worker collects and records detailed information about the problems and lives of previous generations in order to understand the person currently seeking help (such as with a genogram), family development focuses on both a family's current situation and where they want to go. Although it is important to help a person reflect on what has created a current situation, too much emphasis on generations of past problems can prevent a person from seeing present and future possibilities, or from acting on them.

In the process of setting and working toward a goal for increased self-reliance, a person may seek psychological therapy among other necessary services. A qualified therapist can help the person understand how trauma or family patterns have contributed to current problems, and help the individual or family heal.

Commitment

Families often emerge out of the attraction and love two adults feel for each other. Commitment is the glue that holds families together as the two adults' attraction deepens, is shaken, or dissolves. Commitment takes many forms, such as parents' commitment to care for their children; a family's commitment to care for aging parents; or your commitment as a family worker to skillfully, ethically help families set and reach their goals.

Because families take many different forms, as a family worker, it is wise to hold the ideal of committed, healthy relationships for the families you serve, while accepting the family's current reality. For many families, marriage or a commitment ceremony provides an enduring foundation through life's inevitable joys, sorrows, and challenges. There are, however, situations, such as abusive relationships, in which it is healthier not to encourage a long-term commitment, except to any children already created within the union. Helping people make a commitment to their own inner truths—setting and reaching their own goals for a healthy, responsible life—is the cornerstone of your role as a family development worker.

Family development is built on an understanding that people need more than temporary relief from a crisis, that their deep motivation for freedom, self-respect, hope, and the chance to make an important contribution must be honored and reflected back to them, even if they have buried this inherent, deep motivation under layers of dependency.

Agency workers have enormous power in the lives of the people who seek help: the power to give or withhold desperately needed services. But even more important is workers' power to help families restore their sense of hope and ability to care for themselves and their families. *Empowerment Skills for Family Workers* will help you systematically learn and practice the skills you need to use this power responsibly and grow into a highly skilled, effective family development worker who can help families move from dependence on government programs to a healthy, sustainable relationship with their communities.

References

Arden, J. B. (2010. *Rewire your brain: Think your way to a better life*. Hoboken, NJ: Wiley.

Bach-y-Rita, P. (1987). Brain plasticity as a basis of sensory substitution. *Journal of Neurologic Rehabilitation, 2*, 67–71.

Bronfenbrenner, U. (1988). Strengthening family systems. In E. F. Zigler & M. Frank (Eds.), *The parental leave crisis: Toward a national policy*, pp. 143–160. New Haven, CT: Yale University Press.

Camus, A. (1955). *The myth of Sisyphus*. New York: Random Vintage.

Evans, G. W. (2004). The environment of childhood poverty. *American Psychologist, 59*, 77-92.

Evans, G. W., Brauchie, G., Haq, A., Stecker, R., Wong, K., & Shapiro, E. (2007). Young children's environmental attitudes and behaviors. *Environment and Behavior, 39*, 635-659.

Evans, G. W., Eckenrode, J., & Marcynyszyn, L. (2007). Poverty and chaos. Paper presented at The First Bronfenbrenner Conference, Chaos and Children's Development: Levels of Analysis and Mechanisms, October, Ithaca, NY.

Evans, G. W., & Hygge, S. (2007). Noise and performance in children and adults. In L. Luxon & D. Prasher (Eds.), *Noise and its effects* (pp. 549–566). London: Wiley.

Evans, G. W., & Lepore, S. J. (1993). Nonauditory effects of noise on children: A critical review. *Children's Environments, 10*(1), 31-51.

Garling, T., & Evans, G. W. (1991). *Environment, cognition and action*. New York: Oxford University Press.

Hanson, R., & Mendius, R. (2009). *The Buddha's brain: The practical neuroscience of happiness, love, and wisdom*. Oakland, CA: New Harbinger.

Hebb, D. O. (1949). *The organization of behavior: A neuropsychological theory*. New York: Wiley.

Forest, C. (2003). *Empowerment skills for family workers.* Ithaca, NY: Family Development Press.

Forest, C. (2013). *Using new brain research to engage families in reaching their goals.* May 2, 2013. Washington: 40th National Head Start Conference.

Mezirow, J. (1978a). *Education for perspective transformation: Women's re-entry programs in community colleges.* New York: Center for Adult Education, Teachers' College, Columbia University.

Mezirow, J. (1978b). Perspective transformation. *Adult Education Quarterly, 28*(2), 100–110.

Mezirow, J. (1990). How critical reflection triggers transformative learning. In J. Mezirow and Associates (Eds.), *Fostering critical reflection in adulthood: A guide to transformative and emancipatory learning* (pp. 1-20). San Francisco: Jossey-Bass.

Rock, D. (2006). A brain-based approach to coaching. *International Journal of Coaching in Organizations, 4*(2), 32–43.

Schwartz, J. M., & Begley, S. (2002). *The mind and the brain: Neuroplasticity and the power of mental force.* New York: HarperCollins.

Siegal, D. J. (2010). *Mindsight: The new science of personal transformation.* New York: Bantam.

Activities to Extend Learning

Chapter 1
Family Development: A Sustainable Route to Healthy Self-Reliance

A. A bone-deep longing for freedom and self-respect

1. Reflect on your own longing for freedom and self-respect. How do you fulfill it?
2. List people, agencies, organizations, and businesses that your family is interdependent with. Is your family "self-sufficient"?
3. What do you feel responsible for in your own family's life? How did you develop this sense?
4. List some factors that work against people developing a sense of self-reliance.

B. Beyond "providing services"

1. What services have you and your family (or a friend or relative) used or tried to access? How were you treated? Were you treated differently when the service was one that all people of a certain age or from a certain area were entitled to (public school, social security) than when it was based on a problem or inability (probation, food stamps)?
2. Why did you enter human service work?
3. Can you identify three families your agency has helped to reach their goals by providing services? If so, what other factors besides the services provided helped these families succeed?
4. Think of three families your agency worked with who have not reached their goals (or not even set goals), despite the provision of many services. Describe the reasons why, as you see them. If possible, ask the families for their perceptions of the reasons.
5. Describe your successes and frustrations with providing services, whether you do so directly (yourself) or indirectly (through referrals).

C. Does case management empower families?

1. Describe ways that your current job duties relate to the major functions of a family development worker. Do you think your current job title helps or hinders offering family development to families? Why or why not?
2. Why are families sometimes unable to serve as their own advocates? How can workers help families develop skills to be their own advocates?
3. Think of a situation in which you helped a family advocate for services they needed. What did the family do? What support did you offer? What did you and the family learn through the experience?
4. Briefly describe two situations in your life: an experience in which a family professional "provided services," and another in which she/he offered "compassionate presence." How did the family professional's approach affect the way you remember the experience?

D. Core principles of family development

1. For each core principle, describe (1) how it promotes family self-sufficiency and (2) ways in which your agency's work does and does not reflect this principle.
2. List other programs or social institutions (laws, businesses, schools, religious organizations, neighborhood groups) that reflect these principles, giving specific examples of the ways they do so.

3. How do you feel about each of these principles? Why? If you are uncomfortable with some of the principles, describe why.

4. Consider ways that you as an individual, your agency, and any professional organizations you belong to could more fully apply one of these principles. Choose one of these ways and try it out for one month, noting its effects and any challenges encountered.

E. Understanding family development

1. Review the seven steps of family development. Think of an important goal of your own family. Which steps are you focused on right now in pursuing this goal? What is next?

2. Which of the seven roles of a family development worker are you most comfortable with? Why? Which are you least comfortable with? Why?

3. Chart how your own family has moved through the seven steps. You have probably revisited some steps several times and may have stopped only briefly at others. Note what has helped you most at each step, and what has discouraged or harmed your family's development.

4. List examples of each of the seven roles of a family worker from your own work, or from other agencies, community organizations, or businesses.

5. List the ways you and your agency are already using the family development approach. List ways you are not doing so but could with only minor changes. List major changes your agency, and the corresponding state and federal agencies, would need to make in order for you and your co-workers to shift toward the family development approach.

F. Power and family development

1. How do you feel about the idea of a paradigm shift from the provision-of-services approach to an empowerment approach?

2. What are some of the challenges of shifting from a provision-of-services approach to an empowerment approach?

3. List any ways your agency or professional organization (or corresponding state or federal agency or organization) is attempting to move toward an empowerment approach.

4. Were there times in your own life when you felt someone, or a system, had power over you, or stood in your way of receiving help or success? Describe your feelings. Was there any sense of defensiveness, rebellion, wanting to "put one over on the powers that be"?

5. Can you remember a time when someone who could have had power over you shared that power with you in a way that enabled you to set your own direction or make your own decision, even if it might not have been the decision they would have made for you? What feelings do you recall about that time?

6. In what ways do you hold power over the families in your program?

7. List ways that you could share power with families, even if your agency does not yet operate with a family development approach.

8. Describe some of the challenges of using an empowerment approach with families who have a long history of getting services from agencies operating under the deficit approach.

9. What personal changes would you have to make in your attitude and behavior to work more in the empowerment approach?

10. List the strengths you see in the most challenging family you work with.

11. List the advantages and disadvantages of the provision-of-services model to families, workers, agencies, and funders (including taxpayers). Then list the advantages and disadvantages of the empowerment model to each group.

12. Describe the special challenges of doing family development work with families who are mandated to work with your agency. What strategies can you use?

G. The Family Development Plan

1. Write a script describing the Family Development Plan to a family member you are working with. Include what the Family Development Plan is, how to use it, why it is different from other assessments, and some ways it helps families set and achieve their goals.

2. Write a script describing the Family Development Plan to your supervisor. Include what the Plan is, how it promotes healthy self-reliance with families, how it complements other assessments used at your agency, and ways your agency might consider including the Plan in working with families.

3. Reflect on the statement, "Family development is not a quick fix." Describe how you would explain its meaning to someone skeptical about the benefits of family development. What makes family development different from other approaches used by family-serving agencies? Why would an agency want to incorporate an approach to family support that requires continual reassessment?

H. Your Mind and Your Brain

1. Reread the section in this chapter on neuroplasticity and transformative learning. Write a reflection on a personal experience you've had with transformative learning. What impacted the process for you?

2. What steps can you take as a family worker to facilitate the process of transformative learning with families?

3. Reflect on your role as a "coach" with families to help them change unhealthy or problem behaviors. How might you improve upon your coaching role, considering what you have learned in this chapter?

I. The importance of family context

1. Being honest with yourself, what types of families do you feel most comfortable with? Least comfortable?

2. List an example of something you do in a certain way because that's how your family did it when you were growing up.

3. Describe something you do differently than your family did when you were growing up, because you didn't like it and decided to change. How did your change affect the rest of your family?

4. List some ways you can support an individual family member to make a desired change, while retaining the respect of other family members.

5. Why is it important to help families reflect on the factors that contributed to their current situation? How can assessment tools that focus on a family's past limit the family's ability to move forward?

6. What local, state, national, and global trends and policies are affecting families in your area?

7. Are there any ways in which your community is "toxic" to families?

J. Putting it all together as a family development worker

1. Reread the seven steps of family development and the roles of a family development worker, and the section on empowerment. Create two parallel columns, labeling one column "Family" and the other "Family Development Worker." List at least one strategy for sharing power at each step.

2. Reread the roles of a family development worker. For each, list a corresponding role for a family the worker is working with.

3. List professionals who have had great power over your life (doctors, agency workers, judges, principals). Do you think they understood how much power they had in your life?

4. List five ways you can avoid creating a situation in which a family becomes too dependent on you, while still being there for them.

Skills Practices

These skills practices are a suggested list. You may also develop your own skills practice or make modifications to the ones listed below to help you create a meaningful and manageable plan.

1. Discuss the seven roles of a family development with a co-worker. After you discuss them, determine which one(s) come most easily for each of you and which are the most challenging. Did you agree about which were easier and which were more difficult? What steps can you take to help each other work on those that are more challenging or difficult?

2. With a friend or a member of your own family, discuss the difference between using "power over" and "shared power" in a helping or mentoring relationship. How did your friend or family member react to this concept? Together, identify ways that "shared power" relationships benefit the families you work with and relationships with your own family.

3. Use the family development plan yourself to develop steps that will help you achieve the goal of earning the FDC credential. Ask someone from your FDC class to help you serve the role of family development worker as you develop your plan. After you complete the plan, respond to these questions: How will other people in your life be affected by your goal to earn the FDC credential? What type of help will you need from them? How did developing the plan with a family development worker help?

4. Explain to a co-worker or a member of your own family the differences between offering family support using the core principles of family development and the "provision of services" approach. Ask for ideas on how family workers can best help families to set and reach goals of healthy self-reliance.

5. With a co-worker or your supervisor, discuss how your agency is currently using family development or could begin to incorporate using this approach with families. What are the potential benefits to families, workers, and the agency? What might be some challenges to using family development within your agency, and how could you or your agency address them?

Chapter 2
Communicating with Skill and Heart

Objectives

A. Explain why effective communication takes both skill and "heart."

B. Build empathy with others by appropriately sharing something of your own life with the families you work with.

C. Develop more attention to nonverbal communication messages you receive from and send to others.

D. Understand how mutual respect and assertiveness is a way out of the submission-aggression communication loop.

E. Create a listening atmosphere using communication "helpers," avoiding communication "blockers" and reflecting back what you've heard.

F. Learn how to say what you mean clearly and respectfully.

G. Use skillful listening and speaking skills to resolve conflict.

H. Handle blame and criticism.

I. Confront people constructively when needed.

J. Communicate about "hot topics," such as sexuality, domestic violence, and addiction.

K. Work skillfully with families with language barriers or low levels of literacy.

L. Use technology to communicate in appropriate ways.

A. Communicating with skill and heart

Communicating effectively is the most important ability a family development worker can have. You communicate regularly with families, co-workers, people from other agencies or community organizations, and perhaps funders. You communicate through the words you speak and write, through listening, and through gestures such as smiles and handshakes.

You also have a remarkable opportunity to help the families you coach and to learn to communicate with skill and heart. Good communication promotes healthy relationships between parents, and among parents, children, and other extended family members whose opinions often influence family decisions. Parents' relationships have a profound impact on where a family lives, their safety, their finances, their food decisions, and their guidelines for their children's behavior. People have different styles of communicating based on personality, gender, culture, family background, and education.

These differences can lead to problems if you assume that someone else means the same thing you do by a particular kind of communication. For example, you may enjoy giving a warm hug to show you like someone, but that person may feel you are invading his or her "space." Or, you may be used to showing respect by keeping quiet, while another person may show respect by talking a lot to get to know you. As a family development worker, you need to know how to communicate well with everyone you meet.

The best communication takes both skill and heart. On a typical day, workers will need to exercise a wide variety of communication skills, from building empathy to confronting people constructively, from communicating about "hot topics" to working with families with language barriers. You probably already feel quite competent in some of these areas and would like to advance your skills in others. Use this chapter to polish the communication skills you already have and to build new ones to become a top-notch family development worker.

B. Empathy: Putting yourself in their shoes

Before you can really hear what someone else has to say, offer information, or let another person know what you think, it's crucial to build a bridge between yourself and the other person. Empathy, or being able to "put yourself in someone else's shoes," is an important first step in skillful communication. Empathy is being able to understand another person's feelings, or to see his or her point of view (even if you don't necessarily agree with it). Looking for what you have in common is a good starting point for building empathy.

Listening well—instead of trying to get your own point across right away—is an important bridge-builder. Often, acknowledging that you notice that a family is upset can begin to demonstrate that you are listening and understand their feelings. This kind of listening requires that you offer families your undivided attention, or mindful presence (which you will learn more about in Chapter 3).

Whether or not you have successfully handled situations similar to those of families you work with, knowing how to listen skillfully and express yourself respectfully is crucial to building empathy with others. For example, you'll sometimes encounter a person who is extremely upset, raging about something that happened which they perceive of as a terrible injustice, or depressed about something that feels overwhelming. Listening well is a crucial first step before helping them sort out what they want to do about it.

Having had similar experiences can make it easier to empathize with families. When asked about workers who have been most helpful, a family member in our focus groups said:

> The worker who came into my home last year--she was very friendly and open. I guess her own family situation made her more sympathetic to others because a lot of times she was in a similar situation. She was always aware of our needs, and she accepted us for all our faults. She tried to see the good in all of it.

A family worker said:

> I think someone who's had personal experience with what they're working with in another person, can empathize better than someone who didn't have that experience. I know that people who haven't had a particular experience can be kind-hearted and understanding, but it hits right at the roots when you've been there.

Another family worker felt that workers who have not had the same experience as the families they work with can still be empathetic and helpful:

> It doesn't necessarily mean that a person who is not disabled cannot help someone who is. I think there are lessons to be learned both ways.

How much of your own personal life should you share with the families you work with? Families are sharing a lot of personal information with you, and may feel like the relationship is one-sided unless you share something of your own family life. Here are some guidelines to help you decide what to share:

- Be genuine.

- Share your own information in order to build rapport with the family. Be careful not to turn the focus onto you and your family. Remember that this is the family's time. For example, if you're working with a family who is struggling to help their aging mother decide whether to return home after a serious fall, you could say, "I can relate! My mother had a serious operation last year, and my brothers and I had quite a time helping her sort through her options to find a solution we all could live with. Would you like to tell me more about your mother's situation?"

- Keep the goal of family development in mind: to help the family develop the skills to find good solutions to their own problems. If you spend too much time describing your own problems and how you've solved them, the family may feel they should come up with the same solution you did.

- Don't rely on the families to help you solve your own problems. Set up a good support system for yourself so you don't become dependent on the families you serve. When you gain insight into your own life through your work (as you certainly will), do thank the family for the ways they helped you. It is empowering to hear that you've learned from them. You could say: "Hearing about how you got your mother's doctor and physical therapist to work together with you inspired me to encourage my mother to make another appointment with her doctor, to talk about whether physical therapy might help her, too. Thank you!"

- Be prepared for anything you share to be discussed (and possibly distorted) by the family, both among themselves and with other agency workers and people in the community. If you tell a family you work with the details of your personal struggles with your teenager, you (or your daughter) should be prepared to hear from anyone in the community: "Oh, hi. I haven't seen you for a long time. But I heard that your daughter was pregnant. Did she decide to have an abortion, or what? And who is the father anyway?"

To summarize, give enough personal information so families can see that you're "real," but keep the focus on their development. Be careful not to imply from your personal stories *how* they should solve their problems. Maintain a good personal support network in your own life, so you aren't tempted to rely on the families you work with to help you solve your own problems.

C. Understanding nonverbal communication

A lot of important information is communicated without ever saying a word. Paying attention to nonverbal communication can help you put people at ease and understand them better. Nonverbal communication includes:

- facial expressions

- body posture

- awareness of personal space

- intuition

For example, an open body posture (the opposite of having your arms folded across your chest) conveys attention. Have you ever talked with someone who is telling you one thing with words, but whose nonverbal behavior communicates something else? Perhaps a person is saying that whatever you're suggesting is fine, but you feel tension rising, and she quickly cuts off the conversation, unwilling to schedule another appointment. What can you do? First, pay attention to the nonverbal communication. It's real. Use effective communication to check whether your perceptions are accurate. For example, "I'm feeling uneasy about our agreement. You said you wanted to enter the residential treatment program, but I'm picking up on some hesitation and want to make sure I'm not misinterpreting you." Then, reopen the communication channel by saying something like: "Would you like to talk more about what you want to do next?"

Be particularly careful about the nonverbal messages you send. A family worker in our focus group explained that she is careful even about where she sits:

> When I come into a house, a lot of times I ask the family, "Where do you usually sit? Where would you like me to sit?" And I like to notice, when I sit down, how far they sit away from me; it tells me what they are comfortable with.

Another worker said:

> I had to learn to shake the person's hand when I say hello, firm grip, look them in the eye. Watch my posture. Be aware what I wear.

Not all cultures—or individuals—are comfortable with a lot of eye contact. To some people, it is a sign of respect to keep eyes lowered. Notice how the families you work with use nonverbal communication, and look for a comfortable way to communicate that you respect them and want to hear what they have to say. Chapter 5 offers suggestions for communicating respectfully across cultures.

D. Finding a good balance between listening and expressing yourself

Communication requires a balance of listening and expression. People are often stronger in one or the other. People who are stronger at listening often feel drained and burned out, and they eventually become resentful because their own needs aren't met. People who are better at expressing their needs often overwhelm other people, and are seen as controlling or self-centered. Listening is ineffective if you cannot express yourself clearly, and expression is ineffective without skilled listening. Which is your strength?

Most of us would like to be able to say what we think and feel clearly, respecting ourselves and other people. We want to meet our own needs and get along well with other people. Yet often people walk away from a conversation feeling that they haven't gotten their point across, or feeling badly about the way they got it across and are afraid that the other person will try to get back at them. And many people feel guilty about focusing on their own needs or asking for help.

The submission-aggression loop

What's behind this problem is something called the "submission-aggression loop." *Submission* is doing what other people want you to, or what you think they want, while your needs go unmet. *Aggression* is doing something that gets you what you want without regard to its effects on others. Submission and aggression are behaviors; they do not necessarily indicate lifelong personality types. Often people are submissive when they feel they don't have much power in a situation, and they are aggressive when they feel they can get away with it.

Few people can live entirely in one mode or the other. Usually, submissive people who put everyone else's desires ahead of their own eventually become resentful and lash out aggressively or get depressed and withdraw. Aggressive people who get their way at any cost begin to feel pretty lonely and swing around to being submissive. It doesn't work very well, though, because they can't maintain it for very long. Whichever role is chosen, these behaviors amount to disrespectful communication: submissive behavior is disrespectful to self, while aggressive behavior is disrespectful to others. So people go round and round on the submission-aggression loop without ever communicating clearly or respectfully.

Sometimes people remain stuck in one mode or the other. Submissive people put others first and disregard their own needs. They often take on responsibilities that they don't really want, apologize a lot, and often don't even know what they really feel and want. There are many payoffs for this behavior: Submissive people have less responsibility when things go wrong, because they weren't in on making decisions; they avoid conflict; and they are often well-liked and get to consider themselves good, responsible, unselfish, self-sacrificing. Submissive people pay a price for all this: they have to go along with whatever other people choose even if it doesn't really suit them, and they can build up a lot of anger and resentment. Even though submission is intended to keep everything "nice," it can create a lot of anger and dissatisfaction. Our society has generally taught girls and women to be submissive, although this pattern is changing slowly.

Aggressive people are often very skilled at getting what they want, often without considering others. They tend to overpower other people, sometimes without realizing it. There are two kinds of aggressive people: those who are used to getting their own way at all costs, and those who become aggressive because they feel powerless in a particular situation. Our society has generally taught boys and men to be aggressive.

Both the payoffs and the costs of aggressive behavior are high. In many cultures, aggressive people often make more money and have their opinions heard. The costs of aggression may become more apparent over time. Aggressive people make a lot of enemies and alienate people. People fear but don't respect them. Aggressive people get along better within an institution or organization with lots of rules than in friendships or informal arrangements, which depend more on mutual respect. For example, a parent who is aggressive might get along better with a day-care-center arrangement (which has clear-cut rules for pick-up time, payment, etc.) than with informal family day care provided by a relative or neighbor.

Please note that although some religious traditions teach submission to a higher power, this is not the same as being submissive with other people. A person can follow religious teachings about submission to a higher power while using mutually respectful, or assertive, behavior with other people.

Mutual respect: A way out of the submission-aggression loop

Is there an effective middle path between submission and aggression loop? Yes! It's called *mutually respectful communication*, or *assertiveness*. Assertive people make sure that their important rights are respected and their needs met, they express themselves, and they have a genuine interest in the rights and needs of others. The payoffs are high: Mutually respectful people tend to like themselves, have fulfilling relationships, and don't get into as many conflicts because they trust and respect themselves and others.

There are costs to mutually respectful communication: It takes time, work, and effort to change old patterns. And some people, especially those caught in patterns of submission and aggression, may not like your behavior. For formerly submissive people learning assertiveness, it can be a new experience to accept that other people may not appreciate their new-found ability to defend personal rights and express needs. It takes time to learn that a person's survival doesn't depend on everyone approving of their behavior all the time.

Do you think you're primarily aggressive or submissive in the aggression-submission loop, or are you mutually respectful in your present communications? Deciding what your tendency is now will help you know which skills to focus on developing. Aggressive people need to pay more attention to listening well. Submissive people need to learn how to say what they mean more skillfully, without apologizing. If you are someone who flip-flops between the two, you need to learn to recognize when you're in each mode, to listen better when you're tending toward aggression, and to express yourself better when you're tending toward submission. Assertive, or mutually respectful, people can practice becoming even more skillful at working for solutions in which everybody wins. Remember, these are not necessarily lifelong personality types, but reflect behavior we've learned and can thus change or develop.

Communicating in ways that build mutual respect frees you from the submission-aggression loop. The two basic tools of mutually respectful communication are listening and speaking effectively.

E. Listening well

Listening well involves the following skills:

- Creating an atmosphere that will encourage the other person to talk openly
- Using communication "helpers"
- Avoiding communication "blockers"

• Reflecting back what you've heard

Creating a listening atmosphere

It's not always easy for a family development worker to create an ideal atmosphere for listening. You may be meeting with people on the street, in a noisy school, or at a homeless shelter without much privacy. You may have to rely on an interpreter or translator. Even if you meet with families in their homes, the TV may be on when you arrive, or there may be several family members' opinions to hear.

Still, there are ways to convey that you are really listening. Create as much privacy as possible. If you're in your office, don't accept phone calls while you're meeting with someone. Hearing you say, "The machine will get that. I want to listen to what you have to say," conveys a powerful feeling of respect for the family member or co-worker you are meeting with.

If it is not possible to meet without interruptions, create a "listening zone" with your attention. Stand or sit facing the person you're meeting with, with your back to everyone and everything else that might distract you, and your arms relaxed instead of crossed in front of your chest. If the person you are talking with comes from a cultural background that equates eye contact with respectful attention, look her in the eye. If he is from a culture where direct eye contact is a sign of disrespect, you can convey that you are listening, while looking at his child or something else. Follow the body language cues of the person you're communicating with. Your goal is to give the person the feeling that you are "right here" with him. If you must take notes, explain why. A family member relays:

> When we got the kids, she came out to the house and talked to us and started setting up programs and counseling, things like that, which was a big help. She listened to what I had to say and gave me the support that I needed because there were days when I first got them that I just felt like screaming because I didn't know how to control what they were doing and what to do to correct it.

From a credentialed worker:

> Since I took the FDC Credential, I'm a better listener than before because I kept running my mouth and now, every time a client comes to me and just talks. I will find a nice place for us to be comfortable and I will listen to you. When you finish talking I will tell you "I'm not going to tell you what to do." "What do you think you will be able to do?"

Using communication helpers

Three types of communication helpers can help communication flow more easily:

• *Door openers:* Invitations to talk, letting the other decide whether or not to proceed. Examples: "Want to talk about it?" "You look upset. Is something bothering you?"

• *Encouragers:* Statements that draw out the speaker, welcome him or her to continue. Example: "I'd like to hear more about your family's concerns."

• *Open questions:* Questions without a yes or no answer that allow a person to fill in more of the picture. Example: "What do you hope your mother will gain from living here?"

Avoiding communication blockers

Communication helpers can go a long way toward promoting good communication with family members, but it is just as important to avoid the following common communication "blockers":

- *Blaming:* "It's your own fault that you got pregnant." Note that blaming can come across in your tone and body language even if you're words aren't blaming. Blaming feels like an attack to the listener; often people react by shutting down, and cutting off communication.

- *"Always" and "Never" statements:* "You never fill out the forms right" or "You are always telling me what to do." These statements invite argument because they are so extreme, and they are hardly ever accurate.

- *Name-calling:* "That social worker is really stupid to say that." This kind of statement is hurtful and does not convey useful information in a way others can hear.

- *Labeling:* "She is such a typical bureaucrat—she just pushes papers around and doesn't care what really happens to people." This is a version of name-calling.

- *Giving unasked-for advice:* "You just have to go straight to the director when you have problems. That's what I did, and the squeaky wheel gets the grease." This advice may be useful and well intended, but it can be perceived as an effort to tell another what to do, and as such can convey disrespect for another's ability to make decisions.

- *Moralizing:* "Families who really care about their elderly parents keep them out of nursing homes." Judgmental statements are disrespectful and can reflect ignorance of another's personal experience or circumstances. They also fail to acknowledge the other person's feelings; for example, "I think you're overreacting. You're making a mountain out of a mole hill here." They put the listener on the defensive, blocking communication.

- *Giving orders or threatening:* "You get me my check by tonight, or all hell is gonna break loose." Such a statement is a form of verbal violence. When people are threatened, they focus their energies on protecting themselves, not on listening.

- *Diverting or avoiding the other's concern:* Changing the subject; for example, if a client says "I'm worried about my little girl. She's had this rash that won't go away," and a worker responds "Did you get your application for subsidized housing in today?" This change of subject demonstrates disregard for the client's concern; it sends the message that the worker's ideas are more important. One especially disrespectful way of changing the subject is to shift the focus to yourself and minimize the other person's concern. For example, a family member says, "I had a heck of a time getting paperwork through for Medicaid today," and a worker responds, "You think you had it bad! Let me tell you, I had it a lot worse."

- *Excessive questioning:* For example, persisting in collecting details about a subject that a client is clearly uncomfortable discussing. Many family members feel that excessive questioning is a particular problem among family workers.

In our focus group, one family member described her reaction to excessive questioning:

> I don't like it when they ask imposing questions. If I want to tell you something, I'll explain it to you, let you know. I want to be anonymous. Just listen to me.

A worker described how families perceive excessive questioning:

> It's hard sometimes because some families think you are trying to pry into their lives. They don't want you in their business. Especially if they receive social services, they may be afraid you're going to report them for something.

Try to avoid excessive questions. If you need specific information so you can help a family, tell them why you are asking for the information: "I would like to help you make a plan that you can live with comfortably. I don't want to pry into your personal life, but I will need to know your family income in order to know if you're eligible for our agency's services." One health program's "bill of rights" states that families do not need to answer questions they consider intrusive.

Has anyone ever used one of these communication blockers with you? How did that affect your willingness to communicate with that person? If the other person had instead used any of the communication helpers, how would that have changed your communication?

Reflecting what you've heard

Once you're able to encourage people to say what is on their minds, through using Communication Helpers and avoiding Communication Blockers, it is important to respond in a way that lets them know you are really listening. You may have heard of "active listening," in which you give the speaker *feedback* to communicate that you've heard what is being said.

Here are three types of feedback, along with an example of each:

- *Factual:* "You weren't able to make your doctor's appointment because your car broke down. And you couldn't call because your phone got shut off when you couldn't pay the bill."

- *Emotional:* "It's frustrating not to have a reliable car, or a phone. That must be really hard."

- *Solution-focused:* "The woman at the doctor's office said you could reschedule for next week. Did you say your sister works in Middletown? Do you think she'd give you a ride? Yes? Great! Would you like to use the phone here to call her, and call the doctor's office to reschedule your appointment? Once that's set, we can talk about budget counseling if you're interested in finding ways to get the phone company to stop inconveniencing you and turn your phone back on."

Matching your feedback to a person's style

If the person is matter-of-fact in the way she speaks to you ("I want to go back to school"), use factual feedback ("You're interested in going back for more education?") If the person shows some emotion ("My friend just got into a computer course! She's going to be able to get a good job! I want to go back to school, too!"), reflect that back as well ("That's exciting about your friend getting into a computer course! You'd like to do it, too!"). Only then should you focus on solutions ("You'd like a good job, too. Would you like to find out more about computer school, and ways you could pay for it and find good care for your children while you work?").

Too often, people who are trying to help someone else jump right into trying to find a solution. But if you want the family members you work with to feel that you respect them, you'll need to use plenty of factual and emotional feedback first. If they are really upset about a situation, you may need to provide several rounds of emotional feedback.

With practice, you can become so skilled at using feedback that people don't even notice you're doing it. They just feel that you really understand them and want to help them reach their goals. Sometimes the most helpful communication comes from listening so well that you pick up on passing statements that others might miss.

One family worker told her favorite story:

> I was sitting, listening, during a home visit. This mom was talking about her past, and mentioned that a number of years ago when she was in high school, she had thought she wanted to be a nurse. I replied, "Well, you look like a nurse." Within a week, she got herself in school and now she's a nurse.

F. Saying what you mean clearly and respectfully

The listening skills described above can help you understand people and their reasons for doing what they do. While listening is a very important part of communicating, you also need to be able to say what you think while showing respect for others.

The basic format for saying what you mean clearly and respectfully has three phrases:

1. What happened
2. What you feel
3. What you want

When people first begin practicing this format, they sometimes feel (and sound) awkward. But soon they are able to express their feelings about a situation and their needs in a way that seems more natural. It just takes practice. You can practice this skill by modifying the format in ways that reflect your own personality, so it will sound and feel natural.

Begin with a brief description of what's on your mind: "When I come to see you at the time we've agreed on and you're not here, I feel worried, and frustrated that we can't work together if you're not here." You may want to stop there and listen, or you may want to go on to say what you would like to have happen: "If you can't keep an appointment, please call my office the day before so I can use the time with another family." Then use your best listening skills to hear what the other person tells you about the situation. You will learn something valuable, and the other person will feel respected.

Give feedback; for example, "You forgot that we had an appointment last week." If the person offers possible solutions that could work, encourage them: "Yes, I agree that it is hard to remember when I'm coming when it's always on a different day of the week. I could come every Tuesday morning at ten o'clock, or every Friday at two thirty, if you'd rather have a regular meeting time."

If you have ideas of your own, offer them lightly, using this format: "I wonder if you'd like to have a calendar to hang on your refrigerator to write down all your appointments?" Thank the person for working with you; be positive: "I appreciate your willingness to work with me on this. I really want to continue to work with you. You've made such good progress toward your goal. Knowing you'll be here when we have an appointment will be a big help to me."

Notice that there was no judgment expressed about the person's way of handling things, only an expression of your needs in the situation. Imagine how this situation could have unfolded without mutual respect, skillful listening, and saying what you mean clearly and respectfully. For example, don't say, "Where were you last week when I came? You missed our appointment! If you want to stay in our program, you have to be here when I come!" This example may seem exaggerated, but most of us can think of times we have not been as skillful as we could have been in communicating. Good listening and speaking skills are especially helpful in tough situations, when you want to get your message across without blaming.

Typical responses to skillful speaking

There are four typical responses to skillful speaking:

1. Agreement
2. Resistance
3. Emotions
4. Statement of needs without acknowledging yours

The first, which may surprise you when it happens, is agreement: the person does what you ask. When this happens, say, "Thank you. I really appreciate that."

Another typical response is *resistance*. The person blames you or someone else for the problem, attacks your ideas or criticizes you, or gives excuses. If the other person resists your message in these ways, try not to be sidetracked. Use feedback, listen, respond to their needs, and state your own. Work toward a solution; for example, "You feel it's my fault that you don't have an apartment, because I didn't give you the phone number of the housing office." Then listen and respond: "You wish you were on their list already. Would you like to look up the phone number together right now, so you can call and make an appointment? It's important to me to know that you have your name on their list, because I care about you getting out of the shelter."

A third response, which is hard for many people to handle, is emotion: the person starts crying or gets angry. In this case, use this same sequence of feedback, listening, responding to their needs, and stating your own, but be careful to use emotional feedback. "It makes you sad to think of having to move, and scared not to know where you'll be living. You've had so many changes and disappointments to deal with. You have to get out of your sister's place by this weekend. I'm as eager as you are to see you settled in an apartment. Shall we make a list together of what we can each do to help you get an apartment and move?"

A fourth typical response is for the other person to respond with his or her own needs, without acknowledging yours. It would be easy to keep restating your own needs but more productive to use the sequence of feedback, listening, and responding to their needs, before restating your own: "You need a place to live, fast. You have to be out of here by this weekend. You're scared. How would you like me to help?" Now listen, and then state your needs: "The man from the housing office said they could pay a deposit and half the rent if you can find an apartment for under $450? You need my help finding an apartment under $450 that is still in your daughter's school district? I'd be glad to help you go look at apartments tomorrow afternoon. The Pennysaver comes out tonight. Can you get a copy, circle the ads that interest you, and call and make appointments for tomorrow between one o'clock and four thirty? Please call me tomorrow at 11:30 to let me know what you've lined up."

To summarize, you can handle responses in these ways:

1. Agreement: gracious acceptance
2. Resistance: feedback, listening, responding, restating your needs
3. Emotions: emotional feedback, listening, responding, restating your needs
4. Statement of needs: respect their needs, and go for a "win-win"

G. Promoting cooperative solutions to conflicts

Handling conflict is a challenge even for the skilled communicator. What do we mean by conflict? It can range from a mild disagreement that simmers under the surface to nuclear war. We can all think of examples of conflict that was poorly handled, whether in our own families or communities, or in the world. This is why it's hard for many people to realize that there can be benefits to conflict. Conflict can keep things moving in our lives and force us to see how others see things. Many people don't realize that a disagreement shows that someone cares about the situation or about us. When people just don't care at all, they are apathetic or disinterested, and there is no conflict.

Seven steps to resolving conflicts

These seven steps to resolving conflicts rely on skillful listening and speaking:

1. Encourage the other person to describe the complaint fully. Use "door openers," "encouragers," and open questions.

2. Let the other person know you understand their complaint. Use the appropriate type of feedback: emotional, factual, or solution-focused. Don't defend yourself or retaliate with your own complaints.

3. Affirm something you admire in the person. It's best if the quality is something that can help in the situation.

4. Look for the need behind the problem.

5. Together, come up with a list of possible solutions.

6. Together, choose one that meets both of your needs.

7. Agree on a specific time period to try out the solution.

The first step in reaching a solution is to listen well. The three types of communication helpers—door openers, encouragers and open questions—are a good place to start. Next, you need to let the other person know you understand the complaint. That doesn't mean you agree with it, only that you understand it. This feedback will prompt the person to tell you what is on his or her mind. Respond with feedback, matching the type of feedback to the person's complaint. *Remember that you may have to use several rounds of feedback to understand the person's complaint completely.*

Once the other person believes that you've understood the complaint, you can really begin to work together on finding a solution. One of the reasons so many conflicts go unresolved and end up in bitterness is that many people skip this step. Often, this step alone will mitigate a person's complaint, especially if you combine it with affirmation. Affirmation means to mention a quality that you honestly admire in the person. It's best if the quality can be helpful in this situation. For example, if a family member is very angry when you tell him or her you are obliged to call in a report for child abuse, you can combine listening, feedback, and affirmation:

> I understand that you're furious at me for reporting you to the child abuse hotline. You feel betrayed, because you've been trying hard to control your temper around your children. You've even gone into treatment for your alcoholism. I really admire the work you've done on controlling your emotions, and respect how hard you're working to get help with your drinking problem. Yet I can't ignore Michael here with a black eye and welts on his face. I understand that getting reported is a big setback when you've been working so hard, and that you thought I would never report you. I really respect all the hard work you're doing, and I will tell that to the judge.

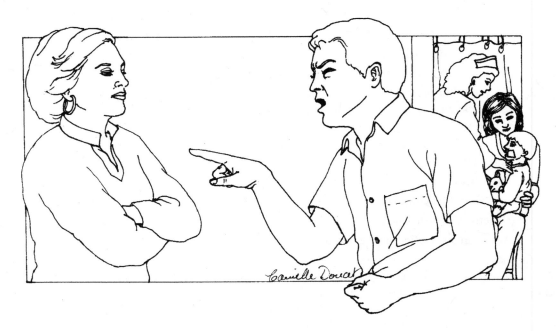

Offering understanding and affirmation can help an angry person move through intense emotion to engage in a cooperative discussion of the problem. Once you have reached agreement on the problem, look for the needs behind it. Too often, people jump to trying to solve the problem before identifying needs. Once you understand what each of you needs, you can work together to come up with a list of possible solutions. Then, together, choose one that meets the needs of you both. The last step is to agree on a specific period of time to try out the solution, and to talk it over again.

Skillful listening and speaking can help resolve all kinds of conflict, whether or not blame and criticism are involved. One example could be that your agency is divided over whether or not to use the family development approach. Some of your co-workers feel that most people receiving the agency's services are trying to take unfair advantage of what is offered. These workers feel that a family worker's main job is to monitor closely the people receiving services to make sure they use as few services as possible for the shortest time. They don't have time to help families develop goals or seek out specialized services that would help families meet these goals. They are already overworked because of all the families who take as much as they can from the system.

Other workers feel that the monitoring approach leads to an endless cycle of services and dependency. They want to build partnerships with families so families will set and reach goals for healthier, more independent lives. These workers see some families who abuse the system, but they see many others who really need the agency's help, and who have some motivation to help themselves.

Skillful listening and speaking can help people in these two factions of an agency understand each other's point of view and find ways to work together more constructively.

H. Handling blame and criticism constructively

One of the hardest aspects of being a family worker may be taking blame or criticism from families you work with, co-workers, or your supervisor. Why is there so much blame and criticism? We live in an adversarial society, in which one of the main messages we hear is that whenever there's a problem, someone is to blame, someone should pay, and you should do everything you can to make sure it's not you who pays. This is an extension of the submission-aggression loop. If aggression or submission are the only two solutions, then someone wins, and someone loses, with the best possible outcome defined as a compromise that satisfies neither person.

It's natural to want to defend yourself! Yet, jumping into defending yourself can easily lead to a spiral of blame, criticism, and bad feelings. Fortunately, it is often possible to find a solution in which each person's needs are met. Not everyone is initially willing to work out such a solution. Some people are so used to looking for a winner and a loser in every situation that they think a solution is too "soft" unless they win and the other person loses.

You are already developing the skills needed to handle blame, criticism, and conflict. Skillful listening and speaking skills can help with the blame and criticism you will inevitably encounter in your work. And ironically, saying what you mean clearly and respectfully can also bring on blame and criticism as a form of resistance to what you're saying.

The next time you're treated this way, try using skillful listening and speaking. Compare these two examples:

Example without skillful listening and speaking

Family member:

> We got an eviction notice last night! We have to be out by Friday! The landlady said she hadn't gotten any rent money for three months! You told me you had arranged for Section 8 housing for us. My children and my elderly mother will be out on the street in two days, and it's all your fault! You're supposed to be helping us! You should be fired from your job! Let me talk to your boss!

Family worker:

> Wait a minute! It's not my fault you got evicted. Did you go down to the Housing Authority like I said and fill out the paperwork? Is all that trash still lying around in your hallway? There are lots of other families who want a good subsidized apartment if you can't be cooperative. I've worked at this agency for six years and no one has ever treated me so disrespectfully!

Example with skillful listening and speaking

Family worker:

> I can see you're furious and worried about being evicted. I'll try to help you, and I'll appreciate it if we can be respectful toward each other. I know getting evicted is scary, and I'll be able to help you best if we're working together on this. Let me make sure I have the facts right, so I can help you straighten this out as quickly as possible. Mrs. Barber said she hasn't received rent from the housing authority for three months? You received a written eviction notice yesterday, saying you're supposed to be out by Friday? Can you remember what kind of paperwork you filled out at the Housing Authority office, and when it was?

This family worker used skillful listening and speaking to sidestep a huge load of blame and criticism, while acknowledging the family member's feelings, getting the facts straight, and focusing on solutions. She also managed to regain a tone of mutual respect.

Handling blame and criticism is like an advanced course in communication skills. Try practicing your listening and speaking skills in calm situations first, so you'll be able to rely on them when the going gets rough.

I. Confronting people constructively when necessary

As a family worker, sometimes you have to confront someone with a situation that he or she doesn't want to face. Using skillful listening and speaking is a respectful way to take this action. For example, let's say an older woman you work with was diagnosed two years ago with diabetes and high blood pressure. You helped her arrange for a home health aide to help her learn how to take her glucose reading and handle her medications for two months. You also arranged for her to meet with a nutrition aide to help her learn new recipes and shopping tips. The nutritionist gave your client information about an easy exercise class near her home and about Meals on Wheels, in case she didn't feel up to cooking all the time.

When you next visit her, she is busy baking brownies for the church bazaar. "I make them every Monday to take to the nursing home, too," she tells you. "Everyone loves my recipe. Would you like to try some?" You can see she has gained weight.

She mentions that she has been having "dizzy spells" and plans to have some tests at the doctor's one of these days. When you ask about the exercise class, she tells you, "My friend goes, and she likes it, but it's not my style. Anyway, it meets on Mondays, when I take my brownies to the nursing home. But weren't we going to work on trying to get someone to help me with my taxes? I can't see well enough to do much close work anymore, so I can't balance my checkbook. My taxes are going to be hard this year because of that." You see what looks like a cut-off notice from the electric company lying on top of her pile of unpaid bills.

You suspect that this charming, independent lady is on the verge of disaster, financially and physically. What can you do? Use your listening and speaking skills:

> It sounds like you and your brownies are very popular at the nursing home. I can easily see why everyone there would enjoy your good company. I do feel concerned to see you making brownies, though, because of your diabetes. It would be very hard for me to bake brownies without wanting to eat them! I care about you, and am concerned that eating brownies may be leading to dizzy spells. I'm worried that you might have a dizzy spell and fall sometime, especially since you live alone.

> Let's talk about finding someone to help you go over your bills and balance your checkbook. And some older people ask the utility companies to send a notice to their sons or daughters or a friend if a bill doesn't get paid on time.

In this way, you can affirm her positive intentions, help her to recognize some facts she may be denying, and offer her solutions based on what she recognizes as the problem. Sharing your perspective in this way preserves her dignity while alerting her to important concerns.

J. Communicating about "hot topics"

The communication skills you're learning here can be used successfully to address any subject, but are especially useful when you need to communicate about a "hot topic"—something that is usually hard to talk about, such as domestic violence, substance abuse, or AIDS. Chapter 8 will help you recognize problems that require such services, and show you how to support families in specialized treatment programs. The communication skills you're learning now are the first step in addressing these "hot topics" that require specialized services.

For example, a person you're working with has many excuses for not making the progress you agreed on together in your goal-setting sessions. His life may be filled with drama and seem much more interesting than a lot of the families you see in your work. He may even be quite intelligent and charming. Yet you have a feeling he is abusing drugs, and seeming to cooperate with your family development program as a way to appease his family members and probation officer. Confront his behavior respectfully:

> Sam, I care about you and your family. I know you've had a lot of hard luck, but I'm concerned because I haven't noticed much progress toward the goals you set when we started working together four months ago. I'm concerned for you and for your family. In order for me to keep working with your family, I need you to have an evaluation session with the Drug and Alcohol center. You and the counselor there can decide how to proceed. Are you willing to go?

You and your agency need to have a policy about what to do when someone you are working with, and suspect has an addiction problem, refuses to seek appropriate assessment and treatment. Ask your supervisor whether your agency has a policy about working with people who will not confront their own addictions (also see Chapter 8).

K. Working with families with language barriers or low levels of literacy

Many agencies use jargon that is hard for people outside that profession to understand, and forms that are hard to fill out. Keep in mind that as many as 25 percent of people in the United States can't read English well enough to fill out a job application because of learning disabilities, incomplete educations, or the fact that English is not their home language.

Using plain language

Practice describing your agency's services and requirements in plain language. Take a look at your agency's brochures and forms with this goal in mind. Too often, agency forms and publicity give much more information than families need or can digest at the first meeting. In addition, it is common for workers to use abbreviations or acronyms (such as "WIC" for Women, Infants and Children Program) rather than the entire name of a program; this can be confusing to people unfamiliar with the programs. Ask several families you work with if they can suggest changes that would help families understand your agency and its procedures better. If there are forms that cannot be changed (or until they can be), you'll need to develop ways to help families fill them out so they can get the services they need.

Many family literacy programs are willing to answer questions from agency staff about how best to encourage families' efforts. Some will sponsor in-service training or conferences to help other agencies promote literacy or help agencies rewrite their brochures and forms at a basic level. Learning to communicate with skill and heart will help you help families in even the most challenging circumstances.

L. Communicating using technology

In today's world, e-mail, cell phones, and other electronic devices are commonplace and serve as a primary way we communicate with each other. Workers in the same office are just as likely to e-mail or text each other than to pick up the phone and talk face to face. Sometimes, though, there is no substitute for talking in person, particularly when dealing with conflict situations. Constantly checking e-mail or phone messages also takes away from mindfulness and our ability to focus on the task at hand. New studies are showing that it promotes multitasking behaviors, which, as it turns out, impede our understanding and ultimate productiveness. Technology has opened new doors and, if wisely used, can be a tremendous help, but it can also waste time and lead to misunderstandings. Keeping technology in balanced perspective is important.

Although technology can help you communicate with the families you coach, realize that many families cannot afford cell-phone plans or Internet access. Similarly, those living in rural areas may not have broadband access. However, for those who do, e-mail and texting may be the best way to contact them to confirm appointments, home visits, or just to check in. You may get a quicker response from a text than a phone message. Most public libraries and some community programs also have free computer access and classes to promote computer literacy that could be beneficial to families, particularly those doing job searches.

Another aspect of technology is social networking. It is not advisable to become personal "Facebook friends" with the families you serve. However, many not-for-profits are using Facebook and Twitter to market their programs and reach out to communities. This is a great way to publicize special events, recruit, or even send out snippets of information. It is amazing how many "followers" you can attract who could be supporters of your program.

You can also help educate the families you serve about the importance of safe use of the Internet. The Children's Online Privacy Protection Act (COPPA) is a federal law designed to prevent businesses or predators from obtaining a child's personal information without a parent's permission. COPPA requires websites to explain their privacy policies on their sites and get parental consent before collecting or using a child's personal information, such as a name, address, phone number, or Social Security number. The law prohibits sites from requiring children to provide more personal information than necessary to play a game or participate in a contest.

Despite this law, unless parents explicitly teach their children not to give any information over the Internet, many children do freely provide such information to play a game or enter a contest. Parents who understand the Internet and its use, keep current, and are not afraid to set limits (which may include not providing electronic devices or removing them, if a child or teenager uses them unwisely) are the best protection. To complicate the issue, many schools now require or promote online homework sites, which require Internet access and therefore necessitate constant monitoring of its appropriate use.

Parents are kids' best online protection and may need help to decipher the opportunities and hazards. According to the American Academy of Pediatrics,[6]

> When you and your family surf the Web it's important to keep the following in mind:
>
> - Online information is usually not private.
> - People online are not always who they say they are.
> - Anyone can put information online.
> - You can't trust everything you read online.
> - You and your family may unexpectedly and unintentionally find material on the Web that is offensive, pornographic (including child pornography), obscene, violent, or racist.

References

Bavelier, Daphne. 2012. Your brain on video games. *TED.com*. Retrieved
    from http://www.ted.com/talks/daphne_bavelier_your_brain_on_video_games.html.
Centers for Disease Control and Prevention. *Kids and technology: Tips for parents in a high-tech world*. Retrieved from
    http://www.cdc.gov/media/subtopic/matte/pdf/cdcelectronicregression.pdf.
Vavricheck, S. M. (2012). *The guide to compassionate assertiveness: How to express your needs and deal with conflict while keeping a kind heart*. Oakland, CA: New Harbinger.

---

[6] http://www.aap.org/en-us/Pages/Default.aspx; accessed 3/17/14):

Activities to Extend Learning

Chapter 2
Communicating with Skill and Heart

A. Communicating with skill and heart

1. List three communication skills you see as your strengths. Describe an experience for each in which you demonstrated that strength.

2. Describe a communication that went wrong, and why. List three communication skills you would like to develop more fully to help you handle situations like this one more skillfully in the future.

B. Empathy: Putting yourself in their shoes

1. List the people you communicated with in your work over the past week. Identify one thing for each person that you have in common.

2. What information about your personal life would you feel comfortable sharing with families? How might sharing information about your own life build empathy with a family?

3. Briefly describe an actual experience in which you shared information about your personal life with a family. Write a reflection on the experience referring to the "guidelines on deciding what to share" in this chapter.

4. How can you, as a family worker, "put yourself in their shoes" and build empathy with families if you have not experienced a similar challenge or struggle in your own life?

C. Understanding nonverbal communication

1. Describe the skills or techniques you use to help put families at ease using nonverbal communication when you meet them for the first time at their home or at your office.

2. Walk around your agency and observe the physical environment (for example, the location and privacy of reception, posters, signage). What nonverbal messages does your agency send?

3. If you meet with families in an agency office, sit where family members usually sit and look at your workspace from their point of view. What nonverbal messages do you send families through the photos, posters, or personal items displayed in your workspace?

D. Finding a good balance between listening and expressing yourself

1. Describe a situation in which you have been submissive or aggressive. Then, describe how you could handle the situation in the future, using skillful speaking.

2. Which of the following is your natural strength in communicating: listening or expressing yourself? What are some advantages of having that strength in your work with families? What steps could you take to find a good balance between listening and expressing yourself?

3. In communicating with others, do you tend to be primarily submissive, aggressive, in the aggression-submission loop, or mutually respectful/assertive? What have been some costs and payoffs for you?

E. Listening well

1. Describe the challenges of creating a listening atmosphere in the places where you work. List three possible ways of improving the atmosphere to support good listening.

2. Identify a communication blocker you use. Describe the results, and how you could have used communication helpers instead. Try replacing this communication blocker with a helper for the next two weeks, and describe the results.

F. Saying what you mean clearly and respectfully

1. Note when someone responds with any of the typical responses to skillful speaking—compliance, resistance, emotions, and statement of needs—without acknowledging yours. Practice handling these responses. Describe the results.

2. Describe an actual workplace situation in which a co-worker was being inconsiderate or behaving inappropriately. Using the guidelines in the chapter, how would you address the issue with them clearly and respectfully?

G. Promoting cooperative solutions to conflicts

1. Think about a time when you had a disagreement or conflict with your own family member or an agency colleague. "Replay" the situation using the seven steps to resolving conflict, and describe what each of you could say and do to come to a win-win solution.

2. Describe a disagreement or conflict in the workplace that was not resolved. Reflect on how you might have communicated differently to get a better outcome.

H. Handling blame and criticism constructively

1. How do you feel when someone criticizes the work your agency does because of a negative experience? Referring to the fourth step to resolve conflict, what might be the need behind this person's problem with the agency?

2. Write how you would respond to the following statement, using skillful listening and speaking: "I'll never go to ABC agency again! I sat there waiting for four hours only to find out we're not eligible for their program. The worker didn't help us at all and didn't even apologize for wasting our entire day!"

I. Confronting people constructively when needed

1. A family you are working with during the winter has extremely high electric bills because their home is poorly insulated and needs a new furnace. You tell them about the benefits of weatherization and offer to help prepare an application, but the family declines. Today, they tell you the electric bill is being turned over to a collection agency. Write a short script using skillful listening and speaking that would help them recognize some facts they may be denying and offer solutions that preserve their dignity.

2. Choose three skills for "communicating with skill and heart." Describe an example of how each could be used by a family worker to help a family handle a situation that they don't want to face.

J. Communicating about "hot topics"

1. List five hot topics that come up in your work. Choose the one you find most challenging and write a script for handling it, using your communication skills.

2. What do you feel have been some hot topics for you to talk about with families? What support do you get from your agency to respectfully talk about these hot topics? What support(s) you need? How can your agency help you?

3. Does your program or agency have a policy regarding working with a family that has an addiction problem they are not facing? How does the policy, or its lack, affect your ability to offer support and services to those families?

K. Working with families with language barriers or low levels of literacy

1. Divide a sheet of paper into three columns. In the first column, list services or programs in your community that are most frequently referred to using acronyms. In the second column, write out the full name of the service or program. In the third column, write a description of that service or program using plain language that families with limited literacy could easily understand.

2. Learn about family literacy programs in your community and services available for adults with special learning needs or disabilities. Use this information to prepare a script to talk with an interested family member. After preparing the script, underline and label the statements that reflect techniques to communicate with skill and heart from this chapter.

L. Communicating using technology

1. How do you communicate with families using technology while maintaining appropriate boundaries?

2. Reflect upon whether you keep technology in a balanced perspective. How might you make needed changes in your use of technology?

Skills Practices

These skills practices are a suggested list. You may also develop your own skills practice or make modifications to the ones listed below to help you create a meaningful and manageable plan.

1. Over a one week period, practice communicating with others using the following communication helpers: "door openers," "encouragers," and "open questions." Describe one situation during the week when you used them and how it went. How did the person respond when you used communication helpers? How did they promote more open and genuine communication?

2. Choose a person who you communicate with on a daily basis. Over a one-week period, practice "skillful listening" and offer factual, emotional, and solution-focused feedback in communicating with this person. At the end of the week, respond to these questions: What steps did you take to practice listening well during the week? How did the person respond? What did you learn about your skills at balancing skillful listening and expressing yourself?

3. Meet with a friend or a member of your own family to discuss a concern. Practice using the format of stating what happened, what you felt, and what you want clearly and respectfully. Use communication helpers and feedback to reflect back what you hear. Write a reflection on the experience and identify strengths you saw in yourself and the other person.

4. Review a brochure, form, or other printed material from your agency that is routinely used with families. Assess whether you think families with language barriers or limited literacy could understand it. If needed, propose how you might revise the text, substitute pictures for words, or make other changes that would help families with limited literacy learn about the agency's services in a culturally appropriate and respectful way.

5. Prepare a list of ways you think you use nonverbal communication with others. Then, ask two friends or co-workers to describe ways they observe you communicate without using words. What messages do you intentionally try to send using nonverbal communication? Did your friend or co-worker observe any message(s) in your nonverbal communication that you didn't think you were sending? As a family development worker, why is it helpful to know how you send messages to others through nonverbal communication?

6. If you feel that using technology (of all types) has created an imbalance in your life, make some intentional changes over a one week period. Describe what you did and reflect on the experience. What will you do differently?

Chapter 3
Presence and Mindfulness: Cornerstones of Healthy Relationships

Objectives

A. Recognize the value of presence.

B. Describe the benefits of increased awareness and mindfulness in your life.

C. Learn about research on mindfulness-based stress reduction.

D. Use simple exercises for mindfulness-based stress reduction.

E. Incorporate natural ways to practice mindfulness-based stress reduction at work.

A. Presence

Helping families recognize and build constructively on their own powerful bone-deep longing is crucial to their future, and to the future of our country and the world. Each person is born with a unique combination of talents, which—if cultivated by parents, caregivers, and schools—will remain strong and grow into her or his exceptional gift to the community and the world. Recognizing and supporting these unique talents requires presence.

Presence is giving focused attention to yourself or another person, without judgment. It is healing, restorative, freeing, and protective. The more present you are to your own life, the more present you can be for others. Presence is the foundation of the work done by credentialed family workers. It allows us to take a fresh look at our own lives, without preconceived ideas or being stuck in old patterns. *The fresh view gained through presence is necessary for transformative learning to take place.*

Many people readily recall someone—a parent, grandparent, friend, counselor, teacher, family worker, or sponsor—whose presence made a major difference in their lives. Through presence, that special person noticed and encouraged their talents, protected them, opened doors.

Too often, however, talents go unnoticed, are ridiculed, or become buried under survival strategies in a chaotic family or neighborhood. Without emotional and physical safety and healthy outlets for unique talents, the child, young person, or adult looks for ways to fit in and find relief. Behaviors that are healthy in moderation can quickly become addictions, as the person seeks to numb the pain of being "different" or living in an abusive, unsafe world. As the quest for numbing relief grows, tobacco, alcohol, narcotics, gambling, severe overeating, or other forms of self-abuse often enter the picture, leading to the downward spiral of addiction.

Presence is the opposite of the numbing that occurs in addiction, and can become a powerful force in a family worker's approach. Presence can also serve as a powerful component of a person's recovery from addiction. How do we become present, as family workers and in our own lives, so we can live healthy lives that express our unique talents and promote health? Mindfulness practice, which you will learn in this chapter, is a great place to begin. Establishing a daily mindfulness practice will help you become more present. Yet presence is more than mindfulness practice. Presence is being fully present to your own life, and in your interactions with the families you coach. Presence is living your own life to the fullest and helping your own family and others in your sphere of influence do the same.

Does a mindful life mean you can't relax, watch a movie, or enjoy eating with friends? Not at all. You can enjoy all this while remaining mindful, as long as you are not consumed by or addicted to these actions. This is the age-old challenge: living life to the fullest while not becoming controlled by it.

Few people have mastered this balance (I certainly have not!). The goal is to incorporate into your daily life practices reminders to help you become and remain more mindful, and—when you begin to lose balance—to know how to regain it.

More than services: Compassionate presence

Providing services can be a waste of time and money if the person providing the services is unskillful, or if the family does not set its own goal. Compassionate presence is the foundation of skilled family development work. Compassion is not simply feeling sorry for the families we work with; it is bringing your full awareness to your work with people. Sometimes simply sitting or standing with a family, offering your full attention, and listening can help them begin to unravel their problems enough to identify what they need to do and what specific help they need.

Even when a family's problems are complex (which is often the case), your compassionate presence can help them sort out their most pressing goals and begin to make encouraging progress. *Empowerment Skills for Family Workers* will teach you how to develop your natural compassion through an approach called *mindfulness: bringing your full attention to each moment*. It will also help you handle the stressful situations all family workers encounter, using the mindfulness-based stress reduction methods developed at the University of Massachusetts Medical Center.

B. Shifting your focus from "doing" to "being"

How do you feel when you are with someone who gives you undivided attention? Imagine how this scenario might feel: no cell phones, no interruptions, just you and the other person listening to one another. This quality of presence, being totally awake and aware each moment, is the essential quality of a family development worker. Although few people are able to sustain this quality of presence for long periods, you can begin today to cultivate your unique capacity to be more fully present with others.

First, practice being present with yourself. Do you arrive at your office breathless, your mind already racing through a long list of "to do's"? There is nothing wrong with having a "to-do" list, but if you want to live more fully, try shifting your focus from getting things done to being fully present with each person you meet and every activity you undertake. Don't worry, you'll still be able to cross those tasks off your to-do list, but you'll do it with deeper understanding and creativity.

Mindfulness is exactly this quality of being and awareness. In the study of creativity, mindfulness is sometimes called "flow." In athletics, it's sometimes called "being in the zone." Mindfulness is not something you have to acquire; you already have it. It is your natural birthright. As a baby, you played, delighting in every aspect of "the moment." But by the time you reached adulthood, millions of (often mixed) messages had blunted the keen awareness and natural intuitive intelligence that you had as a baby. Mindfulness is a practice that can help you recover some of that natural capacity to be joyfully and fully present in your life.

In *The Power of Mindful Learning,*[7] Ellen Langer suggests using mindfulness as an approach to counteract the inclination to think and act in "mindless" and unconscious ways. For example, read the following message, which typically appears at the close of most professional correspondence:

> Thank you for your time and and attention with this matter.

Just a typical closing sentence to a business letter? If you noticed the extra "and" in the middle of the sentence, you were probably reading with a more alert, mindful approach than most people bring to daily life.

---

[7] Ellen Langer, *The power of mindful learning* (Reading, MA: Perseus, 1997).

Mindfulness brings increased alertness to everything and everyone you encounter. This alertness can bring potential problems to your attention while they are still in their early stages, when it is easier to redirect them. *Intuition—your subtle, inner wisdom—thrives in a mindful atmosphere.*

You might be thinking that, even if it were possible to give undivided attention to every task and person, by always being mindful you could never get everything done. However, being mindful is not merely another time management technique. It is an approach that allows you to:

- Appreciate the creativity that both you and the families you work with have to find innovative solutions to problems

- Bring all of "who you are" as a unique individual to your work

- Reframe the outdated and limiting "monitoring" mind-set into a vision of partnership with families who set their own goals

- Transform mindless conditioned responses into fresh, aware living

C. Mindfulness-based stress reduction

As a front-line family worker, you need a stress reduction program that really works. *Empowerment Skills for Family Workers* offers front-line workers practical, effective stress reduction techniques.

Stress reduction has been a popular choice for portfolio work since Cornell issued the first Family Development Credentials in 1996. At first, I was pleased that workers were learning such useful skills, but a further analysis of the FDC portfolios made me realize how inherently stressful front-line family work really is. I asked myself, "Is something more than stress management needed? If so, who in the United States is doing the most effective work in this area?"

This query sent me searching. I found that the University of Massachusetts Medical Center's Stress Reduction Clinic had an impressive record in settings similar to those in which family workers work. This clinic has twenty-five years of research findings from its work in free community clinics, public schools, and workplaces. Using the mindfulness-based stress reduction methods developed at the University of Massachusetts, men and women from a range of cultural backgrounds and life circumstances showed significant improvements in serious stress-related illnesses.

I was intrigued, so I took the professional training offered by the Stress Reduction Clinic's director, Dr. Saki Santorelli, and its founder, Dr. Jon Kabat-Zinn. I learned to bring moment-to-moment awareness—mindfulness—to everyday activities such as breathing, walking, sitting, and eating. I tried the "body scan" developed at the Clinic, bringing gentle awareness to each part of my body. I practiced simple stretching exercises. I felt my knots of stress unwind in ways that twenty-five years of practicing and teaching stress management had not touched.

It doesn't cost anything to practice mindfulness-based stress reduction, nor does it require any special gear. Drs. Kabat-Zinn and Santorelli emphasized that before teaching mindfulness-based stress reduction to others, a person should practice it daily for at least one year. They recommend at least forty-five minutes of practice daily.

I followed their recommendations. A year later, I was so convinced that this simple, yet profound approach could be helpful in the FDC system, that I offered the FDC's first retreat for its facilitators and field advisors. I was not new to mindfulness, having practiced it for two decades, but their methods showed me the benefits this approach could offer FDC instructors and portfolio advisors, agency leaders, front-line workers, and, ultimately, the families we serve.

For a more detailed description of these practices and the body-scan technique, read Jon Kabat-Zinn's book, *Full Catastrophe Living: Using the Wisdom of Your Mind and Body to Face Pain, Stress, and Illness.*[8] This lively book contains many stories from people in all walks of life who have significantly

---

[8] Jon Kabat-Zinn, *Full catastrophe living: Using the wisdom of your body and mind to face stress, pain and illness* (New York: Delta, 1990).

reduced their symptoms of stress-related illness using these methods. It provides a great resource to help you "practice what we preach" in the FDC: learning respectfully from people whose cultural backgrounds and experiences might differ from yours. If you would like to practice mindfulness-based stress reduction, these exercises are a good place to start.

D. Mindfulness practice exercises

Mindful breathing

Perhaps you're ready to try mindfulness practice but wonder how to begin. You won't need any special equipment; just find a quiet spot with a comfortable chair. Start with ten minutes of mindful breathing. To begin, you can close your eyes (although it's okay to keep your eyes open, if you prefer) and bring your awareness to the sounds around you: birds, traffic, people talking, or whatever noises you hear. As you settle in, you'll become aware of more subtle sounds, such as the air conditioning or heating system noises. Let go of these sounds and pay attention to your breathing coming in, then going out. Concentrate on your breathing and experience the sensations of your body as you inhale and exhale.

If thoughts begin to arise during this exercise, gently bring your attention back to your breathing. Feel any emotions that arise, but don't let the story behind the emotion occupy your attention. After a few minutes, and when you are ready, open your eyes and slowly bring yourself back to your external world. Mindful breathing will help you feel refreshed, peaceful, and ready to meet whatever the next part of your day brings. You can gradually increase these sessions to 45 minutes a day.

Mindful walking

Once you're comfortable with the mindfulness breathing practice, try mindful walking. Usually, we gallop from place to place, barely noticing how we arrived. Mindful walking invites you to pay exquisite attention to the usually unconscious activity of walking. Lift one foot gently, slowly, off the ground. Pay attention to each muscle as your foot leaves the earth. Be aware of the miraculous coordination of bones, muscles, and sinews that work with your brain to enable you to lift your foot. Notice where your body weight is resting.

When you're ready, slowly place that foot onto the ground. Feel yourself fully grounded before gradually shifting your weight. Keep breathing. When you're ready, mindfully lift your other foot. Try walking in this way for three minutes, bringing your full moment-to-moment awareness to the process. You will cover very little ground. The purpose is not to get somewhere; it is to be fully present where you are.

Try bringing this same quality of attention to other things you do routinely, such as answering the phone. Instead of leaping to answer the phone on the first ring, you could let it be a signal to be mindful before you answer.

Mindful stretching

Do you spend much of your day sitting in meetings, at the computer, or in a car? Try mindful stretching. Just getting up out of your chair can restore your mindfulness. Start by standing up, stretching your arms overhead, and then letting them fall back to your sides. Gently roll your shoulders forward and then back. A little mindful stretching can do wonders to relax and bring awareness to your body. Better yet, take a class in stretching or yoga, or find an exercise teacher to come to your workplace to offer gentle stretching classes.

Mindful listening

Family workers spend hours each day listening. In Chapter 2 you practiced using advanced-level communication skills to help you say what you mean clearly and respectfully. Listening affords an ideal way to practice mindfulness. Instead of focusing on your reply while listening, bring your full attention to what the other person is saying. Every encounter is an opportunity to practice mindful listening. Imagine that you've never listened to anyone before. Then bring that fresh, curious perspective to listening to the other person.

Mindful living

Mindfulness is not just a skill to practice; it is an approach to life. No one ever lives mindfully in every moment. By practicing mindfulness regularly in focused activities such as mindful breathing or mindful walking, you will develop a habit of mindfulness that will carry over to other moments in your life. You may drive down the street and be keenly aware of the bright red berries on the trees around you, or notice with appreciation a moment of silence in your day. Mindfulness practice deepens with time; it can help you live your life to its fullest and bring forth your natural compassion and intuitive intelligence.

E. Practical strategies for mindful family development work

One way to begin a work day

Subtle changes in your work patterns can help you bring mindfulness into your daily work. I begin each work day in basically the same way. I walk into my office, close the door, open the window, and sit down quietly without saying anything. I don't check my e-mail or use the phone right away. I just sit there, quietly breathing and being aware that I'm alive. I don't deliberately think about things; if thoughts arise, I ask them to take a walk, agreeing to see them later. After a little while, I pick up the notepad I keep near my chair, and make my to-do list for the day. The list usually contains several items left over from the to-do list I made at the end of the previous day, but often it includes a few new items that emerged during my silent mindfulness practice—people to call, something to attend to. Only then do I have conversations with my co-workers, some of these by phone.

I let my intuition guide me. In these quiet moments, sometimes for no obvious reason, I'll feel like calling a certain person—maybe someone I met with a few days before, or perhaps a person I haven't spoken with in years. Most often, something worthwhile comes of following this intuitive guidance. Maybe I call the person I met with yesterday and find out she has had new thoughts about our plan to begin a collaborative project, or perhaps I call a former colleague and discover that he has received a new grant and that the FDC program turns out to be what he needs.

Sometimes I don't know exactly what to say when following up on my intuition. I might just say, "Hi, this is Claire Forest. We haven't talked in a while, and I just felt like calling. How are things with you?" I listen, respond to whatever the person brings up, and if it seems right, bring the person up to date on my life and work. Sometimes the reason for my intuitive promptings becomes quickly apparent, while at other times it remains elusive. When that happens, I politely say, "It was so nice to catch up with you. I'll see you later."

Then I proceed with my to-do list: calls and e-mail to return, tasks left over from yesterday, and those that emerged from the morning's quiet time. The tasks might be the same as they would if I hadn't begun my work day this way, but what I do becomes more mindful and inspired. This peaceful start to my day allows me to focus more clearly on what is really important. During the busiest days, I return to this quiet practice at least once.

You may wonder if it is appropriate for you to spend time this way. You may ask, "Is this a good use of taxpayer dollars?" The answer is a resounding "Yes! This is efficiency at its best!" When you start your day this way, you spend your time doing the really important things while drawing on your heightened awareness, intuition, and creativity. Working in this mode, you will begin to spend much less time in meaningless conversation over the coffee pot, and a greater percentage of time fully engaged in work that matters.

"Can I be mindful and still get things done?"

Although this level of awareness can enhance every area of your life, you will find it especially helpful in your role as a worker or supervisor. When you first consider adding mindfulness practice to your day, it's natural to worry about how you can fit in another activity without neglecting required responsibilities. Working mindfully does not mean you throw away your to-do list. *It means that you strive to bring your full awareness to all of your activities.*

By working mindfully, you will save the time needed to reorient yourself to your task when you get called away or take a break, because you'll be more aware of where you left off. As you become increasingly mindful, you'll naturally feel more inclined to cut out distractions that can take energy away from your real work. You'll have fewer time-consuming mistakes to correct. And, as you bring more mindfulness to interactions with staff members, they will begin to work more harmoniously and efficiently as well. If you choose to become a more mindful worker, you'll still do most of the same things you did before, but you'll approach your work in a profoundly different way.

Not everyone has an office door to close or can let an answering machine take messages for a little while. Some jobs offer little opportunity for quiet reflection. In many work settings, it takes great creativity to find time and space for this kind of mindfulness practice. I worked in a storefront family center in which all staff shared one office, as a home visitor driving around to families' homes, and in a day-care center, where every moment is public time. As a home visitor, I would pause for a moment on the front stoop of a home and "catch my breath" before knocking. Driving between appointments, I would pull over for a few minutes to reflect and return to mindfulness before going on to the next family or meeting.

Try a "mindful minute"

If spending the first minutes of your workday in mindfulness practice is something you can't comfortably imagine right now, try practicing a "mindful minute" during your day between meetings or telephone calls. You can do this almost anywhere. You may think that stopping for only a minute won't do much good, but taking time regularly, and particularly on stressful days, can help you regain the balance you need to work effectively. This is especially true if you regularly make time for longer stretches of mindfulness practice, for example, at home. The longer practice trains your mind so it is easier to recall mindfulness at work.

Here is how to spend a mindful minute:

- Find a comfortable sitting position. Allow your body to relax, drop your shoulders, and rest your arms and legs. Close your eyes or, if you prefer, keep them open and focus on a comforting or neutral sight in your workspace.

- Start by listening to the subtle sounds around you, such as air moving or voices in the background. After a while, notice your breath entering and leaving your body. If thoughts or emotions arise, notice them, but don't follow their story line; visualize them as clouds drifting by on a summer day. Bring your awareness to your body: the sensations of breathing in your chest and the beating of your heart. Become aware of and release any tension in your shoulders or arms. Notice the way that your back rests into the curve of the chair. Stay in that awareness for a few more moments. Notice how it feels to be relaxed and aware of your being in the world.

- Then, gently make the transition back to your day at work. Listen for the sounds of the outside world coming back into focus. When you feel ready, open your eyes and sharpen your focus and attention on the objects you see at eye-level. Then with a final, deep breath, go back to your work or routine and notice the effect that your mindful minute has on your energy, patience, and creativity.

Removing distractions

Modern life is filled with mindless distractions that rob you of energy and keep you from focusing on what really matters. Here are some examples:

- TV, radio, or "scanner" (police-band radio) constantly going in the background
- Cell phones, especially when set to beep whenever a text or call comes in
- Twitter, Facebook, and other social media
- Computer screen savers that stay in constant motion
- Extraneous e-mail we don't want but appears on our screen anyway
- Web "surfing"
- Chatty co-workers
- Junk food
- Junk mail
- Most advertising

For one day, keep a list of all the distractions in your life. Then choose one, and do something to reduce its negative impact on your mindfulness. For example, look at your mail. Does it include items you don't want to receive? Does sorting through useless mail distract you from more meaningful tasks? If so, you could send a firm, courteous letter asking to have your name removed from those mailing lists.

Do you usually turn on the TV or radio as soon as you wake up? Leave it off for one morning and focus on listening to your family members or fully tasting your breakfast. If you live with others, you may need to make this a family experiment.

Your computer has probably filled your life with new and rapidly multiplying forms of distraction. Anyone with a computer can, with a few quick key strokes, send you messages that are equally likely to contain drivel or useful information. Either way, they take your valuable time and attention.

How do you know when you've lost your mindfulness? If someone asks you, "How do you stand it when … ?" and you reply, "I don't even notice it anymore," you may be so enmeshed in that particular distraction that you are no longer aware of its debilitating effect on your capacity to be present and mindful. These effects may have bypassed your mind, going straight into your body and creating ill health, or into maintaining addictions to alcohol, cigarettes, food, drugs, sex, or gambling to numb the pain that comes from not living life fully.

References

Goleman, D. (2012). *Focus: The hidden driver of excellence*. New York: Harper.

Kabat-Zinn, J. (1990). *Full catastrophe living: Using the wisdom of your body and mind to face stress, pain and illness*. New York: Delacorte.

Kabat-Zinn, M., & Kabat-Zinn, J. (1997). *Everyday blessings: The inner work of mindful parenting*. New York: Hyperion.

Langer, E. (1989). *Mindfulness*. Reading, MA: Perseus.

Langer, E. (1997). *The power of mindful learning*. Reading, MA: Perseus.

Santorelli, S. (1999). *Heal thyself: Lessons on mindfulness in medicine*. New York: Bell Tower.

Resources

University of Massachusetts Medical Center's Stress Reduction Clinic
University of Massachusetts Worcester Campus
Center for Mindfulness
55 Lake Ave.
North Worcester, MA 01605
(508) 856-2000
http://umassmed.edu

Activities to Extend Learning

Chapter 3
Presence and Mindfulness: Cornerstones of Healthy Relationships

A. Presence

1. Reflect on the quality of presence in your life. What are some things you might do to enhance it?

2. How do you convey a compassionate presence with the families you work with? How do they respond?

B. Shifting your focus from "doing" to "being"

1. Prepare a sheet with three columns. In the first column, list your routine work tasks (meeting families, writing forms, answering the telephone, etc.). Label the second column "Costs," and next to each task, identify a cost of doing each one in a mindless manner. Label the third column "Benefits," and identify a benefit of doing the task mindfully.

2. How do you feel when you are with someone who gives you undivided attention? What is she/he doing? How is she/he being? What does it mean that "the quality of presence is the essential quality of a family development worker?"

C. Mindfulness-based stress reduction

1. What factors make family development work stressful? What are ways in which you have managed work-related stress in the past? How might mindfulness-based stress reduction help you manage work-related stress in your job now? What exercises are you willing to try?

2. Describe a stressful aspect of your life that is difficult to change. How might using mindfulness-based stress reduction help you cope with that stressor? What steps could you take to practice mindfulness-based stress reduction on a regular basis?

3. Read Chapter 1 ("You Have Only Moments to Live") of *Full Catastrophe Living: Using the Wisdom of Your Body and Mind to Face Stress, Pain and Illness* by Jon Kabat-Zinn. Then write a reflection of what mindfulness-based stress reduction means to you.

D. Mindfulness practice exercises

1. For one week, try each of the mindfulness practices in the chapter: mindful breathing, mindful stretching, mindful walking, mindful listening. Write a reflection on how it went and whether you want to continue the practice.

2. Visit the National Family Development Credential website at http://www.familydevelopmentcredential.org. Click on the tab for Workers' Resources. Print and read a copy of "A Worker's Guide to a Practicing a Mindfulness-Based Body Scan." Read the guide and practice the body scan technique at home. Write a reflection on how the practice went.

E. Practical strategies for mindful family development work

1. List some of the distractions you encounter in daily life (junk mail, e-mail "spam," waiting in line). Describe the benefits to your life with that distraction removed. Choose one and enact a plan to remove it. Reflect on what you learned through the process.

2. Practice a mindful minute when you feel stressed at work, and again when you are relaxed at work. Write a reflection on each.

Skills Practices

These skills practices are a suggested list. You may also develop your own skills practice or make modifications to the ones listed below to help you create a meaningful and manageable plan.

1. For one week, plan 15 minutes each day to practice any form of mindfulness. After one week, write a reflection responding to these questions: What arrangements did you make to include mindfulness practice each day for a week? How did they work out? Was it helpful? If it was helpful, how might you continue to make time for mindfulness practice, no matter how hectic your day gets?

2. Discuss the concept of mindfulness with a friend, co-worker, or family member. How does that person feel about it? Write a reflection on the discussion including both challenges and benefits to practicing mindfulness. How can you support each other?

3. Introduce some strategies to practice mindfulness-based stress reduction with a family member you are working with. How did you approach the concept with her/him? Follow up with her/him to see if it was helpful.

4. Explore resources in your community related to mindfulness-based stress reduction (e.g., Yoga classes, pain reduction clinics). Talk to the instructor or facilitator about what is involved and what the benefits are.

5. For one day, whenever you want to are inclined to repeat a habitual action, stop, notice what you are about to do, and don't do it. Refrain from this activity for one hour, one day, or one week. Notice how you feel at first, and then later on. Write about your experience. Examples of activities to refrain from:

   - checking your e-mail or other electronic device again, after you have already checked it a short while ago
   - eating or drinking something containing sugar or caffeine
   - sitting without getting up to stretch or walk

89

Chapter 4
Taking Good Care of Yourself

Objectives

A. Clarify your personal vision for your work.
B. Learn how to create a support system.
C. Create a healthy support system for yourself.
D. Design a personal stress reduction and wellness program.
E. Understand how to balance work and family life as a family development worker.
F. Learn basics of family financial management.

A. Clarifying a personal vision for your work

It's not easy being a family worker! Families' progress can be discouragingly slow. Agency regulations are often frustrating. Pay is lower than in other professions requiring as much responsibility. Many agencies still use a deficit approach to staff management.

To thrive as a family development worker, it is essential to develop and hold a personal vision, and to take good care of yourself. Developing a personal vision is a way to make a commitment to yourself. It is not so much a description of what you are *doing* as an expression of your true *being*. When you develop a clear personal vision for your work, you realize that each person you work with and each job you hold can support and shape that vision.

Some people already have a clear vision of exactly the kind of work they want to do, and the kind of presence they want to bring to their work. Often this clarity comes from personal experience. Whether you are new to your role as a family worker or have held the same job for years, now is a good time to develop or update a personal vision for your work. Revisiting your vision periodically helps you stay connected to the most important person who can make that vision into reality: *you*.

What if your vision is not quite clear, or has become clouded over time? Take a few minutes now or at a convenient time to step back from your work, and ask yourself these questions:

• Why did I go into this kind of work?

• Are these reasons still important to me?

• What is really important in my life?

• What special talents do I have to offer?

• Is there something I'd rather be doing? And if so, then how can I move in that direction?

B. Creating a support system at work

Think about the people you work with. Some of these you see often: the families you work with, your supervisor, co-workers. Others you see less often: colleagues from other agencies, people in the state and federal agencies who fund or regulate your work. Which of these people do you feel are highly supportive of you and your work? These are the people who trust that you are competent and are doing your best. You don't feel you have to be "on guard" with them. You know they will help you meet your goals whenever possible.

Others are somewhat supportive, but you haven't worked together enough yet to learn to trust each other deeply. Or, they may support your work in some areas, but not in others. Most people also have people they work with who are distrustful, unsupportive, and perhaps even jealous or deliberately undermining their work.

How can you build up your network of people who readily support your work, and turn adversaries into allies? The first step is to appreciate those who believe in what you're doing and who do their best to support you. Let them know, often, how much you appreciate the good job they do, and the "extras" that help you do your job well. Make time to nurture work relationships that you value. When someone you work with is trying to meet a goal, help out if possible. Conduct yourself in ways that help people trust you. Keep your word. Don't gossip.

Working with your supervisor

Sometimes workers feel frustrated when they use an empowerment approach with families, but feel that their own supervisor doesn't understand or use this model with them. If you are taking this course, your supervisor may well have earned the corresponding Empowerment Skills for Leaders credential. Remember that your supervisor has probably never been supervised using a strengths-based approach and may never have seen anyone else do so.

Keep in mind that your supervisor does not have to embrace family development thoroughly, or be perfect, in order for you to use family development with families. If you feel excited about and committed to family development, it can be disappointing to find that your supervisor is more tentative about it, or "talks the talk" but, in your opinion, doesn't "walk the walk." You can still apply all you are learning about family development in your work, offering your supervisor concrete examples of how it helps families.

If you need agency policies to change in order to work with families in this way, explain the need and reason behind it to your supervisor. Be courteous, persistent, and appreciative. Your supervisor may have to work through many layers of bureaucracy before the change you need actually takes place.

Find ways to help your supervisor do his or her job as well as possible. Look for his or her strengths, and reflect them back as often as possible. Supervisors like positive feedback as much as anyone. Share information about family development with your supervisor in a respectful manner, assuming that he or she wants to understand this approach.

Perhaps most importantly, try to understand your supervisor's goals, pressures, and need for support. Make a decision to help your supervisor be successful. For example, share success stories from your work with families, so they can be passed along to the board or funders, or used in a grant application. The more your supervisor perceives you as an ally and sees you on the same team, the more open he or she will be to new ways of working with families and workers. As you and co-workers use the empowerment approach more and more, you may be able to suggest changes in the workplace. For example, workers' performance reviews can be done from a strengths-based approach. Worker's strengths and accomplishments are identified, sometimes independently, by the supervisor and the worker on separate forms, and then discussed in the review session. Then, in a collaborative manner, the worker and supervisor identify goals for the worker to focus on in the coming year. When the National Family Development Credential Program moved from Cornell to the University of Connecticut, I was happy to discover that the performance review process in place there already used this strengths-based approach, which is becoming more common among forward-thinking organizations.

Healthy ways to express your feelings

Expressing your feelings clearly and respectfully is an essential skill for family workers. You will need to handle feelings expressed by others with skill as well. Family development requires you to listen to people who are upset. Even when you don't ask, someone will usually volunteer an opinion or express an emotion. Feelings come with the territory of family development.

Your own thoughts and feelings can arise without notice. In a typical day, you may encounter situations that cause you to feel angry, sad, upset, happy, worried, or frightened. You'll need to make conscious choices about whether and how to express those feelings.

Conflict exists at all stages of life, both at work and at home. It can be tempting to deny that a conflict exists by avoiding it, giving in, or attempting to impose instant solutions. Although many people try to avoid conflict, disagreement can be productive. Skillfully managing small conflicts can prevent big problems from erupting. Disagreement can help people understand and become more open to other points of view. Thoughtful confrontation can lead to needed change.

Of all forms of conflict, blame or criticism can be the hardest and most stressful communication challenge for family workers. Whether the criticism comes from your staff, your supervisor, a board member, or a colleague, it's hard to avoid reacting defensively, or becoming depressed or angry. Some people internalize criticism, seeing it as "all my fault," while others see it as a personal attack and attempt to retaliate. Communication techniques such as skillful listening, paraphrasing, and feedback can help you understand your reactions and express your feelings responsibly and effectively.

Have some fun!

Healthy children naturally find ways to have fun, but this ability too often disappears as we grow up, especially if mind-numbing activities like violent video games overtake this natural ability. One evening my young son proposed watching a movie, a request I declined because only half an hour remained before "lights out." I knew that sticking close to normal bedtime would provide everyone with much-needed sleep and ease the next morning's routine. I offered a longer story than usual, but he was seeking something more lively. Glancing around, we both noticed the flash light on the kitchen counter. "How about we play hide-and-seek with a flashlight?" he proposed.

Adept at the impromptu way children negotiate game rules with each other, he wasted no time suggesting rules on where we could hide. I agreed to all his proposals except atop the counter: "I can't climb up there and you might fall off or break something in the dark," I said. "I won't fall Mom, but if you don't want me up there, okay. Let's get playing! Who gets the flash light first?" Since he'd been so gracious—and I was mindful of bed time—I suggested he go first. I sat on the couch and counted, eyes closed, vaguely aware of scuffles under the table then the shower curtain being pulled aside in the bathroom. I was aware of the wood stove crackling, the scent of supper lingering in the air, my longing to stretch, a car driving by.

Just as I finished counting, silence. "Ready or not, here I come!" Flashlight in hand, I searched, but he was not in the tub or under the table. Stumped, I sat down on the couch, to the squirming peels of laughter beneath me. "Your turn to hide now, Mom," he laughed as he took the flashlight." We were both disappointed when the phone rang, but when it turned out to be his older brother, whose ride home had fallen through, my young son was elated. "He can play flashlight hide-and-seek with us too!"—not to mention stay up a bit longer.

Soon we were back home in our darkened living room, flashlight in hand, laughing as the one who was "it" bumped into walls and fell over sneakers. No cost, no video games, no movies, no one else's life on a screen in our home (at least not tonight) … just some creativity. Sometimes it's organized soccer team practice or a game, sometimes yoga stretching, sometimes running around with friends, but being able to make our own fun without spending money is fun.

Do not stop playing because we grow old;
We grow old because we stop playing.

– Anonymous

When was the last time you remember laughing and just having fun? Hopefully, it wasn't too long ago! As an adult, you may feel that play and work are opposites and that playfulness is childish and immature. But having fun and taking healthy risks nurtures your creativity and provides significant health benefits.

Resilience, optimism, and hardiness

Think of people you might know who personify the qualities expressed in these aphorisms:

- "She's someone who can roll with the punches."

- "He's a person who won't cry over spilled milk."

- "The team went back to work realizing it was water under the bridge."

People with optimistic attitudes tend to cope more effectively with stress. Optimistic people are more likely to use solution-focused coping skills to resolve difficulties. This personality attribute is called "hardiness," an emotional characteristic found in people who feel they have significant control over their lives. They see challenges as opportunities that encourage their creativity and personal growth. Studies have found that commitment to seeing a situation through and having confidence in one's ability to successfully complete a task with an appropriate level of challenge were essential characteristics of individual hardiness.

Cornell developmental psychologist Anthony Ong's research has focused on the capacity of some people to thrive even when faced with adversity. His research delineates how positive emotions can serve as a buffer to life's stressors. Ong suggests that positive emotions can encourage speedier cardiovascular recovery from negative arousal (e.g., anger), and recovery from significant negative life events (e.g., the loss of a partner). He builds his insights into positive emotion not only on his own research, but also on decades of experiments led by Cornell psychologist Dr. Alice Isen.

According to Ong (2014), "positive emotions fuel psychological resilience" (p. 2.). He concludes that

> positive emotions fuel psychological resilience. … The capacity for positive emotional engagement in the context of stress has consequences that are not just emotional but physiological. When our positive emotions are in short supply—when we feel hemmed in by negative emotions such as fear and sadness—we become stuck in a rut and painfully predictable. But when our positive emotions are in ample supply—when we feel lifted by the centripetal force of our closest relationships—we take off and become generative, resilient versions of ourselves. (p. 2)

Compassion and care for yourself

Did you go into human service work because you felt compassion for and wanted to help others? Perhaps you soon learned that it was not that simple. Maybe you began to shut down some of your natural empathy in the face of agency regulations, professional guidelines, and the daily grind of witnessing poverty and inequity. In this process, you may have protected yourself, but you might also have lost some of your initial compassion.

Mindfulness can help you restore your empathy and compassion for yourself and others. Let's start with you. Can you offer yourself the same level of compassion you offer to families? Can you be kind to yourself? As you try to balance the ideals of service with the realities of life, there will be tension between meeting your needs and the needs of other people. Accept the fact that it's impossible to be there for everybody all the time. Recognize that this is not because you have shortcomings, but because life will always ask more of you than you can give.

Try to develop compassion for yourself, realizing that you can't do everything and that it is okay to fall short of your ideals. If you treat yourself with compassion and care, you will have renewed energy to choose what is important and follow through.

Here is a recipe for taking good care of yourself:

- Recognize when stress becomes "overstress."
- Practice mindfulness-based stress reduction most days.
- Share your feelings in healthy solution-focused ways.
- Incorporate some fun into life every day.

Appropriate Intimacy

Mindful relationships with the families you work with can feel very intimate. When you listen mindfully to someone, you offer a kind of intimacy that some people have seldom, or perhaps never, experienced. As a family development worker, you have an opportunity to model such relationships. You can be genuine, honest, and build caring relationships with others while safeguarding your privacy and theirs.

You also have a special responsibility to establish appropriate boundaries because of the inherent power your position carries. Recently revealed abuses of power by athletic coaches, religious leaders, and others have underscored the devastation in clients' or students' lives caused by a person in authority misusing that trust.

The Family Development Credentialing Program developed a Code of Ethics (included at the end of this book) that will help your organization establish ethical guidelines.

Spending your time on what is important

Look at your calendar. Are there things on your schedule that you don't want to do and don't have to do? If so, cancel them right now. Don't be apologetic, just be polite and firm. You might say, "I have been happy to serve on the _____ committee for the past eight years, but I must resign now because of other commitments. Please send my best to the others. It was a pleasure to work with you." Then put something in that time on your calendar that will nourish you and your vision, such as an exercise class, a regular fun outing with your family, time for mindfulness practice, a class at a community college, or a walk in the park. Write these on your calendar in indelible ink. This will help you notice significant discrepancies between which activities you actually do and which you really want to do.

Developing a daily to-do list will also help you prioritize and review your accomplishments at the end of each day. After you prepare the list, take a minute to step back, review it, and ask yourself these questions:

- What tasks must be accomplished today?
- Are there so many things on my list that it will require "superhuman" stamina to do them all today?

Here are some tips to help you use your time effectively:

Set *realistic* goals for your work and personal life. You are probably a "can do" person who routinely performs well under pressure and tight deadlines. Whenever you can, set timelines to finish a task, so you don't end up frantically rushing out the door to mail a grant proposal or make a presentation.

Listen to your intuition. If you have a sense that you should make contact with a family or coworker about something, go ahead and do it. It will save time in the long run. Focus your best energy on what is most important. What time of day do you feel clearest and most productive? Try to schedule your most important work at that time. Concentrate on those tasks directly related to your work; be careful about inadvertently taking on tasks that are the responsibility of others.

Handle routine tasks efficiently. Use technology wisely to save time. If you have voice mail, invite callers to leave a detailed message. If you have e-mail, use it to confirm meeting dates and times.

Take time to learn how to use new office technology. Although this will take time initially, it will allow you to be more productive and efficient in the long run.

"Never touch a piece of paper twice." This is a helpful habit to adopt in tackling paperwork and junk mail. Arrange to have your name removed from lists you don't want to receive. When you receive correspondence that asks for a reply, consider making a quick phone call or sending a brief e-mail, whichever saves you the most time, instead of composing a time-consuming written response.

C. Creating a support system for yourself

You help the families you work with identify and develop their support systems. You deserve the same support in your own life. The Family Circles Assessment, which you will use to help families identify the supports in their life, is just as useful for you. While the version you use with families is focused on helping them build self-reliance, here is a version just for you.

Figure 4-1. Family Circles[9]

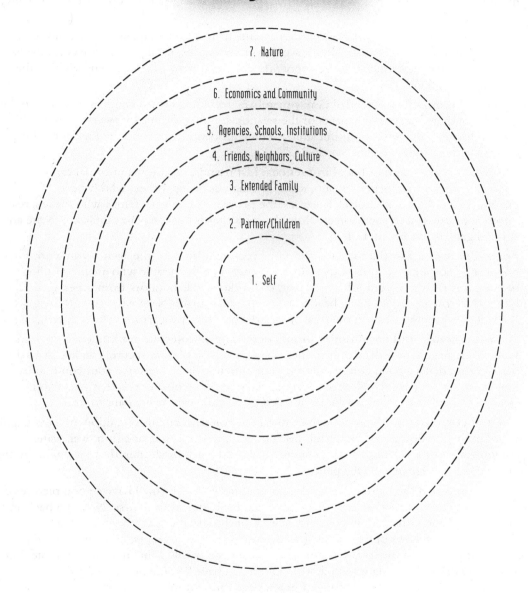

Family Circles

7. Nature

6. Economics and Community

5. Agencies, Schools, Institutions

4. Friends, Neighbors, Culture

3. Extended Family

2. Partner/Children

1. Self

---

[9] Adapted from the Social World Model developed by Moncrieff Cochran and the Family Matters Project, and Urie Bronfenbrenner's Ecological model.

Using the Family Circles Assessment

1. **Self:** At the center of your world is your relationship with yourself (and your inner belief system, if you have one). Note your strengths, hopes, and dreams. Note any conditions or qualities that deeply influence your life (e.g., athletic ability, hearing impairment, sense of humor). Note what you enjoy. If religion or spirituality is an important part of who you are, note that.

2. **Partner and child(ren):** List your partner's name (if you have one), and your child(ren). Describe your partner's and children's aspirations, strengths, needs. Ex-partners can be listed here, or in extended family, informal network, or formal network, depending on how they influence your life.

3. **Extended family:** List extended family members, including grown children who are on their own. Note their qualities or aspects of the relationship that mean a lot to you (e.g., Sophie stays in touch, Shivonne's beautiful smile). These influences can continue for a long time, even after the family member has died.

4. **Informal network and cultural influences:** List friends, neighbors, informal care providers, fellow members of a club, team, or religious group, others who have a relationship with you by choice. These are the people outside your family who make a real difference (stressful or supportive). Note the ways they influence your family life. Note any cultural groups you are part of.

5. **Formal network:** List the formal institutions you are related to (the agency you work for, physicians/hospitals, schools your children attend). List the people who are in your life because it is their job (your job supervisor, co-workers, collaborators from other agencies). Note what you get (a paycheck, health insurance, self-worth). Note what you give (eight hours a day, keeping a car on the road to get to work, time away from your children).

6. **Socio-economic and community influences:** Note socio-economic influences in your family's life (e.g., new federal policies mean your job is less/more secure, you live in a safe neighborhood, it's a good community for your elderly father). Describe your community and how it affects your family. Note local, state, national, and global trends that affect your family's self-sufficiency (video game violence, good child care being hard to find).

7. **Natural environment:** Note how the natural environment and its condition affect you and your family (the flowers are beautiful this summer, the family got sick from well water contaminated by a neighbor's farm chemicals, a child has asthma caused by air pollution, the family likes to relax in a nearby park).

Once you have completed the Family Circles Assessment for yourself, you'll have a good picture of the people and other influences that help shape your life, for better or for worse. Now, go back and look at this "map" of the influences in your life. Is each of the seven circles about as full as the others? If one of your circles is brimming over while another is nearly empty, this may point out an imbalance in your life. For example, if your formal network can hardly contain what you wrote, but your informal network only contains people with whom you have a polite but not very deep relationship, this imbalance may be a source of much stress but not much support.

Now, take two pens of different colors than the one you used to complete the Family Circles Assessment. With the first color, circle all the influences that are supportive; with the other, circle all the influences that are stressful. (The same influence may be both!) When you've finished, take a good look at where the supports in your life are, and where you feel a need to develop more support.

D. Creating your own stress-reduction and wellness program

Stress is a response that varies with each person and each circumstance. The effects of chronic stress have been proven to be uniformly detrimental to long-term health and well-being. There are two types of stress: positive and negative. You might experience positive stress when you become a new parent or send your first child off to college. You're likely to experience negative stress when you're faced with sudden illness or the death of a loved one.

The following analogy may help you distinguish between positive and negative stress:

As a potter presses clay on a spinning wheel, a shape begins to emerge. The rotation of the pottery wheel and the gentle, yet firm hands of the potter work together to mold a mass of clay into a beautiful form. If the potter exerts too much pressure, the clay will break or tear. If the potter exerts too little pressure, the clay will not transform into a piece of pottery.

After the potter is done making the pot, the clay must "rest" before being fired. Like clay pots or vases, we can become our best when we experience enough stress, but not too much. We also need time to rest, especially before and after times of "fire" in our lives.

More and more employers realize that employees do their jobs better when the rest of their life works well, too. That's why so many employers now offer wellness programs, stress management classes, and other choices to help workers stay healthy and balanced. Small social service agencies seldom have formal wellness or stress management programs, so you may need to empower yourself to create your own.

Stress is a normal part of life

Stress can also be a problem. The evidence is clear that when people experience too many major life events such as the death of a spouse, a move, or a job promotion, the chance of illness is increased. Research also shows that life's daily strains such as work overload, rush-hour traffic, and conflicts at home can be equally stressful. Most of us can absorb some hassles each day, but when daily strains become chronic—with no relief in sight—the pile-up can become as stressful as major life changes.

It is important to learn to recognize signs of overstress: when you feel "stressed out," begin to work less efficiently and creatively, complain continually, are irritable, constantly tired, and have more minor illness, sleeping problems, tension, and pessimism. Being overstressed can lead to health problems that can become more and more severe, making it hard to do your job or take care of your family. Health problems cost your employer because you have to take sick time, are less efficient, and use more health insurance benefits. Chronic overstress can lead to disease: allergies, ulcers, heart disease, cancer, and other serious ailments.

In a focus group, a supervisor commented:

> There's the issue of burn-out. There are some people who just do, do it, do it, and then they're gone. But those who have a sense that they are human beings, that they have their own needs, can stay in for the long haul. This helps build trust and continuity. It's about taking care of themselves.

A family worker who is a home visitor said:

> I think the one thing we need to remember as home visitors is taking care of ourselves first. It's very important that we don't carry our work home with us. We empower the parents the best that we can. I carry a caseload of 12 families. And really you know when you build and bond with that relationship, you have to make sure you draw that line that you don't cross into a personal relationship with families. I think if you cross that personal line, you become more affected by everything that happens in their lives and then they're calling you at home, you know, so the job never ends.

Although every family worker has stressful days, if you feel very stressed a lot of the time, consider this a wake-up call! You are worthy of your own care. No one else is going to manage your stress for you: not your employer, your doctor, or your family or friends. How can you manage stress? You can become more aware of how you cope with stressful situations, and you can start your own personal wellness and stress management program.

Here is a list of elements of a balanced personal stress-reduction and wellness program:

1. Daily mindfulness practice

Refer to Chapter 3 for help designing and implementing a daily mindfulness practice that is comfortable for you.

2. Exercise you enjoy enough to actually do

Exercise not only keeps you fit (and better able to handle stress) but also reduces adverse effects of stress. People know they would feel better if they were to exercise regularly and eat healthy food in moderation. Yet millions of Americans lead sedentary lives and overeat unhealthy food. Overweight and obesity are rampant, even among young children (see the Chapter 4 Appendix for more information).

3. Eat healthful foods that you like enough to actually eat

Some foods reduce stress, while other foods exacerbate it. Whole grains, unsweetened fruits, and vegetables help you maintain balanced energy and feel good. High-fat fried foods and sweets can make you gain weight, feel jittery, and contribute to heart disease and diabetes. Skipping meals or consuming too much caffeine (coffee, chocolate, tea, colas) can increase your stress level. High-carbohydrate foods such as bread, pasta, cookies, and other sweets are sometimes called "comfort" foods, but after an initial "high" from rapidly rising blood sugar, as soon as your blood sugar level drops, you'll feel tired again. Eating quickly at your desk can add to your stress, and eating while driving can also be dangerous to yourself and others. Eating without paying attention also increases the likelihood of overeating or eating unhealthy foods.

New scientific research shows that eating well and building health may be simpler than we thought. Harvard School of Public Health has distilled recent healthy-eating knowledge into a "Healthy Eating Plate" diagram (see the Chapter 4 Appendix).

Try an experiment for one week: Write down everything you eat and drink and how you feel each day. Once you see what you usually eat and how it affects you, then you can decide whether you want to make some changes. If you do try some new ways of eating, notice how you feel after eating each new food.

If it's not realistic to give up caffeinated beverages or comfort foods "cold turkey," you can become more aware of how they create or reduce stress in your life. Notice what you choose to eat at the office or during conferences. Try choosing a piece of fruit, instead of a pastry, at the next meeting you attend. Plan to gradually limit caffeine intake. Every way you choose to be kind to your body reduces stress and enhances your overall health and well-being.

4. Friends and family

One of the best ways to handle work is to get away from it. Honor your feelings when you feel "stressed out." Step out of your work role and take a break. "Check back in" with your partner, child or friend. Family members and friends can become so accustomed to your "not right now, maybe later" commitment to work that they stop asking for your time and attention. Then when you come up for a "breather" and want to spend some time with loved ones, they have usually filled their time with other things.

Family members and good friends are often the unsung heroes behind successful workers. The unrelenting pace of a worker's job may leave little time to nurture relationships. Ask yourself, "How much has work drawn me away from my family and friends recently?" Consider scheduling one evening each week just for time with family or friends. Taking care of the friends and loved ones who take care of you is not about what you can provide with your paycheck. Taking care is about giving them the most precious gift: your time, attention, and love.

5. Changing harmful habits

Many people seek to numb the pain and distress in their lives by using or abusing drugs or alcohol, smoking cigarettes, gambling, or eating compulsively. Sometimes it's very hard to recognize when you have crossed the line from user to abuser, especially if a harmful habit has numbed or distorted your perceptions. If you use alcohol or have a cigarette whenever you feel discouraged, then you might not face whatever is making you feel so sad, frustrated, or hopeless. Feeling your emotions is essential to living life fully. If you're angry, it's healthier to express your anger—respectfully and safely—than to ignore it.

If you're hiding your habits from others, or if people who love you have asked you to get help, pay attention and listen! You can't be an effective worker if you have an addiction. If you have the courage to face a harmful habit and work through the recovery process, you will be far more effective in your work and better able to live a healthier, happier life.

6. Counseling

There are times when it's helpful to have a skillful outsider to talk to about life's inevitable problems and challenges. Going for professional counseling can sometimes be hard to do, especially if you feel you should "have it all together." Keep in mind that most people can benefit from seeing a counselor at certain points in their lives—including counselors. It's a sign of strength and wisdom to recognize that you need help. If you call a counseling service, you may be told there is a waiting list; go ahead and put your name on it if you're comfortable waiting for an appointment. You can request to be seen immediately, however, if you are feeling very anxious or distressed. All reputable counseling services will be able to find a counselor to see you right away.

Your employer may offer an Employee Assistance Program (EAP) as a fringe benefit. An EAP usually works with a local counseling service to provide short-term professional counseling without any cost (or at a very small cost). This is strictly a confidential service. Your employer will not be told why you came for counseling. If your employer has an EAP, your family members can probably use it, too.

Your employer, its EAP program, or another community group may also offer free or inexpensive support groups for people affected by common life circumstances, such as providing care for elderly parents, coping with loss and grief, or parenting a troubled teenager. A group like this can be a great support; you'll get to know people with similar concerns and be able to share your struggles, and come up with creative and practical solutions.

E. Balancing work and family life

Live a balanced life
Learn some and think some and draw and paint some
And sing and dance and play and work every day some.

– Robert Fulghum

Most people work for two reasons: to support themselves and their families, and to contribute something of value to the world. Do you ever feel like earning your paycheck doesn't leave you enough time and energy to spend with your family?

Your days at work are long and filled with demands, and yet it may be difficult to justify going home at a reasonable hour when there is still important work left to be done. Perhaps you were at a meeting the night before so you could even leave early, but you have a tendency to "just keep going." This type of behavior isn't good for you, for your home or family life, or even for your organization.

Keeping your work and family life in balance is difficult, especially if you have a strong work ethic. But you benefit from your efforts to achieve a healthy balance. A satisfying family life can help you keep the frustrations at work in perspective and give you the energy to meet another challenging day; and having a fulfilling job can help you cope with the normal frustrations of family life. The skills you develop at work can help you at home, and the empathy and insight you develop as a member of your own family can help be more effective in your job. If you don't care for yourself, you have less to give on the job. Being an active part of your family makes you a better worker.

From a family development worker:

> When I leave work, I have a family of my own, a husband and two children. I have my hands full. I think keeping myself healthy, regular check- ups, taking adequate time off, and I try to take time off that I don't have home visits on, so I'm not having to reschedule home visits and make them up. I try to just keep a mental clear.

What's going well?

Instead of comparing your life to advertisements or movies, try taking an inventory of what is working well as you balance your own work and family life. Here is an example of one worker's inventory:

- My children are happy, healthy, and delighted with life.

- I have a loving, secure, nearby child-care arrangement I can afford. Our children are very happy in this situation.

- I am doing work I believe in and am good at.

- My paycheck covers our expenses, with a little left to save.

- My job benefits include family health insurance. Visits to our family doctor are covered, without me having to fill out a lot of forms or cover the bills until the insurance pays.

- I've learned communication skills on the job that help me in my family life.

- My experience dealing with physical therapy services for my older child has helped me do my own work with families better.

- My employer is paying for me to take training that helps me do my work better, and will lead to a college degree.

Changing what you can

Next, list the aspects of balancing work and family life that you wish you could change. For example:

- Some days I'm so tired when I get through helping all these families with their problems that I don't have much energy left for my own family.

- My job doesn't have a very good retirement plan, so I wonder if I'll have enough money when I'm older.

- I want my children to go to college, but wonder how I'll pay for it.

- Although I am mostly assigned families in the area around our home, on days I have to go to the central office for meetings, I drive an hour each way. Our child-care provider doesn't like to work that late, and my kids are hungry and anxious to get home.

- I've used up my vacation and personal time; my father's health is not good; and I worry about being able to take time off from work if he needs me.

Turning the drawbacks around

- Can you think of ways you can turn any of these drawbacks around?

- Family development work can be very draining. What ways do you have to re-energize yourself? Does exercise help? What foods help restore your energy? Does listening to your favorite music on the way home renew your energy? Do you get enough sleep? Can you get more?

- Preparing for retirement is probably of interest to some of your co-workers, too. Can you work together with your employer to look into group retirement plans that your agency might join?

- Can the guidance counselor at your local high school help you think through potential college expenses and ways to cover them?

- Can someone else pick your children up and give them supper on the days you have late meetings? If only some of your agency meetings apply to your work, maybe your supervisor will be willing to have you attend only those for which your presence is really needed. Or, maybe others you work with also have problems with getting home so late on meeting days and would welcome meetings earlier in the day. Then you could get back to work with the families you see, and get home on time. Can you suggest changing the meeting time?

- The Federal Family and Medical Leave Act allows most workers to take up to three months off, unpaid, to care for a new baby or a sick family member. Workers are allowed to use up their own paid sick and vacation leave for this purpose before taking unpaid leave. Even though you've used up your vacation and personal leave, you may be able to use your sick leave if a family health emergency requires you to take time off from work.

Public policies and community problems

There are many things you can do yourself to resolve work-family problems, especially with the help of others in your support network. However, many work-family problems are bigger than any one worker or family. Economic conditions that require two adults to work full-time outside the home just to provide the basics for a family; neighborhood crime that makes it unsafe for young teenagers or elderly grandparents to stay home alone; difficulty finding good, affordable child care: these are all problems that cannot be solved by one worker alone.

It's tempting to blame yourself, or the person who represents the problem you're facing, instead of seeing your problem as part of a bigger picture. If money is always tight at your house, you may blame yourself for not managing better, or your employer for not paying more. Certainly, it's worthwhile to manage your money carefully, and for agencies to pay the best salaries they can so good workers can stay on. But the bigger issue is: How can you help your elected representatives understand the value of family development and the importance of worker continuity? If an unsafe neighborhood causes you to enroll your young teens in an after-school program, or to look for a day program for your grandparents, it's important to convey these concerns to your elected officials, and to join together with neighbors who are working on local solutions. If you have trouble finding good child care, your elected representatives need to know.

Ironically, the workers who most need support for balancing work and family life have the least extra time to help change workplace, state, or federal policies. Do what you can, and don't feel guilty about the rest. But *do realize* that the problems you experience in balancing your work and family life are probably not because you're less organized, hard-working, or "together" than the families in the movies. It's because your family is *real*, and because we live in a country that is still learning to make families a priority.

F. Family Financial Literacy

What is "financial literacy"? William G. Gale and Ruth Levine (2010) of the Brookings Institution define financial literacy as "the ability to make informed judgments and effective decisions regarding the use and management of money and wealth" (p. 3). They go on to say:

> Financially illiterate households make poor choices that affect not only the decision-makers themselves, but also their families and the public at large, making improvement of financial literacy a first-order concern for public policy. (p. 3)

Family financial literacy is defined by National Family Development Credential Program Director Dr. Claire Forest (2011) as "a set of skills and financial knowledge that allows families to make informed, effective decisions about money, and thus more likely to be able to live a healthy life and pursue their dreams."[10]

In families with more than one adult, different people within the family may earn and spend money, pay bills, and make financial decisions. Family financial decisions are influenced not only by these adults, but also by teenagers, children, grandparents, and other family members. For this reason, *family* financial literacy is more complex than financial literacy for a single person or childless couple.

Family financial literacy requires that a family's decision-makers have accurate information about where the family stands financially, clear goals for their future, and dependable planning resources. This section, and the resources it lists, offers methods for learning to handle your own finances as skillfully as possible, and for helping the families you coach manage their finances as well.

"Wealth" for ordinary families

When you hear the term "wealth," do you picture millionaires or movie stars? If so, reorient your view to focus on your own family enjoying a tasty, healthful dinner, living in a pleasant stable home, getting medical care when you need it, and meeting your goals for education, retirement, and perhaps an occasional affordable vacation. In the FDC Program, wealth refers to ordinary people meeting their financial goals, getting out of debt, and accumulating assets over time by making wise financial choices. As a family worker, you can readily find examples of this kind of wealth: owning an affordable home, and having a savings account and realistic plan for retirement.

How can credentialed workers promote financial literacy?

Credentialed family workers should not provide financial counseling, yet with a basic understanding of money management, they can more readily help families understand the connection between wise financial management and their ability to reach their goals. As a family worker, you can:

• Understand financial literacy well enough to make wise decisions for your own family

• Be aware of resources on financial literacy and money management

• Refer families you coach to qualified financial counselors when needed

---

[10] *Family financial literacy*. Presentation at Family Development Credential Update, June 2011.

- Partner with respected organizations in your area that offer financial literacy education
- Support families as they increase their financial literacy and work toward their own financial goals

Whether you use the federal government's financial management program (http://www.mymoney.gov) or live in a locale such as New York City with good financial management resources (listed at the end of this chapter), the basics are the same.

Simple tools such as tracking all income and spending for one month, and then for one year, can help you get an accurate handle on how much money you have to work with, where spending leaks could be plugged, and how income might be increased. With this essential basic information in hand, you can look into other tools offered on this website. Once you've done this for yourself, you will be in a better position to help the families you coach to become more financially literate.

Of course, your personal finances are your own confidential concern, which you should not share with families you coach. However, once you've worked with these tools, you can share general insights from your own experience with them, such as "These days most people are looking for smart ways to handle their money. When I went to the website mymoney.gov, I realized it would benefit my family if we got more serious about savings. We also looked at ways we could spend less, and how to help our children learn about money."

While any person can benefit from the tools on this site, the Annie E. Casey Foundation's Center for Family Economics focuses specifically on strategies for helping families currently living on low incomes to build wealth. This foundation works with selected urban and rural communities to promote these strategies:

- Jobs
- Asset-building (including saving)
- Wider use of the earned income tax credit available to low-income families.

The Annie E. Casey Foundation's use of the term "wealth" is refreshing, because it refers to ways ordinary people can build a healthy financial future through strategies on how to "Earn It, Keep It, Grow It."

"Working hard in a troubled economy"

In 2008, Michael Perry and Julia Commings of Lake Research Partners, together with Julia Paradise and Tanya Swartz of the Kaiser Commission on Medicaid and the Uninsured, interviewed heads of households in 27 diverse working families throughout the United States. For the purposes of that study, having an income under 200 percent of the federal poverty level (FPL) was considered "low income." This was $42,400 for a family of four. "Middle income" was defined as a family income of more than 400 percent of the FPL (Perry & Paradise, 2009, p. 2).

A theme of this report, "working hard in a troubled economy" (Perry & Paradise, 2009, p. 2), summed up the experiences of those surveyed. Many expressed gratitude to have a job. Some worked more than one job, others were working full time in seasonal or temporary jobs. Lack of job stability was common. Many workers had jobs with little security or future. Most had been in their jobs less than one year. Fewer than half had health insurance benefits from their job.

Transportation was needed in order to work, but many of those surveyed said gas costs and car repairs made it difficult to afford getting to work. Some lived far from their jobs in order to save on housing costs, but this increased time away from home. Child care was a factor for many families. When one parent stayed home to take care of young children, a desire to contribute to the family's income was often expressed, along with the concern about not being able to find work that would cover child-care costs (Perry & Paradise, 2009).

Health care poses a particular financial challenge to families living on low or moderate incomes. Fewer than half of families in this study had health insurance related to their job. Families had a range of health issues, and also a range of health insurance coverage: no health insurance, Medicaid, employer-provided health insurance, or a combination of coverage within the family. Even those with coverage struggled to afford the costs. Many did without necessary medical and dental care because of the costs. Several families in the study reported having daunting bills and debts from pervious medical problems (Perry & Paradise, 2009).

Although families worked diligently and lived simply, most said that their finances were strained and unpredictable. Once families had paid their housing costs through rent or mortgage payment, there was little left to pay for other necessary expenses. Many had utilities shut off due to not being able to pay the bill. These families sometimes resorted to paying basic costs such as groceries, on a credit card, which left them with increased debt and pressure (Perry & Paradise, 2009).

Most families in the study were in debt, and many faced a growing pressure around debt, some of it past medical debt which they were trying to pay off monthly when they could spare $5 or $25. Some considered filing for bankruptcy. Few of the families were able to save. Without a personal "rainy day" fund, one problem (such as a child needed emergency medical care) could quickly grow into a complex web of problems. Many owed huge debts for past medical care (Perry & Paradise, 2009).

On March 23, 2010, President Obama signed the Affordable Care Act, which put in place comprehensive health insurance reforms that will roll out over four years and beyond. The Affordable Care Act has helped millions of Americans to get health insurance, including many who were formerly uninsured.

Get "real" about your financial situation and future

Many families face struggles around money. Often these struggles are related to not earning enough money. Low income can be related to low educational levels, physical or mental health problems, or living in a region with limited job opportunities or unreliable transportation. Some people have financial problems because they lack health insurance and can thus be financially undermined by one family member's illness. Many financial problems, however, are related to inadequate financial literacy.

For example, many people lack a realistic understanding of the importance of planning, and regular savings, in working toward a future financial goal such as one's own retirement. According to a survey conducted by the Consumer Federation of America (2006), 21 percent of those surveyed—including 38 percent of those with incomes under $25,000—thought that winning the lottery was the most practical method of paying for their own retirement! In addition, 16 percent thought winning the lottery was the best way for most Americans to afford retirement.

Helping the families you coach to understand the reality of their being much more likely to retire by investing a small amount each week in their own savings account in an insured bank or credit union than by spending it on lottery tickets is a good use of your time as a family worker. This is an example of how making decisions based on accurate information is a key to financial literacy.

You can help your organization and the families you coach, by researching which reliable organizations in your area offer financial literacy education, then working with your supervisor to form working referral relationships. Hopefully, your supervisor will work with you to invite representatives of those organizations to make a presentation at your agency. In most states, the cooperative extension offers practical low-cost or free financial literacy classes based on reliable research.

The importance of saving

According to Daniel Carrol and Beth Mowry (2010) of the Federal Reserve Bank of Cleveland, in 1982 the personal savings rate in American was nearly 11 percent of "disposable income"—in other words, for every dollar not spent on taxes, Americans saved more than a dime. By 2005, personal savings had plummeted to 1.4 percent of disposable income—in other words, only slightly more than one penny per dollar. In 2009, this rate climbed to 4.3 percent. Although recent increases in personal savings is a positive trend, it falls far short of the 11 percent Americans saved in 1982. How can you, as a credentialed worker, help the families you coach to increase their savings? First, by finding ways, however small, in which you can save in your own life. This will fuel your own belief in savings and provide you with inspiring examples. Next, you can provide families with reliable eye-opening information that demonstrates the power of savings.

The power of compound interest and time

Do the families you coach understand the power of regular savings over time? The following example, developed by the US Securities and Exchange Commission (SEC, 2011), shows how compound interest works:

> If you have $100.00 and it earns 5% interest each year, you'll have $105.00 at the end of the first year. But at the end of the second year, you'll have $110.25. Not only did you earn $5.00 on the $100.00 you initially deposited—your original "principal"—but you also earned an extra $0.25 on the $5.00 in interest. Twenty-five cents may not sound like much at first, but it adds up over time. Even if you never add another dime to that account, in 10 years you'll have over $162.00 through the power of compound interest, and in 25 years you'll have almost $340.00. (p. 1)

The SEC (2011) offers a further example, using the cost of a teenager buying a slice of pizza each week:[11]

> Here's another way to look at compound interest. How much does a slice of pizza cost? Would you believe nearly $65,000? If a slice of plain pizza costs $2.00, and you buy a slice every week until you're old enough to retire, you'll spend $5,200 on pizza. If you give up that slice of pizza and invest the money instead, earning 8% interest compounded every year for 50 years, you'll have over $64,678.87. (p. 2)

The high costs of being "unbanked"

The term "unbanked" refers to a person who does not have an account at either a bank or credit union. Although both banks and credit unions provide services such as a checking account, savings account, credit card, and loans, and insure deposits up to $250,000, credit unions usually add an educational mission to the banking services and products they offer.

Credentialed workers can help "unbanked" families understand the financial benefits—and costs—of having an account at a credit union or bank. According to John P. Caskey of Swarthmore College (2002), approximately ten million American households do not have a bank account. Without a checking account, these "unbanked" consumers often use commercial check cashing (CCO) services located at stores to cash their pay checks or government checks. These people then pay the CCO additional fees for money orders used to pay utility or other bills. CCOs make their services convenient by offering envelopes and stamps (pp. 2–3). According to Caskey (2002), regular use of a CCO's services can cost $400 annually for a person with $18,000 annual take-home income (p. 3).

Angela C. Lyons and Erik Scherpf (2004) of the University of Illinois studied data from the FDIC's Money Smart program and found that

> millions of Americans do not have bank accounts and must rely on high-cost alternative financial services such as currency exchanges and pawnshops to conduct everyday transactions such as check cashing, making payments, and taking out small, short term loans. In a complex financial world, it is easy for the 'unbanked' to fall prey to predatory lenders and financial scams, especially because many lack adequate financial education. (p. 215)

People who do not have bank accounts are more likely to be Black or Hispanic, younger, unemployed, have lower education levels, and/or live in a low-to-moderate income location. (Lyons

---

[11] For more information, visit http://www.sec.gov/investor/students/tips.htm.

and Scherpf, 2004). Immigrants are also less likely to use banks (Toussaint-Coumeau & Rhine, 2000). Immigrants' experiences in their homeland may shape their attitudes toward how they handle money here in America.

Why do millions of Americans still lack a bank account? Some do not believe they have enough money to need or get an account. Some consider the options and conclude that the costs outweigh the benefits. Lack of basic knowledge about how banks work, and the advantages of having an account, often keep people from opening an account.

Yet, even when people learn about the advantages of a bank account and how to handle one, many still do not join America's financial mainstream by opening a bank account or joining a credit union. Studies find that unbanked people seldom complain about high fees. Fewer than 20 percent of unbanked people he surveyed use currency exchanges to cash checks; nearly 75 percent were able to cash their checks at grocery stores, banks, or credit unions, 59 percent without paying a fee (Caskey, 1997; Berry, 2004).

Some people are not eligible for an account or do not want one. Immigrants who do not have a social security card cannot open a bank account. For people living paycheck to paycheck, with no financial reserve and little education in financial management, use of a checking account often results in a "bounced" check. In addition to needing to scramble to repay the bank or the business the check was written to, a bounced check also results in a returned check fee of $25 or more to the bank. The business to which the check was written may also charge a similar amount. Plus, the person who wrote the check will have to scramble to get this banking problem straightened out quickly.

If this happens more than once, the bank may close the person's account. A bounced check may also result in embarrassment if the business to which the person wrote the check posts this bounced check (or the person's name) prominently on a "do not cash" list taped to its cash register. Such an experience can readily convince an unbanked consumer to continue using alternative methods for cashing checks and paying bills.

Credentialed workers can also help unbanked families who decide they want an account gather, understand, and compare information on available options. Rhine, Greene, and Toussaint-Comeau (2006) also suggested that consumers' participation in mainstream financial venues (e.g., banks) can improve their ability to build assets and create wealth, protect them from theft and predatory loans, and help promote stability and vitality in their communities.

The unbanked are less likely to save for the future

Lack of a positive relationship with a bank makes people less likely to save. This leaves them especially vulnerable when they need credit—to borrow money in an emergency or for a major purchase such as a car. Unbanked consumers often borrow at high interest rates from pawn shops, car-title lenders, payday lenders, or private lenders.

Bertrand, Mullainathan, and Shafir (2007) suggested that "unlabeled and easily available money will be spent more freely than money that is accounted for, leading to very low savings rates among the unbanked" (p. 17). Lack of a financial reserve (savings) has forced many people to miss rent, utility, or credit card payments, which caused stress and often a damaged credit rating.

Credit rating

Although a person might not realize it immediately, late or missed payments also result in a damaged credit rating. A *credit rating* predicts the likelihood that a person will repay a loan promptly. Three credit bureaus—Experian, Transunion, and Equifax—collect information from banks, credit card companies, utility companies, and others about each person's borrowing and repayment history, then assign a number (from 300–850) to provide potential lenders with a quick estimate of the each person's credit worthiness. Although individual situations vary, a score below 700 often prompts a lender to refuse a loan request, or to charge a higher interest rate, if a loan is offered at all. Credit ratings are also used by insurance companies to determine premiums, and by utility companies to determine the size of a deposit. Each person is entitled to a free credit report from each major credit bureau once every year. Many financial advisors recommend requesting a report from one of the credit bureaus every four months.[12]

People seeking their credit reports should be careful not to provide information (such as social security number) to other sites offering a credit report, as some may be illicit "imposter" sites "phishing" for your social security number and other personal information.

Once you receive your credit report, review it, and report any mistakes promptly. If your credit report reveals accurate problems such as late or missed payments, you will need to take steps to repair your credit record, such as being very careful to make all payments on time. You would be wise to work with a reliable nonprofit educational organization such as a cooperative extension or your credit union (if you belong to one) to learn how to improve your credit rating and overall financial health. Do not pay for this service, as some unscrupulous advisors take advantage of people's money problems by offering to "fix" bad credit while in fact stealing their identity.

People with potentially complex situations, such as immigrants, may want to consult a trusted financial advisor before requesting a credit report or applying for a bank account. Also, be careful not to cosign a loan with a friend or relative, as this would make you responsible for the loan if the person "defaulted" (failed to pay on time), which would also harm your credit rating and thus make it impossible or more expensive for even you to get a loan.

Staying sane on "soft money"

Many family workers' jobs are funded by grants or by other sources that change from year to year, depending on shifting political priorities. Many people call this type of funding "soft money" (as opposed to "hard money," which is more permanent, reliable funding from institutions). Working hard to help families while not knowing whether you'll have a job next month or next year to take care of your *own* family is tough.

Here are some tips on taking good care of yourself when the future of your work is uncertain. These suggestions recognize three needs all family workers have:

- To support your own family financially
- To feel good about the work you do
- To help the families you work with

Supporting your family financially

Most of us need our jobs to support ourselves and our families. It's hard to make good decisions about important things, such as whether your son can go to college, whether you can buy a newer car, or whether it is wise to invite your aging parent to live with you, when you don't know whether you'll still have your job next year or might have to move to find work in another place. It's a *big* concern if funding for your job is uncertain. Widespread public agency cuts like the recent "sequestration" leave many family workers unsettled, unable to plan ahead, and maybe without a job!

Worry doesn't do you or the families you work with any good. There are many much more productive things you can do. If funding for next year is up in the air, ask the person who writes proposals for your agency how you can help. As a front-line family worker, you can provide spirited descriptions of how the program helps families become self-reliant. You can offer to collect success stories and quotes, taking care to protect families' confidentiality. You can provide accurate information on family development from this handbook.

---

[12] Your credit report can be requested from http://www.AnnualCreditReport.com. A free credit score can be requested from http://www.creditkarma.com.

You can begin looking at alternatives to your current job situation. There are many ways to "do the work." Often, we get so locked into one job or employer that we stop thinking about the many places we could use our family development skills to work with families in empowering, respectful ways.

Being a good collaborator with other community agencies and businesses throughout your years as a family development worker (not just when you think you might lose your job) is the best insurance if you need to look for another job, because other agencies will already know and respect you.

It's also valuable to take a close look at your family's finances, so you will know what you need if you have to change jobs. Most communities have free or inexpensive budget counseling services (often through a cooperative extension). These services offer help with setting up a budget and handling debt.

Putting it all together

Helping the families you coach develop financial literacy will encourage them to get a clear picture of their financial situation, set financial goals, pay off debt, and save for future goals. Please get to know organizations in your community that offer free or low-cost financial management education, and build working relationships, so you can readily refer families to these classes and services.

References

American Heart Association. (2013). Statistical fact sheet: 2013 update. Washington: American Heart Association. https://www.heart.org/idc/groups/heart-public/@wcm/@sop/@smd/documents/downloadable/ucm_319588.pdf.

Bandura, A. (2005). The primacy of self-regulation in health promotion. *Applied Psychology: An International Review, 54*(2), 245-254.

Berkel, L. A., Carlos Poston, W. S., Reeves, R. S., & Foreyt, J. P. (2005). Behavioral interventions for obesity. *Journal of the American Dietetic Association, 105*(supp. 1), S35-S42.

Berry, C. (2004). *To bank or not to bank? A survey of low-income households*. Joint Center for Housing Studies Working Paper Series.

Bertand, M., Mullainathan, S., & Shafir, E. (2007). *A behavioral economics view of poverty*. Working Paper, Massachusetts Institute of Technology.

Booth, K. M., Pinkston, M. M., & Poston, W. S. (2005). Obesity and the built environment. *Journal of the American Dietetic Association, 105*(supp. 1), S110-S117.

Booth, S. L., Mayer, J., Sallis, J. F., Ritenbaugh, C., et al. (2001). Environmental and societal factors affect food choice and physical activity: Rationale, influences, and leverage points. *Nutrition Reviews, 59*(3), S21-39, S57-65.

Carroll, D., & Mowry, B. (2010). *Personal savings up, national savings down*. Federal Reserve Bank of Cleveland. Retrieved from http://www.clevelandfed.org/research/trends/2010/0410/01ecoact.cfm.

Caskey, J. P. (1997). *Beyond cash-and-carry: Financial savings, financial services, and low-income households in two communities*. Report to the Consumer Federation of American and the Ford Foundation. http://www.swarthmore.edu/Documents/academics/economics/Caskey/BeyondCashandCarry.pdf

Caskey, J. P. (2002). *Bringing unbanked households into the banking system*. Washington: Brookings Institution.

Cawley, J. (2006). Childhood obesity: Introducing the issue. In *The future of children* (special issue on Childhood Obesity), *16*(1), 69-88.

Consumer Federation of America & The Financial Planning Association (2006). *How Americans view personal wealth vs. how financial planners view this wealth*. Washington: Consumer Federation of America.

Evans, G. W., & English, K. (2002). The environment of poverty: Multiple stressor exposure, psychophysiological stress, and socioemotional adjustment. *Child Development, 73*, 1238-48.

Faghri, P. D., Omokaro, C., Parker, C., Nichols, E., Gustavesen, S., Blozie, E. (2008a). Dose response of a worksite pedometer walking programs. *Journal of Primary Prevention* (pending review).

Faghri, P. D., Omokaro, C., Parker, C., Nichols, E., Gustavesen, S., Blozie, E. (2008b). E-technology and pedometer walking program to increase physical activity at work. *Journal of Primary Prevention, 29*(1),73-91.

Fulghum, R. (2014). *All I really need to know I learned in kindergarten: Uncommon thoughts on common things* (25th anniv. ed.). New York: Ballantine.

Gale, W. G., & Levine, R. (2010). *Financial literacy: What works? Could it be more effective?* Working paper, Brookings Institute, Washington.

Garbarino, J. (1999). *Raising children in a socially toxic environment.* San Francisco: Jossey-Bass.

Giles-Corti, B., & Donovon, R. J. (2003). Relative influences of individual, social environmental and physical activity correlates of walking. *American Journal of Public Health, 93,* 1583-1589.

Gillespie, A. H., L. Ganter, et al. (2003). Productive partnerships for food: Principles and strategies. *Journal of Extension, 41*(No. 2).

Hill, J. O., & Peters, J. C. (1998). Environmental contributions to the obesity epidemic. *Science, 280,* 1371.

Hill, J. O., Wyatt, H., Phelan, S., & Wing, R. (2005). The National Weight Control Registry: Is it useful in helping deal with our obesity epidemic? *Journal of Nutrition Education and Behavior, 37,* 206-210.

Koplan, J. P., Liverman, C. T. & Kraak, V. (Eds.). (2004). *Preventing childhood obesity: Health in the balance* (p. 436). Washington: National Academies Press.

Lyons, A. C., & Scherpf, E. (2004). Moving from unbanked to banked: Evidence from the money smart program. *Financial Services Review, 13*(3), 215-31.

Olson, C. M. (2005). Food insecurity in women: A recipe for unhealthy trade-offs. *Topics in Clinical Nutrition, 20*:321-328, 2005. http://www.human.cornell.edu/bio.cfm?netid=cmo3#sthash.9LUFIJqe.dpuf.

Ong, A. (2014). *A life worth living: The science of human flourishing.* Ithaca, NY: Cornell University Human Development Outreach & Extension.

Perry, M., & Paradise, J. (2009). *Snapshots from the kitchen table: Family budgets and health care.* Kaiser Commission on Medicaid and the Uninsured.

Rhine, S. L. W., Greene, W. H., & Toussaint-Comeau, M. (2006). The importance of check-cashing businesses to the unbanked: Racial/ethnic differences. *Review of Economics and Statistics, 88,* 146-57.

Sallis, J. F., Conway, T. L., Prochaska, J. J., McKenzie, T. L., Marshall, S. J., & Brown, M. (2001). The association of school environments with youth physical activity. *American Journal of Public Health, 91,* 618-620.

Toussaint-Comeau, M., & Rhine, S. L. W. (2000). *Ethnic immigrants' enclaves and homeownership: A case study of an urban Hispanic community.* Federal Reserve Bank of Chicago, Consumer and Community Affairs Policy Studies, no. 6.

U.S. Department of Agriculture. My Food Pyramid. Retrieved 21 March 2006 from http://www.mypyramid.gov/.

Wansink, B., & Kim, J. (2005). Bad popcorn in big buckets: Portion size can influence intake as much as taste. *Journal of Nutrition Education and Behavior.* Forthcoming.

Resources

Websites

- http://www.sec.gov/investor/students/tips.htm.
- http://www.census.gov/hhes/www/poverty/about/overview/index.html
- http://www.census.gov/hhes/www/poverty/about/overview/index.html
- http://www.mymoney.gov/
- http://www.bls.gov/
- http://www.aecf.org/MajorInitiatives/CenterforFamilyEconomicSuccess/CFESResources.

Mindful eating

Andersen, S. A. Ed. (1990). "Core Indicators of Nutritional State for Difficult to Sample Populations," *Journal of Nutrition, 120,* 1557S-1600S.

Bays, J. C.. (2009). *Mindful eating: A guide to rediscovering a healthy and joyful relationship with food.* Boston: Shambhala.

Hanh, T. N. & Cheung, L. (2010). *Savor: Mindful eating, mindful life.* New York: HarperCollins.

Wansink, B. (2006). *Mindless eating: Why we eat more than we think.* New York: Random House.

Financial Literacy

Recognizing that too many Americans lack the ability to handle their money wisely, the US government launched a web site to educate people on money management at http://www.mymoney.gov/. Topics include:

- Developing a spending plan

- Managing debt and credit
- Planning for retirement
- Saving and investing
- Getting a loan
- Getting insured
- Knowing your consumer rights
- Scam/fraud

In addition, some states and cities also offer financial management resources. For example, New York City established a Financial Empowerment Center, to help city residents learn to manage their money. See their website, http://www.NYC.gov/ProtectYourMoney. This program offers several well-researched Tip sheets. "Top Ten Ways to Protect Your Money" includes details on the following tips:

1. Open a NYC Safe Start account.

2. Track and manage spending.

3. Get control of your debt.

4. Save for the unexpected ... even just a little.

5. Claim every public benefit for which you qualify.

6. Avoid scams.

7. Protect your identity.

8. Report debt collection harassment.

9. File a complaint with Consumer Affairs.

10. Get free professional financial counseling.

Publications and counseling are available in English, Spanish, and Chinese.

Activities to Extend Learning

Chapter 4
Taking Good Care of Yourself

A. Clarifying a personal vision for your work

1. If you are new to family development work, describe the hopes, goals, and vision you have for the way family development could be offered in your community.

2. If you are an experienced family worker, describe how you have clarified your personal vision for your work since you began. How has your personal vision to help families developed with time and experience?

3. Write a letter to "fictional" family who successfully completed your program to congratulate them. Describe the vision for your program and how the relationship helped you see strengths in them and yourself as a family worker, and reflect on ways that it helped you connect with your personal vision for your work.

B. Creating a support system at work

1. What qualities of your supervisor or co-workers support you in doing your best work? Write a note to your supervisor or a co-worker appreciating these strengths and the support. Give the note to them and reflect on their response.

2. Reflect on your program's progress in reaching its goals over the past year. What circumstances helped your program in positive ways? What difficulties hindered your program? What can you do to help your program succeed in reaching its goals for this year?

3. List your own long-term goals for your work, and short-term goals leading to it.

C. Creating a support system for yourself

1. Start each day for the next week by making a "to do" list. At the end of the week, review all the to-do lists together. What things were accomplished as you planned? What things were sidetracked by emergencies or other priorities? Write a reflection on how it went and then answer this question: Would accomplishing all the tasks on my to-do list have required superhuman stamina?

2. Reread "Spending your time on what is important." Post one of the tips in a visible place in your workspace. Practice it for one week. Write a reflection about how it worked in your life for that week.

3. List three workplace, state, or federal policies that affect the decisions your family makes. List ways you can affect these policies, or ways you can limit their affects on your family.

4. Investigate alternatives to your current job. Is there a related (or unrelated) type of work you'd like to do? Find out what kind of training or credentialing it would require. Talk over with your family your ideal "big picture" jobs, schedules, living arrangements, further education, and so on.

D. Creating your own stress-reduction and wellness program

1. Think of an enjoyable stress reduction and wellness goal you would like to accomplish over the next month. Break the goal down into "mini" steps you could do in just a few minutes each day to achieve it. Post the mini-steps on your refrigerator or desk. Read the steps/tasks every morning and try to do one thing each day to bring you closer to that goal. After one month (or sooner if you achieve the goal), write a reflection on how it went and whether breaking the goal down into small steps helped you stick with it to achieve your goal.

2. Prepare a list of ways you can reduce stress and increase wellness in your life in these specific areas:
   a. exercise that you enjoy enough doing
   b. healthful food that you like enough to actually eat
   c. friends and family who care about you (and you about them)
   d. fun
   e. healthy ways to express your feelings
   f. ways to let go of harmful habits

E. Balancing work and family life

1. Do you ever feel like earning your paycheck doesn't leave you enough time and energy to spend with your family? How do you try to balance having a fulfilling work and family life? If changing one thing could improve the balance between your work and family life right now, what would it be?

2. Family development work can be very draining. What ways do you have to re-energize yourself? How can you turn the drawbacks of being a family development worker around to gain more balance in your work and family life?

F. Family financial literacy

1. How would you describe "wealth" for your family?

2. Make an honest assessment of your own family's financial literacy. What are some steps you could take to make improvements? What resources might you access?

3. Reflect on how well your agency promotes financial literacy with families. What professional development related to financial management would be helpful to staff?

4. Describe how uncertain funding affects you, your family, and the families you work with. List steps you can take to (a) promote continued funding and (b) find alternatives.

Skills Practices

These skills practices are a suggested list. You may also develop your own skills practice or make modifications to the ones listed below to help you create a meaningful and manageable plan.

1. Write a statement describing your personal vision for your work: the hopes, goals, and dreams you have for yourself, families, and the future of family development work. Share it with a co-worker or your supervisor. Reflect on your strengths and abilities to step back from your work and determine what is important to you. How can these skills help you set future goals?

2. Use the Family Circles Assessment to assess the strengths, stressors, and supports in your life. Identify the "circles" in your life that might benefit from additional support. What could you do to increase support in these areas?

3. Briefly describe a time in your life when you felt "overstressed." Looking back now, were there any warning signs then that could help you anticipate overstress now or in the future? What steps do you currently take to reduce stress in your life? What are other ways you can take better care of yourself to prevent becoming overstressed?

4. To practice using time more effectively, identify a nonessential task at work that you routinely ask for help with (e.g., unjamming a paper caught in the copier, replacing a fax cartridge, or using a metered-stamp machine). Arrange with a colleague to learn how to do this task so you won't need to have others do it for you. Write a reflection describing the task you identified, the steps you took to learn it, and how it may help you use time more effectively in the future.

5. Write down everything you eat and drink each day for one week, including *when* you eat. Notice how you feel throughout the day. Reflect on whether you want to make some changes and how you plan to go about it.

6. Over a one-week period, prepare family meals according to the Healthy Eating Plate (see the Chapter 4 Appendix). What did you need to do differently? How did your family respond?

7. Create a resource list of financial management services and resources in your community. Have a discussion with someone from one of these services to learn more about their program and how you can promote it with the families you serve. Write a reflection on how you can promote these financial management services in your agency.

Chapter 4 Appendix
Overweight/obesity research and the Healthy Eating Plate

Overweight/obesity research

Some facts about overweight and obesity

According to the Harvard School of Public Health, "the words "overweight" and "obesity" are ways to describe having too much body fat. The most commonly used measure of weight status today is the body mass index (BMI). BMI uses a simple calculation based on the ratio of weight to height (BMI = kg/m^2). Decades of research have shown that BMI provides a good estimate of "fatness" and also correlates well with important health outcomes like heart disease, diabetes, cancer, and overall mortality. So it's a useful tool for clinicians trying to screen and determine who may be at risk because of carrying around too much weight for their height.

What is a healthy BMI? For adult men and women, a BMI between 18.5 and 24.9. Overweight is defined as a BMI between 25.0 and 29.9; and obesity, a BMI of 30 or higher.

Harvard School of Public Health also noted that "abdominal obesity" (extra fat found around the middle) is an important factor in health, even independent of BMI. The simplest and most often-used measure of abdominal obesity is waist size. Guidelines generally define abdominal obesity in women as a waist size 35 inches or higher, and in men as a waist size of 40 inches or higher."

According to the National Centers for Disease Control and Prevention, obesity-related conditions include heart disease, stroke, type-2 diabetes, and certain types of cancer. These are among the leading causes of preventable death. The annual medical cost of obesity in the United States was $147 billion in 2008; the medical costs for obese people were $1,429 higher than those of normal-weight people.

Higher-income women are less likely to be obese than low-income women. The obesity epidemic is the result of a complex interaction between environmental and individual factors. A report by the Institute of Medicine (Koplan, Liverman, & Kraak, 2004) states, "Understanding the causes of childhood obesity, determining what to do about them, and taking appropriate action require attention to what influences eating behaviors" (p. 436).

In order to successfully address this obesity epidemic, the nation needs to develop interventions at multiple levels of environments (Bandura, 2005; Giles-Corti & Donovan, 2003; Booth, Pinkston, & Poston, 2005; Sallis et al., 2001). Because children are influenced directly by their family's eating and activity decisions, parents whose decisions foster their own obesity also predispose their children to obesity. In addition to fostering a healthy family environment and making wise food and eating decisions, families can, with support, influence their child's community and school environment as well (Gillespie et al., 2003). Because of environmental factors such as poverty, job and housing instability, lack of reliable transportation to affordable grocery stores, substance abuse, and "an environment that promotes excessive food intake and discourages physical activity" (Sallis et al., 2001; Hill & Peters, 1998), families living in "socially toxic environments" (Garbarino, 1999) are at especially high risk of maintaining and passing down obesity-prone eating behaviors.

Research and interventions to date have been unable to reverse the trend toward higher levels of obesity. Despite the health community's consensus on the urgent need to reduce and prevent obesity, conventional efforts have not been successful in curtailing the rising obesity rate (Garbarino, 1999; Hill, Wyatt, Phelan, & Wing, 2005; Berkel, Carlos Poston, Reeves, & Foreyt, 2005). Thus, creative approaches to standard treatments are needed.

The Centers for Disease Control and Prevention (2013) reported that 68 percent of Americans are overweight and more than a third are obese. According to the American Heart Association (2013),

> among Americans 20 and over, 154.7 million are overweight (Body Mass Index—BMI—of 25.0 kg/m and higher). Of these, 78.4 million are obese (BMI of 30.0 kg/m and higher). If current trends in the growth of obesity continue, total healthcare costs attributable to obesity could reach $861 to $957 billion by 2030, which would account for 16% to 18% of US health expenditures. (p. 2)

This epidemic takes a financial toll on individuals, families, states, and the nation. The CDC (2013) stated that 35.7 percent of US adults are obese and observes:

The estimated annual medical cost of obesity in the U.S. was $147 billion in 2008 U.S. dollars; annual the medical costs for people who are obese were $1,429 higher than those of normal weight.[13]

Although a wide range of Americans struggle with obesity and its harmful effects, these problems are exacerbated among low-income women. According to the Pew Research Center (2013),[14] obesity is most prevalent at lower income levels: 42 percent of women living in households with income below 130 percent of the poverty level were obese, compared with 29 percent of women in households at or above 350 percent of poverty level.

A study by Cornell University Nutritional Sciences Professor Christine Olson (2005) confirmed this trend, as well as investigated its possible intergenerational foundation. Olsen conducted in-depth interviews with 30 low-income mothers for three consecutive years. She found that 60 percent of these women were obese or overweight. Her analysis also revealed that 80 percent of women in this study were raised in economically poor households. Olsen concluded that growing up in a poor household was significantly associated with being overweight or obese in adulthood. Many factors contribute to the greater likelihood of overweight and obesity in women living on low incomes. These include market factors (Cawley, 2006) and portion size (Wansink & Kim, 2005), family food decisions (Gillespie, Ganter, et al., 2003), the "built environment" (e.g., transportation systems that discouraged walking [Booth, 2005; Booth et al., 2001]), school cafeteria marketing, individual behavior (Berkel, 2005; USDA, 2006), and food insecurity (not being able to rely on having enough safe, nutritionally adequate food).

Despite the health community's consensus on the urgent need to reduce and prevent obesity, conventional efforts have not succeeded in curtailing the rising obesity rate (Hill, 2005). Numerous interventions have been attempted, with varying success. One of the fitness interventions I find most promising for the Family Development Credential Program's clientele, is the ConnectFit workplace walking study conducted by Pouran Faghri, MD, professor of Health Promotion in University of Connecticut's Division of Allied Health Sciences (Faghri et al., 2008a, 2008b).

The ten-week ConnectiFit intervention used a transtheoretical model (TTM) to increase physical activity in two workplaces. After completing a health history questionnaire and assessment, 2006 participants combined a pedometer walking program with Internet-based motivational messages.

There were significant improvements in participants' number of steps per week, level of physical activity, movement through stage of change and other health-related indicators ($p < 0.05$). Work-site pedometer walking programs and e-technology may be effective interventions in improving the lifestyle of employees who might be at risk for developing chronic diseases. For most people, walking is an easy, inexpensive, and convenient approach to exercise. Likewise, a pedometer is inexpensive and easy to use. This study has the added advantage of increasing awareness of one's own health risks, an important step in reducing and managing cardiovascular and other risks of overweight and sedentary lives.[15]

The effect of "socially toxic environments" on obesity

From my viewpoint as director of the National Family Development Program, I hypothesize that women living in "socially toxic environments" (Garbarino, 1999) marked by poverty, limited job and educational opportunities, substandard housing, substance abuse, violence, irregular work hours, and chaos are at especially high risk of unhealthy behaviors that lead to obesity, because the effects of this chronic chaos undermine their ability to set and reach goals for overcoming obesity. Socially toxic environments appear to be prime examples of this type of environment. Because obesity rates are higher among low-income women, it can be concluded that conventional efforts to reduce obesity among this population are especially ineffective.

A study by Evans and English, although it was not focused on obesity, reported that "Chronic stress exposure may disrupt task persistence and produce disequilibrium in self-regulatory behavior" (2002, p. 1239). I hypothesize that the chronic chaos of living in socially toxic environments repeatedly undermines any goals for healthy eating and exercise these women set. I further hypothesize that transformational learning—not simply acquiring new information—may be required to overcome the harmful effects of chaos on goals for achieving and maintaining a healthy weight.

---

[13] Retrieved from http://www.cdc.gov/nchs/data/hus/hus12.pdf#063.

[14] Rich Morin, "Is Child Obesity Contagious?" (Pew Research Center, 11 July 2013). http://www.pewresearch.org/fact-tank/2013/07/11/is-childhood-obesity-contagious/.

[15] For more information on the role of physical activity in adopting a healthy lifestyle, see Centers for Disease Control and Prevention, "Physical Activity" (October 15, 2009). http://www.cdc.gov/healthyplaces/healthtopics/physactivity.htm.

Many universities and government agencies offer web sites and other guidance on healthy eating facts and strategies. I find Harvard Medical School's Healthy Eating Plate to be a simple reminder to eat a variety of vegetables, whole grains, fruits, and healthy proteins, and to drink water and stay active. You and the families you coach can learn more about the Healthy Eating Plate at:

Nutrition Source, Department of Nutrition, Harvard School of Public Health (http://www.health.harvard.edu/plate/healthy-eating-plate).

Chapter 5
Our Diverse World

Objectives

A. Understand cultural diversity in the context of family development.

B. Explain how "culture" is defined in family development.

C. Realize why an understanding of diversity and oppression is important to family development work.

D. Discuss why cultural competence is an important skill of family development work.

E. Learn skills for respectful cross-cultural communication with families and your work with interpreters.

F. Understand how language affects family dynamics and why some cultural groups are reluctant to take "help" when it has hurt them in the past.

G. Learn how displacement and immigration have shaped the experiences of African American, Native American, Hispanic, and Asian American families in our country.

H. Describe four barriers to a cultural competent society and their impact on growth and change for individuals and cultural groups.

I. Reflect on the limitations of "diversity training" to make long-term institutional changes that support cultural competence.

J. Appreciate aspects of your own cultural identity and learn ways to become more acquainted with your own culture.

K. Describe ways that most people learn about culture and consider new ways to expand your understanding of, and sensitivity to, other cultures.

L. Offer ways that your agency can develop and strengthen multicultural competence with families and the community.

A. Living in this diverse world

As technology increasingly brings the world into our living rooms and even into the palms of our hands, people in the United States have become more aware that we are interdependent with the whole planet. Although many welcome the variety and excitement of interacting with new people and places, many are uncomfortable with change. Discomfort is often fueled by stereotypes— images of various groups, portrayed inaccurately by media, by limited experience, or a few negative experiences. And, even when presented with realistic information, many people just do not want to give up privileges, or images, to which they have grown accustomed. Change can be hard! Yet embracing diversity remains a cornerstone of the National Family Development Credential Program. We recognize that credentialed family workers who can skillfully work with people of a wide range of diverse backgrounds, are an asset to the families and agencies of our nation.

Accurate information can help family workers understand the importance of working skillfully with people from diverse backgrounds. According to M. Allison Witt, of the University of Illinois at Urbana-Champaign, "an estimated 32.5 million foreign-born people reside in the U.S., with one million more achieving legal permanent resident status every year."[16]

According to June 2012 U.S. Census Bureau projections,

---

[16] M. Allison Witt, *Journal of Educational Controversy* (2014).

The U.S. population will be considerably … more racially and ethnically diverse by 2060, according to projections by the U.S. Census Bureau. These projections of the nation's population by age, sex, race and Hispanic origin, which cover the 2012-2060 period, are the first set of population projections based on the 2010 Census.

"The next half century marks key points in continuing trends—the U.S. will become a plurality nation, where the non-Hispanic white population remains the largest single group, but no group is in the majority," said Acting Director Thomas L. Mesenbourg. …

The non-Hispanic white population is projected to peak in 2024, at 199.6 million, up from 197.8 million in 2012. Unlike other race or ethnic groups, however, its population is projected to slowly decrease, falling by nearly 20.6 million from 2024 to 2060.

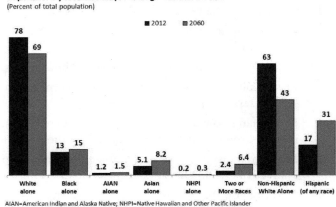

Population by Race and Hispanic Origin: 2012 and 2060
(Percent of total population)

Meanwhile, the Hispanic population would more than double, from 53.3 million in 2012 to 128.8 million in 2060. Consequently, by the end of the period, nearly one in three U.S. residents would be Hispanic, up from about one in six today.

The black population is expected to increase from 41.2 million to 61.8 million over the same period. Its share of the total population would rise slightly, from 13.1 percent in 2012 to 14.7 percent in 2060.

The Asian population is projected to more than double, from 15.9 million in 2012 to 34.4 million in 2060, with its share of nation's total population climbing from 5.1 percent to 8.2 percent in the same period.

Among the remaining race groups, American Indians and Alaska Natives would increase by more than half from now to 2060, from 3.9 million to 6.3 million, with their share of the total population edging up from 1.2 percent to 1.5 percent. The Native Hawaiian and Other Pacific Islander population is expected to nearly double, from 706,000 to 1.4 million. The number of people who identify themselves as being of two or more races is projected to more than triple, from 7.5 million to 26.7 million over the same period.

The U.S. is projected to become a majority-minority nation for the first time in 2043. While the non-Hispanic white population will remain the largest single group, no group will make up a majority.

All in all, minorities, now 37 percent of the U.S. population, are projected to comprise 57 percent of the population in 2060. (Minorities consist of all but the single-race, non-Hispanic white population.) The total minority population would more than double, from 116.2 million to 241.3 million over the period.[17]

What does this mean for our work in the National Family Development Program? First, while we understand that many factors can influence this fifty-year projection, we recognize that these changes are already happening in our homes, schools, agencies, and immigration policies. Our wisest response is to practice more deeply the cultural awareness skills taught in the National FDC program since its inception more than two decades ago: skills to help us understand more deeply our own cultures, to respectfully invite people different from us to help us understand their cultures, to live peacefully in our multicultural world. It is also important to remember that the United States has long been a nation peopled largely by invaders, and immigrants. No one should feel complacent, or superior, in our rapidly diversifying world.

---

[17] For more information, see the U.S. Census Bureau's blog posting at http://blogs.census.gov/2012/12/12/what-a-difference-four-years-make-u-s-population-projected-to-grow-at-a-slower-pace-over-the-next-five-decades/. Accessed 20 July 2013.

It is also worth noting that in most counties in the world, people—even little children, often speak two or more languages, and many speak several languages. At my children's everyday athletic games, young people and their families routinely play, and cheer on the kids in several languages. This is a small example of the many ways our nation is becoming more multicultural. Although there certainly are settings in the United States in which speaking a language other than English is not accepted, or may even be dangerous, shifting demographics have opened the way toward an openly multilingual and multicultural nation. I rejoice in this.

Here's an example from my own life. My son was friends with a boy whose entire family came to watch his soccer games—grandparents, parents, teenagers, cousins, little children—a large supportive family. I sometimes gave the boy a ride to games, and his mother kindly invited my son to play soccer in this family's informal league, which he took as a high honor given their skill level. I once asked the boy what languages he spoke. Nonchalantly, he replied, in excellent English, "Spanish." I pointed out that he also spoke very good English. "Sure," he shrugged.

As I got to know his mom, she mentioned that the whole family had immigrated from Peru. I noticed his grandparents at the games, speaking to each other in a language that was neither English nor Spanish. I mentioned to the teenager's mother, that it was a beautiful-sounding language, and asked if she spoke it too. "Oh, that's Quechuan," she replied, "Only with my parents." She then spoke gently to her toddler in Spanish, while cheering her son in English. The toddler said, "Hola!" to me then, and not getting an immediate response because I was watching the game, tried, "Hi!" Later I asked the teenage boy if he also spoke Quechuan. "A little, not much," he politely replied, then turned back to the soccer game. I mentioned that maybe his grandparents would love to teach it to him.

B. What is culture?

Many people think of culture as ethnic heritage. Ethnicity is an important part of a person's culture, but there are other equally important elements: race, language, gender, sexual orientation, class, family form, age, religion or spirituality, geographic origin, and physical and mental ability. Some aspects of culture—race, for example—stay the same throughout a person's life. Others, such as family form or spirituality, are more fluid and may change. Age certainly changes, bringing people into contact with different aspects of their own cultures over their life span.

Culture is a combination of thoughts, feelings, attitudes, beliefs, values and behavior patterns that are shared by a racial, ethnic, religious, or social group. Although we all have the same basic human needs, there are many different ways in which we meet those needs. Culture influences the ways we decide to meet those needs ranging from the most visible factors—such as diet, dress, and health—to the assumptions people make about themselves, their relationships with others, and their own priorities. Such decisions are influenced (but not determined) by the customs passed down through families, traditions, and cultural groups.

Each person has a unique cultural history. This history includes the history of our relationship with our own culture and others, including the dominant culture. For example, people may adjust their behavior to fit the rules and expectations of the dominant culture without giving up their own ways entirely. We call this process *acculturation*. On the other hand, some people choose to adapt to a new culture by taking on that culture's identity and abandoning their own culture. This is called *assimilation*.

In the United States, we have lost much cultural richness and diversity to an oppressive, often forced, assimilation known as the "melting pot," in which each family's heritage is supposed to be "melted" into one "American" culture. For example, generations of Native Americans, as well as voluntary and involuntary immigrants, were forced by US authorities to replace their native language with English. They were also forced to abandon their customs and religious practices in an attempt to "melt" all these cultures into one based on White European-American culture. Some newly arrived immigrants voluntarily gave up their language and cultural practices to survive or succeed in the United States.

Reclaiming cultural heritage

Recently, many cultural groups in the United States have begun to reclaim their heritage by relearning their native language, studying and passing along cultural history, and returning to native dress and names. These practices can mystify and anger people who are comfortable with the melting pot idea. Some feel threatened by people who are different from them and who are choosing to celebrate their unique cultural heritage publicly.

A family's cultural identity can be shaped over time by changes in the culture as well as by the experiences of individual family members. For example, a Hmong family arrives in the United States after several years of devastating loss in war and refugee camps. They are far away from their native Laos, but they still carry seeds of their original culture in language, customs, health practices, dress, crafts, and preferred family form. Once here, the family devotes itself to establishing a home, learning English, getting jobs, and going to school. Family members begin to incorporate new viewpoints and behaviors into their lives, while retaining some of the old ways. Other Hmong families in the same community, and in other communities, are making similar adjustments. A Hmong-American culture begins to emerge. This emerging culture shapes, and is shaped by, each family's and individual's experiences.

People from different countries can share a common cultural heritage. For example, Jews live in many countries but share a common religion and culture. Each Jewish person's experience of that cultural heritage will be influenced by the country he or she came from, as well as family influences and personal traits.

As your understanding of diversity and oppression grows, remember that each family, and each family member, is made up of a combination of cultural traits, family traits, and personal traits. For this reason, *it is not safe to generalize*—to assume that if one (or even several) people of a particular cultural background behave in a certain way, that behavior is a cultural trait. It may be a family or personal trait instead.

C. Why is an understanding of diversity and oppression important to family development?

As a family development worker, you meet and work with people from diverse cultural groups. Working respectfully with each person and family can be a challenge as you approach the increasingly diverse people of your community. It is not possible to learn everything you need to know about the cultures of all the families and individuals you'll work with. It is possible to expand your understanding of culture one small step at a time.

This chapter will not attempt to describe various cultural groups in detail, because there are hundreds of cultural subgroups today in the United States, and there will be more tomorrow, each constantly evolving. The brief descriptions offered here provide an introduction to some cultural groups here who have been affected by displacement and oppression. While this is useful background information, cultural competence cannot be acquired through reading summaries of the traits of particular groups. It can only be developed by starting a lifelong quest to respect and know yourself and other people more deeply.

A lifelong journey

What is "cultural competence"? It is the ability to learn from and relate respectfully with people of your own culture as well as those from other cultures. It includes adjusting your own and your organization's behaviors based on what you learn. Cultural competence is not something you master once and then forget. It is a lifelong journey.

Honoring a variety of cultures

Cultural competence is not about trying to change others to become more like you. It is about cultivating an open attitude, and new skills, in yourself. Cultural competence involves exploring and honoring your own heritage, while at the same time learning about and honoring other people's cultures. Developing cultural competence is a life-long journey in which you will be tremendously enriched (and will make some mistakes).

Although cultural competence has been seen as the task of individual workers, organizations and systems are responsible for the delivery of culturally competent services. Therefore, to be able to work in this way, your agency should strive to become culturally competent.

A culturally competent organization is one that commits to this work, allocates resources, sets specific goals, and develops policies that support the agency and the staff to work with the cultural differences of the population(s) they serve. Cultural competence means:

- Recognizing the strengths in all cultures

- Respecting cultural differences

- Using cultural knowledge to design and provide services

D. Why is cultural competence important for family development workers?

The family development approach is based on developing and maintaining mutually respectful relationships with families. These respectful relationships depend on your ability to respect and learn from the cultures of the families you work with. This ability is built on a foundation of self-respect for your own culture.

The population is growing more diverse

As a family worker, you need to work skillfully with many kinds of diversity, including race, ethnic background, language, gender, sexual orientation, class, family form, age, religion or spirituality, geographic origin, and physical and mental ability. This diversity can bring a tremendous richness to your life, and to the life of your community. Yet it also can feel overwhelming to deal with people who are different from you, especially if you aren't sure how to get along in mutually respectful ways. In this chapter, you'll learn some reliable ways to establish good working relationships with a wide range of people, and to learn from each other. You'll also learn how to handle gracefully (and learn from) the blunders that are inevitable in an increasingly multicultural world.

Workers must relate to different kinds of people

It is natural to feel most comfortable being with people like yourself, or at least with people who want to be like you. In family development work, you will work with people who are unlike you in some or many aspects of their lives. Some of them will have cultural traits that you don't understand or necessarily like. If you tend to ignore or reject the unfamiliar aspects of their culture, you will not be able to help them, and you'll miss an opportunity to grow yourself.

Family workers need to grow more comfortable responding to the unique needs of different populations. For example, most community-based agencies are staffed by women, and therefore are most comfortable working with women, especially those with young children. Successful family workers need to become more skillful in working with men, teenagers, and elders. You will not be effective working with families experiencing problems such as teen pregnancy, single-parent households, absent fathers, school dropouts, or substance abuse, until you become more comfortable in reaching out and listening to the needs of other groups. Also, reaching out to these groups makes your work with women and children more effective.

Workers need to understand power differences

As you do this, you may find yourself looking at who holds power in the family. It can help to look at your own experiences of family: the power dynamics (the way power works) between husband and wife, mother and father, in-laws, and young people that you have lived with in your childhood and adult life. For example, if you were never allowed to "talk back" to your father or grandmother when you were a teen, this history might affect the way you relate to families with the same or different "rules" as they communicate about family goals.

The expectations workers have of various family members can affect who they invite in to the family development process. At a focus group, a man who is a program supervisor talked about the need to encourage males to take a larger role in the family, and the tendency to assume that they can't or won't be involved.

> I think men need to take some of the caretaking responsibility. Maybe we need a support group for men. Something that addresses that segment society wrongly assumes as incapable of dealing with family problems.

At another group, a worker said:

> The fathers really, really need to be brought in. The kids need these men in their lives, no matter how loathsome the mothers think they are.

Another worker talks about successfully involving a father:

> Now that I'm coming here, dad makes sure he comes home when we have visits. He schedules them around that. It's wonderful, because first I met Dorothy, he was in training for his truck driving school. So, when I met him, his enthusiasm of the program and his dedication to interacting with his child during visits was just wonderful.

Family perceptions of the worker's power

Although you may feel powerless sometimes when faced with people whose culture differs from yours, many of the families you work with feel that you have a great deal of power over their lives. You (or other agency workers that they might confuse you with) have the power to decide if they are going to get some service they really need, whether or not their children get put into foster care, and other decisions that are enormously important to them. If they (or their ancestors and other relations) have a history of being oppressed by people of your culture who have misused power, you may become the target for their stored-up anger. Developing your own cultural competence will help you handle such anger safely and constructively, while maintaining your own self-respect.

At a focus group, a worker talked about his struggle with this problem:

> I think the largest barrier I encounter day in and day out is fear, and preconceived notions on both sides. I think it's hard for people to see and understand each other as human beings. People are stereotyped and [type-]cast, and that's something I struggle with.

A mother receiving services also talked about stereotypes:

> A lot of times we hear someone say, "Oh, how many kids do you have?" and we'll say "four," and then the question that's most asked of me is "Are they all by the same father?" I guess in this day and age, it's very uncommon. We have really hung in there!

E. Language and cross-cultural communication

Culture and language are very closely related. Several skills will help you to communicate effectively in these two situations: Communicating with people when you both speak English but have very different cultural backgrounds, and cross-cultural communication when English is not their home language.

Cross-cultural communication with other English speakers

First, you will need to interact effectively with people who speak English but have different cultural backgrounds. Many of the skills addressed in Chapter 2 will be helpful here. Because you share a common language, it can be easy to forget that this is a cross-cultural exchange. Communication is always affected by the context (circumstances) in which it happens, and by the personal experience of the people communicating. For example, the word "wedding" will convey a different meaning to an Arab, a Mexican, and a Native American because the expectations, ceremonial traditions, and values vary across these cultures. Understanding usually comes from direct contact with others and from knowledge of specifics such as the history and culture of diverse groups, including values, stories, myths, music, and art.

Culture and language are dynamic—that is, always changing, often in response to economic, political, or societal changes. For example, over the past several decades, the preferred term to describe one large cultural group has shifted from Negro to Black to Afro-American to African American, reflecting both political shifts and a reclaiming of cultural roots.

Yet people seldom identify themselves first as belonging to a general category, such as African American. In getting to know families it is ethnic identity, not race, people tend to identify with first. For example, a Haitian is Haitian first and then Black. A Chinese person is Chinese first and then Asian. A Peruvian is Peruvian first and then Latino or Hispanic.

Choosing the terms to use when referring to the cultural groups you work with is not always an easy process. When in doubt, ask the people you are referring to. You could say, "Some people prefer the term Black, and others like to be called African American. What do you prefer?" *It might feel awkward at first, but learning how to ask questions respectfully is a vital skill to develop as you grow in cultural competence.* Once people understand that you sincerely want to learn and be respectful, they are usually very generous with their help. In the example above, you might hear a reply that is not as simple as you thought it might be, and which broadens your understanding. "I'm from Haiti, so I'm Black but not African American" might be the answer.

Second, cross-cultural competence requires knowledge of nonverbal communication. Although there are some universal nonverbal messages, our interpretations of space, touch, appearance, body language and time differ according to culture and context. For example, when feeling embarrassed, Vietnamese children may avoid eye contact with adults as a sign of respect. This behavior in American classrooms may incorrectly signal disrespect and inattention to some teachers.

To increase your awareness of powerful nonverbal messages, you can observe others. You can also ask people you trust from other cultures:

- How close is it comfortable to stand or sit?
- What postures or gestures show respect? Disrespect? What about eye contact?
- How does timing affect communication? Am I talking too fast? Too slowly?
- What do different tones of voice mean?

At a focus group, a supervisor spoke about the misunderstandings that can arise from cultural differences in body language:

> Cultural sensitivity is so important for workers. You take a Haitian family, where the person is talking to you and you see the child is not looking at you straight. It's a sign of respect, but it's the reverse here, where you think they're not paying attention.

A worker related that she had grown in her understanding of how she appears to some people.

We have had Native American children since we border the reservation. When I first started, their parents seemed very stand-offish to me. And I assumed, "Well they don't want to talk to me, that's how they are." Now I realize that I probably drove them insane because my mannerisms are totally foreign, [they had] issues with [my] eye contact, and I'm very boisterous. I think I may have just come in and given them totally the wrong picture. Now I think I would look at how I approach them, less eye contact, talking slower, if there's a space, not having to jump in and fill that space right away. Just being more respectful of space, listening more.

Working with people for whom English is not the home language

As a family development worker, you may need to communicate with families who can only speak in their native tongue(s) or are limited in their knowledge of English. Whether you speak the same language or use an interpreter, use plain language, without agency jargon (words or abbreviations that you probably didn't know before you started this kind of work).

Many family development workers understand the need to provide bilingual services for people in their area who do not speak English. Ideally, every family worker would be proficient in the language, knowledgeable about cross-cultural communication, and aware of the relationship between language proficiency and family development.

However, this ideal is often unrealistic, because bilingual workers—who are also bicultural and understand cross-cultural communication—are not always available. Unfortunately interpreting often falls on relatives, friends, or staff who were hired to do a completely different job than interpreting (for example, a cook in a day-care center being asked to interpret an impromptu parent-teacher conference).

Hiring an interpreter

To be better prepared to work with interpreters, think about the following suggestions:

- Try to hire professional interpreters. When working with a trained interpreter:
  1. Orient the interpreter to the purpose of the interview.
  2. Explain the importance of accurately translating information provided by the family.
  3. Review some of the technical terms that may come up.
  4. Inform the interpreter of potentially sensitive topics that may arise.
     Always explain to the family who the interpreter is and allow time for trust to develop between the family and the interpreter.

- Whenever possible, do not use relatives, friends, or untrained staff as interpreters. If you cannot avoid it, be aware of situations in which the information being discussed would make it inappropriate to use a family member, someone of the opposite sex, or a child. When in doubt, ask the family if they would feel comfortable with a particular person interpreting.

- Develop a language "bank." You can create a list of bilingual people (staff from your agency or from the community) who can be called to serve as interpreters when needed. Provide training to these staff. The quality of language banks needs to be closely monitored so that staff called upon to interpret are well equipped to do this job and are paid for doing it.

- Use phone-based interpreter services. Some companies and agencies offer online telephone interpreter services. Although this type of interpretation is time-consuming and cannot benefit from the nonverbal cues that are such an important part of your interactions, sometimes you may need to use them as an emergency back-up measure or for short follow-up questions. (It may also be used for less frequently used languages when no interpreter is available.)

- If you are translating written material (such as assessment, eligibility forms, and brochures), be sure to "pretest" the material with members of the group that will be using the information. Be aware of the cultural appropriateness of some of the information or questions, pictures, and special dialects.

Working through an interpreter

A professional interpreter should know and follow the following guidelines, but with an informal interpreter you will have to take more responsibility for introducing the guidelines at the beginning:[18]

> Thank you for agreeing to interpret today for my conversation with_____. Before we begin, let's introduce ourselves, and set some simple guidelines to help us work respectfully together. [Introductions.] As you may know, interpreters are bound by three main ethical guidelines:
>
> * Keep all information strictly confidential.
> * Faithfully convey everything you hear, without changing it.
> * Do not advise or add your person opinions.
>
> Ask, "Is this agreeable to everyone?" If everyone agrees, proceed with the rest of the meeting by looking at and talking to the family member. This can take practice, since we're used to looking at the person talking in our language, but it is the best way to convey respect for the family member you're working with. If you're unsure how to act with a person who uses an interpreter, ask the person what he prefers. He'll tell you, through the interpreter.

A family worker at our focus group shared this story:

> We had a father come in who didn't know much English. The teacher was trying to give him some information and she did it through the interpreter instead of to him. I know some Spanish, and I overheard him say to the translator, "Does she think I'm stupid? Why isn't she talking to me?"

F. Language and family dynamics

Speaking a language different from the dominant one has a strong effect on family and individual development. Language is a powerful vehicle for communicating culture. It can be the glue that holds a cultural group together, or a barrier to gaining access to needed resources such as education or jobs. For many families, it is both. People whose culture is at risk of being replaced by the dominant culture struggle to preserve or reclaim their language. Immigrants eager for citizenship and full acceptance strive to acquire English while maintaining their own language.

Language will become an increasingly important issue for family-serving agencies over the next several decades. For example, 10 percent of the population of New York State (20 percent of the

[18] Adapted from Betty García Mathewson, *Language Interpretation Guidelines* (Brockport, NY: State University of New York Migrant Program, 2006), pp. 11-12.

population of New York City) already speaks or reads English poorly enough to need language training.[19]

While you need to be able to refer families to English-language training in your community, it is equally important that you know how to support families in maintaining the richness of their own culture while becoming fluently bilingual.

People who speak the dominant language tend to take it for granted. People born into an English-speaking family in the United States tend to view English as the "natural" language, forgetting that in most other places in the world, English is not the language most people speak. Yet many people speak more languages than the English-only US citizen. In other countries, even people who don't read and write any language often speak several languages or dialects.

The ability of some or all members of a family to speak only a language other than English affects relationships within the family. It also influences the family's connections with the larger community. Those who do not speak English often feel powerless because they can't participate in important decisions (such as those made in school conferences or health clinics). They feel isolated and excluded from the community.

If children are the first to learn English, as often happens, the balance of power within the family can shift as parent and grandparents rely on children to interpret information from schools, landlords, and others. Children are sometimes asked to interpret (or make written translations) in inappropriate situations. As children and teenagers become more fluent in English, they sometimes start refusing to speak the family's native language, troubling the parents and grandparents as well as upsetting family interactions.

When parents feel less competent than their children in a skill as important as language, they can begin to feel out of control. As soon as children learn English at their preschool, most of them stop speaking their family languages at home. This change can happen even when the parents know little or no English. As a result, meaningful communication between parents and other family members can be lessened. This loss occurs more frequently when learners are made to believe that the second language is the key to social acceptance, while their first language is a barrier to it.

Such difficulties can cause family closeness to break down. This breakdown is especially tragic when children reach adolescence. Parents and children who don't have a common language for communicating with each other may, become alienated (distant or foreign) from one another. The parents are unable to influence their children as they grow up. Many parents complain that their teenage children behave disrespectfully toward them. The children regard them as backward and slow because they do not speak or understand English.

Parents will feel that they are losing authority and control over children. The parents' ability to provide guidance, boundaries, support and discipline are undermined when there is no common language between children and parents. Working to assure that youth maintain the home language should be a high priority for family workers working with immigrants.

Maintaining the home language

Immigrant families want to improve their quality of life; it is often their main reason for moving to the United States. They want their children to have a better life. They know that to attain this dream, their children need to learn English. Yet people can maintain their home language while learning English.

At a focus group, a worker said:

> If you can get people, just amongst their own language, to trust each other, and then communication opens up broader and then they can go into helping each other. Sometimes, if you can get some of

---

[19] Wendy Zimmerman, "Teaching immigrants English: Growing needs and shrinking resources," *Migration World Magazine*, vol. 22, issue 2-3 (1994), pp. 13-16.

these people to come in and assist in the organizations, then they see their own, working within the group, and I think that also opens up trust and breaks down barriers.

Another worker said:

> Some of my coworkers say "Speak English," but what they mean is that I don't speak good English, I tell them they need to go and take FDC class because they don't know how to appreciate somebody else's skills. I advise them to take FDC because I think it can teach them cultural competence.

Preserving one's home language while learning English, can support a healthy sense of self. When immigrants lose the home language it is generally the children who lose the language, not the parents. Historically it has been the children of immigrants who first learn English in the United States, not the adult immigrants. This is the first time in our history that we are trying to teach adult immigrants English because our society requires more communication than in the past. Learning a new language is founded on the literacy level of the other language spoken.

When children of immigrants lose the home language, and the family common language, then parents lose their ability to parent their children. In immigrant homes where children have lost the home language, parents and children are unable to communicate. Imagine the impact of this on an adolescent struggling with issues of identity. Imagine parents trying to transmit their knowledge, culture, religion and provide guidance, boundaries, support, and discipline.

Maintaining and developing a children's first language is a critical factor in predicting academic success. Research has demonstrated repeatedly that this higher the literacy in the first language, the greater the transfer of language skills and cognitive ability to the second (or third) language. School-age children learn the new language more quickly than their parents for obvious reasons: the level of exposure and the structure of that exposure.

Foreign language ability is a valued skill in our society and a minimal level of proficiency is required to graduate from high school. Truly bilingual individuals contribute to and enrich our global communities. One of the unfortunate outcomes of replacing children's home language with the language of the school is that when we need bilingual family development workers (and others such as health care workers and teachers), these same people no longer have command of their first language.[20]

Handling oppressive behavior and conflict

Workers who respect diversity need to understand many ways that language can create problems for families. In some situations, language can function to separate people because one language is valued more than another by the dominant culture. In other settings, language can be used as a tool to demean a particular group. The basic skills you learned in Chapter 2 will help you handle two communication challenges specific to diversity:

- Interrupting the oppressive behavior of others respectfully

- Dealing with conflict and anger arising from cross-cultural misunderstandings, or racism and other "isms"

When you're working hard to develop your own cultural competence, it can be hard to listen to racist "jokes" or other put-downs. You can use effective listening and speaking skills to stop these belittling behaviors. For example, "I'm uncomfortable when you refer to Ms. Sallis as a 'chick.' Please call her by her name." If the person retorts with further put-downs (of you, Ms. Sallis, or women), use feedback and continue skillful speaking: "You wonder why women get angry about being called 'chicks.' I understand that you don't mean any harm. Please call us by our names, or call us 'women.'"

As you interact with people who are different from you, you are likely to encounter anger. Again, you can use the skills you learned in Chapter 2. For example, you can use reflective listening skills to

---

[20] Adapted from information provided by Eduardo González Jr., Cornell Migrant Diversity Program.

show your understanding, whether or not you agree with the statement: "It makes you furious to hear Spanish spoken on the streets of New York. You wish everyone spoke English. You wonder what our city is coming to, and what place you'll have in it."

Effective agencies often have staff from the cultures and language groups they are trying to serve who can act as a "bridge" with the dominant culture. They help client families feel more "at home" and help the agency increase its cultural competence. On the other hand, the cultural strengths of these workers cannot be an excuse for other staff to ignore their own need to develop cultural competence. If all workers begin to examine their own culture and privilege, and work on communication skills, then all agencies will have staff members who can work with a variety of families.

Understanding the "help" that has hurt

Family workers who come from a cultural group that has been displaced often understand the reluctance family members feel when an agency worker says, "We're here to help you." They remember their people's long history of receiving "help" that was not only unhelpful but often led to crimes such as the forced removal of children; the tragic losses of cultural languages, customs, and homeland; and other abuses. As one agency supervisor said,

> There's a cultural barrier when we work with the Native American population. We walk into their reservation; we're totally outsiders, and it's very difficult to provide the services we want to, because it's not what they want.

Agencies that use a family development approach find this less of a problem, because family development is not about "delivering services" to people who don't want them. The cornerstone of family development is a partnership in which the family sets its own goals, with the family and worker forming a mutually respectful partnership in which to work together on meeting those goals. Even with this approach, many families will be wary of the help offered, because of the mistrust remaining from harmful encounters with others.

Family workers who lack personal experiences of "help" that has harmed them can often feel hurt or bewildered when people reject their sincere offers to assist. They see hunger that could be relieved by food stamps, illness that needs medical treatment, substandard housing, alcoholism or domestic violence, and wonder why their offers of help are rejected or treated warily.

Being aware of reasons why your assistance may not be readily accepted, and being prepared for that possibility, can help you respect a family's choices, even if they are different from what you expect or hope to find.

At a focus group, a supervisor of an Alzheimer's Support Program talked about working in a rural area where families aren't used to taking help from "outsiders":

> We work hard to gain and maintain trust of rural people, to put their trust in us being there for them. This is our seventh year of operation and we just reached that point with these people.

A supervisor at another group spoke about a similar problem, but this time based on differences in the way some elders look at services:

> In our culture, the African-American culture, we find it's difficult helping seniors. Because they don't want to give us the information that we have to have in order to assist them. I remember going from building to building, trying to assess income to see if folks were eligible for SSI and it turned out that many of them were, but they did not want to go through the process, give us the information needed to get money they truly needed.

Another supervisor added:

> A barrier I think cuts across racial or ethnic groups is the elderly tending to not wanting to services that require giving up their privacy or confidentiality.

G. Displacement and immigration

The United States is a nation made up of people whose ancestors were displaced (Native Americans), brought here as slaves (African Americans), or whose ancestors (or they themselves) immigrated here, often running from persecution or starvation. As family development workers, it is important to recognize the impact of displacement and immigration on our country's history and future. Your work with recent immigrants requires practical skills to help families stabilize their lives. Recent immigrants, descendants of immigrants, and people whose cultures have been involuntarily displaced can use help to reclaim the rich cultural heritages that have often been taken from them or suppressed by the "melting pot" process. These cultural heritages can provide the foundation for healing the wounds of displacement or immigration, and for building a strong future.

Although this chapter could not possibly begin to describe the experiences of each cultural group that has been displaced from its homeland or immigrated to the United States, it does offer very brief glimpses into the experiences of two cultural groups that were either brought here against their will, or forcibly displaced from their homeland here in what is now the United States: African Americans and Native Americans. In addition, it describes the experiences of two other immigrant groups who have suffered forced displacement from what has become their home, Hispanics and Asian Americans. Although everyone in this country has a personal or family history of immigration or displacement, the violent displacement in these groups' cultural history can create particular challenges for family workers trying to "help." These brief histories are in this chapter's Appendix.

A family member in New York City, Haja talks about her more recent flight to freedom:

> I'm from West Africa. I came to Harlem because of the civil war back home. I came with my two kids, then, I had another child here. My husband was here already. I had to leave my country very fast with our children. The day we left, a friend of mine from church called me when the war broke out. Banks and schools were closed. Everybody was in the streets. You hear that this family has been killed. Their house had been bombed.

Factors affecting immigrant families

Understanding the experience of displacement and immigration is an important part of becoming culturally competent. Often, immigrants live and function in two distinct worlds, their past and their present. Some immigrants believe that it is better if the values and experiences of their past remain underground. When this behavior goes on for a long time, people are cut off from their sense of historical identity, and experience self-doubt and insecurity. This can have a bad effect on the children, who miss receiving from their parents solid values of ethnic identity and pride.

To become more sensitive to an individual's immigration experience, you can try asking questions about their original home and family who may still be there. Once trust has been built, the family may be ready to talk about why they came to the United States, how long they've been here, the migration process, difficulties they've faced adjusting to a new culture, and whether they can go back if they want to (many immigrants cannot).

Trauma

For many, the immigration process is a long story of uncertainty and loss. All families immigrating into the United States today are seeking a better life, but the level of hardship and trauma encountered along the way varies. Some have relatives waiting, and a realistic hope of improving their family's future through work and education. Others have encountered incredible hardship in the process of arriving in this country, and arrive traumatized, with little sense of what the future may bring. Many have spent fearsome years in refugee camps where they starved, suffered illness and injuries without medical treatment, were raped (or endured seeing their daughters, sisters, and mothers raped), and lost contact with close family members and their homeland. They arrive distrustful of strangers, yet dependent on whatever help they can find. And, depending on their legal status, they often face hardship getting help.

Fear of deportation

It is frequently difficult to complete a conventional "intake" assessment with an immigrant family, particularly if there are undocumented (illegal) family members. Within an extended family, some members may have green cards (permits to work and live in the United States), some may be citizens, while others may be in this country illegally.

When working with immigrant families, be aware that some of the family members may fear that sharing personal information could get them in trouble with immigration authorities. Families with members who lack legal immigration status may be very reluctant to become involved in community activities because they are afraid of being deported.

Workers who assist immigrants spoke about this issue at a focus group:

> People are scared to death if they are undocumented. They feel they have no rights at all, that if they go to court, they are going to get thrown out of the country because they don't have a green card.
>
> There's the issue of confidentiality in serving undocumented residents. Many agencies do not advocate providing service if the person is undocumented but still have a policy of not turning anyone away.
>
> Sometimes you can't get families to even disclose their family dynamics because they're fearful of saying where their family members are and what they're doing. Are they working? Are they not?

Too many families have experienced the terror of self, husband, wife, mother, father, or other family member suddenly being arrested then deported while at work, in town, or at home. This happens not only to people who've overstayed a tourist visa or are otherwise in the United States illegally, but also to US citizens and to children born here legally. In addition, countless US citizens, when returning home after traveling in another country, are subjected to extra scrutiny because of their race, appearance, name, or the country they've visited.

What can a Family Development worker do? The skills you are learning in the Family Development course—working respectfully with people from diverse backgrounds, communicating with skill and heart, building and keeping up to date your relationships with knowledge of community resources—will help you help families even in this type of emergency situation and beyond.

The language barrier

Immigrants may not speak or read English well enough to understand your questions, or ask questions you can understand correctly. A volunteer who worked with refugee families through her church enjoyed a polite exchange with one immigrant woman. She thought they were finally forming a bond because they were both mothers of three children. The refugee woman ended the conversation by asking the volunteer, "Do you use medicine?" The volunteer told her about a (male) doctor who accepted Medicaid, but the mother never made an appointment. Several months later, seeing the woman was pregnant, the volunteer realized, too late, that she had been asking for birth control information.

A family member in a focus group on immigration issues said:

> The language barrier is the biggest handicap. When you come from a refugee camp straight into this country it is very difficult to adjust to being on the outside again and then in a different culture also. It took a long time for me to learn to adjust and live in this country.

It takes an extra outreach effort, and superb patience, to work with immigrant families. One agency supervisor described the benefits of that extra effort:

> I know once she told me she went to her citizenship class but she didn't pass because she couldn't spell her name. She got so frustrated and she just cannot, she blanked out. But when she was able to do it in a more relaxed atmosphere, she is able to function well. If she had not connected with me and this agency, I think she may have done it later along the line., but she has a lot more help now. I think it probably would have been stressful for her to go ahead with it.

> I went to see Dominicans the other night to talk about the program and we stayed until 10 o'clock. We had to use a translator. The family wanted to ask questions. So what was supposed to take two hours. ... But the next day, here they were. They all needed help, but hadn't known that we could give it to them.

Family roles change

Immigration can change traditional family roles for several reasons. Women often find it easier than men to acquire jobs because domestic work is readily available to people who lack formal U.S. education, English or other qualifications (such as a driver's license). Children and teenagers often learn English faster than parents and grandparents, changing traditional parent-child dynamics.

A supervisor talked about the loss of traditional family roles when immigrants start assimilating into this culture:

> We made a brief study and realized that 40 to 45% of the children here are from Caribbean parents. What we have noticed is, having left the islands, the respect factor is lost. This is because the extended family is now extinct. So we try to help recreate it. We encourage the grandparents to be there, as a second family.

Roles between men and women are often less clearly defined here in the United States than they were in an immigrant's traditional culture. This difference can cause strain as men and women seek to hold on to power within their family.

A family worker described how these dynamics can affect the family development process:

> Sometimes it's a boyfriend or the husband who is holding her back. I'm channeling a lot of women who are on social services into educational programs, but there are significant people who do not want them to further their education, so this is a big battle.

Workers need a range of skills

People working with immigrant families need:

- Patience
- Compassion
- Knowledge of immigration law and Immigration and Naturalization Service (INS) procedures
- Information about refugee services such as ESL (English as a Second Language) classes, Citizenship classes, and job training
- An understanding of the role culture plays in shaping families' decisions
- The ability to speak or learn another language

The family development approach has much to offer immigrant families because of its focus on forming a partnership through which the family can set and reach its own goals. Most immigrant families do have goals: first for the basics of food, shelter, and safety, then later for jobs, education, and a better life. While it may take some extra effort to explain family development to families who have tremendous needs and do not realize that they can have a voice in meeting those needs, in the long run the family development approach holds much greater promise for families eventually becoming self-sustaining.

H. Barriers to a culturally competent society

Discomfort with differences, and fear that you or your own family or group will not get enough of what you want, is at the heart of all prejudice and discrimination. Many people are most comfortable with people like themselves, because they know how to talk and act in familiar ways. It often feels uncomfortable (and even dangerous) to be with people who look, talk, and act different. There is a powerless feeling about not knowing the language and customs of other people. It may seem a lot easier to stay with what is familiar, especially if there is no incentive to change or learn about other cultures. People often go to great lengths to avoid having to be confronted by their own ignorance of other people's cultures.

Discomfort with differences

Our dominant culture supports a fear of human differences. We are not afraid of other differences: flowers, trees, clothing styles. We are taught through socialization to fear human differences, yet not everyone responds in that way. Because prejudice is not natural (we are not born with these attitudes), many of us, through experience, overcome our learned prejudices.

As our society becomes more and more multicultural, it is harder for people to isolate themselves or refuse to learn how to get along with other cultures. As people recognize this fact, some realize that there is a lot to be gained by learning to become more comfortable with other cultures, and are making efforts to increase their own cultural competence. But others, especially people who are used to being in a privileged position, are angry about giving up some of that privilege, and having to pay some of the costs of an increasingly diverse society. They want to see more stringent limitations placed on immigration. They are afraid that they, or their family members, won't be able to get jobs as easily as in the past, or that they will have to learn a new language or new customs.

Privileges are advantages given to some cultural groups or individuals because they belong to certain groups, not because they have done anything special to earn them. Those with privilege often have blind spots about their own privilege, regarding their special position as a result of their own hard work or intelligence rather than seeing that people from other groups work just as hard or are as intelligent, but are denied similar privileges. For example, according to a U.S. Census Bureau 2013 statistic, women were paid seventy-seven cents for every dollar earned by men. And the gap is even greater for African-American and Latino women.[21] Many men attribute this difference only to their own hard work, intelligence, and skill, while many women see evidence of the role privilege plays in men's higher earnings.

Prejudice

As people, we look at everything through the lens of our own experience. This often results in prejudice, or forming a set of beliefs about a group of people based on hearsay, misinformation, or emotions, using one's own group as the point of reference. *Prejudice* (which literally means to "pre-judge") occurs when judgments about a person or group are made without real knowledge.

Treating a person from a cultural group as representative of the group, or an expert on the culture, can also be prejudice. For example, you may meet a person with disabilities and think that everyone with disabilities shares the same characteristics as this person (say, has a good sense of humor or expresses anger). We generally begin learning about cultures as if all individuals of the cultural groups were the same. However, each person interacts with his or her culture in a unique way and is a complex blend of individual, family, historical, and cultural characteristics. When working with a family, you need to learn how each member interacts with the group in which he or she functions, and what the group culture means to him or her, just as you need to be aware that your perceptions are a product of your own professional and personal cultures.

Prejudice against people who are—or are perceived to be—lesbian, gay, bisexual, transgender is called *homophobia*. Homophobic slurs or taunts are also often used against children or adults who don't fit gender role stereotypes; a boy who isn't athletic or tough gets called a "sissy" or "queer." *Heterosexism* is the assumption that everyone is heterosexual, or should be. Many people hold strong religious or personal beliefs about homosexuality. However, for family development workers, the question must be, given that some people are gay, lesbian, or bisexual, how are you going to treat them, and expect other people to treat them?

---

[21] United States Department of Labor, 2001. See the Facts on Working Women website, http://www.dol.gov.

Although several states have passed laws legalizing same-sex marriage, prejudice remains in many areas. Some individuals and families with gay members are "in the closet," afraid to tell even those closest to them—sometimes in their own families, about the reality of who they are. A family you are working with may have a son who has HIV. A "single mom with a roommate" may, in fact, be in a close, committed co-parenting relationship. Many workplaces now offer "domestic partner" designation so that committed couples who cannot legally marry are afforded equivalent health care and life insurance options available to married couples.

Recognizing the reality of people's lives and loves will make you a more effective family development worker.

Discrimination

Discrimination occurs when a person or institution uses power to act on their prejudice. For example, if an individual has negative opinions about lesbians based on incorrect information or personal bias, that is prejudice. If the same person is a landlord, and refuses to rent to lesbians, that is discrimination. There are laws prohibiting some forms of discrimination. Federal law protects people from job discrimination based on sex, national origin, religion, abilities, age, and other similar reasons. In addition to federal law prohibiting discrimination, some states and communities have their own human rights laws, such as a law prohibiting discrimination in housing based on sexual orientation. It is important to know the laws in your community.

Even though there are laws preventing discrimination, as a family development worker you are likely to hear outraged stories of discrimination and be asked for help. You need to be familiar with the resources in your community to help people fight discrimination, such as an Office for Human Rights.

Discrimination occurs at both the *personal* and *institutional* levels. To avoid shopping in a store owned by a member of a cultural group you don't feel comfortable with is an example of personal discrimination. If an employer hires a less-qualified person instead of a well-qualified person with a disability, that is an example of institutional discrimination. Discrimination can often be more subtle than these clear-cut cases. For example, let's say twenty people apply for a position, and twelve are reasonably well qualified. The three people interviewed, and the one selected, belong to the same cultural group as the two people doing the hiring.

At a focus group, a family member currently living at a shelter talked about the way shame can be made worse by discrimination based on economic condition:

> I had gone to an interview. The man took my application and said, "Oh, where is Carleton Avenue?" I looked at him, and I felt so embarrassed in saying where I was coming from. I said to myself, "No, _____, this is not you." I told him, "Arbor Inn Homeless Shelter." He says, "Oh, well I'm sorry but we have to interview some other people and we'll get back to you." ... Never heard from that man again.

Oppression and internalized oppression

The systematic discrimination against certain groups in society is called oppression. Systematic means that it is embedded in the system. A person can "do everything right" and still face discrimination because of his color, or her age. The root word of oppression is the word press: presses are used to mold things, or flatten or reduce them. The experience of oppressed people is that life is confined and shaped by forces and barriers that are not accidental. They are not avoidable or excusable. These forces restrict or penalize motion in any direction. One of the most characteristic and constant features of the world as experienced by oppressed people is *double bind* situations, in which options are reduced to a very few, and all of them expose one to penalty, punishment, or deprivation.

Restrictions and limitations based on racism, poverty, disability, gender, or other forms of oppression can be taken in and made a part of a person's way of seeing the world. When oppressive limits are internalized, the person becomes "self-monitoring"—that is, we do to ourselves what the culture has done to us. This is called "internalizing the oppressor" and is behavior learned as part of the adaptations that feel necessary to survive.

Internalized oppression can lead to lowered self-esteem and expectations for oneself and one's life, as well as low opinions of other members of one's group. When people see mostly negative views of their cultural group on television or in newspapers, magazines, videos, and movies (and have few positive role models in real life), it's not surprising when they come to believe these distorted views.

For example, when a teenage girl sees women valued by men only as sex objects (or objects of scorn or hatred), it is hard for her not to internalize these messages. She begins to think of herself as a sex object, belittling her own intellectual abilities and neglecting her own varied interests, consciously or not, as she seeks male approval. She disrespects herself and other girls and women. In time, she forgets where she picked up this view of women, assuming it is normal.

At a focus group, a worker spoke about the messages young people in their communities are getting:

> We need to let our youth, really our boys, but both boys and girls, know that there's an alternative to carrying a gun and dealing drugs and coming off the street. We have a big struggle with that, being in the midst of a community that does a lot of shooting one another. And for our girls, our barrier is letting them know that they don't have to go to bed with a boy to be somebody, or to feel that they have to get pregnant to have someone to love, because they don't feel love.

Another worker described how the media reinforces racism and internalized oppression:

> One of my concerns is media bias. The media portrays especially a black community as though there is nothing happening here. Scarcely do you find the programs and the good things happening here. There is a lot going on in our neighborhoods. I think we feel that a stereotypical pattern is placed by the media before the eyes of the people. And it fights against what we're doing. If they could portray the better side of our community and what's really happening, it will be better for our people.

People can be strongly affected by internalizing others' ideas of them. A worker said at a focus group:

> Racism is a barrier for the families we work with, and discrimination and prejudice, which I think affects internalized oppression. So that somebody starts to believe what other people say about them and we have trouble motivating them.

For example, a young person from an oppressed group excels in a particular way that is considered unusual for her group—say, a Puerto Rican woman excelling at law. If she pursues that strength, and takes advantage of attention from the dominant group, she can feel and be accused of "selling out" or trying to be different or better than others in her group. Even her family may give her these messages. While pulled in the direction of her interest or talent, she knows that ultimately her strongest and longest-term source of support over the course of her life will be from within the group, and she may not wish to risk their rejection. She may also know that others like her have been given attention as "tokens" by the dominant culture but dropped when their interest wore off. As her family development worker, you might not understand her hesitation in taking advantage of some big opportunity if you don't learn to look at the situation through her eyes. There are no easy answers here, and the most you can do is help her, and her family, look at the choices she faces, as she sees them.

A worker who does peer counseling with differently abled people discussed the way that commonly believed misinformation can diminish what individuals and families think is possible:

> Families of people with disabilities buy into the idea. ... "Oh, my child [even if it's an adult with a disability] is incapable of making decisions, lacks judgment, can't go to school, go out and get a job." They think they need to be taken care of. Even individuals with disabilities absorb that kind of thinking.

She went on to say that believing one can't set high goals, because, for example, of learned stereotypes about people with disabilities and lack of role models, can lead to fear of moving forward.

> I think two of the biggest barriers for us are fear of action and fear of success. They're afraid, not only that they're going to fail, but that if they're successful, that means they're going to go a step further, that they're going to have to be more responsible. And they're afraid of that.

Internalized oppression can lead people to believe that low expectations are acceptable. An agency worker gave this example of a family that had internalized ideas of what it means to be poor, and not have access to health care:

> One family I worked with, the children's teeth were extremely rotten, they were just little pegs sticking through their gums. But the parent's teeth were like that, too. They seemed to think it's okay: "I'm an all right person and my teeth look like that." So what I think helps is to bring them back to how they felt when they were children, "Yes, you survived, but just because your mom and dad let that happen to you, think of the way you felt, the pain you went through, and at this point we need to break the cycle. You see your child is in a lot of pain, and you don't want your child to feel that way. Let's make it better for them."

As this supervisor noted, internalized oppression can make it harder for people to make headway toward their goals:

> A lot of people who have not completed high school are ashamed or embarrassed, especially someone in their 30s or 40s. They may be ashamed to go to a GED classroom and be with a bunch of teenagers or early 20-year-olds. And they may be ashamed to ask a question if they don't understand what the teacher said.

Workers can help family members by reminding them of their genuine strengths, qualities and accomplishments, and by encouraging their efforts to improve their lives. What are some of the other ways you, as a family development worker, can help the families you work with overcome internalized oppression, racism, and other barriers of prejudice and discrimination?

I. Discussing diversity

Talking about diversity can bring on intensely emotional reactions. People often find it difficult to talk about, for fear that their words or actions may unintentionally harm other groups, or that they might be misunderstood and accused of being oppressive. Other times, people used to community outsiders making decisions for them without even consulting the residents of the community, come to believe that outsiders have nothing useful to say about the fate of their children and families. Some call this the guilt-anger dance that goes on between those with the privilege of being from a mainstream group, and those who have been marginalized. This dance doesn't help move us along.

But being from the group that needs to make a decision does not guarantee that a person has the most useful insights or understandings about that group. Nor does being from a different group imply that a person has no understanding at all. Your challenge is to encourage a useful dialogue that builds understanding of multiple points of view, with people willing to share power and find common ground.

As a family development worker, you may need to advocate for the needs of those who are being left out, even if it means bringing up a topic that others find uncomfortable or politically "hot."

Limitations of diversity training

Many agencies have developed or contracted for "diversity training" for their staff. Diversity training cannot be a one-time effort. Developing cultural competence is a life-long process that requires an ongoing commitment from agencies and individual staff. Secondly, most of these short workshops or trainings focus on providing information about people from particular cultures. This information may help individuals to change personal prejudices, and can sometimes lead to institutional changes.

Although important, these changes do not replace the continuous knowledge gained from life experiences (for example, making the effort to develop friendships with people from different groups than your own) or the long-term institutional changes needed to support cultural competence. In addition, these trainings are seldom evaluated to see whether they result in positive changes.

An agency's cultural competence depends on attitudes, structures, policies and practices. These features can be supported by quality diversity training programs focused on specific areas. For example, an agency can provide ongoing professional development that helps staff to understand the complexity, based in oppression, of our diversity in the United States. Cultural competence also requires an understanding of the social and political environment in which the agency operates. This environment includes the agency's funding, state and city policies and laws, and the ethnic populations it serves.

Overemphasis on culture

In our zealous and well-intentioned efforts to become more sensitive to other cultures, we sometimes categorize people as quickly as possible and assume they have particular cultural characteristics. We speak about the elderly, people with disabilities, or Mexican Americans as if we know a lot about them because they are in this group. We must remember that people in the same group vary enormously. It is important to avoid substituting one set of stereotypes for another (for example, changing the negative prejudice of Asian Americans as "the yellow peril" to the positive prejudice of the "model minority"). Any overgeneralization, whether positive or negative, reflects cultural insensitivity.

Also, it is important to recognize that overemphasizing culture can limit growth. When people are overly rigid about doing things the way their group has always done them, they resist change, missing opportunities for development and growth. Many times, values that have served people in one place and time can be less helpful in the United States, or in a specific agency or program. While the comfort and familiarity of one's own group is important, sometimes fear or distrust of outsiders can prevent cooperation with other groups who can provide resources ranging from friendship to financial support. Closed-mindedness can cause conflicts both within and among different groups.

J. Exploring your own culture

Whew! How can you move yourself and your agency toward greater cultural competence? Cultural competence begins with understanding and appreciating your own identity. You are a culturally rich person, with your own blend of race, ethnic background, language, gender, sexual orientation, class, family form, age, religion or spirituality, geographic origin, and physical and mental ability.

Your personal cultural inventory

If you were describing yourself in each of these areas to a close friend, what would you say?

- race
- ethnic background
- language
- gender
- sexual orientation
- class (poor, working class, middle class, wealthy, etc.)
- family form
- age
- religion or spirituality
- geographic identity (rural or urban? Eastern, Southern, Western, Midwestern?)
- physical and mental ability
- other

Now, imagine that you are describing yourself and your culture not to your best friend, but to someone who has power over your life, power to say "yes" or "no" to a resource you or a family member really needs (like acceptance to school or long-term care, or affordable housing). When you describe your culture to this person, are there aspects you leave out, or try to make "fit" what you think is more acceptable? If you have to do that often, what happens to these parts of yourself? How do you feel? Most people have some aspects of their culture they are knowledgeable about and like to discuss, and others that they either don't know much about, or want to keep private from people they feel will judge or discriminate against them.

If you are going to be able to support others and appreciate the significance of their culture, it is important that you offer the same consideration to yourself. As you learned in Chapter 4, we cannot help others without at the same time caring for ourselves. People who are or have been traditionally oppressed do not need your guilt or sympathy; what they need is a fully functioning ally who takes pride in his or her own culture and background. Here are some ways you can become more acquainted with your own culture:

- Talk with family members and others. Ask questions about ancestors, relatives, places, immigration, celebrations, losses, heroes and heroines. Video or write down what they tell you. Consider researching your genealogy (family history), or at least documenting what the elders in your family know. Ask them to review what you've written or recorded, and correct or add anything they want to make the history more accurate.

- Visit important places in your cultural history. Introduce yourself to people there, telling them you're learning about your own cultural history. Ask for their help.

- Read about your culture and history. Realize that what you read (and what you learned in school) might not be accurate. It takes a conscious effort to replace misinformation with correct information, in your own mind and in the minds of others.

- Listen to or make the music of your culture. Enjoy art and crafts from your culture. Prepare and eat foods, and wear clothes that reflect your cultural heritage. Share these cultural expressions with others. Talk with the people you meet along the way—people who can help you find food, clothes, music, crafts, art from your culture. Ask them questions in a respectful way. Let them know you want to learn.

K. Expanding your ability to work respectfully with other cultures

A growing understanding of, and pride in, your own culture is a strong foundation for expanding your understanding of other cultures. Everyone views life through a personal lens. Much of what we think we know about other cultures is inaccurate, based on misinformation and lack of real contact. How have you learned about other cultures? How do you learn about other cultures now?

Here are some of the ways most people learn about other cultures:

- Media: TV, movies, songs, advertising
- Schools: teachers, books, experiences
- Our own perceptions: what we hear and see growing up in our families and communities

What have we learned through these channels? A blend of stereotypes, incorrect information, and some accurate information. Family workers often work with the most troubled families within a culture. The families who show up in agency offices are seldom the strong healthy role models within a cultural group. Yet family workers often base their opinions about a whole cultural group on their experiences with the most troubled members of that group.

Learning about other cultures

In order to expand your cultural awareness accurately, it is important to get to know strong, healthy people within a cultural group. Political, educational, and religious leaders within a community usually recognize the value of educating agency workers, so they are often generous in providing accurate information. Cultivate relationships with these leaders as well as with people you meet through work, your neighborhood, schools, personal or professional interests. These people can help you grow more comfortable with and knowledgeable about their culture. As you strive to learn more about the culture of families you work with, be cautious of making overgeneralizations. Be aware that individual differences exist within all cultures. Traits that you observe in a person or family may be personal quirks rather than cultural characteristics.

Here are some other ways to begin to expand your understanding of and sensitivity to other cultures:

- Attend public cultural events, or private gatherings to which you are invited. If you're invited to an event, go, be courteous, and thank your hosts. You will sometimes feel uncomfortable in unfamiliar settings, but eventually you'll make friends and become more at home.

- Read the literature of a culture, listen to the music, eat foods associated with the culture.

- When you've made enough of a connection with people in a cultural group different from yours, respectfully ask them questions. People are usually willing to answer sincere questions asked in a respectful manner. For example, "I've been admiring your beautiful hair. How do you braid cornrows? Do you have to re-braid them often?"

- If you're willing to follow through, ask for advice on how to learn more about their culture. If a book is recommended, read it, and then discuss it with the person who recommended it. Your efforts show your guide that you are sincere about learning, and open the way for deeper communication.

Leaning about family dynamics

As a family development worker, you'll probably be especially interested in family structures and dynamics. Many cultural groups place a higher value on interdependence with extended families than European Americans, who tend to value independence more highly. Sometimes it is hard for a family worker from one cultural group to understand the family structure of another culture, especially when the culture's traditional family structure has been disrupted by immigration or another major change.

For example, you may be unfamiliar with families made up of people not related by blood. Sociologists have special names for non-blood-related, extended family members of some cultural groups: "fictive kin." To the people who live these relationships, families are defined more by love than by official bloodlines, and have no need to question whether an "auntie" is "real." Where the auntie fits on the social worker's form is not the family's problem, but it can be if workers put that relationship in a category that makes it "less than family."

Family development workers need to be able to work respectfully with all families regardless of form. Some common family forms include:

- a mother and father with their biological and/or adopted children
- one parent with children (sometimes with a new partner)
- a remarried mother or father with joint custody or frequent visitation
- blended families to which parents bring children from previous marriages (and often go on to have more children together)
- same-sex couples, without children, or with children from a previous marriage by one of the parents or through adoption or artificial insemination
- a husband and wife without children
- foster families
- families who temporarily or permanently do not have custody of one or more of their children
- families with young adults who have remained or returned home (sometimes with their children)
- grandparents raising grandchildren with or without the presence of the children's parent(s)
- families who have a great deal of interaction with and are very influenced by extended family members
- families with a grandparent living with them (possibly needing care) as well as raising children
- individuals living alone or in group houses or shelters, who have varying amounts of contact with members of their extended families
- transgender couples

This complexity of family forms can be very challenging for family development workers, who may have strong opinions about the "best" family form(s). The most successful workers are those who accept that the form of a family is much less important than the stability and love with which family members support each other. The respect communicated by this acceptance, and the workers' focus on helping families clarify and attain their goals of self-reliance, provide a rich ground for collaboration and growth. When workers pass judgment on a family based on its form, they communicate disrespect, which blocks the trust building necessary to an effective working relationship.

It is also important to remember that every family is unique, even if the family form appears similar to another family. Every family is a distinctive blend of personalities and biological, cultural, economic and social influences which change over time.

For example, you may work with two families who appear to be headed by single mothers. As you gain their trust, you may find that one of these families is actually headed by two women in a stable, loving relationship, who share child-rearing, money-earning, and household responsibilities very competently, and enjoy a strong network of helpful friends and extended family. An overworked single mother heads the other family with little help from others. Although both families may look similar when you first meet them (because they apparently have the same form), their needs and resources are actually very different.

Understanding the power of language

Language has enormous power to degrade or uplift people. The words we use may come across as oppressive without any bad intention on our part. One word may have different meanings in different cultures. Language develops as part of a group's historical, economic and political evolution. It reflects that group's attitudes and thinking. Language actually shapes thoughts.

We do not consciously realize how much our attitudes have been conditioned since early childhood by the power of words to glorify or condemn. Negative language seeps in from the time we first learn to speak. To recognize the oppression in language is an important step in cultural competence. We may be aware of and ready to speak out against slurs about our own group but laugh at jokes that make fun of other groups, having heard these references all our lives. We may not be able to change the language most people use, right away, but we can definitely change the way we use language. We can avoid using words that degrade people. Also consider the message you send to families through the posters, magazines, books, and decorations in your office.

Most of all, as you approach families, be humble and aware that ultimately you cannot and will not know what needs, strengths, and goals they will bring to your partnership. That knowledge can only come from listening and planning together. If your client is an immigrant in a wheelchair, the issues he wants to discuss may not have to do with either of those factors. Instead, he may be a new father dealing with abuse in his own childhood, fearing that he will become abusive to his child. What he needs from you is an open mind, full respect for his humanity, and good listening. Based on trust and belief in your willingness to help, people will tell you what they need. Together with them, you can help them reach their goals.

L. Helping your agency to develop cultural competence

Your personal efforts to become more culturally competent will be much more effective if your agency also makes an organizational commitment to this process. As a front-line worker, you will probably not be able to transform your agency overnight, but over time you can influence your organization in that direction.

The two most important ways to move an organization toward multicultural competence are through *staffing* and *advisors*. It is critical to think about who is included and who is excluded, and what you do to assure that your organization is welcoming to people from varying cultures. *The organization needs to let its culture adjust and evolve, rather than expect the families you serve to do all the adapting.*

Since affirmative action laws went into effect, most human service agencies have hired some people of color. Too often, these are still "tokens": one Asian American among a staff of five social workers; Hispanic paraprofessional home visitors supervised by white nurses in a family health program. When funding cuts hit, a "last hired, first fired" policy often applies, hitting women, people of color, and people with disabilities the hardest since they were often the most recently hired.

Increasingly, organizations are setting up advisory councils that represent their clients. If only a few clients serve on these councils, they are easily intimidated by the professionals who outnumber them, and who are accustomed to speaking out and being heard in meetings. You may want to have informal advisors, such as the key advisors that will be discussed in Chapter 8, who can help plan outreach efforts. Focus groups with representatives of cultural groups you want to reach including families who are already working with your organization, are an excellent way to listen and get feedback. It may help if the person leading those groups is not from your agency.

Organizations committed to cultural competence make a serious effort to diversify staff whenever an opening occurs. They also look carefully at the diversity of the Board of Directors, advisory councils, and others who make decisions for the organization, and then take steps to increase diversity in those areas.

Acknowledgments

The substantial contributions to this edition by the following diversity consultants are deeply appreciated:

Evelyn Arce White, MAT, of the First Nations Development Institute
11917 Main St.
The Stores Building
Fredericksburg, VA 22408
(540) 371-5615.
E-mail: Info@firstnations.org.
Website: http://www.firstnations.org.

Ms. Arce White reviewed this chapter in its earlier edition, making insightful suggestions throughout. Specifically, she drafted the "brief history" sections in this chapter's Appendix and provided the national demographic data, and provided extensive resource lists. Her extensive knowledge, and her professionalism and responsiveness even in the midst of moving to accept her new position with the First Nations Institute, was much appreciated.

Eduardo González (primary liaison), Kathy Castania, and Betty García Mathewson of the Cornell Migrant Program Diversity Project.

Mr. Gonzalez and Ms. Garcia Mathewson reviewed this chapter in its earlier edition, making insightful suggestions throughout. Specifically they suggested replacing the earlier title "Cultural Competence," provided extensive resource information, provided detailed new information on working with interpreters, and updated the earlier edition's section on helping families retain the home language. Their extensive knowledge, professionalism and responsiveness to my questions are much appreciated. It was a joy to have this opportunity to work in-depth with these long-time colleagues, whose work I had previously respected from afar.

Contributions carried forward from the first edition by the following diversity consultants continue to be appreciated:

Dr. Ednita Wright, formerly of Syracuse University, Syracuse, NY.
Ms. Elena Cohen of the National Family Impact Seminar, Washington, D.C.

Any mistakes in applying the consultants' suggestions are the author's.

Resources

Using language that accurately tells the story of the experiences of excluded groups is critically important when discussing issues of difference.

African American

The following resources are useful in gathering additional perspectives on the history of Africans, the systematic enslavement of African peoples and the lingering legacy of slavery in the United States on African Americans and whites:

Castania, Kathy. *Diversity—what is diversity?* Fact Sheet #1. Available from Cornell Media and Technology Services Center, 7 Business and Technology Park, Ithaca, NY 14850 ([607] 255-2080; e-mail: resctr@cornell.edu)

DeGruy-Leary, Joy. (1994). *Post-traumatic slave syndrome: America's legacy of enduring injury.* Videotape available through the University of Massachusetts, Amherst. (Dr. DeGruy-Leary is also the author of a doctoral dissertation, *Axiology and post-traumatic slave syndrome.*)

Hall, Edward. (1959). *The silent language.* New York: Anchor.

Hassan-El, Malik Kashif. (1999). *The Willie Lynch letter and the making of a slave.* Chicago: Lushena.

Johnson, Albert. (2001). *Power, privilege and difference.* Boston: McGraw Hill.

Loewen, James W. (1994). *Lies my teacher told me: Everything your American history textbook got wrong.* New York: Touchstone.

Robinson, Randall. (2000). *The debt: What America owes to blacks.* New York: Plume.

Nieto, Sonia. (1992). *Affirming diversity: The sociopolitical context of multicultural education.* White Plains, NY: Longman.

Zinn, Howard. (1999). *A people's history of the United States: 1492 to present.* New York: Harper Perennial.

You can contact the national chapter of the NAACP and the Southern Poverty Law Center for information on local chapters that can help people fight discrimination:

National Association for the Advancement of Colored People
    8 W. 26th Street
    Baltimore, MD 21218
    (410) 366-3300
    http://www.naacp.org/

Southern Poverty Law Center
    400 Washington Avenue
    Montgomery, Alabama 36104
    (334) 956-8200
    http://www.splcenter.org/splc.html

Teaching Tolerance—A Project of the Southern Poverty Law Center. Free resources and films with teaching
    guides. http://www.tolerance.org/?source=redirect&url=teachingtoleranceresources

Puerto Rican/Latino American

Center for Puerto Rican Studies
    Hunter College
    695 Park Avenue, Rm. E1429
    New York, NY 10021
    (212) 772-5688
    http://www.centropr.org/index.html

Puerto Rican Legal Defense and Education Fund
    99 Hudson Street, 14th Floor
    New York, NY 10013-2815
    (212) 219-3360 / Toll free: 1 (800) 328-2322
    http://www.prldef.org/

Latino-Americans. PBS videos coproduced by WETA (Washington); Bosch and Co., Inc.; Latino Public
    Broadcasting; and Independent Television Service. http://www.pbs.org/latino-americans/en/watch-
    videos/#2365075996

Bilingualism and second-language learning

Center for Applied Linguistics
    4646 40th Street, NW
    Washington, DC 20016-1859
    (202) 362-0700
    http://www.cal.org

CREDE-Center for Research on Education, Diversity and Excellence
    University of California, Santa Cruz
    1156 High Street
    Santa Cruz, CA 95064
    (831) 459-3500
    http://www.crede.ucsc.edu

National Association for Business Economics
    1233 20th Street NW #505
    Washington DC 20036
    (202) 463-6223
    http://www.nabe.org

General resources on diversity

Cross, Elsie Y. (2000). *Managing diversity: The courage to lead.* Westport, CT: Quorum.
Loden, Marilyn. (1996). *Implementing diversity.* Chicago: McGraw Hill.
PBS. (2003). *Race—The power of an illusion.* Online companion to California Newsreel's three-part documentary
    about race in society, science, and history. http://www.pbs.org/race/000_General/000_00-Home.htm
Southwest Educational Development Laboratory (SEDL). (2005). *Reaching out to diverse populations: What schools
    can do to foster family-school connections.* http://www.sedl.org/connections/

State University of New York (SUNY) Brockport. (2012/2014). *Opening Doors Diversity Project*. A source of training and resources, including *Authentic Voices*, a trilogy of training DVDs with educational materials focusing on strategies for communicating through interpreters, and advocacy resources for Migrant Education. http://cc.brockport.edu/

Sue, D. W. (2010). Microagressions: More than just race—Can microagressions be directed at women or gay people? In D. W. Sue & D. Rivera (Eds.), *Microagressions in everyday life*, http://www.psychologytoday.com/em/50612. Accessed February 12, 2014.

Thomas, R. R., Jr. (1991). *Beyond race and gender: Unleashing the power of your total work force by managing diversity*. New York: Amacom.

Thomas, R. R., Jr. (1996). *Redefining diversity*. New York: Amacom.

Thomas, R. R. & Woodruff, I. M. (1999). *Building a house for diversity: How a fable about a giraffe and an elephant offers new strategies for today's workforce*. New York: Amacom.

Activities to Extend Learning

Chapter 5
Our Diverse World

A. Living in this diverse world

1. Reflect on the diversity in your community and how it has or has not changed in recent years. How have attitudes about diversity changed?

B. What is culture?

1. How do you define "culture?" How did your family describe its culture to you during your childhood? How much reliable information do you have about the culture of your ancestors?

2. How did your family relate to the surrounding community in terms of culture during your childhood? What cultural identities from your childhood do you continue to identity with as an adult? What cultural identities have you changed?

3. Compare your generation with your parents' or your children's. What important events, innovations, and influences have shaped the experiences of recent generations? What thoughts, feelings, attitudes, or values have stayed the same for generations? What has changed?

4. If you could reclaim an aspect of your cultural heritage or identity, what would you choose and why? How would your life be different if you were able to include this newly reclaimed aspect in your current cultural identity?

C. Why is an understanding of diversity and oppression important to family development?

1. Think about a cultural group that is having a greater presence in your community. How has your community responded to their emerging presence? Write a short script as if you were talking to a community member who is fearful about their presence. Explain why understanding diversity and oppression is important for people to relate respectfully with each other in your community.

2. *"A culturally competent organization is one that commits to this work, allocates resources, sets goals, and develops policies that support the agency and staff to work with cultural differences of the populations they serves."* Use this statement to assess your agency's current level of cultural competence. List ways you can help your agency build and strengthen its' cultural competence.

D. Why is cultural competence important for family development workers?

1. How comfortable are you working with men (if you are a female family worker) or with women (if you are a male family worker)?

2. What are some assumptions that families may have about family workers based on their gender or culture? How do you earn families' respect and trust in order to become more culturally competent in serving them?

3. Assess your agency to determine how father- or elder-friendly it is. For example: What are the expectations? How do you find out what a specific group wants or needs? Do you display images of the population in the brochure, on walls, in publications? What is the staff's skill level to work with this group? What are the hidden barriers?

E. Language and cross-cultural communication

1. Tune your TV to a channel that transmits a program in another language, including sign language. Observe nonverbal language and gestures. Can you make sense of what's happening? How do you feel about not understanding?

2. What is your reaction when you hear people close to you speaking a different language? Why do you think you feel that way? Have your feelings changed over time?

3. Describe an experience communicating through an interpreter. Reflect on suggestions in this chapter as well as your own experience, what suggestions do you have for working with families for whom English is not their home language?

F. Language and family dynamics

1. If you live in a bilingual home (with family members who speak English as well as another home language), describe how this works for your family. Does nonverbal communication differ based on the language spoken? How does the ability to communicate in two languages enrich the culture of your family? What, if any, are the challenges?

G. Displacement and immigration

1. Have you ever moved from one place of residence to another? Can you describe the experience, feelings, coping skills? List things that you could have done to make the transition less difficult.

2. Choose one of the brief histories for family workers presented in the Appendix of this chapter. Describe something new that you learned by reading it, or if you are a member of that cultural group, give your reflection of the information provided.

3. Why is it important for family workers to know some history of displaced and immigrant groups? How can this understanding of past history help families you work with today?

H. Barriers to a culturally competent society

1. Choose one of the barriers to a culturally competent society in the chapter, and share an example from your own life of how it affected you or your family.

2. How do you think the media influences our perceptions about diversity? Watch a news broadcast or read a news article and reflect on whether it may have suggested a bias about an individual or group.

3. What are some ways that you, as a family development worker, can help families you work with overcome the barriers discussed in the chapter?

I. Discussing diversity

1. Why is it often difficult to talk about diversity? Share an example from your life when you tried to discuss diversity and others tried to change the topic of conversation. How did you feel? How did you respond?

2. Explain the "guilt-anger dance" and how it occurs in your own words. How might this dance be characterized in the relationship between families and the family support delivery system? Share an example from your own experience as a family worker when you felt the guilt-anger dance occurred with a family your agency was working with.

3. Why is it important for family workers to know some history of displaced and immigrant groups? How can this understanding of past history help families you work with today?

J. Exploring your own culture

1. Review the definition of culture presented at the beginning of the chapter. Write the heading "Who Am I?" on a sheet of paper and describe who you are based on the thoughts, feelings,

146

146

attitudes, beliefs, values, and behavior patterns you share with a racial, ethnic, religious or social group. How does this description of "who you are" differ from describing yourself through physical or visible characteristics?

2. Listen to or make the music of your culture. Enjoy art and crafts from your culture. Prepare and eat foods, and wear clothes that reflect your cultural heritage. Share these cultural expressions with others. Talk with the people you meet along the way—people who can help you find food, clothes, music, crafts, art from your culture. Ask them questions in a respectful way. Let them know you want to learn.

K. Expanding your ability to work respectfully with other cultures

1. Read the literature of a culture other than your own, listen to the music, eat foods. Write a reflection describing why you chose to learn more about this culture, what you did, and the strengths you learned about this cultural group by expanding your understanding.

2. Have you ever received inaccurate information about another culture through newspaper, television, or movies? How did your personal experience with a person of that cultural group change a stereotype or misperception you had?

3. Do you belong to a cultural group that, at some time, has been misrepresented in the newspaper, television, or movies? What misinformation was given? What stereotypes or misperceptions about your cultural group might it have led to? What would you want people to know instead?

L. Helping your agency to develop multicultural competence

1. Look around your organization's staff, volunteers, Board, advisory groups, families you work with. Then look at the community. Are you representative? Consider staff hiring and turnover. How does your organization welcome and support people different from those already there? How could it be more supportive of diversity?

2. How do you feel about affirmative action (laws requiring employers, colleges, and other institutions to increase their representation and support for members of cultural groups that were prevented equal access to employment, education, or excluded in the past)?

3. If your agency has a board of directors or other voluntary governing body, learn more about how the members are appointed and the cultural groups they represent. As directors, do they represent a geographic district, a target population or constituency, or a sector such as business, government, or special interest? How does the composition of the board promote or hinder the agency's ability to build or strengthen multicultural competence?

4. Think about how your life is enhanced, and can be even better, because of the diversity of people in the world and in your life. Talk with a friend about the ways you can grow over your lifetime as you make close connections with people who are different from you.

5. How has working with families from different cultural groups supported you in your own journey of cultural competence? What do you enjoy most about working with families from different cultures than your own? What has been challenging for you?

6. As a family worker, have you ever been invited to attend a wedding, religious rite, or other special event of a family you are working with? How did it feel to be invited and to participate in the celebration of that family's culture? How did that celebration differ from your own culture's tradition? What did you learn about the meaning of "family" in their culture?

Skills Practices

These skills practices are a suggested list. You may also develop your own skills practice or make modifications to the ones listed below to help you create a meaningful and manageable plan.

1. Interview a family elder about your own family history and the values that were passed down to her/him. After your interview, consider the values you hold today. Reflect on the ways that some of the values you inherited from your family have continued to influence your life, culture, and family today.

2. Choose someone you trust from an ethnic identity different from your own. Share information about aspects of your ethnic identities with each other, and ask questions about each other's ethnic identity. Then, take turns describing positive aspects of your ethnic identities that you would like others to know. What things did you learn using this format that you couldn't have learned through just observing and interacting with other cultures?

3. Arrange to meet with a co-worker and discuss the benefits and challenges of supporting a family's ability to maintain their home language while they are learning English. Write a reflection summarizing the benefits and challenges you discussed. How do feel about the efforts of groups to maintain and reclaim their cultural identity and heritage?

4. Arrange to interview a family that immigrated to this country. Using open-ended questions and active listening skills, ask them about their experiences: What was helpful, and what was difficult? How can you incorporate what you learned into your future work with immigrant families?

5. Review the section on taking a personal cultural inventory, then write a description of yourself in each of the areas. Then, arrange to share and discuss it with a trusted friend. Write a reflection on the information you shared with your friend. Were there any areas you felt uncomfortable sharing? Reflect on how you might feel to be asked to share the same information with someone who had power over your life (for example, someone who could grant you admission to school, a job you really want, or affordable housing).

6. Talk with someone who immigrated to the United States and became a naturalized citizen about their experience and the process. Write a reflection about their experience and any challenges they encountered. How can family workers assist with the process?

Chapter 5 Appendix
A brief history of African, Native, Hispanic, and Asian Americans for family workers

African Americans

The three most significant issues that affect African Americans in all aspects of their lives are slavery, separation from the Motherland, and racism. Africans were stolen from their country and brought to the United States beginning around 1619 and ending in 1808, 189 years later. Immigration of African people has been limited ever since then.

It is important to remember what makes African Americans different:

1. Africans who were brought to America came from a country that had values very different from the American way of life.
2. They spoke different languages and had different cultural practices.
3. They came in bondage.

Prior to being brought to this country, Africans lived in culturally rich communities. Living was communal, hence the saying "I am because we are," rather than the more common "I think, therefore I am." The diversity of the African communities they came from made it even more difficult for Africans to bond together and withstand the abuse they met here, because unlike immigrants who arrive together from a particular country, their languages were often different, families were separated, and children and spouses were sold.

As they attempted to adjust to the hostile environment of America, Africans were unable to recreate aspects of the society they had known, which is what other immigrants often do. They were forbidden by Government policies to learn to read. They were "counted" by law as three-fifths of a person. The basic right of a citizen, the right to vote, was denied African Americans in many places from the days of slavery until the civil rights movement of the 1960s.

A turning point in the civil rights movement came when a brave member of that movement, Rosa Parks, would not stand when a white person demanded her seat on a bus. She knew the community of activists she was connected to would support her. From this one action, the bus boycott and other boycotts became a common group activity for African Americans to draw attention to the second-class treatment they were still receiving in the United States. Many followed in the footsteps of leaders such as Ms. Parks, Dr. Martin Luther King, Malcolm X, and Angela Davis. The civil rights movement led to affirmative action, which tried to correct the inequality in our schools, colleges, and other institutions. Yet it remains controversial today.

The lasting effect of slavery plays a part—in fact a much larger part that most of us might realize or admit—in how African Americans see themselves today. The basis of family they had known in their native land was kinship group, blood ties, common interests, and mutual assistance. In this land, they were not allowed to maintain a family unit as they had known. Over the many generations they lived under slavery, they always lived with the threat that the family could be separated at any moment.

When working with African American families, it is important to be aware of this history, and the way it could shape families' feelings toward you, a person they could perceive as having the power to hurt rather than help them. This is especially true if you are not African-American yourself.

Native Americans[22]

> *If the Great Spirit had desired me*
> *to be a white man*
> *he would have made me so*
> *in the first place.*
> *He put in your heart*
> *certain wishes and plans;*

---

[22] Adapted from information provided by Evelyn Arce White, MAT, First Nations Development Institute.

*in my heart he put
other and different desires.
Each man is good
in the sight of the Great Spirit.
It is not necessary,
that eagles should be crows.*

– Sitting Bull (Teton Sioux)

Five hundred years ago, when the first European settlers came to the "New World," there were over ten million Natives in the Northern Hemisphere. With the new settlers came many diseases that decimated most of the Natives, sometimes whole tribes and peoples.

Today there remain more than 600 different Native American nations throughout the United States, each with its own language and culture. The 2000 US census figures reported over 4.1 million people identified themselves as Native American/American Indian, comprising 1.5 percent of the country's population.

In Northeast America, from the banks of the Hudson to the shores of Lake Erie, there is a group of people that call themselves Huadenosaunee, or People of the Longhouse. They have a system of democracy called the Iroquois Confederacy, which is comprised of five nations: Mohawk, Oneida, Onondaga, Cayuga, Seneca, and Tuscarora. This confederacy is a complex system of government that was adopted by America's founding fathers in drafting the US Constitution.

The Iroquois had a matrilineal system; women in the native culture had many rights, such as the right to be landowners. Each tribe's clan mothers elected representatives, or chiefs, which comprised a council. The Iroquois Grand Council was the gathering of all of these chiefs to discuss affairs that affected all of the nations collectively, such as war, peace, resources and the protection of smaller tribes. All of them had an equal voice and equal authority.

The Great Law is the founding constitution of the Iroquois Confederacy. Codified in a series of wampum belts now held by the Onondaga Nation in Syracuse, New York, it defines the functions of the Grand Council and how the Native nations can resolve disputes between themselves and maintain peace.

Throughout the 1600s, 1700s, 1800s, and even to the beginning of the 1900s, Native peoples were forced to sign treaties that were eventually broken. Native tribes throughout the centuries lost over 95 percent of all their land. Europeans saw the Natives as obstacles to be eliminated or used for a workforce. The new settlers did not want to integrate Natives into their society so they formed reservations, which first had fences to keep the Natives out of general society. Ironically, this reservation concept was used by Adolph Hitler during WWII. Today less than half of Native Americans live on reservations.

One of the biggest negative influences for Native families was the disruption caused by religious and government boarding schools. The founder of the Carlisle Indian School in Pennsylvania, Captain Richard Pratt, was famous for his motto for: "Kill the Indian, save the Man." Pratt and others felt that the Natives must have their inherited culture stripped away in order for them to become productive members of society.

In many of these boarding schools, as on the reservation, the health of many Indian people was in peril as a result of contact with Euro-Americans. Some students were stricken with tuberculosis or smallpox and died. These institutions were intended to assimilate Native people into dominant society and eradicate Native cultures. Administrators and teachers cut children's hair; discarded their cultural garments; changed their diets, and their names; and subjected them to militaristic regimentation, discipline and at times physical and mental abuse. Educators suppressed tribal languages and cultural practices by forcing children to eat lye soap for speaking their tribal languages and paddling them for having Indian medicine bundles. They sought to replace their language and religion with only English and Christianity. They instructed students in the industrial and domestic skills appropriate to European American gender roles and taught them manual labor.

For many Indian children, this cultural assault led to confusion, alienation, homesickness and resentment, which at times led to suicide. By 1931, nearly one-third of all Native American school-age children, about 24,000, were in boarding schools. It was not until the 1950s that these schools were revamped and their mission of acculturating Native young people to the Anglo perspective was changed. The attempted eradication of Indian cultures is still a source of pain for many American Indians.

Economically, Native Americans continue to be the poorest sector of the US population. Based on a 1999–2001 national average, over 800,000 American Indians and Alaska Natives live below the poverty line. In addition, the Native population has the highest percentage of high school dropouts, unemployed people, alcoholics, and environmental pollution-related health issues.

The portrayal of Indians in the media perpetuates stereotypes that affect relationships with non-Indians. Most people are seriously uninformed about Native Americans because of distorted textbooks, misguided movies and biased history books. Seldom have people been able to hear directly from recognized traditional people to counteract the negative racial and cultural stereotypes perpetuated by American popular culture.

It is important to recognize the enduring differences between white and Native culture, differences that have consequences for the environment and human well-being. Native people make decisions based on consequences for the Seventh Generation in order to secure the well-being of the human population and Mother Earth. The Chiefs deliberate on the serious matters of the Council; they are to consider the impact of their decisions on the Seventh Generation into the future. This way, they are to proceed cautiously, thinking of what effect their decisions will have on the welfare of their descendants.

This form of decision-making requires a special attention to the future. It also produces a sense of stability. In November 2001, Cornell University in Ithaca, New York hosted a conference called An American Indian Millennium: Renewing Our Ways of Life for Future Generations, inviting dozens of Native leaders across the continent to send their message to the Seventh Generation.[23]

Hispanic Americans[24]

The word Hispanic originates from *España* (the Spanish name for their country), which led the conquest of the New World. It is the most used government term but some prefer the term Latinos, which is derived from the geographic area of Latin America. Still, many prefer to be referred to according to the country they come from, such as Mexican American or Puerto Rican American.

Even within the Hispanic group, there are important regional, socioeconomic, cultural, religious, and racial differences. Hispanics are the most diverse group in the United States; they can trace their ancestry to twenty-two different nations. Hispanics are unique in that they are classified by their language, Spanish, and not by a specific culture, racial background or geographic area. The three largest Hispanic groups in the United States are Mexican American, 18 million (56% of the total Hispanic population), Puerto Rican, 2.7 million (10%) and Cuban, 1.2 million (5%).

Five hundred years ago, the soldiers of the Spanish empire came to the western hemisphere and intermingled with Native nations such as the Tainos, Mayans, Aztecs and other pre-Colombian civilizations. This combination produced the majority of the Hispanic population. Spanish conquerors exploited the mineral wealth of the land, using as laborers the native population and a growing mestizo (mixed race of Indian and Spaniard) class. In 1821, Spain accepted Mexican independence; turmoil and corruption marked Mexico's early years.

The American expansionist ideology of Manifest Destiny, which proposed that all United States citizens had the God-given right to take and rule land (including that occupied by Mexicans and Indians) led to the Mexican-American War in 1846. The war took two years, cost Mexico half of its territories, and ended with the signing of the Treaty of Guadalupe Hidalgo on February 2, 1848.

The Treaty ceded territory in the Southwest to the United States for $15 million and promised to forgive any debts owed to the United States. The treaty also promised to respect the cultural and property rights of Mexicans living in the territory and to allow them to become US citizens. Mexican Americans settled for the most part in the areas of Texas, New Mexico, Arizona and California.

Mexican American workers, many of whom were US citizens, were deported in great numbers during the 1930s. Over 400,000 were deported to Mexico, having been accused of usurping "American" jobs during the Depression.

Puerto Rican Americans represent a mixture of races, cultures, languages and religions. They draw their unique heritage from their native people, the Tainos, from the Spanish and from Africans. Ceded to the United States by the terms of the Treaty of Paris in 1898, Puerto Rico became a commonwealth. In 1917, The Jones Act

---

[23] Proceedings of this conference were published in the Fall/Winter 2002 issue of *Native Americas Journal*, published by the First Nations Development Institute, 11917 Main St.-The Stores Building, Fredericksburg, VA 22408 (phone: [540] 371-5615; e-mail: Info@firstnations.org; website: http://www.firstnations.org).

[24] Adapted from information provided by Evelyn Arce White, MAT, First Nations Development Institute.

granted full citizenship to Puerto Ricans and gave them the right to travel freely to the continental United States and the right to vote only on the mainland. Over half of Puerto Rican Americans have made New York City their home.

The first Cuban Americans arrived in the 1960s after Fidel Castro ousted the Batista regime. Most of them were political refugees who were educated and middle-class. Most Cubans have made Miami, Florida their home and have become economically successful.

Discrimination against Hispanic Americans was common. The 1986 Immigration Reform and Control Act (IRCA) allowed large fines against employers who hired illegal workers. In theory, this promised to be a good deterrent against the hiring of "illegals," but Hispanic civil rights activists argued that such a measure would encourage discrimination in the workplace: employers would not hire Hispanics for fear that they might be illegal. The General Accounting Office (GAO) reported three years later that the IRCA had led to employment discrimination against Hispanic workers. At the same time, however, it also granted legal status to illegal aliens. By 1992, over 2.3 million Mexicans became legalized.

The US Latino population already equals the African American population and will soon make up the single largest ethnic group in the country. In 2012, the US Hispanic population was at 53.3 million, and is predicted to reach 128.8 million by 2060—one Hispanic person for every three US residents. With a growing number of Hispanics in this country, we are seeing greater political clout for this group.

Asian Americans[25]

The history of Asian Americans has been marked by cultural conflicts, political alienation, and a stream of economic and social injustices. American images of the Asians have changed from highly unfavorable in the nineteenth century, to the currently held view of the "model minority." The population of Asian Americans was 15.9 million in 2012 and will grow to 34.4 million by 2060, climbing from 5.1 percent of the total population to 8.2 percent.[26]

The Chinese were the first Asians to migrate to the United States during the California gold rush of 1849. The exploration of these areas demanded an abundant supply of cheap labor. During this time, over one hundred thousand Chinese settled on the west coast of the United States.

The implementation of the Chinese Exclusion Act in 1882 significantly decreased the numbers of Chinese immigrants. It was the first law in US history to specifically bar a race of people from America and from citizenship by naturalization. It is only with the implementation of the 1965 Immigration and Naturalization Act and more recent laws that we see an increase of Chinese immigrants and family reunification.

The Act ended discriminatory quotas favoring Europeans over Chinese and other non-European immigrants and consequently, a diverse population of Chinese was able to immigrate to the United States. Most came from three main areas, Taiwan, the People's Republic of China, and Hong Kong, to escape political persecution and lack of employment opportunities at home.

Between 1890 and 1920, most Japanese immigrants arrived in Hawaii to work as cheap laborers in many of the same areas in which the earlier Chinese immigrants had worked. In 1924, another exclusion act was passed by the US Congress prohibiting further immigration from Japan.

After Pearl Harbor and during the spring and summer of 1942, the United States Government carried out one of the largest controlled migrations in history. This was the movement of 110,000 people of Japanese descent from their homes in an area bordering the Pacific coast into wartime communities and camps constructed in remote areas between the Sierra Nevada Mountains and the Mississippi River. President Roosevelt started the evacuation of these people with the signing of Executive Order 9066.

Two-thirds of the people in the centers were American citizens, born in this country and educated in American public schools. Many of them had sons, husbands, and brothers in the United States Army. Most of these people had lived in the United States for two decades or longer, but were denied the privilege of gaining American citizenship.

Japanese Americans left behind an estimated total of approximately $200,000,000 worth of real, commercial and personal property, ranging from household appliances to extensive commercial and agricultural holdings.

---

25 Adapted from material provided by Evelyn Arce White, MAT, First Nations Development Institute.
26 U.S. Census Bureau, http://www.census.gov/newsroom/cspan/pop_proj/20121214_cspan_popproj.pdf/.

The detainees held numerous demonstrations; six thousand renounced their US citizenship. Gradually, several thousand college students and workers on special agricultural assignments were released from the camps. Ironically, others were released to go into the US army. In March 1946, the last of the camps was closed down. Many Japanese Americans then returned to the West Coast where they found most of their possessions had been stolen or ruined.

By the 1960s, Japanese Americans had gained many Americans' respect because of their economic prosperity. Japanese Americans have a lower unemployment rate than whites and other Asian Americans. This is when the stereotype of the Japanese and Asians overall became the "model minority." They were seen as good assimilators into white American society. Unfortunately, Asian Americans have also been used as scapegoats for US economic problems because they tend to be successful in business.

In 1987, the US government officially apologized to Japanese Americans for the suffering they endured during World War II internment, and paid each surviving internee $20,000 in reparations. Washington State has taken another step: On July 1, 2002, Governor Gary Locke signed into law a bill that prohibits the use of the word "Oriental" and requires use of the word "Asian" (when referring to persons of Asian descent) on all state and local government statutes, codes, rules, regulations, and other official documents.

Chapter 6
Strengths-Based Assessment

Objectives

    A. Understand what assessment is and why agencies still use deficit-oriented assessment.

    B. Apply the seven principles of strengths-based assessment in your work.

    C. Protect families' information and privacy and know the three exceptions to confidentiality.

    D. Know when to offer the Family Circles Assessment to families to help families identify the strengths, supports, and stressors that affect their ability to reach their goals.

    E. Work with your agency to review and, if needed, adapt its assessment forms to support family development.

A. What is assessment?

There are many kinds of assessment in everyday life. A dentist might assess your child's teeth to decide whether braces would help. A mechanic will assess your car's brakes to see if they are safe. If the dentist recommends braces, you might assess your checkbook to decide whether you can pay for the dental work now.

- The dentist uses his or her *professional judgment*, and possibly a *diagnostic test* like an x-ray, to assess your child's teeth.

- The mechanic might use two forms of assessment: a *standardized measurement* of how much brake pad is left, plus his professional judgment about how long it will last.

- You assess your own finances by getting a current balance on your account, then thinking over what bills you have to pay, and how much money you have coming in. If you have a partner, you probably talk over the situation. You collect information on the costs of the dental work. These are all steps in an assessment.

There are other examples of assessment in everyday life:

- If you or someone you know earned the Family Development Credential, you produced a portfolio and took an exam. These were assessments.

- If you own your house, an assessor comes around periodically to estimate the value of your house. Your taxes are based on this assessment.

In all these examples, an "expert" (e.g., dentist, mechanic, tax assessor) made the assessment. Sometimes you take the expert's advice and make your own decision (the mechanic told you your brakes were bad but you could get another opinion, decide to do without a car, get the brakes replaced, or buy a different car). Sometimes your only alternative to living with the expert's opinion is to go through a major appeal process, as in a tax appeal. Sometimes both the assessment procedure and the assessor's judgment of you are nonnegotiable.

As a family development worker, you will need to use assessment to help families decide on their goals and how to reach them. Sometimes you will also need to assess (determine) whether a family is eligible for your agency's services. If you are a protective caseworker, you'll need to assess whether it is safe for the child or adult to stay in the home. Many agencies require families to fill out handfuls of forms, and workers to go through a range of assessment procedures with their various forms.

Many agencies still use deficit-oriented assessment

While the goal of assessment is to help families, often assessment forms and procedures work against the family development process. Sometimes they are still being used because no one has reviewed them since the agency decided to use a family development approach, or because there are few examples of assessment forms based on strengths. Often a state or federal funder requires the agency to use these forms. Many of these forms and assessment procedures are more appropriate to the deficit-oriented service delivery model than to the family development approach (see Chapter 1).

In this chapter, you'll learn seven basic principles of empowerment-oriented assessment. These principles can help you and your agency decide if your forms and procedures are promoting family development, or working against it. This chapter also offers two assessment forms that follow these principles of strengths-based assessment. The Family Development Plan (introduced in Chapter 1) and the Family Circles Assessment (Chapter 4) are useful when you want to help a family gain more insight into the ways extended family, friends, and community affect their lives. A blank copy of this form is included in this chapter's appendix.

B. Basic principles of strengths-based assessment

1. *Assessment, like family development, is an ongoing process.* Each family's goals, needs, and resources will change over time, and they share more with you as trust develops.

2. *Focus on the family's strengths, current situation, and future goals.* When you help families evaluate past experiences and influences, focus on how they affect the family's current situation and future goals.

3. *Effective assessment is family-driven, not agency-centered.* The primary goal of assessment is to help families become healthier and more self-reliant. Although agencies do need to collect information about their own effectiveness, this requirement must not become more important than helping families assess their own needs.

4. *Assessment with families is much more effective than assessment of families or for families.* Write down information with families, in plain language, and make sure they have a copy, too.

5. *Collect only the information you need, and treat it with great care.* Ask the family's permission to share their information with someone else. When you ask, be specific about what, who, and why. Have the family sign a release form if you are going to share their information.

6. *Assessment must be respectful and culturally appropriate to the family you are working with.*

7. *There are sometimes good reasons to use standardized assessment,* such as collaborative agreements between agencies to make it easy for families to get services, or research/program planning to improve services. Yet often, particular families benefit more from an individualized assessment.

Each of these principles is discussed in greater detail below.

1. Assessment, like family development, is an ongoing process

Each family's goals, needs, and resources will change over time, and they will share more with you as trust develops.

Perhaps a family member initially comes to your agency because her son, who is disabled, wants to get a job. As you work with this family, the son finds out about a supervised apartment where he could live. The family's goals change as the son becomes interested in living more independently. Learning life skills such as budgeting and taking the bus become more urgent than getting a job. Once the son learns these skills and settles into his new apartment, his desire for a job resurfaces with renewed vigor. His mother is also considering job training, now that she has less daily responsibility for her adult son's needs. Once she begins to trust the family development worker, the mother also reveals that both she and her son were abused by her husband.

In a conventional assessment, it might appear that this family had made no progress toward their original goal of getting the son a job. At first it might even look like their situation was worse than before. Several steps needed to be taken before they could reach their goal of a job for the son, and a serious problem (abuse) came to light. For a time, this family will need more services, not fewer. If necessary services are available, they will probably reach not only their original goal, but also other goals they set along the way (such as a more independent life for the son, a job for the mother, and a home without abuse).

Assessment must be flexible

Assessment tools and procedures must be flexible enough to take into account a family's changing goals and situations. Families should not be labeled failures, and their services cut off, if they take a detour from the goal they describe at "intake" (the first time you meet). On the other hand, agencies do need assessment tools and methods that encourage families to make progress, so that valuable agency resources are not tied up with families who lack the motivation necessary for the family development process.

As families grow to trust you more, they usually share more information with you over time than they did at your first meeting. Many agencies rely too heavily on information a family provided during intake and then expect them to keep the agency posted on any relevant changes. Agencies using a family development approach now recognize that families will change in many ways during the family development process, and so use *ongoing assessment*.

Familiarity with assessment tools

During the ongoing assessment process, you will need to use assessments specific to each family you work with. You don't have to know how to administer many different types of assessment yourself. You do need to be familiar with other commonly used assessment tools so you can determine whether they help or hinder the family development process. Often, you will refer families to another agency or service for assessment.

For example, if you or a father you're working with are concerned about his child's development, it will help if you are familiar with the growth charts family physicians and health departments routinely use. It will help you to help the family if you can explain the term "percentile" when the father asks you about the chart after he returns from a visit to the doctor. If you know what usually happens in a well-child visit, you'll be better able to encourage this father to take his child for regular check-ups.

2. Focus on the family's strengths, current situation, and future goals

When you help families evaluate past experiences and influences, focus on how these affect the family's current situation and future goals.

Most assessments focus on problems rather than on family strengths. For example, "risk assessment scales" are much more common than "strengths scales." There are important reasons for a worker and family to assess risks and problems accurately. For example, a Child Protective Services caseworker must be able to make an accurate judgment about the risk of a child remaining in the family home following a report of suspected child abuse.

Such scales can be useful in crisis situations. When a family is not in crisis, and the goal can be supporting a family to move toward healthy self-reliance, the worker must help them focus on family strengths even while looking realistically at family problems. At a focus group, one worker said:

> While you're doing family assessment from the strengths perspective, you need to strengthen some things in the client. Sometimes we forget that people have strengths, you need to draw from that individual's strengths. You might ask that individual, "What do you want?" "Well, I want an apartment." And you can respond, "That's good. You already made yourself a goal that you want an apartment."

Some widely used assessment tools work against family development

Instead of focusing on current strengths, many workers have been trained to do a "thorough assessment" focusing on past problems before beginning an "intervention" with a family. This conventional approach is inappropriate for many families entering the family development process.

First, it is important to recognize that conducting an assessment is an *intervention*. The way the worker treats the family, the kinds of questions asked and the way they are asked, the way the information is handled all send powerful messages to the family about the kind of "help" they might get from this agency, and the way the agency thinks the family should regard itself. If this first meeting focuses on analyzing the family's past, it will be hard to then shift the focus to their current situation and their future goals.

Many widely used assessment tools are based on the deficit model of family practice, and are rarely appropriate to family development. For example, the genogram is an assessment tool in which workers ask families in-depth questions about past generations, and then record potentially harmful information about families using a code that only trained social workers understand.

One woman described how she felt when an agency worker used a genogram to assess her family:

> The social worker asked me about my grandparents, my parents, my sisters and brothers, the whole family. I thought she was really interested, so I told her all about my family—like that my mother's aunt and uncle had raised her after her mother died, and since her father later remarried, I have two sets of grandparents on that side (plus my grandparents on my father's side). I always felt lucky to have so many grandparents to love me! But it was clear the social worker thought this was weird. She was taking notes all the time, in a kind of secret code I couldn't understand.

> It took her an hour to get around to asking about my husband and me, and then I had to point out to her that we have a good marriage, and also a great community of friends where we help each other a lot with our children. If I hadn't pointed it out, she never would have asked. I guess there aren't codes for "friends" or "community." She was only interested in what she thinks of as family.

> I went into that interview feeling very positive about my family, and came out feeling like a freak. And the worst part was, she had a lot of power over what happened to our family! To her credit, she was willing to let me read her report and make corrections, but I had to ask. It took her over two months to get it to me, and then she wanted our comments within twenty-four hours!

Insoo Kim Berg, MSW, director of the Brief Family Therapy Center in Milwaukee, has commented on the potentially discouraging effect of the genogram. In an interview published in the Summer 1993 newsletter of the National Association for Family Based Services, she remarked:

> The genogram is an example ... of how a problem is traced through three or four generations. Instead of putting a lot of energy in feeling out where the problem lies, my immediate focus is "What is the solution? Where do we need to go? What does the client want? Then, what to do about it?"

> The longer they talk about the problem, the more generations (of problems you focus on), you imply to them this is a very long, deep-rooted problem. (You're saying that) there's a long history to this problem [and it's] therefore hard to solve. ... You would have to fight against three generations of having been one way.

Help the family focus on solving current problems and setting attainable goals

Family development is based on the philosophy that the pull of the future can be stronger than the push of the past. Family development assessment does not ignore the past, but also does not focus on it. Instead, the focus is on learning to solve current problems and reaching for future self-reliance and health.

At a later point in the family development process, it may be valuable to help a family understand how past experiences are shaping their current actions and future goals. At first, however, it is essential to set a strong focus on solving present problems and setting attainable goals for the future.

For example, a pregnant mother may be reluctant to seek out preschool for her children or a prenatal care program for herself, but if she is suddenly in danger of become homeless, she is likely to seek out a subsidized housing program. If workers in that program help her get a safe affordable apartment quickly, she is likely to consider their offer of a referral to Head Start and the Community Health Program. But if workers require her to go through assessment procedures focusing on her past problems instead of her current housing need, she will be out the door before they can help find an apartment or talk about other current needs.

Families may be used to meeting with workers and focusing on problems, hoping an "expert" can "fix it." Moving the conversation to discuss their own vision for a better future, or improved circumstances, can be difficult. Maybe no one has ever asked them what it would look like if their problem(s) no longer existed. They may have difficulty even imagining such a future.

3. Effective assessment is family-driven, not agency-centered

The primary goal of assessment is to help families become healthier and more self-reliant. While agencies do need to collect information about their own effectiveness, this requirement must not become more important than helping families assess their own needs.

Ineffective assessment is one reason why so many families stay on government assistance for a long time (sometimes even for generations) without developing healthy self-reliance on their own resources. Too often, workers meet with a family, talk over a goal, make referrals to services, record information about the family in a file, and then expect the family to reach the goal.

In this model, the worker sets the goal, although the family might say they agree with it. Families often agree to what the "expert" recommends, either because they are afraid they'll lose their children or services they need, or because they are so used to the deficit model that they really don't have goals of their own. If the family doesn't follow through on the worker's goal, they are labeled "noncompliant."

One worker at a focus group commented:

> Some people aren't ready to be transformed. Sometimes they want you to know what their problems are but that's as far as they want to go with it. And that's a problem. I mean, you want them to get that problem solved. Sometimes I go home at night saying, "I can't understand why that person didn't do what I told them to do." And they're not ready. They're not ready to make that move. We have to be able to understand that.

Few of us would want to "make that move" either, relying on someone else's idea of what we "should" be doing.

Focus on the family's goals

You may find that a family member honestly cannot think of a goal. It can take time for the family to brainstorm ideas together and make suggestions. Brainstorming their own ideas makes it less likely that they are just going along with an idea to please you.

Because the deficit orientation has been so widespread, many families don't know at first what their goals are, or have realistic ideas about how to reach them. If they do have goals, they may not trust an agency worker enough to share them honestly.

A front-line worker in a focus group said:

> My goal is to find out what the family's goals are. That's not an easy task a lot of times, because people have been conditioned by a system that has traditionally told them what their goals are and how they are not meeting those. So my primary goal is to create an atmosphere where there's a sense of partnership and mutual discovery about what this family believes will be best for them.

A credentialed front-line worker said:

> The second thing I learned from FDC is they ask you not to make goals for the family. But the way the system is built, they make you believe you have to set all the goals for the family. So, the first time I see the family I let the family write something if she or he can. Some questions, I don't answer them. I let the family answer. And then when I do the assessment, I turn the computer around so they can

see what I write. As we look at the computer, I say this is what you said last time. We do it together. I don't do and then give them the paper and have them sign it.

Even though it is often discouragingly slow to help a family identify its own goals, it does not help a family for the worker to decide what the family needs to do. And in our diverse society, it is unrealistic to think that a worker will "know" each family's values and situation well enough to plan for them.

A worker said:

> We have to keep in mind—and it must be kept very clear--the uniqueness of each client and each family and counselor. [If they are immigrants, we] have to keep in mind the variety of countries our clients are coming from. What may be normal in one country may be something totally different in another country. If we try to help everybody in a fixed way, we will end up doing more harm to certain types of people than helping them.

The worker's role is to help family members decide on a long-term goal and short-term goals leading up to it, help the family find the resources they need, and list the steps the family and the worker will take to help the family achieve those goals.

The problem with agency-centered assessment

If several agencies were to assess the same family's situation, it is likely that they would list different goals and needed services, depending on the services their own agency provides. For example, an agency that provides Section 8 housing subsidy might encourage a family to move into subsidized housing in order to solve its financial problems. An agency that provides budget counseling might encourage the family to stay in its current housing while negotiating overdue rent payments with the landlord. A family literacy agency might focus on a longer-term solution of better education for the parent. A job training agency would focus on getting the parent a job so she could pay the rent regularly.

In reality, the family probably needs most or all these services, some as short-term solutions, others focusing on longer-term goals. This family really needs a family development worker who can respond to the family's needs and goals with knowledge of all these services, instead of steering the family toward services the worker's agency provides.

Team planning, in which workers from several agencies meet with the family to provide information, can be useful *if* you can help the family member remain in charge. Too often, team planning or "case conferencing" takes place without the family. Even when workers from various agencies may have useful insights to offer, this approach will be of limited use unless family members are invited to the session and supported in voicing their own goals and perceptions.

4. Assessment *with* families is much more effective than assessment *of* (or *for*) families

Write down information with families in plain language, and make sure they have a copy, too. Agency "ownership" of client files is slowly beginning to change as they realize that for family development to occur, families—not agencies—must "own" the assessment process. Successful family development depends on families taking an active role in defining what their needs are, what they want to accomplish, what it will take to get there, and what resources they can bring.

At a focus group, a worker said:

> I believe in setting goals with clients, because each client is an individual. I sit down with a client—say, a person who has been into substance abuse and they've been homeless as well as HIV positive. When they're coming to a program for the first time, they've dealt so much with the different systems, that they come and say, "OK, what do you want me to do?" It's like they're saying, "What are you going to do to me now?" And, so you sit down with the person and say "Look, I'm not here to tell you what to do. I'm here to work with you, so that you can find out what you want to do."

If *workers* assess what a family needs and what a family should do about it without genuine involvement from the family, the plan is not likely to work. This is especially true if workers use an assessment tool that families don't understand or are not allowed to see, and record information in language families cannot understand or don't have an opportunity to correct and update.

Filling out forms with families

Many families have grown used to agencies filling out forms *about* them. Few agency workers show their files to the families they work with, so families never have a chance to update or correct information. Many agencies have kept records in a kind of professional shorthand, using jargon that families would not understand even if they saw their own records.

The Family Development Plan is designed to use with (not for) families. This form of assessment gives them ownership of their own family development process. Meeting after meeting, they see clearly written, in their own words, what they say their goal is, and the steps they've agreed to take to work toward that goal. They keep a copy of this information; you do, too. This way, you both have a clear reminder of what you've agreed to do.

Sometimes you will have to use forms that are filled with acronyms (letters that stand for several words, e.g., "DSS" for Department of Social Services). Instead, say and write out the whole name along with the acronym. That way, the family member will have the information needed to speak knowledgeably to agencies in the future. Remember, the goal of family development is to restore a sense of responsible, healthy self-reliance in families.

Workers in focus groups talked about the change they saw as families set goals and took steps to reach them:

> When I first started working with them, I saw them as frightened, isolated, angry, feeling out of control, feeling that they had no rights, and feeling that they themselves had no ability to fix what was wrong, that somebody outside of them had to do it. And I saw that turn around.

A family member talked about her progress:

> Every time Jill comes, we go over my goals. My goals haven't changed; we're still working on them. To make sure that the money's coming in and I'm paying the bills. Now that my husband has a job, we don't get food stamp benefits anymore. I have to spend my bill money on food. Then it's very hard to pay my bills.

At a focus group, a man who was HIV positive and had been homeless stated an often-repeated but still powerful thought when he said:

> Where I went before they told me to go here and told me to go there, to try to get an apartment. But here, they taught me how to do it, and showed me where to go. You get a lot farther when you teach a man to fish, instead of giving him the fish. And now I have a place to live.

Instead of filling out forms for families, ask them to fill out the forms with you whenever possible. At minimum, ask them to look over the form and point out anything that is incorrect. Then ask them what it should say, and change it together. If you do planning and note-taking with families, you won't have to spend time alone in your office trying to recollect what happened, and you can spend more time with the families.

When asked about barriers to being as effective as he'd like to be, a worker said:

> Too much of my time is devoted to keeping up the progress notes. We work with so many clients, two or three times a week and there is no time!

Giving families a copy of their forms

Whenever possible, give families a copy of their forms. It is frustrating for families, and expensive for the government, when families do not have a copy of their own records.

One woman told the story of how she tried to get her medical records:

They did all these tests, but refused to tell me the results. I called my doctor's office, and they said they couldn't tell me over the phone, that I would have to make and appointment and come in. I got really worried. I took time off from work to go see the doctor about my tests. He said they were basically fine.

Later that year, when I kept having the same problem, they sent me to a specialist. I couldn't explain what tests had been done, because I didn't have my records. He ended up doing all the same tests again, plus some others. When I asked him to explain the results, he said I couldn't understand because I wasn't a doctor. He was very insulting. He just gave me a prescription. All those tests hurt, and took a lot of time off from work, plus cost my insurance company a lot of money. It's my body! I care more about it than anyone else. I hoped there was something I could do, myself, to improve my condition.

Helping families take responsibility for their own assessment process is key to promoting their growing sense of self-respect and self-reliance.

5. Collect only the information you really need

Treat information you gather from a family with great care. Ask the family's permission to share their information with someone else. When you ask, be specific about what, who, and why. Have the family member sign a release form if you are going to share their information.

Agencies tend to collect a lot of information about families, often more than is really needed in order to help them effectively. This information is stored away in file cabinets (or computer files). It is not always accurate. Often, many people have access to this private information about families: the caseworker, agency secretaries, student interns. Even after the family stops working with the agency, this information can often be kept on file for a long time.

Families have different ways of coping with this reality. Some people never go to an agency for help because they know they will have to give the agency a lot of information, and they value their privacy. Others (probably most families) tell the agency worker what they think she or he wants to hear, giving out as little information as possible while still giving enough to get the desired services. Other families have grown used to giving out information in order to get services, and tell more than is necessary.

A family worker told this story about her first meeting with a woman seeking help from the agency:

The client was having a lot of problems. When I met her, the first thing she did was to pull out her ID cards. I was astounded and said, "Wait a minute, we need to sit down and talk." She replied, "Oh, I thought you just wanted to do an intake, and I'll just give you all my cards and we'll take it from there." I asked her, "Well, what are some of your issues? What do you want help with?" After a while, she started talking about being HIV positive, and that her daughter was HIV positive also. Another agency had sent a homemaker in to help her, but she felt the homemaker wasn't doing her job. That was a concern to her because she said she really needed help with her daughter.

The approach that I took with her was, "You tell me what you want to do." And, then we sat down together and talked about what she wanted to do. She said, "Okay, so let's make a plan." And I said, "Let's call the supervisor of the agency, who sent the homemaker to your home, and we'll get together at your house. We'll sit down and we can all see whatever ideas we can come up with." And she seemed a little more relaxed. Her IDs were still laid out all over the table. But she said, "Okay, I think we can really work with this."

This approach worked very well. She was able to start opening up a little bit, and one of the things that we just started to deal with, as I started to get to know her towards the end of last year, she decided that she's going to do something about her domestic violence problem. And she filed a complaint. We worked with Victim's Services. She got an order of protection. She started to realize, "Look, my life is in danger. My kids are going to be exposed to this." As a matter of fact, she became part of the job-training program. So she had some goals. I think that was a real incentive because she said, "Well, if I'm part of a job-training program, I'm going to work towards something."

This worker was able to use the family development approach to help restore this mother's sense of responsibility for her own life. The mother started out by laying her ID cards in front of the worker, as if to say, "Okay, here's all my information; now, you fix my life." Instead of playing into this situation, the worker created a mutually respectful relationship with this mother, asking what help she needed, and how she wanted to proceed.

By the number of ID cards this mother had, it was clear that she had given out lots of information to a wide range of workers. Yet all the agency files of information represented by those ID cards had not led to this mother's success in solving her own problems, or restored her sense of self-respect and self-reliance. In fact, giving out all that information to a number of agencies may have contributed to her expectation that agency workers could solve her problems for her.

Collecting only really necessary information helps the family as well as you to focus on their goals, instead of getting sidetracked with a lot of unrelated information.

Treat the information with great care

To get your help, the families you work with entrust you with a great deal of very private information about themselves. Treating this information with great care is an essential part of the family development process. Treating the family's information as worthy of great respect helps them respect themselves, and builds trust between you.

Be careful not to leave a family's forms or files lying around on your desk or in your car, where others might see them. Follow your agency's confidentiality guidelines carefully. Some people (like the mother who laid out her ID on the worker's table) are conditioned to give strangers all kinds of private information about themselves. Even if their past experiences have led them to give out information freely, it is still important to treat them (and their information) with deep respect. Treating their information respectfully will help them have a sense of self-respect.

Write carefully so that family members, your supervisor, and any worker who comes after you can easily read the form. This might seem obvious, but many workers do not write legibly, which leads to important family information being lost or misinterpreted.

Filling in assessment forms with family members as part of your visits or meetings helps you keep up with paperwork, so you don't have a backlog to finish at the end of each day or week.

You will learn more about confidentiality later in this chapter.

6. Assessment must be respectful and culturally appropriate

Unfortunately, many widely used assessment tools are considered intrusive and disrespectful by families. The questions asked or the way they are asked can lead to a bad start, even if you or your agency mean well. Family members won't necessarily tell you what they think of your assessment; they may just drop out of (or not enroll in) your program. Or, if you offer a service they absolutely need (or they are mandated to participate in your program), they may seem to go along while resenting you quietly, or complaining to their friends and neighbors.

Many families feel powerless to resist assessment that they find disrespectful. It is up to agencies using a family development approach to make sure assessment occurs in a respectful way, to listen and act on suggestions or complaints from families. Some agencies have a client "bill of rights" that says families have the right not to answer questions they find intrusive, and to ask the worker why a particular question is being asked.

Most assessment forms and procedures were developed by professionals trained in the deficit model. These widely used assessment tools are not necessarily appropriate within (and are often harmful to) the family development process. Deficit-based assessment tools may be particularly harmful to families of cultural groups other than the white middle class.

7. There are sometimes good reasons to use standardized assessment

"Standardized" assessment means that the same forms and procedures are used with every family you work with, and the answers are recorded in a way that makes it easy to see trends across many families. Some states and cities are experimenting with standardized intake forms so that a family only has to fill out one form and then can receive services from several agencies. This type of collaboration agreement between agencies can make it much simpler for families in crisis to get needed services (and for agencies to avoid duplication of services). It also saves families the exhausting, demoralizing experience of repeating their problems to several different agency workers.

Standardized assessment forms also make it easy to collect and evaluate program information from many families. Sometimes standardized assessment forms are used with thousands of families across a whole state, or even nationwide. This makes it easier for program developers, researchers, funders, or policy makers to decide what works with lots of families, what changes need to be made in programs, and what should get funded. While it has these benefits, one drawback of standardized assessment is that it usually doesn't promote the development of individual families as well as a more personalized assessment form.

The Family Development Plan was designed primarily to collect information in ways that help individual families reach their goals. Information collected using the Family Development Plan is usually much more specific than on a standardized form where a family just checks "yes" or "no," or rates their situation on a numbered scale. The Family Development Plan is reviewed and updated at every meeting, so it is always current. This provides more specific information than most standardized assessments.

C. Confidentiality

As you do family development work, you will find out all kinds of things about the families you work with: their hopes, dreams, fears, secrets, things that give them feelings of shame or guilt. You will hear and see much more than you might want an agency worker to know about your own family! You will see families at their best and at their worst.

If you want families to trust you, you need to treat all the information you gather about them with the greatest care. In the best sense of the word, *confidentiality* means treating everything you learn about a family in a way that will allow them to continue to have confidence and trust in you.

Too often, confidentiality means that family workers write down information about a family (including the workers' own observations and judgments) in a file. The families seldom see this file. Yet the workers' supervisor, co-workers, the agency secretary, student interns who came along after any confidentiality training the agency offered, and other workers who may come years later, have easy access to these files. In many agencies, workers often talk with each other about the families they are working with, by name, without the family's explicit permission. In the worst situations, agency workers talk about the families they work with to their own family and friends, or anyone from another agency who asks. In a Cornell University review of state and national family support staff training programs, the ethical and legal issues associated with confidentiality were not addressed at all by the majority of programs reviewed. Overlooking the importance of confidentiality can result in loss of trust between families and workers, which can make progress more difficult or even impossible.

It is a great privilege to be allowed into families' lives enough to do meaningful family development work. Respecting this privilege by treating the family's information with great care is crucial to maintaining the trust you have worked so hard to establish. You should apply the same degree of care to information the family tells you as you do to things that you observe yourself.

Three important questions regarding confidentiality

When deciding whether to share information you know about a family, ask yourself:

1. *Does this person need to know this information?* If not, but I just feel a need to share it with someone (maybe because it is so "heavy" for me), is there a way I could do it that would protect the confidentiality of the family?
2. *Is this information accurate and verifiable, or just my personal judgment?*
3. *Do I need to get the family's permission to share this information?*

Some agencies have a policy that they will keep all information confidential. They keep notes to a minimum, and all notes are kept locked. They do not tell others (outside of their immediate co-workers) what families they are working with, unless there is a need to know, and then they are cautious about what they share.

Three exceptions to confidentiality

There may be three exceptions to strict confidentiality. It is important to let all families know when about these exceptions when you begin working together:

1. Being mandated reporters to the State Child Abuse and Maltreatment Reporting Center, workers will report suspected child abuse and neglect.
2. If subpoenaed, they will cooperate with the court, releasing files and testifying.
3. They have a "duty to warn," which means that if a family member is dangerous to self or to others, they will take steps to ensure safety.

Other than these circumstances, do not reveal that you are working with any particular family or share any information about the family without their written permission (i.e., a signed release of information form that specifies what information can be released and to whom).

This may be a stricter policy than your program thinks is necessary, depending on the types of services provided. You could also ask the agency director to schedule agency-wide training to review the agency's policies on confidentiality.

Release forms and your own personal confidentiality policy

Before sharing information about a family with someone else, ask for permission from the family, and request that they sign your agency's release form. If your agency doesn't have a release form for sharing information, offer to work with your supervisor to create one and to establish guidelines for its use.

Many agencies ask families to sign a "blanket" release form when they first begin working with the agency, which may allow you to share information with co-workers and with other agencies or professionals such as doctors. However, it is much better to ask families for specific permission to release information to a specific person or agency.

Although a blanket release form gives you some legal protection, it does not necessarily help you build and maintain trusting relationships with families. If you release information to someone without talking it over with the family, and they hear about it, they may lose trust in you, no matter what piece of paper they have signed. You may hold yourself to a higher standard by creating your own personal confidentiality policy in which you always discuss the release of information with a family. You might say something like: "My co-worker Edith Hasper has been working with other families with situations similar to yours. Would it be all right with you for me to discuss your situation with her, and ask if she has ideas? She would respect your privacy, just like I do."

Protecting families' privacy can mean resisting others' requests for information. For example, say that one of your co-workers is weatherizing a family's home. You told the family about this service, made the referral, and at their request, helped them establish eligibility for weatherization services. While working in the family's home, the weatherization crew notices a man staying with the family who is neither husband nor brother. One of the weatherization crew members asks you, "Is Jaime Gonzales living with Maria Sanchez now? He is always there when we get there in the morning to work on the house." Maria told you that she was taking in boarders in order to increase her family's income. Is this confidential information? Yes! How do you respect her confidentiality, while still maintaining a good working relationship with the weatherization crew? You could say, "I always try to leave any information I learn about families in their homes when I leave. That way they trust me enough to keep working with me. If you need to know who is living there in order to do your work, please ask Maria."

One final thought about confidentiality: Even after your official relationship with a family has ended, you still owe them confidentiality. If you meet former clients in a store or at a community gathering, greet them and introduce them by name to others you are standing with, but don't add something like "The Phillipses used to be in our family development program." Let them decide how much they want to reveal about your relationship.

D. The Family Circles Assessment

When working with a family on their Family Development Plan, there will be times when you (or they) feel it would be helpful for them to look more closely at how other people, institutions, and social trends affect them. That's when you can invite them to fill in the Family Circles Assessment (see Chapter 4). This exercise provides a good opportunity for people to reflect on how they are influenced by their immediate family, extended family, friends, neighbors, co-workers, community institutions, culture, the economy, and natural environment. It is especially helpful in the following situations:

- The family seems too dependent on agencies.
- The family seems to lack informal social supports such as friends, relatives, neighbors, voluntary community organizations.
- The family's relationships with others seem to bring more hindrances than support.
- The family lacks an awareness of how outside influences affect its ability to reach its goals.

The Family Circles Assessment offers the same major benefits as a genogram, while providing some significant advantages: it is recorded by the families in everyday language, and it recognizes that while family systems have a major influence, so do many other factors such as culture, economics, community, and the natural environment.

A blank Family Circles Assessment form and guidelines for its use can be found in Chapter 4.

E. Helping your agency choose strengths-based assessment tools

Tools such as the Family Circles Assessment are designed to assist families in becoming healthier and more self-reliant. It is important that your agency review its assessment forms and procedures to determine whether they support or undermine this goal. Your agency may find that many of the principles described above are reflected in its forms, or you may find that some changes are needed. Many were developed over a long period of time, keeping old tools while adding new ones. The result is often that workers and families have to fill out so many forms that it is hard to get going on the family development process. Also, many of these forms are based on families' deficits rather than focused on their goals and strengths.

How can you assess your agency's assessment tools? Take a copy of one form, and instructions for its use. Put it beside a copy of the seven principles of strengths-based assessment. Consider how well your assessment tool (or an assessment tool you're considering using) applies to each principle. Make a list of the ways it does and doesn't meet each principle. That will help your agency decide whether to use (or keep using) that particular assessment tool. If an assessment tool meets most of the principles but not others, it may be that the tool can be adapted by making a simple change (for example, by completing the form with families instead of for them).

You may want to ask your supervisors to consider appointing a committee to do this review together. The committee will be most effective if it includes several family members served by your agency, as well as workers from other agencies with which you collaborate.

Activities to Extend Learning

Chapter 6
Strengths-Based Assessment

A. What is assessment?

1. Briefly describe an experience you have had with each of the following kinds of assessment: a professional judgment (e.g., a doctor's visit), a standardized measurement (e.g., a driver's license exam), and an individualized assessment (like financial planning for a personal goal such as home, car, or education). What did you think and feel during each experience? What factors made each assessment different from another?

2. If the goal of assessment is to help families, why are many agency's forms and assessment procedures still focused on using a deficit-oriented service delivery model? How does using deficit-oriented assessment forms affect your ability to build a worker-family relationship based on family development?

3. Why do family-serving agencies do assessments? How do agencies benefit? In your opinion, how do most families feel about completing assessments? What are the benefits and costs to families who complete agency assessments?

B. Basic principles of strengths-based assessment

1. Give an example of a family's goals, needs, or resources changing over time. Did the family keep this goal, or did they reorder priorities along the way? If the family re-assessed their goal over time, how did that affect the ultimate outcome? Did they achieve their goal? If the family reordered priorities and changed their goal, how did this affect them?

2. Why do think families often agree with a goal set by a worker? Why is it important for families to set their own goals?

3. How do you feel when a family sets a goal you don't like? How do you feel when a family doesn't seem to have any goals?

4. Ask three families you work with: Who do you feel "owns" the information you've given to our agency? Why do they feel this way?

5. Review your agency's policy on confidentiality. If the agency doesn't have one, offer to help develop one with your supervisor.

6. The next time you want to share information about a family with someone else, ask yourself:

   • Does this person need to know about this information?

   • Is this information accurate and verifiable, or just my personal judgment?

   • Do I need to get the family's permission to share this information?

   Write a reflection on the responses to these questions.

C. Confidentiality

1. Think of a time when someone told someone else something about you or your family without your permission. How did it affect your trust of that person?

2. Why is confidentiality important to family development work?

3. Write a personal confidentiality policy that you would follow. How does this compare with your agency's official policy?

D. The Family Circles Assessment

1. Write a script about offering to help complete a Family Circles Assessment with a family. Include a description, in everyday language, of what the Family Circles Assessment is, why you think it would be helpful for this family, and how to complete it.

2. Apply the basic principles of strengths-based assessment to the Family Circles Assessment. For each principle, describe how that the Family Circles Assessment fulfills that condition of strengths-based assessment. Provide an example to explain how the form helps families assess their strengths, supports and stressors.

E. Helping your agency choose strengths-based assessment tools

1. Why is it difficult for some agencies to choose and develop strengths-based assessment tools? What can agencies do to help funders support strengths-based assessment?

2. If you could design a strengths-based assessment tool for your program or agency, what would it include? How would its design and information differ from the current assessment forms used at your agency?

3. Some interagency collaborations have developed or considered developing a single standardized intake or other assessment so families wouldn't have to give the same basic information to each individual agency. What do you think about this idea? What might the advantages and disadvantages to families? What issues might arise if multiple agencies possess confidential information?

Skills Practices

These skills practices are a suggested list. You may also develop your own skills practice or make modifications to the ones listed below to help you create a meaningful and manageable plan.

1. Review your organization's confidentiality policy. If there is no policy, or if it differs from your own personal confidentiality statement, draft one using the section on confidentiality in the FDC Code of Ethics as a guide. Share the draft with a co-worker or supervisor and ask for feedback. Identify steps you can take to help develop or refine a confidentiality policy for your agency.

2. Use the Family Circles Assessment with a family to help them assess the strengths, stressors, and supports in their life. If they identify gaps in their supports, brainstorm with them to identify supports in those areas. Describe how the family responded and how it was a useful assessment for them.

3. Develop a new assessment tool or review one of your agency's standardized forms using the principles of strengths-based assessment. If you develop a new assessment tool (such as an agency intake or goal-setting form), describe how the new form incorporates specific principles of strengths-based assessment. If you review one of your agency's standardized forms, propose revisions if you think the assessment can be more strengths-based, and cite the principle(s) you used in offering your suggestions.

4. Before your first meeting with a new family seeking help from your agency, prepare to discuss with them how you and your agency will protect their confidentiality and privacy. When you meet with them, include discussing your agency's confidentiality policy. Respond to their questions and ask how they feel about the agency's policy. Write a reflection on what you did to prepare, how the discussion went, what you think you did well and what you might do differently in the future.

5. Arrange to meet with an agency co-worker who is not a front-line family worker (for example, staff who provide clerical support, bookkeeping or human resources services) to talk about strengths-based assessment. Explain the difference between deficit-oriented and strengths-based assessment. Describe the basic principles and explain how ongoing assessment with families helps promote healthy self-reliance. Invite your co-worker to ask questions or share comments. Write a reflection on preparing for the meeting, the discussion itself, and your co-worker's thoughts and feelings about strengths-based assessment.

Chapter 7
Helping Families Set and Reach Their Own Goals

Objectives

A. Learn ways to establish and build relationships with families based on mutual respect and trust.

B. Practice techniques to help families identify their strengths.

C. Set healthy boundaries in relationships so families won't become dependent on you.

D. Know when and how to end a relationship in a way that supports ongoing family development.

A. Establishing mutually respectful, trusting relationships with families

Helping families restore and live from their own sense of self-respect is the cornerstone of successful family development work. Establishing a mutually respectful relationship with families—where you respect them and they respect you—is your first and most important challenge and make your job much easier. You cannot help them become more self-reliant until you establish a mutually respectful relationship.

Family development will not work unless you establish a relationship built on mutual respect. If your relationship with families is built on you holding the power, families may appear to go along, but they will never truly invest themselves in the process enough to set real goals and do the hard work of reaching them.

If you are successful in establishing a mutually respectful relationship, it may develop into trust. A partnership based on mutual trust will enable the family to go much further toward meeting their goals. Many families have good reasons not to trust or even to respect agency workers, since their past experiences have taught them to be cautious:

* Workers who promised help but did not provide it

* Programs that have ended just as families were beginning to make progress toward their goals

* Workers who "let them down" or betrayed their trust

Overcoming this past history and any personal family history that inhibits their ability to trust people in authority is a major challenge to building trust.

Start with family needs and their own dreams, not your agency's services

Too often, well-intentioned human services workers have gone into communities with their own "bag of tricks" based on their funder's goals or their professional training, imposing solutions that neither the community nor the families really wanted. One worker said,

> I think one thing is just establishing the trust between the family worker and the family, because a lot of families have histories of hooking up with an agency and either being dropped because they didn't do what the agency wanted them to do, or they will tell their whole life story to one social worker who will leave in six months and then they will have to tell it all over to another one. So I don't think anything can happen until that trust is started.

One family member talks about her frustration with workers who never followed up:

Mercedes is helping me out so much; there is so much less stress now. None of the workers from other agencies ever got back to me. I don't need a lot of attention but I do need some help because of so many factors like transportation and stuff. It just keeps leaving me in the same spot. I think if they had gotten back to me I would have a house by now.

Families usually find themselves seeking help just when their self-confidence is at its lowest and their sense of hopelessness at its highest. Understandably, they are cautious when a stranger offers to help. Do not expect the families you work with to trust you completely right away. You wouldn't trust a stranger with your innermost hopes, dreams, and problems right away, either. For now, begin working to develop *mutual respect*.

First meetings between family development workers and families take place in many different places: their home, your office or van, at a clinic or neighborhood center, on the street, in a school. Any of these can offer you a place to begin developing a mutually respectful relationship.

- If you have an appointment, be on time. If you must keep the person(s) waiting, apologize, saying that you know their time is valuable. This helps establish a feeling that you respect the family, and also lets them know, politely, that you also value your own time, and expect them to make an effort to be on time, too.

- Treat the family members politely. Smile and say hello. If they are visiting your agency, say, "Welcome." Introduce yourself. Ask what they would like you to call them. If you expect to be called by a title (Ms., Mrs., Miss, Mr., Dr., Rev.), offer the same courtesy to the adult family members you work with. In many cultures and families, it is disrespectful to call people by their first names unless you are very close. If you prefer to be called by your first name, you can say so, while still offering the families you work with a respectful choice about what you call them. Offer to hang up their coats.

- Establish your humanness. If you can honestly compliment the person on something like how smart or healthy the children seem, or can mention that you also have a teenage daughter, say so simply, without going into it at this point. If the weather is awful, compliment the family for arriving at the appointment on time despite the weather.

- Briefly explain the purpose of the meeting, introduce your agency's goals, and explain the way you and the agency work.

- Ask how you can help. Then *listen* (see Chapter 2).

- If you and your agency can help, describe how.

- If you can begin an initial assessment with the family using the approaches described in Chapter 6, then do so.

- If possible, try to help the family establish a clear-cut goal. Sometimes families asking for help have very clear-cut goals: get money for food, get help paying for child care, get services for a family member with a disability, get home health care for their mother who just had a stroke, get the teenage son out of jail, get dental care. Making clear progress toward identifying these goals during the first meeting, or soon after, will help establish mutual respect. The family will feel that you are a person who understands their needs, and helps in a respectful manner. You know that helping a family "fix" a crisis is not very helpful in the long run. Yet responding to the family's immediate need respectfully and efficiently right now can help you develop the kind of relationship you will need in order to begin more in-depth family development work together.

- Brainstorm with the family what steps might be taken toward reaching their goals between now and your next meeting. Tell the family that brainstorming means putting out any idea that comes to mind, without thinking it is too crazy or unrealistic. Only after a list of possibilities has been made should the family narrow it down to realistic possible steps. The value of brainstorming is that even one of these "crazy" ideas might spark a creative solution that is realistic.

- Decide together what steps it makes sense for you to take and what the family can do. Ask the family to prioritize. (What seems like the most important first step to you might not be the family's priority. If the priority is their own, they are much more likely to follow through.) Ask them to write it down, or offer to write it down yourself, using the Family Development Plan,. Write down what you will do. Make a copy for each of you.

- Close the first visit on a positive note. Tell the family members you are glad to work with them, and feel hopeful (or positive) about their ability to reach their goals.

- On the Plan, write your name, agency and phone number where you can best be reached, and give it to the family member. If there are certain times you can be reached more easily, tell him or her that too, and write it down on the paper. Remember that families may be calling you from a pay phone, or a friend's phone, sometimes with great effort. Let them know that if they miss you when they phone, it's helpful if they leave times when it would be best for you to get back to them. If they do not have a phone, ask if there's a friend or neighbor you could leave a message with.

- If you can't help with this family's goals and needs, don't take up their time. Courteously describe other agencies in your community that may be able to help. Write down the agency's name, address, phone number, and what kind of help they can offer. Remember that this person may have told personal family problems to many people in hopes of getting some relief, and may be struggling with many slips of paper containing phone numbers by now. Say that they can call you back or come and see you again if they need more information.

In this chapter, you will learn to use the Family Development Plan to make notes with the family at each meeting; establish a way of filing these notes that will protect each family's privacy. Review the notes several days before your next meeting, so you can remember each family member's name, the goals described to you, and what you were each going to do to achieve them. Make sure you've done what you said you would.

During the first few meetings, all you can realistically expect is courtesy, and some progress (however small) on doing what you each agreed to do. *You cannot expect real trust at this point.* Trust develops over time, as you prove yourself by keeping up your end of the agreement, and being knowledgeable about community resources that are useful to this family. When the initial pain that brought the family to seek help begins to ease, and they see real progress toward a better life, trust can grow.

And even if this particular family doesn't come to trust you now or ever, you have conducted yourself in a way that will earn you and your agency a good reputation. This family may come back later because you were considerate this time, or they may tell a friend about you. Word of mouth is by far the most effective advertising for your agency. A good reputation is built simply, slowly, one step at a time.

Building mutual respect

If a family member you are working with is disrespectful to you (for example, cursing or calling you names), you could say, "I can see you are upset, and I understand you are facing a very difficult situation. I would like to offer you my respect, and ask the same of you." Applying the listening, skillful speaking, and conflict resolution skills from Chapter 2 would be helpful in this situation.

Remember that some of the family members you work with will have been deeply hurt by disrespect. They may have faced continual ridicule, prejudice, physical or emotional abuse, rape, or sexual abuse in their own childhood, or watched helplessly as their children suffered. Many people have lost crucial self-respect through their inability to provide for their families, or by living with the constant threat of neighborhood violence.

Some of the families you see today are living with these harsh realities every day and night. You may or may not be able to help them with their problems and goals. But you can treat them respectfully. *Respect is a great gift, the power of which you should not underestimate.*

Most family workers find some families easier to respect than others. Keep in mind that respect means respecting each other as human beings, respecting the person's and family's potential as well as where they are right now. You do not have to agree with their choices in order to respect them as people.

For example, you might feel that families should care for aging family members at home whenever possible, and have a hard time respecting a family who chooses nursing home care. You will need to suspend your "shoulds" (i.e., "families should do this and should not do that") in order to work successfully with a family who makes decisions you would make differently in your own life. You can still respect many things about this family—they cared for Grandma at home for two years, they chose a nursing home with great care and visit every week, they are raising three well-balanced school-aged children, they maintain a welcoming home, they work steadily and pay their bills. It is also important not to let other agencies impose their "shoulds" on you and the families you work with, particularly those agencies that may not share your belief that families need to set their own goals.

Don't take lack of trust personally, but do continue to set a tone of respect for the family and yourself. Do what you agreed to do. It will help the ongoing family development process, and it will help build respect and, eventually, trust.

When asked about the skills and abilities it takes to do family development work, two focus group participants made these comments:

> The ability to establish rapport, to be able to create a comfortable atmosphere, build trust, be nonjudgmental, and treat people with dignity and respect.

> People who have looked at their own issues and their own feelings about the problems of the families they work with, so that they have acknowledged and have been honest with themselves about that.

Two family members commented:

> When Sue's coming was suggested to us, all we were told was she's an outreach worker, which at the time really didn't mean anything to us. We didn't know what we were getting into. Right from the first day she came, it was very comfortable. She makes it very easy to sit down and talk with her. That is really important because if you don't feel comfortable enough to tell her what's really going on, it is really kind of a waste of time. It's really working out well now. Sue made the difference.

> The day I met her, it was still a time when I didn't want to associate with people. Her and another lady from this organization stuck out in my mind because they came in and they were just so flamboyant or bubbly and welcoming. They had a lot of life!

It is inevitable that some of the families you work with will not trust you, primarily because their own problems run so deep, and so many families have been burned by the deficit-oriented human service systems. Ask for support from your supervisor and co-workers if you feel discouraged about building trust with families, so you can avoid the burnout that comes from working hard with little positive response.

B. Helping families build on their own strengths

Because the deficit approach has been so widespread in schools, human services, and religion, as well as in family systems, many families are much quicker to identify their problems than their strengths. One of the most important skills you'll use as a family development worker is the ability to help families identify and build on their strengths. Every interaction you have with families provides an opportunity to reflect their strengths back to them, if you can train yourself always to think "strengths."

As one focus group participant put it:

> Most of the people we work with don't feel they have any power or control over the environment, over the community, over their own lives. They feel like they are being done to, because that's the experience they have had in their entire life. So when they start making a connection between "Oh my case manager thinks I can do this, I really can," or they actually go out and do it and report back they felt good about it, they make connections between the things the worker's pointing out, their strengths, and the things that are happening in their lives.

A credentialed worker commented:

> In FDC, instead of being negative, we try to enforce the strengths of a family instead of just looking at the negatives. That's important. Generally, if you open a newspaper, you always see the bad news on the top. Because bad news is a business; people are nosy, they want to know. And the good news is in a little corner of the newspaper. Society does that sometimes to people. They always try to put you down instead of lifting you up. This is different in the FDC training point of view. Everybody can get a chance to repair a mistake and move forward. There is always a dream somebody can achieve. Instead of putting down people, its lifting them up. I tell that to families.

Working from the strengths perspective doesn't mean you ignore real problems. It means you deeply believe that all families have strengths, and that they can use these strengths to solve their problems and meet their goals. Even traits that seem negative usually have strengths behind them. They were often developed as a way to survive in a bad situation. Any strength taken too far becomes a fault. Your job is to help families recognize their own strengths, and find healthy ways to build on them. Rather than a particular skill, it's more a way of looking at the world.

Turning negatives into strengths

Consider patience, for example. Family members caring for an elderly person with Alzheimer's disease will find their own patience an invaluable strength. Yet, the time may come when too much patience causes the caregivers not to see their own need for an occasional break from this demanding work. They may not accept their own healthy need to talk regularly with others who understand the strains they face every day and night, people they can be honest with about having some feelings of anger and resentment. As a family development worker, you can reflect back to them the strength the caregivers' patience illustrates, while also helping them to see that by getting more support they can take good care of themselves, too. Your part of a conversation with the main caregiver might go something like this:

> Mrs. Roscoe, I deeply admire your patience in caring for your husband yourself. It is a very difficult job, and it is important to take care of yourself, too. Are there others you know who could help each week?

> Your daughter Julie used to help out but now she has a new baby? You don't have any other family nearby? I know you used to be very active in your church. How would you feel about calling your minister? You could ask if there are church members who would come at regular weekly times to stay with Mr. Roscoe. Then you could get your hair done the way you always used to, and maybe have lunch with a friend. What do you think?

> I'll also leave this pamphlet about the Office for Aging's Alzheimer Caregiver's Support Group, which meets each Thursday noon at the Methodist Church. It's free. Here's another pamphlet about the Visiting Nurse Service over on Tenth Street. They have trained nurse's aides who can come in to help take care of people with medical needs. You could talk it over with Mr. Roscoe's doctor. He might think it would be helpful to have a nurse's aide help you out, especially since you said it's getting harder to take your husband's sugar reading lately. Your doctor can talk with you about whether Medicare may be able to pay for an aide.

> You are a very patient woman, and I respect that. I also want to see you take care of yourself, so you'll be able to go on as long as possible with this difficult job, and also have some energy left over to enjoy your grandchildren. Did you say your Julie just had a new baby?

In another example, an agency worker might visit a rural family whose front yard contains several unlicensed old cars. The worker might conclude that the residents are disorganized, thoughtless neighbors who don't value what they have enough to take care of it. Looking at their strengths will give a different perspective. If you gained the trust of this family and asked them about the old cars (or if you had lived this life yourself), you would see this family's resourcefulness, pride, and skill. Rather than accept welfare, they "make do" with what they have. They rely on their skills to get one of the cars going (with free parts from the others) whenever they need to, or to help a friend get a car going. Occasionally they sell a repaired car or part when they need some money.

If this family told you that money is tight, you could help them think through the marketable skills family members have and help them practice interviewing for jobs, which might lead to one of them getting a job at a local garage. Having built trust through this success, the family might bring up the problems they were having with neighbors about their yard with a new openness to finding solutions. Your ability to see and help the family build on its strengths could make all the difference, especially since they are used to agency people (and neighbors!) who see only a yard full of old "junk" cars.

Developing "peripheral vision"

It helps to develop "peripheral vision"—the ability to see a wider view. Straight ahead you see the reality of a yard filled with old cars, and a family who is having a very hard time making ends meet. But taking a wider view, you can see that these cars represent resourcefulness, potential job skills, and much-needed income.

Sometimes a family's problems seem so overwhelming that it is hard to see their strengths, and even harder to reflect them back to the family. For example, a stressed-out third generation welfare mother gives birth to her second baby before her seventeenth birthday. She has long since dropped out of school, and no one in her family finished school or has an adequate job. She did not get appropriate prenatal care, and the baby is sickly. Her boyfriend abuses drugs as well as her and the toddler. She wonders if her toddler is all right because all he ever says is, "No!" The neighborhood is filled with violence. She tells you it's okay if you want to come see her, but they might be gone by next week because they just got an eviction notice.

How can you see strengths here? If you see any, how can you reflect them back to the family, and help them build on these strengths? This mother still has her two children with her, and a deep commitment to keeping them together. She has food in the house. She is concerned about her child's constant "No"s and interested in learning about normal behavior for toddlers. She likes a clinic in her old neighborhood, where she went regularly when her toddler was younger, and where she returned just before and since the baby was born. Her toddler's immunizations are nearly up to date. She has made arrangements to move her family in with her grandmother if they get evicted. Her grandmother has a telephone. She is thinking about leaving her boyfriend because she doesn't want her children exposed to his drug abuse and violence. She receives AFDC and food stamps, knows she is eligible for job training and childcare, and has thought about what it would be like to become a beautician. Her friends all come over so she can fix their hair. She has friends who may be able to offer her various kinds of support.

Let's say you work for a family preservation program that allows you to work intensively with only two families at a time. One of the families you have been working with just "graduated" yesterday, so you now have an opening. This young mother is willing to have you try to help. Can you find strengths? Can you help her see how these strengths can help her to deal effectively with her problems? Can you work with this family from a strengths perspective, while still realistically seeing both their urgent and their long-term needs?

Even if you see a family's strengths, it may be challenging to help the family recognize and build on them. Many families are so overwhelmed by their daily responsibilities and challenges, or so accustomed to seeing deficits, that they may not believe you when you reflect a strength back to them. They may not know how to build on existing strengths. *Your own belief that families have strengths, and can move in positive directions, is your most powerful tool as you work with them.*

Restoring the natural ability to envision

Human beings are born with an ability to use a wide range of intelligences (cognitive reasoning, intuition, emotional intelligence, body wisdom) to perceive and act on information. Yet by the time people reach adulthood, especially if they have experienced trauma, many people's vast intelligence has narrowed to a small shadow of what it could be. Many families will at first have a very constricted sense of their possibilities. When asked their goals, they are likely to name only the most urgent needs, or reply with what they think you want to hear. Knowing how to help them free their conditioned mind-set enough to envision creatively is a crucial skill. *Your first job is to help them rekindle their ability to dream of a better life.*

Techniques for defining a family's vision and goals

Sometimes family members may need to tell you what's difficult, and feel that you have really heard them, before they can move on to think about goals. You can use skillful listening to satisfy that need. Sometimes, a looming crisis needs to be resolved before other goals can be set. Other times, the focus on the negative and hopelessness can be a long-ingrained habit. If "venting" about problems seems to be a habit, you can ask questions family members may never have been asked, or thought to ask themselves, such as "What would you like to be doing in five years?" Your next step is to affirm their vision, and follow up with a discussion of the resources and information required to make this vision a reality.

Promoting a miracle

Social worker Insoo Kim Berg developed a highly effective tool called the "miracle method" to help families move past their "suck" mind-set. For some, it can feel like it would take a miracle for their situation to improve. Start by asking, "Suppose while you are sleeping tonight, a miracle happens. The miracle is your problem is somehow solved. What would be different tomorrow morning that would tell you a miracle has happened?" You can follow up with a series of questions encouraging the family member to envision this reality as clearly as possible. As they describe these differences, they may begin to develop the idea that things could change. With that faith, identifying goals becomes an easier next step.

Follow-up questions can help to develop clear, concrete goals that focus on the positive. For example, if the answer to the miracle question is "I wouldn't be lonely," you can reshape the goal in a positive direction by asking, "What would you be doing instead?"

Focus on their dreams and strengths

As the family begins to imagine what it wants, be careful not to impose your own ideas. Years ago I told my high school guidance counselor I wanted to become a home economist. I held the Cornell University catalog in my hand as we spoke. I still remember her frozen face as she tsk-tsked her reply: "Now dear, you are too intelligent to become a home economist. You should become an elementary school teacher, and maybe you could even become a guidance counselor some day." Her ignorance of the vast teaching potential of the field of home economics, and of the exciting professional developments then taking place in the field of Home Economics, steered me away from the education that would have led me efficiently to my intended work. Despite her short-sighted "guidance," a serendipitous series of events eventually steered me to my ideal career at Cornell University's College of Human Ecology (formerly the College of Home Economics), where the Family Development Credential Program was born and nourished. Had this counselor known and practiced the principles of family development, she would have followed my lead:

> You're interested in becoming a home economist? What draws you to this career? You like children and their families? Yes, I've noticed you volunteering in the kindergarten. Would you like me to help you find catalogs from colleges of home economics? You could read through them to find out if you could earn a degree to work with children and their families. I see you have the Cornell catalog in your hand. Mrs. Mitchell graduated from Cornell. I'm sure she'd be happy to talk with you about her experiences. You are friends with her granddaughters? Why don't you ask her about Cornell? And while you're at it, would you also like to see this catalog for the Home Economics program at _____ University? You could get into either, and scholarships are available. Let me know if you'd like me to write you a letter of recommendation. And keep me posted. This is exciting!

See how my guidance counselor's "professional knows best" mind-set nipped my dreams in the bud, narrowing my possibilities? No doubt she considered our meeting a success; after all, I did end up going to college and starting a career through which I could support myself. Yet often, the seeds of a deeper success can be watered by promoting skillful visioning. The Family Development Plan provides a highly effective process for envisioning, setting, and reaching one's own goals.

Another way to help families think and talk about their strengths is to ask them how they have coped so far. You can also ask them to tell you about times they've experienced exceptions to their usual struggles. For example, if a single mother tells you how hard it is to keep a job while raising two children, you might ask her to tell you about times when it has worked out, and how she has done it, then help her transfer those skills to other situations.

To keep the "big picture" focus on the positive, you can begin sessions after the initial meeting by asking, "What progress can you see?" You can follow up by asking for details that uncover and affirm family members' strengths. The Family Development Plan is designed to encourage this focus on progress and strengths.[27]

Help them bring their dreams to fruition

The Family Development Plan encourages the person to write a clear goal, and steps leading to this goal. Offer these practical tips:

1. Since it will take a lot of effort and time to reach your goal, make sure it is worthy of the effort you'll expend. Make sure your goal is what you want.

2. Realize that reaching your goal has two purposes: to reach that goal, and to develop your capacity to accomplish other goals in the future. Developing capacity is as important as reaching any particular goal.

3. Gather together the tools and resources you'll need to reach your goals.

4. Share your goal only with people you're sure want to help. Sometimes family members, friends, or professionals whose job it is to help you, may purposefully or unwittingly undermine your goals.

5. Follow your goal through until it is fully met. Abandoning a goal or shifting gears in the middle, may sometimes be necessary but can weaken your ability to reach that goal or future ones. If you find you must abandon or change a goal midstream, make a conscious decision to do so. Find a natural wrapping-up point, celebrate what you've accomplished, and consciously decide to stop there.
Unfinished projects drain your energy, keeping you from accomplishing that goal or any other. For example, if your closet contains a box of crocheted squares that needs five more in order to finish the full-sized afghan you started for your baby niece, recognize that she is now at your door selling Girl Scout cookies. Revise your goal and wrap it up: Either invite her in to crochet the remaining squares and finish the afghan together, or decide to make the squares into a small lap robe that can be completed tonight using the squares you already have. Either way, you'll have a sense of accomplishment and freedom to pursue a fresh new inspiration.

C. How to avoid families becoming dependent on you

Sometimes family development workers are so effective at establishing trust and being available that people become too dependent on them. For example, a family might start to call their family worker

[27] For more information on supporting families to focus on their strengths, imagine a positive future, and define specific, concrete, attainable and measurable goals to build that future, see Insoo Kim Berg, *Family-based services: A solution-focused approach* (New York: Norton, 1993); Peter DeJong and Scott D. Miller, How to interview for client strengths, *Social Work, 40*(1995): 729-36; Steve DeShazer, *Clues: Investigating solutions in brief therapy* (New York: Norton, 1988); Scott D. Miller and Insoo Kim Berg, *The Miracle Method: A radically new approach to problem drinking* (New York: Norton, 1995).

when their child gets sick, instead of calling a doctor. This behavior should signal the worker to help the family establish a good working relationship with a family doctor.

Your job is to work with the family to gradually help them build a healthy interdependence with family, friends, and community support systems. By helping the family develop their own ability to get information, make good decisions, and build support networks, you will be supporting their empowerment. Rather than having learned that they must depend on you alone, they will have built the skills to find several good options whenever they need help.

One focus group participant stated a preference for being given information to help herself:

> When they tell you about these resources, it helps if they have pamphlets or written information they can give you. I mean it's different when you read something. It makes you really stop and think about it, instead of just being told about it. It helps you feel that you don't have to depend on them, because that person is not going to be [working] on your case forever.

As a family development worker, you serve your families best when you are genuine and reasonably accessible while still maintaining a balanced life yourself, encouraging them to find their own solutions whenever possible. It's often hard to say no when asked to help, even when you feel it is not a good idea to step in and take over. But saying no helps keep the relationship from becoming unbalanced. It helps the family develop their own coping skills. It also keeps feelings of resentment from growing in you and getting in the way of the relationship.

Setting healthy boundaries

In Chapter 4, you read about setting boundaries so that you can stay well while still being helpful to the families you work with. In the focus groups, workers frequently talked about the need for this balance: *The ability to know what your own abilities are and not push yourself beyond that limit; that's a skill that needs to be developed.*

It helps to be clear from the beginning of the relationship about what you can help with and what you can't. Although every family situation requires some flexibility (especially when there is a crisis), it helps to tell families about your agency's guidelines in the beginning, and to follow them. Some families have several agency workers coming in and get confused when one worker is able to help them with one task, while another can't or won't.

If you are a home health aide, you may be able to help people with personal grooming and light housekeeping, but not with balancing their checkbook. If you are a nutrition educator, perhaps you can help people shop, learn to garden, and prepare nutritious, inexpensive meals, but not cook their meals for them. If you are a Head Start home visitor, you might work with the children and parent together, but should not babysit while the mother goes shopping. If you are a respite worker in a developmental disabilities program, you *can* care for a child while the parent goes out.

The degree of emotional involvement that workers have with families in a family development program is likely to be greater than when doing short-term or crisis-oriented work. This closeness can require some delicate boundary setting.

Here is a dialogue between two workers at a focus group:

> This aloof attitude, staying apart from the situation, doesn't work. (worker A)

> I think you've touched on the core of the work. When I forget one of the children's birthdays, it's like my own children. I'm the grandmother and I have forgotten their birthday. I become such an integral part of that family group. Although there are certain things I must keep away, I do occasionally share my own pain, and I think that is necessary. You're always vulnerable. You're never set apart. We are together in this and we have to love it. I think it's a problem when people have been put into this family development model without being aware of what is required from them. (worker B)

Knowing what to share, when to be there with a family, and when to step back in order to ensure that you are not enabling unhealthy dependency is a highly refined skill of family development work.

Avoiding the "enabler" role

While there can be affection and mutual caring in the relationship between family development workers and families, it is crucial to keep your role in the family system clear and separate, to avoid another kind of dependency: codependency. The term *codependency* arose from work with families with alcohol or other substance abuse problems, but applies to many families. In many family systems, there is a "person with a problem"—alcohol, drugs, a violent temper, depression. Others in the family system, and even their family workers, can (without being conscious of it) start arranging their lives and their behavior around not "upsetting" the person with the problem, and covering up for him or her. Often, family members unconsciously deny that this is happening.

Codependent people—those who cover up for the "one with the problem"—may be seen as the family heroes. They may see their overprotectiveness as essential to the family's survival. Their actions may actually he "enabling" the behaviors to continue by keeping the whole system in place, and preventing the person and the family from recognizing that things need to change and the person needs to get help.

Sometimes workers can be enablers when they see a family as too fragile to be able to follow through on their commitments, lacking the strength to move forward on their goals or deal with the consequences of their actions. The more the family "needs" them, the more important the worker feels. To check on whether you are falling into codependent patterns, ask yourself these questions:

1. How much progress has this family made? If little progress is occurring, ask yourself whether you might be unconsciously supporting their inertia.

2. How burned out am I? Would my own health and life be much better if I took less responsibility for this family?

3. Have I overstepped healthy boundaries, for example by inviting troubled families to live with me, borrow money, clothes, or my car?

4. How much of my self-esteem comes from working with deeply troubled families, and how much comes from my own life well-lived (satisfying personal relationships, wellness, community involvement)? If bailing out troubled families is a major source of your own self-esteem, consider this painful thought: maybe the families you work with would be better off if you "get a life" of your own.

Although it can be painful and frustrating, you may have to allow the family to flounder, and to deal with the consequences of their actions, before they will see that they need to confront their own ongoing problems.

Other workers, even supervisors or board members, may unwittingly enable a family in unhealthy ways. Jorge, director of a large community organization, trained Kevin, the organization's maintenance man, in carpentry and plumbing skills, as well as basic work habits. At first Kevin did pretty well at most tasks, but then his family problems began to spill over into work. His wife asked him to move out, saying his temper had flared once too often. One day when Jorge arrived at work a neighbor was waiting, fearful because Kevin had threatened her. Jorge dropped his planned tasks to mediate, ending with an agreement from Kevin to leave the neighbor alone. Jorge took the issue to his personnel committee, of which some members asked the organization to "give Kevin another chance."

Jorge was interrupted more and more often with complaints from other staff, whose list of undone maintenance tasks grew. Kevin began to appear later at work, and leave earlier. He asked for two weeks off to take a vacation with his new girlfriend. When this was approved, he took three. Soon after Kevin's return, another neighbor appealed to Jorge, saying Kevin had threatened her sexually. Jorge called an emergency board meeting, where most members recommended seeking a police order of protection, and firing Kevin. However, one board member named Sandy, a social worker from another organization, invited Kevin and his girlfriend to move into her home.

Despite her own social work training, Sandy appeared to have a blind spot when it came to enabling Kevin as well as undermining the work of a skillful director. Had she taken the FDC training and worked in an organization steeped in family development, Sandy would have understood that she could best help Kevin by helping him see the results of his anger management problems, and then set goals for his own life.

Sorting out these issues can be confusing and complex. A staff that supports each other, and supervisors willing to listen, can help workers talk when they are feeling stuck or frustrated. By expressing feelings and sorting out what's going on, workers can remain empathetic with the family, but detached enough to clearly see a family's situation and needs. These workers care about the families, but don't live their lives for them. Workers have full personal lives of their own.

D. When and how to end the relationship

There are four reasons to end a family development relationship:

1. The family has achieved its goals.
2. They don't want to work with you any longer.
3. You no longer feel you can help.
4. The funding or their eligibility ended.

Let's look at each of these reasons, and how an effective family development worker can handle each one.

1. The family has achieved its goals

This happy reason calls for a transformation of your relationship with the family, not necessarily an ending. You will no longer be their family development worker, but you may continue to work with them in other ways. For example, they can become peer support counselors helping other families within your agency or serve on your agency's advisory board. Then you can develop a peer relationship. Even if you have no formal relationship in the future, this family may invite you to a graduation, ask for a job reference, send you an announcement when a grandchild is born, or stop in from time to time to keep you up to date on family progress.

How do you skillfully handle the transition from family worker to friendly supporter within the community, once a family has reached its goals? When you first begin working with a family, you describe how your agency works and you begin to find out what the family wants help with. That is the time to tell them that you will look forward to working with them, and also to the time when they have met their goals. This creates an expectation both that you will be there solidly with them during the most intensive part of the family development process, and also that a time will come when they will be busy with a new job or accomplishing some other goal they have set. Then you will no longer have the same kind of relationship. If you are only allowed to work with families for a certain length of time, make that clear.

In Chapter 6, you learned how to help families identify their strengths and their needs; in this chapter, you are learning how to help them set and reach their goals. This continually unfolding process is the essence of the family development process. It provides you and the family with regular checkpoints that will make it clear, both to the family and to you, that progress is being made toward their goals (or that the goals need to be revised). As the family progresses, there will naturally come a time when you will work less intensively with them.

For example, an elder who contacted your agency after breaking his hip in a fall needed frequent visits at first. He needed your help to line up home health care and physical therapy, to assess whether it made sense to continue living at home, to come to terms with the financial and social realities of his current stage of life, and to make longer-term arrangements for help from family, neighbors, and agencies. He will probably need frequent help at first, and may occasionally need intensive help again later if new crises develop. But as he learns to manage on his own, a time will come when you and he will talk about transitioning to less frequent visits, or to stop meeting altogether.

By the time this point is reached, it is vital that you have helped the family to set and make progress toward their goals, to identify other services, and to learn and practice the skills they need to move toward their goals without you. At every meeting, it helps for you to find ways to reflect the family's strengths and progress to them, however slight.

Never do anything for a family that they could do for themselves unless they are facing a real emergency. It might seem easier to make a phone call for the family instead of giving them a referral, or bringing them loaner equipment like a wheelchair instead of helping them get to the agency or person that loans equipment. The family might prefer that you take care of things for them, but until they have made the call or picked up the equipment several times, they are unlikely to learn how to do it for themselves. This is often one of the hardest guidelines for family development workers to follow, yet it is essential in order for families to become self-reliant.

Planning the last meeting

Your last meeting should never come as a surprise to a family, but instead should be the natural next step. If the family says outright or begins to hint that they don't need you to come any more, pick up on their cues. More often, you will be the one who will need to help the family find ways to celebrate their accomplishments. A mother who has finally been able to reach her goal of getting a safe, affordable apartment for herself and her children might want to plan a housewarming with friends and relatives. This is a way to affirm her ability to care for her family, as well as to strengthen her informal support network. Explore new roles with this family member. Perhaps she can become a board member, staff person, key advisor, or peer support counselor.

As families "graduate" from your program, let them know both that you have great confidence in them, and that they can call you if something happens in the future that they need help with. Leave the door open, but don't give them the impression that you think they'll be back tomorrow. If they call, don't automatically jump right back into the same relationship you had before. Sometimes all it takes is a brief telephone conversation where you help them clarify the problem, ask for their ideas about solutions, and provide encouragement and perhaps a referral.

Handling new problems that arise near "graduation"

Sometimes families will develop new problems just as they are about to "graduate" from the family development worker-client relationship, because some part of them doesn't want to let go of you or the services you help them get. They may or may not be aware of their feelings. If you ask them if this is a hard transition, they may protest and go into great detail about the new problem they need your help to solve. If this situation arises, you may need to extend the worker-client relationship a bit longer, with a strong emphasis on helping them identify and use resources on their own. Focus on their strengths, and your confidence in them.

2. The family doesn't want to work with you any more

Families will let you know in a variety of ways that they are finished with your help, even if you don't think they've met their goals. If they end up with your agency again soon, be careful not to treat it as a failure. Instead, focus on helping them clearly set realistic goals, and on helping them build the skills and confidence to reach them.

More often, families who don't want to work with your agency any more will just fade away, especially if family development work is not a requirement of receiving a service they really need. This family will often not be home when you arrive for a scheduled home visit, or will miss many appointments at your agency. They may seem to go along with your suggestions, but not follow through or make any real progress over several months. There are several possible root causes to this situation. This family may have a long history in the deficit-oriented service delivery loop, and may not really understand or believe in the empowerment-oriented family development approach, which requires them to take a lot of responsibility for their own lives. They are used to going along with whatever an agency worker says. They have had very few experiences that have given them confidence in their own ability to dream of a good future and then make it a reality. Consider asking the family directly how much they want to reach the goal they set, and what they're willing to do to reach it.

With this family, it may be necessary even after several months to repeat your introductory description of the family development approach, how it differs from what they've been used to, what is in it for them, and what it takes from them. Tell them you are happy to work with them if family development fits their goals, and that it will require them to do a lot of work themselves. Describe again the kinds of steps they will need to take. Tell them the choice is theirs: you can do this work together, or, if it doesn't fit their goals, you can go your own separate ways. Tell them you can respect one other even if you decide not to work together at this time. Say that either way is fine with you, but you need a clear answer.

If they choose to work with you, you need to spell out the conditions for working together, such as keeping appointments (or calling to cancel), and focusing on what you can offer. Ask them to think it over for a week and let you know by a specific date. Say again that you will respect them either way. Some families will take this as a "wake-up call" and will make the commitment and begin to make real progress. Others will try to fade away. With them you need to follow up politely, making a clear decision together not to do the work now, and informing them that if they change their minds in the future, your agency will be glad to hear from them. This way you can spend your time with another family who is ready to make a commitment to family development.

3. You no longer feel you can help

Many human service workers understand with their minds that they don't need to "fix" people's problems, but in their hearts they still want to play that role. They will stay too long with a family they really are not helping much. If a family's goals don't fit what your agency can offer, focus more on referral to other services and supports. For example, let's say your agency works primarily with families with young children. It took you a while to realize that one family's most pressing needs come from the financial, emotional, and time adjustments they are making since their grandmother died suddenly, when they began caring for Grandfather at home. You may not know the details of Medicare eligibility, whether Meals on Wheels can meet the special dietary guidelines of this family, or other information that a family worker immersed in elder issues deals with every day.

If a strong, trusting relationship has been built with this family, it may make sense to stay with them briefly while bringing in a partner from another agency. Or, it may be more helpful to recognize your own limitations and strengths, and help the family build a strong relationship with another worker.

In our focus groups, a family development worker said:

> It's important to have an administration that is willing to be realistic about what we can do. Sometimes you get into families and there's nothing you can do, and you have to be able to step back. It's not necessarily your fault. This is a process, not an event. You need to realize that and have an administration that's willing to realize that.

4. The funding or the family's eligibility ended

This is the hardest reason to have to end a family development relationship, especially when the family is making good progress. Family development workers can deal with this situation on two levels. On one level, you can help the family note the progress they have made, and identify next steps. Connect them with other services that will still be available to them. If you feel frustrated about having to stop working with them while still in the midst of the family development process, say so. Reflect their strengths to them, and help them think through how these strengths will help them in the future.

On another level, and at the same time, take every opportunity you have to educate funders and decision makers about the family development process. You can discuss how family development differs from crisis-oriented services, both in the length of time it sometimes takes, and in the long-term outcomes. Join organizations that promote family development.

Activities to Extend Learning

Chapter 7
Helping Families Set and Reach Their Own Goals

A. Establishing mutually respectful, trusting relationships with families

1. What traits or behaviors in families do you find hard to respect? How does this interfere with your ability to be a successful family development worker?

2. Think of two families you work with: the one most "successful" and the other who has made the least progress. List some reasons why you respect each one and reflect on how you convey your respect to the family.

3. How does it help your ability to continue doing your work well when there is a tone of mutual respect with people you work with: families, co-workers, supervisors, colleagues from other agencies, politicians?

B. Helping families build on their own strengths

1. List your roles in life (for example, man, father, family worker, breadwinner, brother, son, friend, softball coach, neighbor). List several strengths that you bring to each. How easy or difficult is it for you to recognize strengths in yourself? Why?

2. You are helping a family member who is has many complex problems. You say, "Suppose while you are sleeping tonight, a miracle happens. Your problem is somehow solved. What would be different tomorrow morning?" The family member replies, "All the overdue bills would be paid and we could start living like a real family again!" Write a script to continue the conversation for another minute with a few follow-up questions from the worker and responses from the family member.

3. Describe some aspects of the most challenging family you work with. Then, using "peripheral vision" (seeing the wider view), list 10 of their strengths. If you responded to activity 2 of topic A above, choose a different family.

C. How to avoid families becoming dependent on you

1. When you have felt overextended or taken advantage of in your personal life. How did you feel? What can you do to notice when this starts to happen so you can set boundaries?

2. Why might it be easy to become codependent with a family served?

3. There is a saying: "Give a man a fish and he will eat for a day. Teach him to fish and he will eat for a lifetime." How does this apply to the work you do with families?

D. When and how to end the relationship

1. How do you want the families you work with to feel about you? In relationships with families you work with, how you do meet your needs to feel good about yourself?

2. What are the signs that you might be enabling a family instead of helping them?

3. Review when and how to end relationships, then describe an experience when a relationship with a family ended due to one such situation. How did you feel? How did the family respond? Why is it important to learn about when and how to end relationships?

4. How does your agency acknowledge the progress families are making toward their goals? Does your agency or program celebrate families' accomplishments? If so, how? How do you and your program/agency help families prepare for closure with your agency? If the agency doesn't offer this opportunity, what suggestion could you make to create it?

Skills Practices

These skills practices are a suggested list. You may also develop your own skills practice or make modifications to the ones listed below to help you create a meaningful and manageable plan.

1. Help a family rekindle their ability to dream of a better life by asking if they would like to create a "Vision for Our Family" collage. If so, prepare a packet of paper, markers, tape, magazines, and arts and crafts items to bring on a home visit. During the visit, talk with the family about creating a collage to describe their hopes, goals, and dreams through drawings, in words, or with pictures and text from magazines. You can help the family get started or ask them to work on it between visits. When the collage is finished, ask a family member to share it with you. Help the family identify their strengths from the collage. Write a reflection on what you learned and whether you think the collage helped rekindle their ability to dream of a better life.[28]

2. Using the Family Development Plan, ask a family to choose a goal for your work together and decide on steps toward that goal. How did the family react to setting their own goal? If the family's goal is different than what you would have chosen, how did that feel? Choose a different family than the one for which you are completing the three Family Development Plans, as part of your portfolio.

3. Ask a family you are working with to identify strengths in their family and discuss with them the strengths you see in them. How did the family respond? How do you think a focus on strengths makes your relationship with a family stronger?

4. Use the miracle method to think about a problem or concern in your own life. Consider specific aspects of your life that would be different if the "miracle" happened. Discuss your experience with a friend or co-worker. What steps could you take to make this "miracle" happen?

5. Ask two separate friends or co-workers to talk with you about an important goal in their lives and how they reached the goal. Using techniques you learned in chapter 2, ask what steps and planning it took to achieve. Ask about people that supported them in reaching the goal, and what challenges occurred along the way. Ask about the personal strengths they gained through the process. What did you learn about the types of help and support people need to fulfill their dreams?

6. Develop a plan to prepare for a last meeting with a family you have been working with. Talk with the family about the idea; together, plan a meaningful way to spend your last visit together. During your last visit, affirm the family's strengths, talk about their accomplishments, and, if appropriate, explore new roles members of this family may have with your agency or in the community. Share your confidence in them and describe the help you can offer in the future. Write a reflection on how you and the family felt about this last meeting and how it went.

---

[28] Thanks to FDC Facilitator Nancy Hess, of Plattsburgh, NY, for suggesting this skills practice option.

Chapter 8
Helping Families Access Specialized Services

Objectives

A. Understand your role as a family worker in helping families access specialized services.

B. Offer accurate referrals to services and programs.

C. Discuss the need for specialized services with families in a respectful and supportive way.

D. Learn steps to make referrals and follow through, that help families access specialized services

E. Support family members through the initial steps of using a specialized service.

F. Help families recognize the need for specialized services in the following areas:

- Developmental disabilities and specialized learning needs

- Common mental health disorders

- Domestic violence (including child abuse and elder abuse)

- Alcohol and drug dependency

- Limited literacy

G. Support military families and veterans.

H. Gather information about other commonly needed services provided by community agencies.

I. Work skillfully with families who have many complex problems.

A. Helping families use specialized services to become self-reliant

Many of the families you work with will need specialized services to reach their goals. It is not your job to *provide* all these services. Your job is to:

1. Know what services are available

2. Recognize the need for specialized services

3. Make referrals, and support families as they follow through

4. Support families as they use specialized services, making sure the services support the family's self-reliance goals

Let's look at ways you can be very effective at each of these steps.

B. Identifying specialized services and helping families gain access to them

To meet the needs of families entering your programs, you need to have up-to-date knowledge about services and opportunities available in your community, and positive relationships with people working in those programs. Many of these will be services provided by your own or other agencies, but be careful not to become so immersed in your "agency worker" mind-set that you forget about other informal supports or opportunities not usually considered "services."

For example, in one town a group of older women rent out wheelchairs, hospital beds, and other equipment for one dollar per month to anyone who requests it. They store the equipment in their garages. They tell local doctors and hospitals that the equipment is available, and that they accept donations of used equipment. They don't have any income eligibility guidelines.

One creative Family Development Credential Instructor invited New York State Electric and Gas Corporation (NYSEG) Customer Service Advocates to attend the interagency FDC course, even though NYSEG is not an "agency." NYSEG responded wholeheartedly by sending their "Power Partner" workers statewide to earn the Family Development Credential, as well as funding and distributing the FDC documentary video "Finding Strengths." NYSEG quickly embraced the family development approach, realizing that customers who set and reached their own goals for self-reliance would be more likely to be able to pay their electric and gas bills.

In the wake of the September 11, 2001, tragedies, the New York City Police Department began sending community police officers to earn the FDC. Wise leaders in this overworked Police Department realized family development was a good investment in healthier communities and families.

Referrals

Being able to offer accurate referrals to other services and opportunities is one of the most valuable services you can provide to families with whom you work. Your referrals will be most useful if you can offer complete information on eligibility requirements, a contact person's name and phone number, the location and hours of the office, costs, and so on.

Over and over in focus groups, family members emphasized the importance of having workers who can "point them in the right direction" to access needed services:

> What I've appreciated the most is someone just knowing what the community has to offer, and being able to follow through for you.

> What has been the most useful? Information for referrals to different agencies or places that could help me with either parenting issues, budgeting issues, time management, task management, information about alcoholism, even information about college degree programs outside of colleges, external degrees.

> I wish there was one main number, like 911, one place you could call that would point you in the right direction.

> I noticed that the biggest problem I've had with the family workers is they don't know everything even in their own little town. They are not fully aware of all the different things that are there. I found out about a Thanksgiving food giveaway from a friend of a friend. And our worker knew we didn't have any money but she didn't know it was there.

> What do we need to move toward our goals? The resources to help you get there: schooling, financial aid, day care, training programs, transportation. Help with figuring the system out.

A worker shared a family's experience:

> If this family hadn't ended up with a Family Development agency, I don't think that this mom would take the initiative to make the phone calls or even to know who to call. This family was already in the CPS system. If they hadn't been referred to my agency, I think this mom's stress levels would have stayed really, really high.

Attending interagency FDC classes will help you get to know people from a wide variety of family services who are all using this approach. Your class may also choose to organize a community forum of family service providers in which you introduce the family development approach, and ask service providers—both those in your group and others—to describe briefly their services, their locations, hours, costs, etc. Your agency could also join together with others to hold a monthly rotating series of informational brown bag lunches at different agency offices, with that month's host agency providing an overview of its own programs. In some communities, such interchanges have led to the formation of a networking group such as a family development coalition in which family members are invited to participate, along with others whose work influences families such as school personnel and county legislators.

Creating and maintaining an up-to-date resource file

Developing a resource file of family services and opportunities available in your community will help you serve families well. Remember that some valuable services can be accessed from anywhere in the state via a toll-free telephone number.

Find a way of keeping your resource file that is comfortable for you, easy to carry along on home visits or access electronically. A separate page for each service, organized into sections by types of service, works well.

On the next page is a sample resource-file page:

Family Development Services and Opportunities Available

Type of service:

_____

_____

_____

Agency, school, or business name:

_____

_____

_____

Address, phone, fax, e-mail:

_____

_____

_____

Website:

_____

_____

Contact person:

_____

_____

Who is eligible?

_____

_____

Days, hours of operation:

_____

_____

Costs:

_____

_____

Notes:

_____

_____

_____

_____

Because being able to quickly provide information about other services a family might need is such an important part of your work, it is worth taking time to create an accurate, complete resource file, and taking a few minutes to update it whenever you learn of a new service or find out that the contact person, eligibility requirements, or something else about one of your resources has changed. Being able to quickly provide accurate, complete information about other services a family might need is a vital part of your work.

It is worth taking time to update your resource file whenever you learn of a new service, or find out that the contact person, eligibility requirements, or some other feature of your resources has changed. It is also worth checking with the services periodically to make sure you still have up-to-date information, especially in this era of funding cuts. The right name and phone number can make all the difference, because a family that is overwhelmed or hesitant is apt to give up on the first try if it doesn't yield the service they need.

As you work with a family, teach them how to find phone numbers for services themselves. Keep in mind that this is not always an easy process, even for people who read English and know how to use a phone book. For those families with internet, looking up phone numbers on the agency's website or just "Google-ing" it may be easier than the phone book.

C. Recognizing the need for specialized services

Families will often ask you directly for help in getting a service. Sometimes they can identify their need clearly, but aren't able to meet it by themselves. For example, a family whose father was laid off can't pay their rent and is about to be evicted. They ask for your help in finding a new place to live, and finding temporary help to pay for it. In this situation, your job is to (1) know about affordable housing and rental subsidies in your area (and how to access them); (2) give the family easily useable information about these services; (3) advocate for them if they run into snags in obtaining the services; and (4) help the family continue to set and reach their goals for self-reliance, once they are stabilized in a new home.

Often, a family's need for specialized services is more complex. For example, the family just described may also be dealing with other problems. The family's own resources may be spread so thin during the time of unemployment that they are no longer able to take care of other vital needs, such as specialized care for a family member with a health problem or disability. Alcohol, drug, mental health, or violence problems may surface. Depending on the type of agency you work for and the economic and social conditions in your community, many or most of the families you work with may have several complex needs that require specialized services. *You may very well be the one to recognize the needs and begin the process of helping the family meet those needs.*

You need to recognize the warning signs of common problems, refer families to specialized services dealing with these problems, and support the family while they're working with the specialized service(s). Depending on the type of agency you work with, you'll see different types of common problems, but *all* family workers need to be able to recognize, refer, and support people for these problems:

- Developmental disabilities and specialized learning needs
- Common mental health disorders
- Domestic violence (including child abuse and neglect)
- Alcohol and drug dependency
- Limited literacy

Many families feel embarrassed about needing a specialized service. Services that many families are eligible to use—like public schools—don't carry a stigma that something is "wrong" with people who use it, but many other services do. You will be most helpful to families if you take a matter-of-fact, accepting approach to specialized services. Remember, you don't need to know how to evaluate or provide treatment. Your job is to recognize the possible need for services, know what services are available, refer families, and support them while they are working with specialized services.

D. Making and following through on referrals

Whether you first recognize the need for a specialized service and suggest it to the family, or they ask for your help in getting a needed service, you'll still need to help families decide where to go, and sometimes make a referral. You will need to:

- Gather information on available options (and/or help them find it themselves) and share the details about the services that you have gathered.

- Decide *with* the family on the appropriate referral.

- If necessary, communicate with the agency that you are referring the family.

- Follow up. Make sure the family was able to get the service they needed, and that it is helping them meet their goals. *This is a critical step.*

Getting started

Sometimes a referral is straightforward, but often it isn't. For example, let's say a young family with three children has a low income. They struggle with mounting bills. The children are sick more and more often. The father takes on more overtime at the fast food restaurant where he works, but the bills still pile up. The mother, already tired, isolated, and short-tempered, is pregnant again. She is having a hard time shopping for and making nutritious meals on the money left over after paying the rent. Both parents are worried about their eighteen-month-old son who still shows no signs of walking.

This family could benefit from any of these services:

- Head Start
- Budget counseling
- Job training (so the father can get a better-paying job)
- W.I.C. (Supplemental nutrition program for Women, Infants, and Children)
- Department of Health Community Health Worker program
- Cooperative Extension Food and Nutrition Education Program

- Local family resource program
- Department of Health, Early Intervention Program
- Library's parent/preschooler hour

Where do you start? This family is already nearly overwhelmed. You would overwhelm them if you referred them to *all* of these services. *Begin with their strengths, and their own concerns and goals.* Since they are worried about the youngest child's development, tell the family about a service that will help them learn if their son needs extra help, and how to get it if he does. Refer them to the Early Intervention Program (through your county Health Department).

That may be all that is needed for a family who is comfortable reading, has a telephone, and has access to transportation. For this family, you could simply ask the next time you see them whether they decided to consult with the Early Intervention people to help them learn whether their son needs extra help. If testing has occurred, ask the family member how it went, and what was recommended. Talk over with them their feelings about going ahead with the recommendations.

Providing support—Enough but not too much

For other families, though, you'll need to give more information and support before they'll take any steps. You may need to offer to give (or help them find) a ride, help them arrange child care, stay with them while they make the phone call, even offer to make the phone call yourself. An important guideline to remember: *Encourage the family to do as much for themselves as possible. Remember that you are not only helping them with today's situation but are also teaching them how to handle similar situations themselves next time.*

A front-line worker spoke about supporting family members to take action:

> At our agency we try to empower our clients to do for themselves. It's easier to write a referral, and send you on your way. Instead, we try to take the time to ask, "What do you think you should do? How would you handle this situation?"

Formalizing a referral

What if the family tries to follow through on your referral but isn't able to obtain the services they need? You may need to formalize the referral by contacting the agency yourself. You'll need the family's written permission to take this step; check with your supervisors about your agency's referral policies and forms. Often a phone call to the other agency or service will help:

> - Hello, this is Winona Roberts from the Family Health Agency. May I please speak with Alan Winter?

> - Hello, Mr. Winter. This is Winona Roberts from the Family Health Agency. I have been working with the Chappas family here in Monroeville. I have a release form from Mrs. Chappas allowing me to explain their situation to you. Mrs. Chappas is concerned about her eighteen-month-old son, Oscar. She says that Oscar does not show any signs of walking. I gave Mrs. Chappas the "Early Intervention Can Help" pamphlet with your agency's name and phone number. She told me she called there last week, asking for help, but just received another copy of the pamphlet instead of an appointment.

> - We thought I might be able to help explain what it is Mrs. Chappas is requesting. She wants someone from your agency to test Oscar to see if he needs extra help. She would prefer testing in their home, but could come to your office if necessary. Mr. Chappas is gone all day with the car, and often works overtime, so it would be much easier if you could send a worker out to their home. It might help you to know that the Chappas family has two older children, a five-year-old who just started kindergarten, and a three-year-old daughter, who I think would benefit from Head Start, and Mrs. Chappas is expecting another baby in the summer. Would you be able to send a worker out to test Oscar?

> - Yes? Thank you, I know the Chappas family will appreciate that, and I do, too. Let me give you their phone number and address. It's 123-4567, and the address is 343 Chambers Street, Monroeville.

Chambers Street is two blocks west of Main Street, on the north end of town. Is there anything else you need to know? ...

- Thanks again, Mr. Winter. I'm glad I reached you. I would be very appreciative if you would get back to me with the results of the testing. I'll be seeing Mrs. Chappas again in two weeks (on April 9). I'm Winona Roberts from the Family Health Agency. Would you like my phone number, or is it easier for you to fax a report to me? Fax? Here's my number: 555-6778. Our fax machine is always on. Just in case you need to call me again, our phone number here at the Family Health Agency is 333-4444.

Notice that this worker is courteous, yet persistent. She doesn't blame the agency for not yet providing the services Mrs. Chappas was seeking. Instead, she gives more information, which will help them do their job well. She asked the person at the other agency to get back to her, and makes it easy for him to contact her. She is appreciative. She understands that building a good working relationship with Mr. Winter and his agency is as important as getting testing for Oscar Chappas, because she will probably refer other families to his agency in the future.

Mr. Winter may ask her for a written referral, perhaps on his agency's form. If he does, she will provide it promptly. Once Oscar Chappas has been tested and recommendations made, Ms. Roberts should get back to Mr. Winter:

- Hello, Mr. Winter? This is Winona Roberts from the Family Health Agency. I wanted to let you know that I really appreciated your sending a worker out to visit the Chappas family, and test their son Oscar. I don't know whether the worker has had a chance to bring you up to date on this, but I wanted to let you know that Mr. and Mrs. Chappas have decided to follow your worker's suggestion about physical therapy for Oscar, and have applied for services through the Early Intervention Program.

- Your worker also suggested Head Start for Oscar's 3-year-old sister, which Mr. and Mrs. Chappas are looking into. I had also suggested Head Start, and it was very helpful to have that idea reinforced by your worker. I believe that Betty White from Head Start is meeting with the Chappas family tomorrow evening about Head Start enrollment for the fall.

- Thank you, Mr. Winter, for helping this family. I think early intervention will make a big difference for Oscar, and if Head Start works out, it will be great for his sister and for the whole family. It's been a pleasure to work with you, Mr. Winter. Please let me know if there are ways the Family Health Agency can help you in the future.

If you think Mrs. Chappas can manage another responsibility in her full days, it would be even better to ask her if she would like to call Mr. Winter herself to thank him. If she is interested, you could offer her his phone number and name. Tell her that she might not get right through to him, and help her practice the kind of message she would leave if she doesn't.

Following up on a referral

Once you have made a referral, ask the family how it is going. Maybe what you thought they'd be able to get wasn't really available. Then you will need to update your resource guide and try another referral.

At a focus group a worker said:

A service will say they offer a certain thing but yet when you go to access it, you have to do 15 other things first. Maybe you have a family in crisis that lives out in the boonies, has no transportation, no telephone and three kids at home. They get a ride in, fill out a form, wait an hour or two before seeing anyone, that's a major problem and I don't blame her if she doesn't want to go there again.

When referring to a service offered by several different providers (for example, doctors, counselors, day care), offer the family several choices. Even when a family begins using a service you've recommended, it doesn't always work out well. You might think family counseling would be a great help for a family struggling with a defiant teenager. Yet the family might get up their nerve to call the service, wait a month for their first appointment, and then be assigned a counselor whose approach doesn't work for them. They may begin to wonder how useful you are in their life, too; after all, you recommended a counseling service that didn't help them!

When this happens, ask the family what didn't work, what did, and make another referral that takes this new information into account. Maybe they are still interested in counseling, but they want a counselor who is of the same cultural background as the family. Do your homework: call people in your network who might know counselors of this cultural background, call the counselors to get information, then offer it to the family.

Perhaps they don't believe in counseling and think things would improve if their teenager had a job. Talk with the teenager about her interests, and collect information about job training, placement, and mentoring programs. Don't get discouraged by referrals that don't work out. Ask yourself if there are ways you could have made a better referral, and try to make another, more appropriate referral for this family.

E. Supporting family members in specialized programs

Families usually have a range of feelings about using a specialized program or service. Some of these include:

- Relief to be doing something about the problem
- Pride at making real changes
- Fear of losing control
- Anger (and later grief) at having to face the problem
- Weariness with all the new appointments and meetings to manage, and arrangements for child care and transportation
- Embarrassment about having to tell strangers their problems
- Upset about criticism (or jealousy) from other family members or friends because of the attention one is getting or the changes one is making
- Worry over the cost or outcome of the services
- Frustration with services that don't work smoothly or that aren't helpful

Once you've made a referral (or the family has chosen on their own to use a specialized service), it's part of your job to support them. This task includes giving the family a chance to air their feelings. Use the communication skills you learned in Chapter 2. Don't let the family go on and on griping; use the three types of feedback (factual, emotional, and solution-focused) to move on to "What do you want to do now?"

Sometimes, when a person has finally gotten help with a long-standing problem, he will have a missionary-like zeal for the service that helped him. There is no need to criticize this tendency. The person may need to behave this way for a while as a form of self-protection, especially when others around him are criticizing his involvement with the program and encouraging him to resume his old ways.

Remember that services exist to help families reach their goals for healthy self-reliance. Services are not ends in themselves. Some workers in other agencies may forget this fact. Families may need your help in asking this question:

How does this service help me meet my goals for becoming better able to take care of myself and my family?

Together with the family, decide what your role should be once a successful referral has been made. Perhaps you don't have any further appropriate role with the family. Perhaps your role will change. If this seems true, review the guidelines in Chapter 7 for ending or changing your relationship with a family. Your ability to carry out each of the following steps in the process is the mark of a successful family development worker:

1. Help a family recognize their need for services.
2. Refer them appropriately.

3. Support them through the initial stages of using a specialized service.

4. Gracefully say good-bye (while leaving the door open to further possible contact).

F. Recognizing, referring, and supporting families needing specialized services

This section will discuss ways you can work with families seeking help for the following problems:

- Developmental disabilities and specialized learning needs
- Common mental health disorders
- Domestic violence (including child abuse and elder abuse)
- Alcohol and drug dependency
- Problem gambling
- Limited literacy

Recognizing, referring, and supporting families

Developmental disabilities include a variety of conditions such as learning disabilities, autism, cerebral palsy, epilepsy, and other neurological impairments that may be apparent at birth, as well as some, like learning disabilities, that may become noticeable during childhood. Developmental disabilities can occur before, during, or after birth, and are due to a variety of causes. Some people have more than one disability. They may not learn as quickly as others or express themselves as clearly. Others may have a limited ability to take care of their physical needs, or limited mobility. They sometimes need special assistance and supports to learn, work and become more independent.

Applying the term developmental disability to an individual does not tell us what the person can or cannot do, or what he or she likes to do. Because people have differing capabilities, it is important to use an individualized approach to identifying their personal strengths and needs, including their families in the process.[29]

Your state's Office of Developmental Disabilities may offer help for families seeking information or services for a family member with a developmental disability. Such offices may have information on family support services such as family reimbursement, respite, and sibling services; family and individual counseling and recreation; help with transportation, supported employment, and living independently; and links to other families as well as service providers.

There may be a parent-to-parent network for parents to receive support from other parents with children who have similar needs. Knowledge of the basic stages of child development will help you encourage appropriate parenting among the families you work with, and will also help you recognize possible developmental disabilities.

A sample referral

Often, a family member you're working with will bring up concerns about a child's development. For example, a grandparent might ask you:

> Do you think Howard is okay? He's nearly one and a half and doesn't walk yet, or talk, really. He's so little, too, and his face looks different from my other grandchildren. My daughter was under a lot of stress when she was expecting him, and I think she drank a lot.

Perhaps you immediately suspect Fetal Alcohol Syndrome (FAS), but it would be inappropriate for you to make a diagnosis. You can reply:

---

[29] This section was adapted from information provided by the New York State Office for Mental Retardation and Developmental Disabilities, and the New York State Developmental Disabilities Planning Council.

I'm not an expert in child development, but there are people I know who can check to see if Howard might need some extra help. Here's the phone number of the local Early Intervention Program). They will tell you the name and phone number of a specialist who can evaluate Howard for free, and if they think he needs help, they'll help you find it for him.

You could call for information and then talk with your daughter about it, or you can give her the number if she wants to call. Next week when I see you, you can let me know what you found out, and what you want to do. I'll also bring you a free brochure that shows what is normal for little children to be able to do at each age. That could help you and your daughter decide whether you think Howard needs extra help.

Individualized Education Plans

Many families are concerned about a school-aged child, and are confused or intimidated by the school's Individualized Educational Plan (IEP) process. You can best help families if you understand the basics of school-based special education.

The Individuals with Disabilities Act (IDEA) of 1990 guarantees the right of all children ages 5 through 21 in the United States to a free, appropriate education in the least restrictive environment. "Least restrictive environment" refers to a classroom or other learning setting that enables the child to have involvement with nondisabled peers, is close to home, and meets the student's needs. This law also provides for parents the right to help plan for their child's education, and to challenge any recommendation from the school that they don't agree with, for whatever reason.

In some states, each public school district has a Committee on Special Education (CSE), which is responsible for helping parents obtain free, competent evaluations to determine if their child has special learning needs. It is also charged with helping the parents and school develop and carry out an IEP, which must be reviewed with the parents at least every six months. Parents can also call for a more frequent review.

Parents sometimes feel intimidated by the meeting at which their child's IEP is reviewed. Often five or six professional specialists attend the meeting, using jargon parents may not understand at first. Parents have the right to bring others with them to the IEP meeting: other family members, other parents with more experience in the IEP process (or who have a child with a similar disability to the one their child has), or others. Families may ask you to attend an IEP meeting with them. The IEP process provides an excellent opportunity for family development as you support the family to gather information, plan for the meeting, keep good notes, and follow up.

If a family you are working with would like their child evaluated, encourage them or accompany them to talk with the child's teacher and principal. They can explain their concerns and ask how to start the process of an evaluation to see if their child qualifies for services through the CSE.

Resources for people with developmental disabilities and specialized learning needs

Many resources exist for families who have a member with a disability. Check your state service directory for special education training and resource centers that provide information to family members, teachers, and others about the following issues:

- Understanding disabilities
- Managing behaviors
- Adapting learning environments or curricula
- Assessing student learning styles
- Home teaching techniques
- The IEP process
- Current laws and regulations
- Preschool programs for children ages 3–5

Sometimes the disabled person is an adult. For example, a parent might say to you:

> My daughter has Down's Syndrome. When she was in school, I could turn to her teachers for help, but now that she's twenty-two, I don't always know where to find help. She takes the van every day to her job at the sheltered workshop over in Middle Town.
>
> She met a young man from Mayfield House who also works at the workshop, and now they're falling in love. It's nice to see her so happy, but I need help explaining sex, and pregnancy, and how to avoid getting a sexually transmitted disease. We need to think about birth control. I raised these questions to our family doctor, who seemed shocked at the thought that a young woman with Down's Syndrome is interested in love and sex. He wasn't much help! Do you know someone who is more knowledgeable, and could help us?

You might refer this mother to your state's Developmental Disabilities Services Office (DDSO), where she will find people knowledgeable about developmental disabilities and committed to helping people find the resources they need to live full lives. There may be family support services associated with the office that can help with crisis intervention, counseling, behavior management, supported employment, respite, recreation services, home modifications, specialized equipment, and help dealing with medical needs.

This office may also help connect families with a case management program that helps people with developmental disabilities obtain the services they need, even if a waiver of usual Medicaid guidelines is required. Since many developmentally disabled people are medically frail, with multiple and complex needs, it can be very helpful for families to contact this office for assistance.

Raising your concerns with families

Sometimes, you will need to bring up a concern about a possible developmental disability, even if the family doesn't raise any questions. Perhaps you've noticed that the three-year-old boy in a family you're working with seems particularly aggressive. Once you've built trust with the family, use skillful speaking to convey your concerns. For example:

> I know that young children often play alone, and don't always do what we want them to. I have three sons myself! But I am concerned about how Robert will get along once he goes to school, especially since you said he hardly ever plays with other kids. Whenever I come to see you, I've noticed that he seems to be in a world of his own, playing killing games with his toys.
>
> Do you think it might help him to be in a group with other children his age? Have you heard of the Special Children's Program? It's for families who have some concern about their child's development, and who want the best for their children. They have a great preschool classroom program. There's a free bus that picks up the kids and brings them home, and you can go as often as you like to help in his classroom if you want to. Or, some families choose to have a home visitor come to work with them and their children each week.
>
> One of my own boys went there, and I'm glad he did. He's doing very well in school. The Special Children's Program is registering families for next year, and I could ask one of their home visitors to come to see you and explain the program if you like. What do you think?
>
> You're not sure? Well, here, I'll write their number down for you, and you can think it over. Call them if you want more information. When I come next Thursday at 10:00, we'll talk more about it if you want to.

Support for parents

It also helps to tell families about parenting programs available to all parents as well as support groups for families whose children have a disability. One excellent resource is Parent to Parent, an organization that matches parents with trained and experienced veteran parents of children with special needs, providing emotional and informational support (http://www.p2pusa.org). Parents as

Teachers is a nationwide home visiting program providing early childhood education and parenting education (http://www. parentsasteachers.org).[30]

A worker at a focus group talked about the ways that having a child with a special need can create emotional stress for the parent:

> Often, there's more than one disability, so there's a lot going on. The parent is exhausted. They call me and say, "I've been up for three days. My child is sick. I don't know where to go. Tell me, who's going to take care of this kid if I conk out?" It means looking for respite for her. Advocating. Trying to help make everything in the house function decently. Trying to create a network that the parents can use.

At another focus group, a mother talked about the stress in her life:

> Another thing I found helpful is the Parenting Assistance line. When the kids are not cooperating. ... A seven-year-old who is depressed, has asthma, and all kind of medications that make him hyperactive, and he's constantly laughing like he's just strung up, and you're telling him to get ready for bed and he just sits there. And my eighteen-month-old daughter is in the bathroom pouring shampoo all over, and I'm depressed, and angry, that's when I'm pushing those first three numbers of the Parent Assistance line. I go to support groups too, for ADD [Attention Deficit Disorder].

One mother of a teenager who has been disabled since birth described some of the extra stresses in her life:

> *Physicians*: There are too many to deal with and often they do not see your child as a whole person (meaning they only want to treat their part of him/her). A family may be dealing with many different specialists and several hospitals, including some out of state. Some families deal with clinics where they spend minimal time with the child and parent. There are so many reimbursement forms to keep track of—believe me, you need a file cabinet just for all those forms (if you know how to deal with it at all).

> *Community acceptance*: Simple things everyone else takes for granted are difficult for us. Going out to eat or to the mall or a store, you have to find out: Can we park close to the door? Is there a wheelchair-accessible bathroom? Can the wheelchair get through the store aisles?

> *School*: Getting the best education for your child will be a constant battle from start to finish. Parents need to know their rights and become an advocate for their child.

> *Family*: The family goes through more than most people can imagine. There is the constant personal blame: "What could I have done differently to have avoided this?" Siblings sometimes feel that they don't get enough attention, no matter how the parent tries. The doctors' visits get to everyone. The extended hospital stays take their toll. Simple things like going to the grocery store take major planning.

> *Work*: Most families these days need both parents to be employed (if there are two parents). However, when a family has a disabled child that may not be possible. And if it is, all the days missed for illness or doctors' appointments can become an issue with employers. Child care is next to impossible.

> *Rest*: Very important, but sometimes nonexistent. Respite (having someone else take care of your child so you can get a break) is sometimes the only thing that holds a family together and keeps them sane.

> *Socialization*: The child may not be very well accepted, so may have few chances to make friends or do things with other children. In a small town, there may be few children with a similar disability. School is not that great for socialization.

> *The future*: Is always on your mind. What opportunities will my child have in the future? Just when the country and the state were beginning to treat people with disabilities as full people, now everyone is talking cuts, cuts, cuts, in services. How can families with a disabled member survive without the few services we get now?

---

[30] See also *Each Mind Matters: California's Mental Health Movement*, http://www.eachmindmatters.org/great-minds-gallery/; and *A New State of Mind: Ending the Stigma of Mental Illness*, a documentary produced by PBS and the California Mental Health Services Advisory (2013), at http://www.eachmindmatters.org/great-minds-gallery/view-the-film/.

Your job as a family worker is to recognize potential disabilities, refer the family to appropriate services, and support the family. Sometimes this means helping them work through the grief of realizing that they may be facing a lifetime of insensitivity from others, restricted choices, and lost dreams. Often one of the most helpful things you can do is to put the family in touch with others who have learned to live creatively and well with a family member's disability.

Recognizing, referring, and supporting family members seeking help with common mental health disorders

Mentally healthy people can:

- Develop good relationships with others
- Adapt to change
- Control impulses
- Handle a reasonable amount of frustration
- Handle disappointment
- Deal positively with routine problems
- Respect themselves
- Respect others

Most people have trouble in some of these areas some of the time. Everyone has days when routine problems seem "too much." The bus is late, so you're late to work. Your supervisor complains about not being able to rely on you, then hands you a gigantic assignment that needs to be completed by the end of the day. Your teenage daughter gives you a hard time, ending with the observation that her coach is a lot smarter than you. When you change into old clothes to cook dinner, your jeans pop a button, reminding you that you haven't kept up on your New Year's resolution to exercise more. You put on sweat pants and go into the kitchen to cook dinner anyway, but discover that the electricity is off. A quick call to your neighbor reveals that the whole street is without power; a car hit a pole earlier this afternoon. You sit down next to the window to read the mail, and discover an angry letter from your landlord, saying your rent is overdue. (You know you paid it on time; maybe your check got lost in the mail.)

Do you feel frustrated? Of course. This is not a sign of mental illness; this is a normal, healthy response to everyday frustrations. What do you do? Laugh? Call a friend? Take your son out for tacos? Take a nap? Look through the community college course for courses you might take that would lead to a better job? These are mentally healthy responses to frustration.

Or, do you beat your son? Smash windows? Call your landlord and curse him out? Go to sleep and not get up for two days? Get drunk? These are unhealthy responses to daily frustrations, and point to the need for mental health care.

Just like you, all the families you work with will go through hard times, and some of them, at some time, will need the help of a mental health professional. Adults, teenagers, children, can all suffer from mental health problems and need the help of a professional. Many factors help determine a person's mental health:

- Physical factors (prenatal alcohol or drug use, diet, medicines and drugs taken, accidents or abuse that may have altered brain chemistry)
- Family and community factors (childhood abuse, loss due to family death or divorce, violence, trauma, and so on)
- Heredity
- Stress

As a family development worker, it is not your job to treat mental illness. Your job is to recognize when a family member you're working with needs mental health help, and to be able to refer appropriately. The following description of five common mental health problems will help you make these referrals.

Post-traumatic stress disorder

People who have experienced, witnessed, or are threatened with death or serious injury feel intensely scared, horrified, or powerless. They can keep reliving the traumatic event through distressing memories or thoughts, which may include flashbacks when dreaming or when intoxicated. Children may play act the traumatic event. Post-traumatic stress disorder (PTSD) affects people who have experienced an intensely threatening event. They may avoid reminders of the trauma, may start to feel emotionally numb, and are unable to have deeply loving feelings. Traumatized people may not expect to have a good job, relationship, children, or to live a normal life. It is hard for them to fall asleep or concentrate, and they may express themselves in angry outbursts. They may become too careful and startle easily.

PTSD has become more widespread in the United States. If you or someone you're working with has experienced traumatic stress and shows any of these signs, get help from a mental health professional who specializes in post-traumatic stress. PTSD can be treated with highly effective therapies. Do not allow yourself or the families you serve to suffer in silence.

Any traumatic event (such as a car accident) can send a person into a physical and emotional tailspin. Widespread disaster strains not only individual and family coping mechanisms, but also those of an entire city, nation, or the world. Your ability to recognize and refer people to treatment for PTSD can help promote individual and community healing.

A man who walked out of the Pentagon (he was a bookkeeper there) following the attacks on September 11, 2001, told me that strangers' acts of kindness (e.g., offering him a cell phone to call home) helped restore his faith and enabled him to take a fresh look at his life following the attack. A year later, he had made meditation a daily part of his life, and within a few years had decided to change careers, while also retiring to his quiet boyhood hometown where he felt a sense of community. He took yoga teacher training, then after retirement established a small yoga studio in his hometown.

Depression

A depressed person may behave in different ways. She or he may:

- no longer enjoy the company of family, friends, neighbors, or others
- lose interest in activities that used to bring pleasure
- neglect basic personal care—or, if a parent, that of children (i.e., dressing, arranging hair, showers or baths, shopping, preparing food)
- keep window shades drawn all day
- sleep all day or suffer from insomnia

Some of these signs might be appropriate for a short time after a significant loss. For example, an elderly woman whose husband died last month might have a hard time summoning the energy to cook meals, or getting out her summer clothes as the weather warms up. She might sleep a lot, and not call her grown children unless they call her. These can be normal, healthy responses to grief. If she is still not cooking or getting dressed appropriately six months later, the people around her need to be alert for the possible need for mental health support.

Depression can be life threatening when suicide starts to look like an option. This is an increasing danger in young and older people. When a person mentions suicide or refers to "ending it all," starves him- or herself, or starts to give away valued possessions, workers and families should seek help from suicide prevention counselors or mental health workers. It is dangerous to dismiss references to suicide as "just a way of getting attention." They are usually cries for help, and should be taken very seriously.

At a focus group, a parent of two grown children and a ten-year-old still at home talked about her experiences with depression:

> When my husband and I separated after 25 years, I had a nervous breakdown. It just threw me for a loop, and I went into a state of serious depression and had to go on disability. I started going to Mental Health, and then I was able to get assistance from [a family development program]. Because of what I've been through and the emotional state I was in, I needed people that would support me emotionally. And I got it through them. When I started with them, I was in a serious state of depression. I didn't want to do anything; I couldn't even function. And now here I am, and I'm working too, part time, but at least I'm working.
>
> That's one of the things I wanted to do, was get back to work. And now I am. [Later she added that workers need knowledge about child sexual abuse, because she had been abused by her grandfather and didn't receive any help until she was in crisis as an adult.] As a child, I was introverted. I felt dead and didn't want to do anything. Later I did work, off and on, but I was never able to accomplish what I wanted to accomplish and I felt like a failure. Workers should be on the lookout for [child sexual abuse]. Children need protection.

A woman with a chronically sick child described her depression:

> I was just nothing but a mess. My kids were begging me to play with them but I'm doing nothing but sleeping because I'm so depressed. I just felt like at that point it was going to be easier for them and me to end it all. I didn't know if things were going to get better, not so much Jimmy's illness, but it was really the money. It was overwhelming. Nobody gave me a break. The problem kind of tumble-weeded. I closed us all up for like a year. I didn't let nobody inside. It was hard to go anywhere. I didn't want Jimmy to get sick again.

Anxiety/panic disorder[31]

Everyone feels anxious in some situations. If you can identify the source of your anxiety and do something about it, it is probably not a mental health problem. Anxiety becomes a mental health problem when a person repeatedly feels anxious without really knowing why, or reports symptoms of anxiety (such as chest pain, jitters, heart pounding, lack of concentration, insomnia) that a doctor's examination can't explain.

Panic disorder is a more severe form of anxiety. People with panic disorder have unexpected and repeated episodes of intense fear accompanied by a set of unexplained physical symptoms, such as chest pain, heart palpitations, shortness of breath, dizziness, or abdominal upset. They often fear that they are dying or losing control.

One-third of panic disorder sufferers begin to avoid situations where they fear an attack may occur or where help is not available. This condition is known as agoraphobia. About half of the people with panic disorder will need professional help for depression at some time in their lives. People with panic disorder often turn to alcohol and drugs in an attempt to alleviate painful mental and physical symptoms. Twenty percent of people with panic disorder attempt suicide at some point in their lives.

Panic disorder is one of the most treatable of all mental illnesses, yet it is apt to go unrecognized or be misdiagnosed. Before getting the help they need, many people with panic disorder visits as many as 10 doctors and undergo expensive unnecessary medical tests.

Between 3 to 6 million Americans will have panic disorders in their lifetimes. Between 1 and 3 million people have panic disorder right now, with women twice as likely as men to develop the problem. It typically strikes in young adulthood. Anxiety or panic disorders can interfere with the family development process by making it extremely difficult for the person to deal with the changes that are part of the process.

---

[31] Information for this section was adapted from *Facts about Panic Disorder* (Bethesda, MD: National Institute of Mental Health, 1999). Available at www.nihm.nih.gov.

Hoarding

Hoarders accumulate and keep items most people would consider useless. Their living spaces are so cluttered that they cannot fulfill normal daily functions (e.g., cooking, sitting down, sleeping, using the bathtub or shower, finding reasonably clean clothes). They wind their way through the disorder via narrow pathways. Some hoarders stockpile animals, which magnifies the health issues of hoarding as animal wastes mix with human food. Some experts consider hoarding a type of anxiety disorder, although others associate hoarding with Obsessive Compulsive Disorder (OCD).

While any family with children has days when school papers, clothes, dishes, sports gear, books and entertainment items pile up, mentally healthy families have at least a basic system for handling food, keeping bedding clean, storing clothes, washing, toileting or diapering, and keeping tracking of important items like bills, medical matters, and homework. A key that distinguishes hoarding from normal clutter, is the hoarder's inability to discard items that are no longer relevant. Hoarders do not do "spring cleaning," as each season rolls around, they just look for unused nooks in which to wedge new items they've accumulated.

Risk factors for hoarding include poverty, impaired functioning which makes it difficult for the hoarder to notice when clutter gets out of hand or develop and carry out a corrective plan of action. Impaired functioning can arise from illness, substance abuse, trauma, developmental disabilities, or other causes. Homelessness may prompt either exceptional organizational skills, or hoarding (e.g., in a car).

Hoarding tends to "run in the family." Children and teenagers learn housekeeping methods from parents or other adults in their family. A clutter level unacceptable to other families, seems normal to someone raised by a hoarder. Children of a hoarding family soon learn to avoid normal social interactions such as inviting school mates over to play or "hang out."

I recall that one of my son's friends, a pleasant boy, accepted a ride home but when I suggested stopping in to meet his mom, said frankly, "It's too messy in our house for people to come in. It's nothing about you." Being no stranger to the normal assortment of kid clutter myself, I wondered if there was another reason for his hesitation, but the boy seemed healthy and attended school regularly, so I shrugged it off. Later his mom phoned to thank me for giving him a ride home. As we chatted, she mentioned that her husband was a stay-at-home dad, so I could always drop the boy at home. She said he suffered from depression, and "has always saved things … lots of things."

Sometimes what begins as healthy frugality, saving items that might later prove useful, can develop into hoarding. Many people who lived through the "Great Depression" developed the habit of saving each potentially useful item "for a rainy day." Such thrift—"use it up, make it do, or do without"—is a valuable trait that could benefit today's families. However, occasionally thrift combines with anxiety or cognitive impairment to become hoarding.

I recall, from my early childhood, a very elderly great aunt whose farmhouse seemed filled with nearly everything that had ever come into it: an eccentric combination of useful kitchen and garden tools, interspersed with an entire room of empty oatmeal boxes, buttons, goose feathers (for making quill pens—she was very elderly). To my childish eyes, it was a treasure trove! It took me decades to understand my parents' anguish (and stress), as they sorted out this childless widowed relative's cluttered home so they could pay for her health care. Living alone since her husband's death many years earlier, this great aunt had slowly developed dementia, as well as a penchant for hoarding.

Hoarding is often treated with cognitive behavior therapy, to help the person explore why s/he feels compelled to accumulate and keep items that are no longer needed. Therapy often includes homes visits, when the therapist works side by side with the hoarder to learn to discard, organize, and decide what to keep and what to discard. Therapy often also involves learning relaxation methods. Antidepressant medication is sometimes prescribed, although not all people with hoarding disorder are depressed or respond well to medications.

Delusional disorder

In the Family Development process you will encourage a healthy use of imagination—"What would you like your life to be like in five years?" Yet, occasionally, you'll encounter a person whose imagination has gone awry. This person thinks he or she is being followed, poisoned, infected, loved by someone who shows no outward signs of a relationship, or believes she is being deceived by a partner when there is no realistic reason to hold this belief. Delusional disorder may be one of the trickiest to recognize in family development work, for you are likely to work with people whose partners actually may deceive or harm them.

Bizarre delusions (like hearing voices in the mind) require a professional diagnosis for possible schizophrenia. Forms of delusion include phobias, paranoia, and hypochondria.

Phobias

We all feel afraid sometimes, often with good reason (especially when living in a neighborhood where violence is common). A *phobia* is an irrational fear of a specific thing, or place, which interferes with daily living. For example, some people are afraid to leave their houses. This phobia is known as *agoraphobia* (literally, "fear of the marketplace"). People with agoraphobia are not able to hold a job outside the home, go to the doctor's office, attend children's school events, or go shopping without experiencing intense fears. They may not be able to do these things at all. People who suffer from agoraphobia or other paralyzing fears need mental health help.

Paranoia

It's a good idea to be aware of what others think of you, but people with paranoia has irrational fears that everyone (or specific people) are "out to get" them. They think the neighbors are spying on them, stealing their mail, or putting spells on their pets. They may feel that everyone (or someone specific) wants to hurt them, and may imagine elaborate schemes to protect themselves. People with paranoia shut themselves off from others, resisting the efforts of family and friends to encourage more interaction. Because of this suspicion and distrust, people suffering from paranoia have great difficulty building healthy relationships, which are a cornerstone of mental health.

Hypochondria

Some people feel that they have a serious illness that no doctor has yet diagnosed (even though they have been to many competent doctors). They frequently identify new symptoms in themselves, which lead to more doctors' visits (but not to any specific diagnosis or helpful treatment).

They often take many different drugs prescribed by different doctors. This practice can lead to actual physical problems resulting from drug interactions or inappropriate prescribing from doctors who haven't been told about the other forms of medical care the person is receiving. This person might have hypochondria, and need a mental health professional's help more than another doctor.

Problem gambling

The National Council on Problem Gambling (20013) defines problem gambling as

> gambling behavior which causes disruptions in any major area of life: psychological, physical, social or vocational. The term "Problem Gambling" includes, but is not limited to, the condition known as "Pathological," or "Compulsive," Gambling, a progressive addiction characterized by increasing preoccupation with gambling, a need to bet more money more frequently, restlessness or irritability when attempting to stop, "chasing" losses, and loss of control manifested by continuation of the gambling behavior in spite of mounting, serious, negative consequences.

Since millions of people in the United States have gambling problems, family workers should be alert that gambling may be at the root of a family's financial struggles along with other related problems. People who are compulsive gamblers tend to focus only on gambling, ignoring their other responsibilities including the resulting financial and family issues. Yet gamblers often do not connect these problems with their gambling. The person with a gambling problem may deny how much time and money has been spent on these activities.

Sometimes gamblers do recognize the problem, and have mixed feelings: on one hand, gambling advertisements offer a miraculous hope for a better life, but when gamblers lose money—sometimes large amounts ,their family's entire savings, or even the family home or car—gamblers feel strong remorse. They have a hard time accepting the reality that they will never win back what's been lost.

People with a gambling addiction often become secretive, isolating themselves from family, friends, and neighbors. They often promise to quit but are soon gambling again.

Gamblers keep hoping for the "big win" that will solve all their problems. However, gambling is like other addictions. Until the person recognizes the depth of the problem and family impact, and seeks help, the gambling is likely to continue. Only when gamblers face the extent of what's been lost, and give up all hope of recovering it through gambling, can they start regaining their life.

Often, the gambler has only a vague idea how much money has been lost until they hit "rock bottom"—multiple credit cards maxed out, no money for food or gas, furniture or car reposed, bankruptcy, the landlord or sheriff arriving with an eviction notice or handcuffs. Gambling might have been a family affair, but very often family members had no idea what's been going on.

Suddenly losing money, possessions, even the family home from gambling is likely to propel the family into crisis. The gambler's partner and others who loaned money feel scared, confused, angry, and betrayed. The gambler, and his/her family members, may also feel ashamed. Often, a spouse or partner feels so betrayed that there is a lack of desire to be emotionally or physically close with the person who hurt them. The problem often ripples out beyond the immediate family, as partner and children need support from extended family and friends, who then become angry and may end the relationship when they don't get repaid for loans.

There are also health consequences. The gambler, and the family member who is coping with the situation, may lose sleep, experience stress-related illness, or develop mental health problems such as depression or anxiety.

According to a 2013 study led by John Welte of University of Buffalo's Research Institute on Addictions, adults in the United States are more likely to become dependent on gambling than alcohol. Welte studied many types of gambling including lotteries, office pools, bingo, Internet gambling, and raffles. According to Welte, gambling problems increase after age 21 and peak in the thirties. Welte found that 1 to 5 percent of US adults have a serious gambling problem.

The study may be comparing apples and oranges by ranking people with both severe and less severe gambling problems against those with more severe drinking problems, said Christine Reilly, executive director of the Institute for Research on Gambling Disorders, the research arm of the National Center for Responsible Gaming.

The study included both "compulsive" or "pathological" gamblers, who show withdrawal symptoms similar to drug addicts, as well as "problem gamblers" who experience gambling-related problems such a relationship or financial problems because of their gambling.

Why do people start gambling? State and federal governments normalize gambling, making it seem like a good idea by using a portion of lottery ticket income to fund public education.

It is also easy to gamble—lottery tickets are readily available in grocery and convenience stores. Online gambling makes it easy to gamble at home, interacting only with a computer, paying by credit card or PayPal. Casinos offer bus tours so even those without transportation can gamble. According to Gerda Reith and Fiona Dobbie of University of Glasgow's School of Social Work (2011), children and young people are often initiated into gambling by parents, relatives, neighbors, and co-workers, who teach the young person the logistics of where and how to gamble.

Although credit card overuse is not gambling per se, I suggest that it shares some characteristics with gambling; unwise credit-card use can lead to similar situations. It is important to distinguish between careful credit card use (for example having one credit card paid off in full monthly) and problem behavior. However, utilizing multiple credit cards which one cannot pay off monthly, can lead to problems similar to those brought about by gambling. This is especially true with a joint credit card, in which one spouse charges large debt for which the other spouse is responsible. And, although credit card debt can be spent on anything, if one spouse is racking up debt for gambling or, for example, a shopping addiction, not only are large sums spent, but both individuals' credit rating will plummet, if the debt is not promptly paid, making it difficult or even impossible to borrow money for medical emergencies or other legitimate uses.

Attention deficit hyperactivity disorder (ADHD)

Attention deficit hyperactivity disorder (ADHD) is a serious public health problem which affects children, young people, adults, families, communities, and work places. According to the National Centers for Disease Control, ADHD is "one of the most common neurobehavioral disorders of childhood." ADHD is described by most experts as resulting from abnormal chemical levels in the brain that impair a person's impulse control and attention skills.

Symptoms of ADHD include:

- *Inattention* (often has trouble paying attention, does not pay close attention to details, frequently makes careless mistakes, does not listen when spoken to directly, does not follow through on instructions, loses focus, has a hard time organizing and completing tasks, gets sidetracked, often loses necessary tools (school books, sports gear, mobile phones)

- *Impulsivity* (fidgets, squirms restlessly, talks incessantly, blurts out observations or answers, often interrupts and intrudes upon others, unable to adhere to normal boundaries; in children, unable to play quietly)

It is important to note that many of these characteristics are considered normal in young children, particularly if they are confined overlong in settings in which opportunities for physical activity are inadequate. However, testing for potential ADHD is recommended if these characteristics persist, if many symptoms are present over time, and if these interfere significantly with usual school, home, and participation in community and recreational activities.

A child who sometimes gets bored at school, squirms when waiting in line with a parent at the grocery store, forgets a jacket on the bus, and would rather play with friends than do another math assignment, probably needs a healthy snack, some active recreation, and perhaps a slightly changed daily routine, not ADHD testing. However, if the child or teenager consistently cannot focus, complete school work, or get along with other children and teachers, and has these problems in more than one setting (e.g., both in school and at home), it is worth talking with the family doctor about the situation.

ADHD changes over time—children mature, teenagers deal with flooding hormones, each school year brings new teachers and expectations. Yet if inattention and impulsivity persist or become a growing problem, it is important to seek a professional diagnosis, beginning with the child's physician. Depending on the diagnosis, treatment can include cognitive therapy, establishing healthy routines and eating habits, pinpointing situations that trigger ADHD-like symptoms and learning to de-escalate a problem situation (e.g., a restful hot shower before bed instead of "screen time").

The American Psychiatric Association states that 3 to 7 percent of school-age children have ADHD. However, recent parent surveys show that that approximately 9.5 percent of children 4 to 17 years of age (5.4 million) have been diagnosed with ADHD as of 2007. The percentage of children having a parent-reported ADHD diagnosis increased by 22 percent during 2003–07. Rates of ADHD diagnosis increased an average of 3 percent per year during 1997–2002, and an average of 5.5 percent per year during 2003–07. Boys (13.2%) were more likely than girls (5.6%) to have ever been diagnosed with ADHD.

According to an April 1, 2013, article in the *New York Times*, which quoted a forthcoming report by the CDC, an estimated 6.4 million children ages 4 through 17 had received an A.D.H.D. diagnosis at some point in their lives, a 16 percent increase since 2007 and a 41 percent rise in the past decade. About two-thirds of those with a current diagnosis receive prescriptions for stimulants like Ritalin or Adderall, which can drastically improve the lives of those with A.D.H.D. but can also lead to addiction, anxiety and occasionally psychosis.

Even more teenagers are likely to be prescribed medication in the near future because the American Psychiatric Association plans to change the definition of A.D.H.D. to allow more people to receive the diagnosis and treatment. CDC director, Dr. Thomas R. Frieden, likened the rising rates of stimulant prescriptions among children to the overuse of pain medications and antibiotics in adults.

"We need to ensure balance," Dr. Frieden said. "The right medications for A.D.H.D., given to the right people, can make a huge difference. Unfortunately, misuse appears to be growing at an alarming rate."

According the CDC's recent study, medications—primarily Adderall, Ritalin, Concerta and Vyvanse—can help those with severe ADHD develop and maintain the concentration and impulse control needed to lead relatively normal lives. Because the pills can vastly improve focus and drive among those with perhaps only traces of the disorder, an ADHD diagnosis has become a popular shortcut to better grades, some experts said, with many students and parents unaware of or disregarding the medication's health risks.

Family workers also need to know that although ADHD symptoms often change, sometimes for the better, as children mature or parents find a more appropriate routine or educational setting for the young person, sometimes ADHD persists into adulthood. Also, because ADHD was seldom accurately recognized or adequately treated years ago when today's adults were children and teenagers, many adults (and their families) are living with the adult's undiagnosed (and untreated) ADHD.

According to the Mayo Clinic:

Adult attention-deficit/hyperactivity disorder (ADHD) is a mental health condition exhibited by difficulty maintaining attention, as well as hyperactivity and impulsive behavior. Adult ADHD symptoms can lead to a number of problems, including unstable relationships, poor work or school performance, and low self-esteem.

ADHD always starts in early childhood, but in some cases it's not diagnosed until later in life. It was once thought that ADHD was limited to childhood. But symptoms frequently persist into adulthood. For some people, adult ADHD causes significant problems that improve with treatment.

Treatment for adult ADHD is similar to treatment for childhood ADHD, and includes stimulant drugs or other medications, psychological counseling (psychotherapy), and treatment for any mental health conditions that occur along with adult ADHD.[32]

Common problems of Adults with ADHD include anxiety, chronic boredom, chronic lateness and forgetfulness, depression, difficulty concentrating, difficulty controlling anger, impulsiveness, mood swings, poor organization skills, inability to handle frustration, low self-esteem, mood swings, and sometimes substance abuse or addiction. Some adults with ADHD can concentrate when they are interested (for example with a compelling hobby), but have trouble with tedious tasks. Adults with ADHD often have a history of sporadic employment and broken relationships. They may attempt to calm their distress through being withdrawn or by social relationships that border on compulsivity. Adults with ADD also tend to have more money and relationship problems than other adults.

These behaviors may be mild to severe and can vary with the situation or be present all of the time. Some adults with ADHD may be able to concentrate if they are interested in or excited about what they are doing. Others may have difficulty focusing under any circumstances. Some adults look for stimulation, but others avoid it. In addition, adults with ADHD can be withdrawn and antisocial, or they can be overly social, going from one relationship to the next.

Yet there can be a positive side to ADHD or ADD in children, teenagers, or adults, if the condition is accurately diagnosed, understood, and treated either with education and if necessary with medical

32 From "Definition," *Diseases and Conditions: Adult ADHD.* http://www.mayoclinic.org/diseases-conditions/adult-adhd/basics/definition/con-20034552

treatment. Parents who understand ADHD or ADD can help their children, and the whole family, by establishing and keeping a predictable daily routine (healthy meals, homework management, simple chores, bedtime), both for their children and for themselves.

Many children, teenagers, and adults with ADD or ADHD can offer creative solutions for their own lives. The goal setting process using the Family Development Plan, periodic meetings, and coaching that form the basis of the National Family Development Credential Program, are useful for any families, but may offer essential structure for a family in which ADD or ADHD is present, either in the children or adults.

Treatment for various mental health problems

Get to know the mental health services in your area so that you can refer the families you work with, and support them as they receive care. Ask how they handle referrals. Do they prioritize the calls they receive based on urgency? If so, how long will it take for a person you refer for non-emergency mental health services to see a mental health professional? Knowing this information will help you support family members who finally get up their courage to call a mental health agency, only to hear that they must wait several weeks for their first appointment.

Recognizing, referring, and supporting family members seeking help for domestic violence[33]

Domestic violence is a pattern of one person in a family abusing "power over" others in the family (or a former intimate partner). Abuse comes from one person's need to dominate and control another.

A crime against women and children

It is *very* likely that domestic violence (including child abuse) is a problem in some of the families you work with. Nearly 25 percent of all women in the United States will, at some point in their lives, be abused by a current or former partner. Between two and four million women in the United States are abused each year. Most adult domestic violence involves men abusing women, but don't overlook the possibility of a woman abusing a man, or domestic violence in gay and lesbian couples—it does happen. In this handbook we will say "woman" and "she" when talking about domestic violence (in order to keep the writing simple), but keep in mind that the abused person may be a man.

While economic stress may increase the chances of domestic violence escalating, abuse occurs in families of all socioeconomic backgrounds. It also cuts across all races, cultures, educational backgrounds, and religions. People who grew up with abuse are more likely to abuse or be abused as adults, but not all people who were abused as children continue the cycle. And people who were not involved in domestic violence as children can also abuse and be abused. Often the abuser promises to stop after the first incident, but most commonly, the incidents continue and become more severe.

---

[33] Sources for information in this section were provided by the New York State Office for the Prevention of Domestic Violence (OPDV), and include *Diagnosis and Treatment Guidelines on Domestic Violence* (Chicago, IL: American Medical Association, 1992), available at http://www.ama-assn.org; Susan Schecter, *Guidelines for Mental Health Professionals* (Washington, DC: National Coalition Against Domestic Violence, 1987), available at http://ncadv.gov; *Office for the Prevention of Domestic Violence Bulletin: Special Health Care Edition* 5, no. 1 (Spring 1994).

Forms of abuse

Domestic violence takes several forms:

- *Battering and physical injury* (pushing, shoving, slapping, punching, kicking, choking, assault with a weapon, holding or tying down, leaving her in dangerous places, refusing to help when she is sick or injured)

- *Psychological abuse* (intimidation, threats, humiliation, calling her names and constantly criticizing, insulting and belittling her, false accusations, blaming her for everything, limiting her contact with friends, neighbors, or relatives, lying and breaking promises, driving recklessly to scare her)

- *Willfully depriving her* (of food, money, clothing, shelter, friends, transportation, health care, employment, social services, or other basic needs)

- *Rape* (including forced sex within marriage; trying to make her perform sexual acts against her will, including sex with other men, for money or because her partner wants her to; hurting her physically during sex; coercing her to have sex which exposes her to pregnancy or sexually transmitted diseases; criticizing her sexuality and calling her sexually degrading names; forcing her to have an abortion, or promoting a miscarriage through physical abuse or forced physical labor)

Women in the following categories are at higher risk of domestic violence:

- Single, separated, or divorced women (and those planning a separation or divorce)
- Women ages 17–28
- Women who abuse alcohol or drugs (or whose partners do)
- Pregnant women
- Women whose partners are excessively jealous or possessive

What to ask if you suspect domestic violence

Sometimes women will tell you they are being abused, and ask for help. Other times, you may suspect domestic violence and have to ask. It is wise to start with one or two of the following questions to begin with, and then choose others according to the answers you receive. Many women will quickly deny that any abuse is occurring, but if you seem supportive and approachable, they may come back for help later on.

If you suspect abuse but the woman denies it, don't press, just give her some information about the frequency and what help is available. Keep in mind that the abuser may be in the next room listening, even if she says she's alone. Never ask a woman about abuse if the suspected abuser is around (even in the next room). Always interview her alone. You can ask:

- Is anyone hurting you?
- Is anyone in your family hitting you?
- Does your partner ever threaten you?
- Does your partner prevent you from leaving the house, getting a job or going back to school?
- What happens when your partner doesn't get his way?
- Does your partner threaten to hurt you when you disagree with him?
- Does your partner destroy things that you care about (family photos, your clothes, your pets)?
- Are you forced to have sex that makes you uncomfortable?
- Do you have to have intercourse after a fight to "make up"?
- Does your partner watch your every move? Accuse you of having affairs with everyone? Keep you from seeing your relatives, neighbors, or friends?

- You mentioned that your partner uses drugs (alcohol). How does he act when he is drinking or on drugs? Is he ever verbally or physically abusive?

- Are there guns in your home? Has your partner ever threatened to use them when he was angry?

Responding to domestic violence

What should you do if a woman tells you she is being abused?

1. First, validate her experiences: "Thank you for being willing to tell me about this. It sounds very hard."
2. Tell her that no one deserves to be hurt, and that you will help her.
3. Help her explore her options.
4. Advocate for her safety.
5. Help her build on her strengths, like her determination to keep her children safe, friends or relatives who might help her, job skills.
6. Respect her right to make her own decisions, and let her know where she can find help in the future.

Understanding why women stay

Many abused women stay in abusive situations until they feel strong enough to make the break (or until the abuse becomes too unbearable). Don't "drop" a woman because she refuses to leave (or goes back) to an abusive situation. Continue to say that no one deserves to be hurt, and to offer her options and help.

Recognize that many women leave and return to their abusers many times. Don't regard this action as a failure (either for you, or for the woman). One woman will leave after one abusive incident, where another woman will endure years of abuse (and seeing her children abused) without leaving.

The difference lies in her sense of personal power, her perception of the situation, and the resources available to her: Does she believe she can make a new life? Does she have money, a job, and a place to live? Does she have people willing to help? Does she fear that he will stalk her, or even kill her, if she tries to leave? How emotionally dependent is she on her partner? Is her family pressuring her to stay in the marriage? Is she part of a culture or religion that believes women should "stick it out," no matter what happens? Has she heard about (or experienced herself) police or judges who have not believed the woman's story of abuse, or have not come to her aid in time? Has she tried to leave, and found she couldn't make it without her partner?

Supporting a woman to find help

Ask her, "What do you want to do?" and "How can I help you?" Then listen to her answers, and try to help her in the way she asks. This might be very different from what you think she ought to do. For example, she might say, "Please pick my daughters from school, and take them to my mother's," when you think she should get herself to the hospital and then to a shelter. Respecting her sense of what needs to happen will make her more open to other help, now or in the future. You could say, "Would you like to call your mother from here, and then call the school to let them know I'll pick them up today?"

Once she is assured that her daughters don't have to go home to a potentially abusive situation, you can say, "You deserve to see a doctor. Do you have a doctor you want to see, or do you want me to help you find one who could see you today?" If she wants to see a doctor, help her do that.

You can also explore with her what she wants to do next:

> Do you feel safe going home? Is there someplace else you can go? There is a shelter downtown for women and their children. I've visited several women there. It's clean and safe. The women who run it are nice, and used to helping women who are trying to decide what to do next. They won't judge

you. They won't tell anyone that you're there unless you want them to. You can stay there for free for up to a week. Many women think you have to have bruises to get into the shelter, but that's not true. The shelter is for all women who are afraid of being abused. Do you want to call them now? You're not ready to go there now? Here, I'll write their number down on this slip of paper, and just mark it "home." Then you can put it in your purse in case you ever need it. You can call them any time of day or night.

At a focus group, a young mother talked about how important it was for her to be able to go to a shelter:

> I went around Christmas time and I really liked it there. They have a really nice set-up for day care. They provide the transportation and bring you back. You can just be there, talk with the other moms, and you're not alone. They have counselors who give you all kinds of ideas.

You can give her the phone number of the state or local domestic violence hotline where she can get help and information about local resources. Offer to write the number on a plain slip of paper, or on some other card she has in her purse. If she doesn't want to write the number down, it may be because her partner checks up on her by looking through her purse. Show her where she can find the number in the local phone book.

Few abused woman can change their lives overnight, but many abused woman can get out of abusive situations and build a safe life. It takes a lot of support from someone who believes in them, and often takes many specialized services. Just being able to talk about the abuse with you, and to begin to make plans for a better life, is a success for you and for her.

Identifying services

You need to know what services are available in your area to help women and children get out of abusive situations, both emergency services like police protection and shelters, and services needed over time as a woman works to build a safe new life for herself (and, in many cases, for her children). Review your Resource File. Does it contain up-to-date information about the services needed to help someone leave an abusive situation and build a new life? Make sure you have phone numbers, addresses, names, eligibility information, and costs for the following types of services:

- State and local domestic violence hotlines

- State Child Abuse Reporting Center ("Child Abuse Hotline")

- Police (or, in rural area, possibly the local sheriff)

- Domestic violence services

- Order of Protection (from family and/or criminal court)

- Rape crisis hotline (despite the word "rape" in the name, many rape crisis hotlines are available for any kind of abuse). Know what kinds of problems hotlines in your area are skilled in handling.

- Emergency medical and dental services (especially those that will treat a woman who can't pay at the time services are received, or will accept Medicaid). These are rare. Many abused woman must use the emergency room of a public hospital (either because their injuries are so severe that they require this level of care, or because waiting periods for doctor's appointments range from several days to several months, especially for women without insurance or money)

- Transportation services (especially in rural areas)

- Counseling services offered by counselors who understand domestic violence issues (This service is usually most appropriate for the abused woman and her children, but not appropriate for the couple.)

- Intervention programs for batterers (of varying lengths; generally, the longer ones are more successful)

- Temporary income (welfare)

210

- Emergency food (food pantries, food stamps, soup kitchens)
- Housing (assistance finding, furnishing, and paying for affordable housing)
- Job training and further education
- Child care (assistance finding, furnishing, and paying for affordable child care)
- Advocacy services

Recognizing child abuse

According to a 2014 study of 3,142 US counties, conducted by John Eckenrode and colleagues at Cornell University's Bronfenbrenner Life Course Institute, higher income inequality (poverty) for all the counties was significantly associated with higher county-level rates of child maltreatment. The findings contribute to the growing literature linking greater income inequality to a range of poor health and well-being outcomes in infants and children.[34]

As a credentialed family worker, you are likely to encounter families who are abusing or neglecting their children. Raising children takes a lot of energy, resourcefulness, and patience. All parents get stressed and frustrated sometimes. Some parents "lose it" in the face of daily stress, and abuse their children. Other parents are so stressed that they can't provide the basic physical and emotional needs of their children, which results in child neglect.

All children cry, get dirty, and fall and bump themselves. All homes with children in them look messy and unkempt at times. How do you tell the difference between the normal wear and tear of family life, and child abuse or neglect? Here are some signs of child abuse and neglect:[35]

A child's appearance

- unexplained or unusual bruises, welts, bite marks, or fractures
- frequent injuries, even if explained as accidental
- often dirty, tired, listless, hungry
- clothes dirty or wrong for the weather
- wears long sleeves or other concealing clothing to hid injuries
- needs glasses, dental care, or has other obvious medical needs which are not being attended to

A child's behavior

- wary of physical contact, avoids other people including children, seems to be alone frequently for long periods of time
- appears too anxious to please, allows other people to say and do things to him or her without protest
- unpleasant, hard to get along with, demanding
- often doesn't obey
- shows no enjoyment in other children or toys
- cries often or little with no expectation of being comforted
- avoids physical contact with adults
- seeks affection from any adult
- engages in delinquent acts or runs away

[34] John Eckenrode, Elliott G. Smith, Margaret McCarthy, and Michael Dineen, "Income Inequality and Child Maltreatment in the United States," *Journal of Pediatrics* 133 (2014): 454-461.
[35] Mary Jane Cotter, Rosaleen Mazur, and Patrick Tooman, "Signs of Child Abuse and Neglect," reprinted from *Protecting Children in New York State* (Ithaca, New York: Cornell Cooperative Extension, 1995).

A parent's or caretaker's behavior

- has unrealistic expectations of the child
- uses discipline that is cruel or unsuitable for the child's age, sex, or behavior
- offers an explanation of the child's injury that doesn't make sense or doesn't fit the injury, or offers no
- explanation at all
- is isolated from friends and neighbors or cannot be located
- seems unconcerned about the child, seldom touches or looks at the child
- keeps the child confined for long periods of time
- experiences severe stress because of a crisis such as the death of a relative, arrest, relocation, or marital
- problems
- leaves the child alone, unattended, or without adult supervision
- lacks an understanding of the child's physical and emotional needs

Recognizing child sexual abuse

Unfortunately, child sexual abuse is very common, and the abuser is more often a trusted relative or friend than a stranger. In the United States, one out of three girls and one out of five boys is sexually abused by age 18. Of these children, 85 percent are molested by a family member or authority figure; only 4 percent of children under 12 are sexually abused by someone they don't know.[36]

A mother who is working with a credentialed worker expresses her concern about her children:

> I think my eight year old son was molested by his grandparents, my husband's mom and dad. Jill (the worker) and I are working on that. There's so much. And my daughter was just molested three months ago by the neighbor.

It can be hard to tell the difference between sexual abuse and emotional or physical abuse. Denial—the tendency not to believe something that is very painful—can also make it harder for adults to recognize the signs. A sexually abused child may show some of these tendencies:

- fear of certain people or places
- problems with bedwetting, nightmares, sleep disturbances
- sexual knowledge inappropriate to age (or bizarre sexual behavior)
- denial of pain that seems obvious to adults
- self-mutilation (cuts him- or herself)
- lack of display of emotion
- seductive or extremely modest behavior
- telling stories about a "friend" who has been sexually abused
- drug or alcohol abuse

Forced prostitution—"sex trafficking" or "sexual slavery"

Any abuse of a child or teenager robs innocence, and often causes lasting psychological and sometimes also physical damage. Abuse or neglect leaves a child wondering who to trust.

An even more ominous type of abuse has recently come to light in the United States: forced prostitution, or "sexual trafficking." On July 8, 2013, Connecticut Children's Medical Center sent all

---

[36] U.S. Bureau of Justice Statistics, 1992.

its doctors and staff an alert which stated, "Human Trafficking—The sexual exploitation of American children and women … on its way to becoming one of the worst crimes in the U.S." That notice was followed by an informational seminar, as well as *Vanity Fair's* 2011 article entitled "Sex Trafficking in America—The Girls Next Door." This article quotes girls as young as 13, who were lured into prostitution by a "pimp" (man who offers another person's sexual services for money, which he keeps).

How do these unscrupulous men get a girl or woman under their physical and physiological control? Often these young women are vulnerable in some way—hungry for food, a place to stay or attention, inadequately supervised, running from an abusive home, in a bad foster home, these girls and young women are vulnerable to a man who compliments her, offers a meal and a bed, or a "good time." Although the women sometimes meet these men in person, they often first "meet" on Facebook or other social media sites, an online dating service targeted to teenagers, or even at or near school. The breakdown of healthy societal bounds encourages violent lyrics and movies, songs and clothing that that promote early sex, and too often leave children and teens unsupervised at home and on the Internet, while parents are absent from working long hours, or impaired by drugs and alcohol.

The pimp begins by complimenting the girl, then inviting her to "party" with him and his friends. Alcohol and drugs lower inhibitions and may leave the young woman so drugged that the pimp can simply load her into a car and drive her to an unknown location. Or, the girl sometimes travels voluntarily with a man who promises to get her away from her abusive or "controlling" parents, boring job, school failure, etc. He promises to take care of her, love her, buy her presents. However, as soon as the young woman is in his control, he begins blatantly abusing her.

Although some form of this scenario is not new, Internet social networking gives predators a far wider reach, allows them to fabricate their identify, making it difficult to detect who they really are, or to trace them if they leave town with the girl or hide her in a house, apartment, or garage, sometimes for years. Some predators enslave the girls for their own personal use, but more are pimps who force the girls into prostitution.

According to the article by Tina Frundt,[37] girls and young women forced into prostitution are often forced to have sex each night with as many "johns" (paying customers) as it takes to earn the quota set by the pimp—often as much as $500. A girl quoted in Frundt's article explained that even after she earned that money for her pimp by having sex with numerous men, the pimp sent her back to the street for the rest of the night, then locked her in a closet to "teach her a lesson." He made it clear that if she did not do what he told her, he would sell her to another pimp.

Sexual slavery is not found only in big cities. A case reported in July 2013 in rural upstate New York allegedly involved a man who sat down next to a young woman on a public cross-country bus in California (where she was visiting relatives), began talking with her, asked her some personal information which she readily gave. During the bus ride he allegedly intimidated her into traveling with him to his "grandparents" house in rural upstate New York, by threatening to harm her and her family if she tried to leave. There were no "grandparents" at the house to which she was taken, only another man. According to the woman's report after her escape, the alleged kidnapper forced her to sleep on the floor beside his bed, raped her frequently, and stomped on her hand with his steel-toed boots.

Within weeks she planned and carried out her escape. She pretended to have an asthma attack so was taken to a rural hospital. Once the "asthma attack" was "stabilized," nurses attempted to send her "home." She pleaded to stay in the hospital, and explained the situation to the nurse. Police were called, who soon arrested the man who'd held her captive. It is also important to note that boys and young men are also being abused in similar ways.

---

[37] Tina Frundt, *Enslaved In America: Sex Trafficking in the United States* (Women's Funding Network, 2013, http://www.womensfundingnetwork.org/resource/past-articles/enslaved-in-america-sex-trafficking-in-the-united-states).

What can credentialed workers, and FDC organizations, do to combat this monstrous crime, and to help its victims heal? First, learn about this phenomenon, be alert to the possibility of this insidious practice in your own area, understand the dynamics of how sexual trafficking works, and don't blame a young woman if she falls prey to it. A respected family-serving organization can also help bring awareness.

Elder abuse

Elder abuse (the abuse of older family members) occurs for reasons similar to child abuse. Family members facing the relentless all-day and all-night care of an elderly family member sometimes lash out violently. Especially when caring for a family member with Alzheimer's or another form of dementia, even the most loving caregiver can lose patience. Be alert for caregivers' need for a break, and help them find others who can help out sometimes. If you believe abuse is occurring, ask your local Office for the Aging for guidelines on how to help, and report the suspected abuse to your county Department of Social Services.

Making referrals for families with domestic violence problems

While most referrals are voluntary (you provide information to the family and they decide whether and how to follow through), reporting child abuse and neglect is an especially intricate form of "referral." Reporting abuse to authorities will undoubtedly change your relationship with the family. They may feel betrayed that you have reported their situation to authorities who have the right (and responsibility) to keep family members safe even if doing so means removing a family member from the home, or getting a family member arrested and jailed. In some states, the law allows an abusive partner to be prosecuted for assault even if the victim does not want to bring charges.

Ask your supervisor to provide you with training in your agency's policies about reporting domestic violence, including assault by a partner, and child abuse and neglect. Most agencies working with families realize that reporting suspected abuse or neglect to the state Child Abuse Reporting Center ("hotlining" a family) will radically and quickly change the worker's relationship with the family, and so have developed polices to help maintain trust while making sure children are kept safe. Some agencies, for example, recommend that workers tell a family when they are about to make a hotline report about the family. The rationale behind this policy is to help the worker maintain an honest relationship with the family, even if the worker feels she must do something that may anger them (like reporting suspected child abuse). As a worker, you need and deserve the support of your supervisor and agency in handling hotline reports and their aftermath with the families you must report.

Reporting child abuse or neglect

When there is violence within a family, children are especially vulnerable. While you have an ethical responsibility to try to help anyone you work with who is struggling with domestic violence, you and your agency have specific legal responsibilities to report child abuse. People in specific professions such as teachers, medical practitioners, social workers, and day care workers are "mandated reporters." When mandated reporters observe child abuse or neglect, or have a reasonable suspicion that it is occurring, they are required by law to report it to the state Child Abuse and Neglect Reporting Center (the Child Abuse Hotline).

Because workers from many different professions and paraprofessionals serve as family development workers, you may be unclear about whether you are a "mandated reporter." If you are unsure, ask your supervisor if you are a mandated reporter. Whether or not you are a mandated reporter, your agency probably is (or should be). You can check with your State Department of Social Services to learn about specially trained, certified local training providers who offer detailed training on recognizing and reporting child abuse.

Anyone who suspects child abuse or neglect, not just mandated reporters, should call your state's Child Abuse Hotline. Trained staff, answering the call, will ask for as much information as possible in order to refer the call to the child protective services unit of the DSS in the county where the child lives. Callers who are not mandated reporters do not have to give their names.

The Child Abuse Reporting Center then immediately refers the call to the appropriate local CPS unit, which investigates the report within twenty-four hours (sooner if the child appears to be in immediate danger). The CPS worker, who may be accompanied by police if necessary, determines whether the report is "indicated" or "substantiated" (abuse or neglect has occurred or is occurring).

If the case is indicated or substantiated, the CPS worker must decide whether the child is in immediate danger and needs to be removed from the home. If so, the CPS worker determines if there is a relative, neighbor, or friend who can provide safety for the child, or whether the child needs to be placed in foster care. If foster care is needed, the CPS worker must make arrangements to take the child to a foster care family who has previously been screened and trained by DSS.

If the child does not appear to be in immediate danger, but conditions within the family are so highly stressed that the child is in future danger of abuse or neglect, the CPS worker may offer the family "preventive" services, such as a combination of day care and parent education. Sometimes families are offered a choice between foster care and "intensive home-based services" in which a trained family worker meets intensively with a family—often daily or every other day for a period—to help the family make the changes needed to provide safely for their child(ren).

Families who have been reported to the Child Abuse Hotline are understandably scared and often angry. How can you best support a family you coach who is reported?

- Provide fast, accurate information on what will happen.

- Encourage them to seek legal advice right away, and have a list of names and phone numbers of attorneys or legal clinics that will provide a free initial consultation,

- Encourage the family to be courteous to Child Protective Caseworkers or police who are investigating a report. They are required by law to investigate a report promptly (usually within 24 hours), and write a report that may be used by CPS. The court, or others to make important decisions such as whether the case is "founded" and whether the children can remain in the home. Even though the family is scared, they should be polite. Shouting at or criticizing the CPS worker or police officer will cause them to write negative comments in the report, and may result in the children being immediately removed to foster care. If the family can remain calm and courteous (a hard task, given the situation), this is likely to work in the family's favor.

- Encourage the family to answer questions truthfully, but not to provide more information than is asked.

- Encourage the family write down the name, title, and contact information of the person filling out the forms, and to keep in a safe place copies of any forms they are given. If they were not given or lost these forms, help them get copies.

- Encourage the family to courteously request copies of all reports or other documents, including "case notes." Many families do not realize they are entitled to this information. When they see the case notes, they might discover that inaccurate information which, if corrected, could change the outcome of the situation. Challenging an inaccurate report is tricky, so should be done with the help of an attorney or other knowledgeable advocate.

Recognizing, referring, and supporting family members seeking help for alcohol and drug dependency[38]

Alcohol and/or drug abuse or dependency is a destructive pattern of alcohol or drug use that leads to significant social, occupational, or medical impairment. Substance dependence affects not only the substance abuser but the whole family as well. A family member's dependence on drugs and/or alcohol is often a major obstacle to the process of family development, because the dependence is not easily overcome. In addition to using drugs, the person may also be selling, or even manufacturing, them. The cost of supporting an addition sooner or later propels the addict into desperate means of getting money to support the habit.

Drug use, addiction, and manufacture is not limited to inner cities. The growing "meth" epidemic thrives in rural areas, where a key ingredient in this highly addictive substance's manufacture can readily be legally purchased in agricultural supply stores. Although farmhouses and rural apartments usually house people—while barns and sheds usually shelter cows, tractors, and pick-up trucks—occasionally these dwellings hide a sophisticated "meth lab."

One family member's drug or alcohol use or addiction does not mean that you should not work with families in which drug or alcohol dependency is a problem. It does means that you need to:

- Understand the power of alcohol and other drug abuse and dependency. Addiction is a life-long health condition. Addicts do not get "cured" of an addiction.

- Yet millions of people are "in recovery" from addictions, and lead happy, responsible lives with ongoing support of groups like Alcoholics Anonymous. An addiction is a chronic health problem which requires ongoing treatment, often through a self-help group.

- According the "Big Book" of Alcoholics Anonymous (which has been adapted by Narcotics Anonymous and other self-help programs such a Gamblers Anonymous, Debtors Anonymous, and Overeaters Anonymous, addictions are "fatal, progressive, and cunning." Until an addict is solidly in recovery, he is likely to be "in denial," to claim that although he drinks, uses drugs, and so on, he can stop whenever he wants to. Addicts are often charming (until their lives become in such disarray), lie and steal to support their habit, and blame others for their problems. Be careful not to be an "enabler" who covers up the addiction.

- Listen and try to help in the way family members ask. This might be very different from what you think they should do. Maybe you think they should start attending AA, when in fact their disease has already so overshadowed their lives that what they want is help finding an in-patient treatment facility ("rehab") and figuring out who will care for their children while they are gone.

---

[38] This section was adapted from information provided by the New York State Office for Alcohol and Substance Abuse (OASAS).

- Develop a network of skillful collaborators in alcohol and drug treatment agencies and volunteer groups (such as AA, Al-Anon, Ala-Teen, and NA). Learn about these groups by attending some "open" meetings where newcomers are welcome, and reading the literature provided.

- Learn to support those members of a family who are willing to deal with a substance abuse problem, even if the abuser isn't.

- Enlist help from your state licensed alcohol and drug agencies in determining assessment for the alcoholic/drug abuser (when you suspect a family's repeated crises are the result of substance abuse).

Offering family development to families dealing with alcohol and drug dependency

When alcohol or drug dependency ("substance abuse") may be present in a family you're working with, your challenge is to encourage family members—and with help, the abuser—to consider treatment, while making sure the basic needs of other family members are met. Often, assessments focus on problems rather than on family strengths. As discussed in past chapters, it is important that the way a worker treats the family, the kinds of questions asked, and the way they are asked, the way information is handled, all send positive messages to the family about the kind of "help" they might get from your agency, and the way the agency thinks the family should regard itself.

Begin where they are

The key to any work with families is to begin where they are. A family may come to your agency needing financial assistance, health care, or a job. If early meetings focus exclusively on the possibility of substance abuse, it may be hard to establish the mutual respect and trust needed to address their current and future goals.

At a later point in the family development process, after trust has been established, it may be valuable to help the family recognize the effects that substance abuse is having on their current actions and future goals. At first however, it is essential to set a strong focus on solving present problems and setting attainable goals for the future.

Even though it can be discouragingly slow to help a family identify its own goals, it does not help a family for the worker to decide what the family needs. Helping families restore and live from their own sense of self-respect is the cornerstone of successful family development work. As we've stated in past chapters, establishing a mutually respectful relationship with the families you work with, where you respect the family and they respect you, is your first and most important challenge. You are unlikely to learn of substance abuse problems in the family unless mutual respect and trust are established.

Building relationships based on mutual respect

At the same time, *mutual respect* is critical. If you are interacting with a family member who is under the influence of drugs and/or alcohol, you are not receiving respect. Respectfully helping the individual to know that you look forward to working with her at a later date when she can respect your need to have conversation that is not influenced by drugs and alcohol is taking good care of yourself.

Families usually find themselves seeking help when their self-confidence is lowest and their sense of hopelessness is highest. Generally substance abuse disorders are associated with other problems whether it be alienation from friends and family, impaired school or work performance, financial or legal problems, or impaired health problems. Substance abusers who experience a severe life crisis (such as the loss of an important relationship, loss of housing, incarceration, or medical side effects of substance use) are generally most motivated to seek treatment. This is a significant juncture when external support is critical to maintain their motivation to consider or continue treatment

Helping families develop and set goals

A family with substance dependency may need help repairing relationships, developing social and vocational skills, and getting and keeping a job. Establishing a mutually respectful relationship around one of these goals, set by the family, may lead to addressing a substance abuse problem that stands in the way of reaching the goal.

Few of those with alcohol or drug dependency can change their lives overnight, but many can move out of dependence and build a healthy life. It takes a lot of support from someone who believes in them, and often takes specialized services. Just being able to talk about dependency or abuse with you and to begin to make plans for a better life is a success for you and for them.

Identifying substance abuse

It is often hard for substance abusers to address their problems and decide to enter treatment. They are likely to be defensive, based on the belief that they have their drinking or drug use under control. Family members and friends may complain about the alcohol or drug use, but can often unwittingly protect the abusing family member by covering up when she can't get to work, or by taking on more than their share of the family responsibilities. Also, the physical and emotional effects of alcohol or drugs are constantly pulling the person to continue the abuse. Most alcohol and drug abusers have lots of experience quitting-they've done it many times. *Staying* sober or clean is the challenge.

Sometimes alcohol or drug abuse is not so obvious. If you are working with a family that seems to be continually in crisis, and never seems to meet its goals, ask yourself if drug or alcohol abuse could be a problem here. Until the abuser reaches "bottom," he may not recognize the role his abuse plays in his life. "Bottoms" are brought on by crisis situations for which the alcohol or drug abuser cannot escape responsibility. Members of the alcoholic's or drug abuser's family may unwittingly "enable" the user by accepting responsibility for the crisis. Family members may need assistance to detach (while still loving the person), and let the consequences fall upon the alcohol or drug abuser.

There are helpful ways to identify families that may be in the grips of alcohol or drug abuse. You can identify substance abuse through observation (which takes place during your normal agency work with the family) and incorporating a screening tool during the agency's broader intake and evaluation process.

1. **Observation**: Family members struggling with alcohol and drug abuse may send a number of signals during routine interactions with you and your agency. Here is a list to keep in mind:

   - A family pattern of being in and out of crisis
   - Lack of follow-through on agreed-upon plans
   - Missed appointments
   - Inability to meet agreed-upon goals
   - Spouse's covering up or making excuses
   - Children in trouble at school, at home, or with the police
   - If home visits are made, obvious signs of use or abuse, including track marks, paraphernalia, or "empties" cluttering the home (Balance observation with your own good judgment: One missed appointment, a child struggling at school, a six pack of empties waiting to go back to the grocery store—these do not necessarily signal the presence of a substance abuser in the home. Yet observing a pattern of these indicators can alert you that substance abuse may be a problem.)

   A family member tells about her experience:

   I grew up with a family that my father and my mother both used drugs and were alcoholics, so when I first noticed the signs with my baby's father, I just stopped seeing him. I noticed when he was coming home acting funny and he took my daughter's Girl Scout cookie money. Things like that. And he wasn't working. I was working, so I told him to leave.

2. **Agency screening**: If your agency wants to be proactive in identifying families with alcohol drug abuse problems, a simple question can be folded into the established intake/assessment process. Ask your local Alcoholism Council for questions that your agency could add to its routine screening, that would point toward further assessment, intervention, and referral by professionals experienced in alcohol and drug abuse. Also ask about full assessment services to which you can refer families where alcohol or drug problems are present.

Treatment programs

Treatment programs are licensed by state offices of Alcoholism and Substance Abuse. A directory of all licensed programs is available from your state. It is critical that your agency form a relationship with an agency that can offer a comprehensive individualized assessment regarding the extent of a person's substance abuse problem. That assessment should include all family members. It will form the basis for referral to the most appropriate type of treatment.

Get to know the alcohol and drug treatment programs available to residents of your community. Ask your supervisor if staff from some of these programs can meet with your agency's staff to describe their services and give their recommendations for helping abusers and their families enter treatment and stay sober or "clean." These local treatment programs may also be able to train staff from your agency on recognizing and working with behaviors typical of people using particular kinds of drugs. New drugs, and new variations or ways of using old drugs, are constantly emerging. The drugs that are popular and available vary from community to community. Staff of local drug treatment programs can give your agency up-to-date information on the drugs being used in your community.

Because alcohol/substance abuse is a "family illness" when a family member begins treatment, the family may need your help in working through the many issues that surface as a result of this change in the dynamics of the family system. For example, an individual may require "detoxification" from the toxic effects of drug abuse and may also need inpatient or residential treatment. Either type of treatment would mean being away from home. The family will require support during this period. In most cases, though, the individual will be referred to a community outpatient treatment program. The family will need support of a different kind during this type of treatment, in order to understand and cope with the changes that will arise.

The family systems of alcohol and drug abusers are complex and, like most other well-established patterns, resistant to change. Family members have usually spent years "coping" with the user's behavior, such as covering up the user's condition when he or she can't make it to work, or managing the whole household and family in ways that don't require support from the family member who is unreliable because of alcohol or drug use. The roles of these family members (sometimes called "codependent") may change when a user becomes "clean" and sober. For example, the sober person may take on more family responsibilities, altering the hero role that may have made the codependent feel needed and important. Codependent family members may resist the user's recovery for this reason.

A woman remembers her childhood:

> I knew what drugs are from the time I was like seven. When I got older, I would wake up; there would be needles out and stuff. I would clean it all up before my younger brothers got out of bed. Then, I would get everybody off to school. When my parents' friends came over they would bring their kids with them, so I would have babies to take care of at night, they would be crying

Regardless of whether the alcohol or drug abuser gets into treatment, family members can—and should be—connected to resources for themselves. In fact, family members are often more receptive to accepting help than the individual with the primary problem. This help can be in the form of outpatient treatment at a licensed alcohol or substance abuse clinic, a council on alcoholism and substance abuse, or self-help groups. When family members get help for their problems, it often creates the impetus for the alcohol or drug abuser to seek help for his or her problem.

Residential programs

Some alcohol and drug abusers need *residential* treatment programs, especially at the beginning while going through the detoxification process, which is often physically and emotionally very difficult. Many communities also offer *outpatient* nonresidential treatment programs such as counseling and methadone treatment programs (for people recovering from heroin addiction). Residential treatment programs have the advantage of immersing the person in treatment (away from the influences which have supported alcohol or drug abuse). Non-residential programs (including AA and NA) have the advantage of allowing people to maintain their jobs and family life, and to practice their new way of life in the midst of their daily responsibilities.

There is a wide variation in quality and methods among outpatient and residential rehab programs. Ask colleges, as well as community members, what they know about various programs. You might need to be assertive to help get your client into a program with a good reputation. This is particularly true if there is a business relationship between the local out-patient program which does assessments ordered by courts or schools, and a particular residential program.

Self-help groups

Self-help groups are a valuable resource for people who want to recover from an addiction, or for their family members. The "twelve step" programs based on Alcoholics Anonymous, provides anonymous free "meetings." and "sponsors" who have been "in recovery" long enough to be solid in offering voluntary help to a newcomer who wants to "work the steps."

They offer ways to cope with issues brought up by being part of a family affected by drugs or alcohol. These self-help groups are nonjudgmental, and run by volunteers who are successfully dealing with similar issues. Specifically, Al-Anon is recommended for relatives and friends of alcoholics. Ala-Teen is intended for teenaged family members or friends. The Nar-Anon program is suggested as a means of helping the family to cope with situations created by drug abuse.

The family member who has completed treatment will need support in order to maintain his or her recovery. Self-help groups such as Alcoholics Anonymous (AA) or Narcotics Anonymous (NA) have a proven record in helping people maintain their recovery. Most treatment programs encourage their families to connect with a self-help group. In addition to recognizing alcohol and substance abuse problems, referring families appropriately, and supporting them while in treatment, your agency may also want to offer space for AA, NA, or affiliated self-help groups to meet, and offer to provide child care. Many agencies that supply family development services can provide the nonthreatening, comfortable atmosphere conducive to support group meetings.

Many districts operate school-based alcohol/substance abuse prevention programs that target at-risk students. Participants receive alcohol/drug education, learn to build on their resiliency skills, and join in support groups. However, effectiveness of these programs varies widely.

In addition, an Alcohol/Substance Abuse Council is located in many communities. These councils combine prevention-oriented services for all members of a family, and can help the family assess its problems and ways to deal with them.

Many recovering abusers have both drug and alcohol problems, and go to both AA and NA meetings. AA and NA meetings are accepting, nonjudgmental places where people from all backgrounds call each other by first name. Most towns have one or several AA meetings at different times of the day and evening. In big cities there may be dozens or hundreds of "meetings." People who decide to get sober (from alcohol) or "clean" (from drugs) work their way through twelve steps in which they acknowledge that their problem is out of their control, and that they need help. Eventually, they begin to repair their relationships. They take "one day at a time," often with the help of a "sponsor" (another recovering alcoholic or addict) who helps them work through the twelve steps, and supports them to stay sober when they feel the urge to drink (or do drugs).

Recognizing, referring, and supporting families seeking help with literacy

According to the US Department of Education, 21 percent of US adults can't read at a 5th grade level. That's 32 million adults, many of them parents who must support themselves and their children. How can they get and keep a job, figure out their pay check, find housing, select food in a grocery store, read a note sent home from their child's school, pass a drive test, or understand a medicine label? Seventy-five percent of unemployed adults have problems reading or writing.[39] According to the National Council on Family Literacy (2013),

> literacy is at the root of a person's ability to succeed, and the family is at the heart. ... Children's reading scores improve dramatically when their parents are involved in helping them learn to read. Low income and a mother's lack of education are the two biggest risk factors that hamper a child's early learning and development.[40]

While much is being done to address literacy issues in schools, we have a long way to go. Results from the National Assessment of Educational Progress (NAEP) test for reading, given to 12th graders in 2009 reported the following percentages of high school seniors who scored at or above proficiency levels (Asian/Pacific Islander, 49%; White, 46%; Hispanic, 22%; and Black, 17%).

Families where one or both parents struggle with low literacy often have other problems too, such as getting and keeping a good job, finding and paying for safe housing, and keeping the family healthy. Even when people are able to keep a job despite not being able to read and write English very well, it is harder to set and reach goals for a better life.

Therefore, it is important for family workers to know about family literacy, to be able to refer people to local family literacy programs, and then to support them as they become better readers and set and reach their own goals. If you are helping single adults set goals and find services to meet them, you may want to refer them to programs such as Literacy Volunteers that help adults become better readers. When you are working with a parent or grandparent who is caring for children, a *family literacy* program may be more appropriate. Here is the Federal definition of *family literacy services*:[41]

> Services that are of sufficient intensity in terms of hours and of sufficient duration to make sustainable changes in a family and that integrate all of the following activities:
> 1. Interactive literacy activities between parents and their children
> 2. Training for parents regarding how to be the primary teacher for their children and full partners in the education of their children
> 3. Parent literacy training that leads to economic self-sufficiency
> 4. An age-appropriate education to prepare children for success in school and life experiences

"Sufficient intensity . . . to make sustainable changes" means that people spend enough time in the program to make changes that last.

Rebecca King and Jennifer McMaster of the National Center for Family Literacy have different names for the four components listed in the Federal definition:[42]

1. PACT (parent and child together) time
2. Parent time
3. Adult education
4. Children's education

PACT time includes activities like reading to babies, toddlers and preschoolers, and helping school-age children with their homework. Children who are read to at least three times a week by a family

---

[39] National Institute for Literacy, 800 Connecticut Avenue, NM, Suite 200, Washington.

[40] http://www.famlit.org. Accessed Sept. 2, 2013.

[41] These services include Head Start Act, Reading Excellence Act, Elementary and Secondary Education Act (Even Start), Workforce Investment Act, Community Service Block Grant Act (CSBG).

[42] Rebecca King and Jennifer McMaster, *Pathways: A Primer for Family Literacy Design and Development*. Louisville, KY: National Center for Family Literacy, 2000.

member are almost twice as likely to score in the top 25 percent of their class. Parent Time gives parents a chance to share ideas and concerns with other parents, and to encourage each other with things like parent education and job leads. Adult education often focuses on learning English, studying for the General Equivalency Diploma (GED), and job training.

According to the National Assessment of Adult Literacy, three types of literacy are needed to succeed today:

- *Prose literacy:* the knowledge and skills needed to search, understand written material such as books, brochures, news stories, editorials.

- *Document literacy:* the knowledge and skills needed to find, understand, and use such documents as job applications, payroll forms, bus schedules, maps, prescription directions, food labels.

- *Quantitative literacy:* the knowledge and skills needed to do math computation, understand numbers in written materials, balance a check book, fill out an order form including the right amount and calculate a tip.

Referrals to the right program

It is important to learn about and stay up to date on literacy and family literacy services in the communities you serve. Add this information to your resource file.

Once you know about the literacy services near you, how will you know that you should refer someone to a literacy or family literacy program? When an adult without young children says he lost his job because he doesn't have a GED, the right referral may well be to a program that connects him with a trained volunteer who can help him assess his reading skills and improve them, then prepare for and pass the GED test. When someone says he wants to learn to read and write English better and to help his child get ready for school, a referral to family literacy is obvious.

But often the direction will not be so clear. For example, when a woman says her husband or boyfriend hits her and she needs help finding a safe place to live, of course you will help her with the immediate problem in ways described earlier in this chapter. Once you have helped her reach safety, it would be wise to help her think about her longer-term goals, which may include continuing her education and helping her children with their own education. A referral to a family literacy program might help this family create a routine that will help them regain their sense of safety while furthering their educations.

Or, a family who has trouble paying bills may need an immediate referral for food stamps and a debt counseling service, but when you help them consider their long term goals, referral to a family literacy program might help them break a long cycle of poverty by focusing on parents' as well as the children's education.

Adults with literacy problems have often developed such effective coping strategies that you may not even realize literacy is the issue. Someone might say, "Darn, I forgot my glasses! What does this say?" Or they shop at the same store for years, buying the same products based on the pictures on the containers. Sometimes parents and grandparents ask a child, or you, to read forms and fill them out. Or a family simply does without needed services instead of facing the embarrassment of not being able to read brochures and forms.

Supporting a family enrolled in a family literacy program

Once you have referred a family to an appropriate family literacy program, check back with them to see how it is working for them and their children. You will need to help them decide whether the family support services provided by the family literacy program serve all of their needs. If so, it may make sense for them to stop working with your agency. You can suggest to the family that they, you, and a worker from the family literacy program meet together to plan next steps. You could also suggest to the family member that bringing their Family Development Plans would help the worker from the family literacy program see the family's goals and progress. If the family decides to make the family literacy program their primary agency, use guidelines in the "When and how to end a relationship" section of Chapter 7.

Congratulate the family on their progress. Point out the strengths you see in them. Give them your card and let them know you will be happy to hear from them in the future, either to help them celebrate their successes (like earning a GED), or if they need help the family literacy program can't provide.

G. Supporting military families and veterans

Unless you live in a military community, it is difficult to appreciate the magnitude of sacrifice that military families have experienced and will continue to experience in the Global War against Terror. The current War on Terrorism is the first time in our Nation's history of voluntary military service that the United States has attempted to sustain such a large fighting force for such a prolonged period of time. The resulting stressors placed on military families are significant.

According to the office of the Deputy Undersecretary of Defense (2005), more than half (55%) of active military members are married and many (about 43%) have children (40% of whom are younger than 5 years). About 700,000 children in the United States today have at least one parent who is deployed (Military Child Education Coalition). Of particular, note are the over 1 million citizen-soldiers who are members of the National Guard and Reserves sprinkled across the country. More than half of them are married with children. Multiple deployments, of 12 months or more, to Iraq and Afghanistan have been commonplace with thousands being called up three or more times.

Aside from the separation, military families live in the constant fear that their loved one will be killed or injured. Soldiers often return, having experienced trauma and suffering from post- traumatic stress. Often, reintegration into family life is just as stressful as the absence.

There are other unique characteristics of military families. Many of the enlisted ranks are very young, often in their teens and married with young children. These families may find themselves far from their usual support network, adjusting to a new location, coupled with a deployment. Inexperience managing a household, lack of parenting skills and poor financial literacy can create the need for families to reach out to community services. Although military installations do provide resources, families are often reluctant to request them for fear of being labeled or stigmatized. Others live a distance away from the base and it just isn't practical to access on-base services.

Veterans too, often face daunting challenges. Some are recovering from a severe injury, amputation, post-traumatic stress, and/or substance abuse. Others are simply having a difficult time adjusting back to civilian life. The rates of homelessness, unemployment, and even suicide are alarmingly high among veterans.

So, what can family development workers do? First and foremost, just as with any cultural group, know your community and what resources are available. Don't make assumptions that military families have other resources and be sensitive to their unique circumstances. In one study, only about half of spouses of enlisted members felt they coped well during their most recent deployment (Orthner & Rose, 2006). In a national sample of National Guard spouses, about one third (37%), said they were well prepared for the separation issues of deployment (Caliber Associates, 2003).

Not surprisingly, some of the same things that help non-military families have been shown to be helpful with military families, such as having a strong support network. Research on military families suggests that informal supports are preferred by both family members and service members (Orthner & Rose, 2007). There are some indicators that without adequate supports, the Hispanic community tends to be at higher risk, perhaps because when not in the military they typically do have strong connections. Having strong support networks can buffer the craziness of life. The Family Circles Assessment is a great tool to utilize in identifying these supports.

There are a multitude of resources and programs available to family development workers to assist them in working with military families. In 1995, Army Child and Youth Services began partnering with National 4-H Headquarters to create youth development programs at all Army installations. One outcome has been the establishment of over 400 4-H clubs on Army installations worldwide (see http://www.4-hmilitarypartnerships.org). Operation Purple Camps provide a free week of camp to children in military families, available in locations across the country. In my own community, public schools offer support groups for children in military families, including a weekly evening of supervised activities so the remaining parent can run errands, attend school, or see friends. Soldiers, who are parents home on leave from deployment, attend school events in uniform.

Operation: Military Kids (OMK) has been implemented to support military-affiliated children, youth and families wherever they may live, to the benefit of National Guard and Reserve families experiencing deployment It provides recreational, social and educational programming, assistance with school-related issues, camps and networking with other youth and families also experiencing deployment. They also distribute "Hero Packs" to youth in acknowledgement and appreciation for the sacrifices they have made during their military parent's deployment.

Another resource is a strength-based curriculum called "Essential Life Skills for Military Families," focusing on both the relational and practical challenges of military life. Topics include (a) preparing together for the unexpected, (b) making ends meet, (c) facing legal challenges together, (d) fostering family resilience and strength, and (e) parenting together and apart. For more information about these and other resources and programs to support military families, check out the following websites:

- http://www.4-hmilitarypartnerships.org/
- http://www.Extension.org/militaryfamilies
- http://www.militarychild.org
- http://www.militaryonesource.com
- http://www.MilitaryImpactedSchoolsAssociation.org
- http://www.cyfernet.org

H. Other specialized services commonly needed by families your agency works with

In addition to disabilities, substance abuse, domestic violence, mental health and literacy problems (which all family workers need to know how to recognize and refer), each type of family work has particular types of specialized services that it uses frequently. If you are working primarily with homeless people, you need up-to-the-minute information on housing programs, soup kitchens, food stamp eligibility, and emergency medical care. If you are working with elderly people, you need information on home health care, specific medical conditions that affect older people, and the latest on Medicare eligibility.

No matter whom you are working with, it will be helpful to find local resources on handling loss and grief, since these experiences are part of the fabric of life. Many hospice organizations can provide or refer families to counseling, support groups, and other services for people dealing with all types of grief (not only grief for a dying family member).

Ask your co-workers, and the families you work with, what information would be most useful to them. Then gather as much information as you can on those specific services so you'll be ready to offer valuable referrals. Be sure to include self-help support groups as well as professional services.

I. Families with many complex problems

Often, families struggle with an interconnected complex of problems. Even after you successfully help them focus on their most urgent problem (and they make some progress with that), other problems keep emerging, like peeling back the layers of an onion. As a family worker, it's easy to get overwhelmed. This is particularly true in these times, when many urgently needed services are just not available. What can you do when a family's problems seem overwhelming?

- Use an ongoing assessment process like that in Chapter 6, so that the family can continually reassess its most important goals and priorities, given changing life conditions. Sometimes it gets overwhelming for them and for you when too many goals are being addressed at once. It can help to put some on hold when other needs arise, and come back to them when life calms down a bit.

- Keep current on the services that are available so that you don't waste families' time chasing around after services for which they are not eligible or which will not be helpful to them. It's better to say, "I'm so sorry, that service just isn't available in our community. It makes me mad, too. I'm doing what I can to urge the people who decide how to spend the money to refund that service. The closest thing I know about is _____. Is that of any use to you?"

- Remember to consider the possibility of alcohol or substance abuse, which affect the entire family system in complex ways. If alcohol or substance abuse is present, encourage family members to seek help for themselves even if the alcoholic or drug abuser denies the problem.

- Keep in mind that you can help the most families over the long haul if you keep yourself in balance. Practice the suggestions offered in Chapter 4 for stress management and well-being. Take care of yourself!

References

Hoarding

Black, D. W., Monahan, P., Gable, J., Blum, N., Clancy, G., & Baker, P. (1998). Hoarding and treatment response in 38 nondepressed subjects with obsessive-compulsive disorder. *Journal of Clinical Psychiatry, 59*, 420–425.

Bratiotis, C., Sorrentino Schmalisch, C., & Steketee, G. (2011). *The hoarding handbook: A guide for human service professionals.* New York: Oxford University Press.

Sorensen, R. J. (2001). Hoarding disorder (compulsive hoarding): A comprehensive literature review and professional training to prepare clinicians to treat problematic hoarding. *Professional Psychology Doctoral Projects, 1.* Retrieved from http://ir.stthomas.edu/cgi/viewcontent.cgi?article=1002&context=caps_gradpsych_docproj

Steketee, G., & Frost, R. O. (2006). *Compulsive hoarding and acquiring: Therapist guide.* Treatments That Work series. New York: Oxford University Press.

Tolin, D.F., Frost, R. O., & Steketee, G. (2007). An open trial of cognitive-behavioral therapy for compulsive hoarding. *Behaviour Research and Therapy, 45*, 1461-1470.

Tolin, D. F., Frost, R. O., Steketee, G., & Fitch, K. E. (2008). Family burden of compulsive hoarding: Results of an internet survey. *Behaviour Research and Therapy, 46*, 334-344.

Problem gambling

Bowen, S., Witkiewitz, K., Dillworth, T. M., & Marlatt, G. A. (2007). The role of thought suppression in the relationship between mindfulness meditation and alcohol use. *Addictive Behaviors, 32*, 2324-2328.

Boyer, M., & Dickerson, M. (2003). Attentional bias and addictive behaviour: Automaticity in a gambling-specific modified Stroop task. *Addiction, 98*, 61-70.

Carlbring, P., & Smit, F. (2008). Randomized trial of internet-delivered self-help with telephone support for pathological gamblers. *Journal of Consulting and Clinical Psychology, 76*, 1090-1094.

de Lisle, S. M., Dowling, N. A., & Allen, J. S. (2011). Mindfulness based cognitive therapy for problem gambling. *Clinical Case Studies, 10*, 210-228.

Di Dio, K., & Ong, B. (1997). The conceptual link between avoidant coping style, stress and problem gambling. In G. Coman, B. Evans, & R. Wooton (Eds.), *Proceedings of the 8th National Association for Gambling Studies Conference: Responsible gambling: A future winner* (pp. 91-100). Adelaide, Australia: National Association for Gambling Studies.

Dowling, N., Smith, D., & Thomas, T. (2006). Treatment of female pathological gambling: Efficacy of a cognitive-behavioural approach. *Journal of Gambling Studies, 22*, 355-372.

Dowling, N., Smith, D., & Thomas, T. (2007). A comparison of individual and group cognitive behavioral treatment for female pathological gambling. *Behaviour Research and Therapy, 45*, 2192-2202.

Dowling, N., Smith, D., & Thomas, T. (2009). A preliminary investigation of abstinence and controlled gambling as self-selected goals of treatment for female pathological gambling. *Journal of Gambling Studies, 25*, 201-214.

Hodgins, D. C., Currie, S., el-Guebaly, N., & Peden, N. (2004). Brief motivational treatment for problem gambling: A 24-month follow-up. *Psychology of Addictive Behaviors, 18*, 293-296.

Hoppes, K. (2006). The application of mindfulness-based cognitive interventions in the treatment of co-occurring addictive and mood disorders. *CNS Spectrums, 11*, 829-851.

Kessler, R. C., Hwang, I., LaBrie, R., Petukhova, M., Sampson, N. A., Winters, K. C., & Shaffer, H. J. (2008). DSM-IV pathological gambling in the National Comorbidity Survey Replication. *Psychological Medicine: A Journal for Research in Psychiatry and the Allied Sciences, 38*, 1351-1360.

Ladouceur, R., Lachance, S., & Fournier, P. M. (2009). Is control a viable goal in the treatment of pathological gambling? *Behaviour Research and Therapy, 47*, 189-197.

Lakey, C. E., Campbell, W. K., Brown, K. W., & Goodie, A. S. (2007). Dispositional mindfulness as a predictor of the severity of gambling outcomes. *Personality and Individual Differences, 43*, 1698-1710.

Linehan, M. M. (1993a). *Cognitive-behavioural treatment of borderline personality disorder.* New York: Guilford.

López Viets, V. C., & Miller, W. R. (1997). Treatment approaches for pathological gamblers. *Clinical Psychology Review, 17*, 689-702.

May, R. K., Whelan, J. P., Steenbergh, T. A., & Meyers, A. W. (2003). The gambling self-efficacy questionnaire: An initial psychometric evaluation. *Journal of Gambling Studies, 19, 339-357.*

McCusker, C. G., & Gettings, B. (1997). Automaticity of cognitive biases in addictive behaviours: Further evidence with gamblers. *British Journal of Clinical Psychology, 36*, 543-554.

National Research Council. (1999). *Pathological gambling: A critical review.* Washington: National Academy Press.

Pallesen, S., Mitsem, M., Kvale, G., Johnsen, B., & Molde, H. (2005). Outcome of psychological treatments of pathological gambling: A review and meta-analysis. *Addiction, 100*, 1412-1422.

Petry, N. M., Ammerman, Y., Bohl, J., Doersch, A., Gay, H., Kadden, R., . . . Steinberg, K. (2006). Cognitive-behavioral therapy for pathological gamblers. *Journal of Consulting and Clinical Psychology, 74*, 555-567.

Petry, N. M., Stinson, F. S., & Grant, B. F. (2005). Comorbidity of DSM-IV pathological gambling and other psychiatric disorders: Results from the National Epidemiologic Survey on Alcohol and Related Conditions. *Journal of Clinical Psychiatry, 66*, 564-574.

Petry, N. M., Weinstock, J., Ledgerwood, D. M., & Morasco, B. (2008). A randomized trial of brief interventions for problem and pathological gamblers. *Journal of Consulting and Clinical Psychology, 76*, 318-328.

Reith, G., & Dobbie, F. (2011). Beginning gambling: The role of social networks and environment. *Addiction Research and Theory, 19*, 483–493.

Sauer, S. E., & Baer, R. (2009). Responding to negative internal experience: Relationships between acceptance and change-based approaches and psychological adjustment. *Journal of Psychopathology and Behavioral Assessment, 31*, 378-386.

Tavares, H., Martins, S. S., Zilberman, M. L., & el-Guebaly, N. (2002). Gamblers seeking treatment: Why haven't they come earlier? *Addictive Disorders & Their Treatment, 1*, 65-69.

Toneatto, T., Vettese, L., & Nguyen, L. (2007). The role of mindfulness in the cognitive-behavioural treatment of problem gambling. *Journal of Gambling Issues, 19*, 91-100.

Volberg, R. A. (2002). The epidemiology of pathological gambling. *Psychiatric Annals, 32*, 171-178.

Walker, M., Anjoul, F., Milton, S., & Shannon, K. (2006). A structured clinical interview for pathological gambling. *Gambling Research, 18*, 39-56.

Walker, M., Toneatto, T., Potenza, M. N., Petry, N., Ladouceur, R., Hodgins, D. C., . . . Blaszczynski, A. (2006). A framework for reporting outcomes in problem gambling treatment research: The Banff, Alberta Consensus. *Addiction, 101*, 504-511.

Wardle, H., Sproston, K., Orford, J., Erens, B., Griffiths, M., Constantine, R., & Pigott, S. (2007). *The British Gambling Prevalence Survey 2007.* London: Stationery Office.

Wells, A. (2002). GAD, metacognition, and mindfulness: An information processing analysis. *Clinical Psychology: Science and Practice, 9*, 95-100.

Westphal, J. R. (2008). How well are we helping problem gamblers? An update to the evidence base supporting problem gambling treatment. *International Journal of Mental Health and Addiction, 6*, 249-264.

Whelan, J. P., Steenbergh, T. A., & Meyers, A. W. (2007). *Problem and pathological gambling.* Cambridge, MA: Hogrefe.

ADHD

Centers for Disease Control and Prevention. (2010). Increasing prevalence of parent-reported attention-deficit/hyperactivity disorder among children—United States, 2003 and 2007. *Morbidity and Mortality Weekly Report, 59*, 1439-1443.

Getahun, D., Jacobsen, S. J., Fassettet, M. J., et al., (2013). Recent trends in childhood attention-deficit/hyperactivity disorder. *Journal of the American Medical Association Pediatrics, 167*(3), 282-288.

Owens, J. A. (2005). The ADHD and Sleep conundrum: A review. *Journal of Developmental & Behavioral Pediatrics, 26*, 312-322.

Sarkis, S. M. (2011). *Ten Simple Solutions to Adult ADHD.* Oakland, CA: New Harbinger.

Sarkis, S. M., & Klein, K. (2009). *ADD and your money: A Guide To Personal Finance For Adults With ADD.* Oakland, CA: New Harbinger.

Sarkis, S. M., & Quinn, P. O. (2011). Adult ADD: A guide to the newly diagnosed. Oakland, CA: New Harbinger.

Strine, T. W., Lesesne, C. A., Okoro, C. A., McGuire, L. C., Chapman, D. P., Balluz, L. S., & Mokdad, A. H. (2006). Emotional and behavioral difficulties and impairments in everyday functioning among children with a history of attention-deficit/hyperactivity disorder. *Prevention of Chronic Disease, 3*(2), A52. Retrieved from http://www.ncbi.nlm.nih.gov/pmc/articles/PMC1563970/.

Additional resources

General adult health

Division of Adult and Community Health
    National Center for Chronic Disease Prevention and Health Promotion
    Centers for Disease Control and Prevention
    4770 Buford Hwy NE
    Mail Stop K-66
    Atlanta, GA 30341, USA.
    E-mail: tws2@cdc.gov.

Parental help for divorce/separation

The NYS Unified Court System has resources, including a Parent Handbook to educate parents who are divorced or separated on the best practices for co-parenting. There are many communities across the country who also offer classes on Parenting After Separation and Divorce that family development workers may refer to. For more information, see http://www.nycourts.gov/ip/parent-ed/.

Problem gambling

Gamblers Anonymous is a fellowship of men and women who share their experience, strength and hope with each other that they may solve their common problem and help others to recover from a gambling problem (http://www.gamblersanonymous.org).

Gam-Anon is a self-help organization for the spouse, family or close friends of compulsive gamblers (http://www.gam-anon.org).

Your First Step to Change Online Workbook is a guide to help people understand gambling, figure out if they need to change, and decide how to deal with the actual process of change (http://basis.typepad.com/basis/selfhelp_tools.html).

The *National Certified Gambling Counselor* (NCGC) directory includes only clinicians who have applied for and met the NCGC criteria. There are likely additional counselors certified through other entities in your state, contact the local affiliate or state health agency for more information.

Inpatient/Residential Treatment Locator. Programs must be licensed or accredited to provide treatment; have a gambling specific track or protocol; and have at least one full time clinical staff member who is a certified gambling counselor.

In addition to the resources listed above, there are many additional resources for problem gamblers throughout the National Council on Problem Gambling site, http://www.ncpgambling.org/i4a/links/?pageid=3364&showTitle=1.

For links to publications, including those of the NCPG, see http://www.ncpgambling.org/i4a/ams/amsstore/category.cfm?category_id=6.

Real Voices provides stories of individuals who have been affected by problem gambling, including problem gamblers and their family members, friends, colleagues and employers; treatment providers; advocates; and others (http://www.ncpgambling.org/i4a/pages/index.cfm?pageid=3320).

Or, you can write to:

The National Council on Problem Gambling
    730 11th St, NW, Ste 601
    Washington, DC 20001
    Phone 202.547.9204
    Fax 202.547.9206
    ncpg@ncpgambling.org
    http://www.ncpgambling.org
    Toll-free 24-hour confidential hotline: (800) 522-4700

Activities to Extend Learning

Chapter 8
Helping Families Access Specialized Services

A. Helping families use specialized services in order to become self-reliant

1. Describe the role of a family development worker in helping families use specialized services and the steps involved. Give an example from your experience of helping a family seek and use a specialized service.

2. Describe ways you can help avoid or overcome the negative stigma attached to specialized services.

3. Describe an experience in your own life when you and your family used a specialized service. How did you (or your family) recognize the need? How did you gather information you needed? What choices did your family make in choosing a specialized service? How did using that specialized service support your family's healthy self-reliance?

B. Identifying specialized services and helping families gain access to them

1. Choose one area of family support that you are not familiar with (such as food pantries, senior nutrition, early childhood programs, etc.) and gather information about services and programs available in your community. Prepare a Family Resource Form for each service. How will you be able to use this information?

2. Learn more about local community resource guides available in print or on the internet (consult agencies such as United Way). Review the guides and briefly describe how the resources help families learn about specialized services. Or, conversely, explain why they are difficult to use. What could be improved upon?

3. Learn about the types of community-based support groups available in your community. What are some ways that families using specialized services can get support from other families who share similar experiences?

C. Recognizing the need for specialized services

1. Why do family development workers need to be able to recognize, discuss and refer for issues that your agency doesn't directly address?

2. Have you ever helped a family recognize a need for specialized services that was uncomfortable for you or the family to talk about? What steps did you take to prepare and how did you discuss it with the family?

3. When a family has many complex problems, how do you help families decide which need comes first? What if a family decided to seek a specialized service that you didn't think would meet their needs? What would you say and do?

D. Making and following through on referrals

1. Make three columns and label them, "Steps," "Enough," and "Too much." Then, identify a specialized service that a family involved with your agency might use. Under Steps, write the tasks you would do to help the family follow through on a referral. Under Enough, describe what you think is "enough" help you would offer to the family. Under Too Much, describe what would be offering "too much" help for a family. Reflect on the differences between "enough" and "too much" in promoting a family's healthy self-reliance.

2. When a family has a choice of several providers offering a specialized service, how would you help them decide which was the best option?

3. Have you ever referred a family to a specialized service that wasn't helpful for them? Describe what happened and reasons you think the referral didn't work well. What insight did you learn about that service that will help you refer families more effectively in the future?

E. Supporting family members in specialized programs

1. Think of a family who is using a specialized service. How do they feel about using that service? What support does the family need from you now to help them continue toward reaching their goals of healthy self-reliance?

F. Recognizing, referring, and supporting families needing specialized services

1. Reflect on the prevalence of domestic violence in your community including what the contributing factors may be. What domestic violence services are available in your community?

2. Contact your local courts (family and criminal) to find out how an individual would get an order of protection. Write a summary of the process. What other steps might an individual take?

3. Reflect on the prevalence of child abuse and neglect in your community including what the contributing factors may be. What prevention strategies are needed or in place?

4. Reflect on the prevalence of child sexual abuse in your community including what the contributing factors may be. What prevention strategies are needed or in place?

5. Reflect on the prevalence of problem gambling in your community including what the contributing factors may be. What services are available in your area to assist individuals with gambling addictions?

6. Where would you encourage a family member to turn if there was a concern about depression and potential suicide? Describe the process you would use to communicate your concern and make the referral.

7. How would using the family development approach help a family with alcohol or drug dependency? How might this approach lead to the family seeking services for alcohol or drug dependency? What factors make helping families with addictions more complex?

G. Supporting military families and veterans

1. What special programs or services are available for military families in your community? How does your agency reach out and promote these services to military families or what could be done to do so?

H. Other specialized services commonly needed by families your agency works with

1. List and briefly describe the other specialized services commonly needed by families your agency works with. How do you access these services?

2. Select the five most common services needed by families your agency works with. Prepare a Family Resource File booklet to help families learn more about those programs.

3. Contact a family literacy program in your community. Ask how to recognize and talk with families about the need for family literacy, and how to refer and support families. Request a program brochure. Write a memo to your supervisor and co-workers describing ways that your program can help recognize, refer, and support families in seeking help with family literacy.

I. Families with many complex problems

1. How might using ongoing assessment through tools such as the Family Circles Assessment and Family Development Plan help families from being overwhelmed by complex problems?

2. How do you take good care of yourself when working with families who have many complex problems?

Skills Practices

Here are suggestions for skills practices for this chapter. You may also develop your own skills practice or make modifications to the ones listed below to help you create a meaningful and manageable plan.

1. With a co-worker or supervisor, role play a conversation you might have with a family member if you suspected domestic violence or substance abuse. Reflect on how you felt doing this role play. What was difficult for you to talk about? What respectful speaking skills did you use to communicate about a difficult issue?

2. Arrange to meet with substance abuse counselors in your community. Prepare questions in advance about identifying possible substance abuse, agency services, and how to refer families for substance abuse services. Share what you learned at a staff meeting at your agency.

3. Talk with a child development professional to learn more about services which you are not already familiar with, that help children with specialized needs. Ask about the types of services and support groups available in your community and how you can refer families concerned about their child's development. Discuss what you learned at a staff meeting at your agency.

4. Learn more about how to support family members seeking help for alcohol dependency. Arrange to attend an open AA or Al-Anon meeting in your community Write a reflection about your experience and describe how this self-help program supports family members and others seeking help to deal with their own or a family member's alcohol abuse.

5. If not already available, develop a resource guide of agencies in your community that provide mental health services. Determine how these providers' services differ in terms of services, cost, location, inpatient or outpatient programs, short or long term treatment plans. If you were working with a family seeking help for mental health problems, how would you help them determine which service or agency to choose?

6. Follow up with a family that you referred to a specialized service. Ask a family member if the service is helping them to meet their goals. If the service has been helpful, ask the family for suggestions about ways you could help other families work with this agency. If the service hasn't been helpful, talk about what isn't working and help them explore another service provider. Write a reflection on what you learned and why it's important that family workers follow up with families referred to a specialized service.

Chapter 9
Home Visiting

Objectives

A. Understand the advantages of home visiting.

B. Use the family development approach in making effective home visits.

C. Build a mutually respectful relationship with families during unannounced and first-time home visits.

D. Establish a positive and clear purpose for home visits.

E. Take practical steps to increase your safety when making home visits.

F. Handle the practical challenges of home visiting.

G. Use a family development approach for home visits in child protection or other domestic violence situations.

H. Keep ongoing visits productive using the Family Development Plan to focus on the family's goals.

A. Home visiting: A unique relationship

Home visiting has some advantages over the work you do with families in your office or family center. You can:

- Reach families who wouldn't come to your office

- Work with more of the family members

- Work with families in their own setting, where they are apt to be more at ease

- Gain greater understanding of the family's life and strengths

- To begin to understand home visiting, it helps to think about the people who visit your home:

  - relatives

  - friends

  - family members' friends

  - caregivers for children or family members with disabilities

  - neighbors

  - repair people

  - members of a group you or another family member belongs to

  - clients (if you or a family member has a home business or profession)

  - members of a religious or spiritual group you belong to

These are all people you or a family member has invited into your home. If they are in your home to conduct some business (like repair an appliance), the relationship is clear. They are providing a service, you are paying. A caregiver for your children or for a family member with a disability is there to give you time away to work or relax. You are cordial, appreciative, and clear about your expectations (and you may become friends, over time).

If you or a family member conducts a business at home, the people who come are there to get their hair cut, take music lessons, or obtain whatever service you provide. People from a religious or spiritual organization you belong to might visit you for fellowship or to help out if someone in your family is sick or dying. Relatives, friends, fellow members of voluntary groups, are in your home as your guests. Your role is to help them be at home and enjoy your time together. Most likely you visit in their homes, too.

These are traditional reasons for visiting someone's home. You both have a pretty good idea of what to do (and what not to do). Everybody in the family knows not to put their feet up when Aunt Mary visits, your son knows he must be on time when he goes to his guitar teacher's house, and your babysitter knows it's okay to watch TV but not to invite her boyfriend over.

Some families also call people to their home during an emergency, such as the police during a family fight, or an ambulance attendant following an accident. In these situations, families are highly stressed, looking for protection or help, yet they may be scared of the person making the "home visit." The family member making the call wants help fast, but doesn't want to form an ongoing relationship with the "home visitor."

Relationships between agency home visitors and families are less clear-cut. The people you visit might not know whether to treat you like a guest, a repairperson who has come to fix their problems, a trusted friend, or an enemy. They may not have asked you to visit in the first place. They are probably more nervous than you are, and eager to make a good impression on you. If you are visiting families in their homes, you are in a unique relationship. You will need to establish the purpose of the visiting relationship, set a mutually respectful tone, and help the family set and reach goals for the visits.

B. A family development approach to home visiting

Many agencies make home visits, but not all agencies use a family development approach. Today's home visiting is founded on the nineteenth-century tradition of nurses and teachers making home visits to "the poor," a tradition built on the deficit model. Although many modern home visiting programs have tried to incorporate some empowerment and family support principles, in reality many current home visiting programs are a mixture of deficit and empowerment orientations.

The skills you've learned in this book will help you make effective home visits using a family development approach. You've learned how to develop a vision for your work and create a support system for yourself. You've learned how to build mutually respectful relationships with families, maintain confidentiality, and help families assess their situations, and set and reach goals. You've learned how to communicate effectively with families and co-workers, and how to increase your cultural competence. All of these skills are vital for home visitors. In this chapter, we will not repeat these skills, but will focus on practical ways to apply them in the unique role of home visitor.

Home visiting programs with a family development approach often employ home visitors who live in the community in which visits will be made, or at least come from the same cultural background and speak the same language.

C. How to enter a family's home respectfully the first time and on future visits

Your first visit establishes the tone for your ongoing relationship with a family, so it is worth some advance thought. Your approach to a first visit with a family who is expecting you differs from a visit in which you show up "cold" at their door. A family may be expecting your visit after meeting you at a clinic, group meeting, or place they visit frequently (like a church, school, or senior center). They may have met you, heard about what you can offer, and agreed to your visit at a specific time. They may expect your visit after a referral from someone else. They may have requested your visit. In any of these circumstances, your entry into their home is eased by their agreeing to your visit because the family had a choice about whether to have you visit.

Preparing for the visit

It helps to confirm the date, time, and purpose of the visit ahead of time. You could give or send the family member a small, friendly-looking card with your name, agency name, address, and phone number, plus the date, day of the week, and time of the home visit. Write "home visit" on the card so they understand that you will come to their place. Add, in your own handwriting, "Please call if you can't keep the appointment." Avoid jargon. Write "I'd like to talk with you about ways we might help you with your heating bills," not "We want to determine your eligibility for a federally subsidized weatherization initiative for low income households." If the families you visit speak languages other than English, your agency should print cards and brochures in those languages.

Ask the family member for directions as well as the home address. Ask for any landmarks, and where to park (or which stop to take if you're using public transportation). Ask if there's anything else you should know, like whether there will be a dog, or if you will need to announce your arrival through an apartment building intercom and wait to be let in by the family member. When making your first visit, leave yourself extra time to find their home.

The clothes you wear for home visiting help form an impression of you and your agency. Your clothes should be clean and professional looking but not fancy. Wear clothes suitable to what you'll be doing with the family. For example, if you'll be sitting on the floor with preschool children, dress comfortably. If you'll be doing physical activity or therapy, wear clothes that allow you to move easily. Wear comfortable, sturdy shoes. If you have expensive (or expensive-looking) jewelry or purses, leave them at home. We do not suggest that you hide your personality, but advise you to help yourself fit easily into a family's home environment.

Arriving unannounced

It's much harder to get your "foot in the door" when you arrive without any prior arrangements. Since violence has become so widespread, many people are reluctant to allow a stranger into their home, or even answer the door unless they're expecting a visitor. We strongly encourage home visiting agencies to extend initial outreach in public settings where families already go, and to vigorously network with others in the community who are in a position to make referrals.

When you do end up at a family's door unannounced, there are several things you can do to increase your chances of being invited in. Carry your agency's brochure in your hand. Wear or carry a name badge with your name, photo, agency name, and phone number. Knock, ring, or buzz. When the person answers, say, "Hello, I'm Betina Lacrosse from the Community League. I'm walking (or driving) through your neighborhood today to talk with people about ways to get help insulating their homes and paying their fuel bills. If you'd like me to come in to talk, I'd be glad to. It will take about twenty minutes. If you want to call the Community League first to verify who I am, that would be fine. Or, we could make an appointment for another day if you'd prefer." Then wait for the family member to invite you in, call your agency, say, "No, thank you," or make an appointment for another day.

Asking a respected community member to accompany you is one way to increase your success rate on cold calls. For example, a religious leader who is concerned about elderly community members' difficulty paying winter heating bills might be willing to accompany you on first home visits. Alternatively, they might be willing to ask a respected congregation member to accompany you. People in the neighborhood will open their doors to this person, who can then introduce you:

> Good morning, Mrs. Taro. How are you doing? I'd like you to meet Ms. Lacrosse, from the Community League over on Bushwick Avenue. Ms. Lacrosse and I are visiting with older people in the neighborhood, to talk about ways to get their apartments insulated and get help with fuel bills. Is this a good time for us to come in?

Meeting outside

In warm weather, you might conduct many of your home visits outside, in the family's yard, or on their porch or stoop. Be aware of the family's privacy by using a quiet voice (unless you or a family member has a hearing impairment), and by creating a "zone of privacy" around you and the family member through body language. Ask, "Do you feel comfortable meeting out here, or would you rather meet inside or at our agency?" Families have many reasons for meeting outside, which may range from convenience and comfort while children are playing outside on a hot summer day, to a hostile family member asleep or drunk inside. Follow the family member's lead.

Keep good notes of your attempted visits, even if you don't connect with the family. Note people who were not home, or who seemed interested in a visit but were not ready to invite you or make an appointment at that time.

The first visit

It sends an important message of respect when you arrive on time. Approach the home in whatever way is customary in that region and community: knock, ring the bell, or buzz, and then announce yourself over the intercom, or when appropriate, call out (in a warm climate where windows are always open, for example). If you're announcing yourself within earshot of the neighbors, use your name, not your agency's, to preserve the family's privacy. "Hello, Mrs. Taro. It's Betina Lacrosse." Then, allow a moment for the family member to invite you in. If she doesn't, ask, "Is this a good time for me to come in?"

Every home visitor hopes the family will remember the appointment, be at home, and welcome her in. Experienced home visitors know that doesn't always happen. Maybe you will need to remind the family member of the purpose of your appointment.

> It's nice to see you again, Mrs. Taro. I'm Betina Lacrosse from the Community League on Bushwick Avenue. I enjoyed talking with you at the Senior Dinner last Thursday, and now I've come to visit as we agreed. I brought the information about insulating your apartment, as we talked about. The Community League helps older people get their homes insulated and makes arrangements for help with fuel bills if that's needed. Is this still a good time for me to visit?

While some families do have urgent reasons for not being home when you arrive for an appointment, many others use this as a technique for avoiding having to deal with you or make changes in their lives. Often, someone else is pushing them to work with your agency; they feel they can't say "no," but they are not really very eager to have you come.

Be polite and persistent but not pushy. If the family member doesn't seem to remember the appointment but is willing for you to come in, proceed with the visit. If she doesn't want you to come in, offer her a flyer about your agency's work, saying she is welcome to call for information or to schedule another visit. (Your agency should have an easy-to-read flyer, and you'll need to have it in your hand, not buried in the bottom of your purse or briefcase, or out in the car.) Leave the door open for future contact, but don't push yourself on the family. The family development approach only works if a family is ready to take some initiative and responsibility for their own progress.

If the family member allows you to come in, ask her where she would like you to sit. She may motion you to a particular spot, or may reply, "Oh, anywhere." At a focus group, a worker talked about paying attention to where people sit, so she could judge their comfort with physical closeness, which can vary in different cultures:

> We go into their homes and a lot of times we ask them, "Where would you like us to sit? What's most comfortable for you?" If [they] hesitate, I'll ask, "Where do you sit the most?" and then I'll choose another chair. Or I'll notice, once I've sat down, where they sit down, how far away they sit from me. It's important to respect those boundaries.

Family members often apologize for the messiness of their house, especially if they weren't expecting you. You can say something to put them at ease such as mentioning something positive about the family's home: "Are those pictures of your grandbabies? What beautiful children!" or "Did you crochet this afghan? It's so colorful!"

D. How to establish the purpose of the home visit

Once you've introduced (or reintroduced) yourself, are inside (or have "created space" outside for a visit), and have said something positive about the family or its home, get right to the point of why you're there. For example:

> We want you to be warm, and able to pay your heating bills this winter. I have information here about saving money through insulating your home, and about ways to get help with high heating bills. [If the person seems to be from another country where insulation isn't common, you'll need to explain what insulation is.] Heating bills can be an average of $_____ per month lower, once a house is insulated, although the actual amount varies according to how much insulation you already have, how you heat your home, and what kind of winter it is.

> The Community League receives money from the federal government to pay for insulation, and to pay workers to put it in. The government knows that insulating homes is a good bargain, because it keeps people in their own homes instead of having to move to subsidized housing. So, our League helps people figure out if they are eligible, and if they are, we arrange a convenient date for our workers to come to your home to measure how much insulation will be needed. Then, they come back later to put it in. We may also be able to help pay part of your heating bill if it gets too high. Are your heating bills a problem?

It is not always easy to decide whom to include in the home visit. Sometimes when you arrive, several people are there, and others may drop in during your visit. If you have the name of one person from a referral, and have located that person and been allowed in the door, ask him or her whom to include in the visit.

> Mrs. Taro, is there another family member or anyone else you'd like to include in our conversation? Your son helps you with maintenance on your house? Shall I explain this all to you, and then leave you with information you can talk over with your son? If he has questions, I could come back to talk with you both, or you or your son could call me with any questions.

E. Safety issues

Home visitors need to be alert to personal safety. It is likely that you will go into some unfamiliar or risky neighborhoods. You may be entering homes in which not all family members welcome your visit. You may be alone with families much of the time. There are practical steps you and your agency can take to increase your safety.

If you drive to home visits, your agency should consider supplying you with a cellular phone, which you can carry with you into the home if you're going into a neighborhood where you might want it for safety, or where the phone is in danger of being stolen from your car. Program 911 (or other local emergency number) into your phone's autodial memory, so you just have to push one button to get help.

Carry only what you'll need on that day in your bag; leave your credit cards, checkbook, and other personal valuables at home. Don't carry a big bunch of keys to your office or home with you. Put a single car key on a key ring or chain, and keep it in your pocket, easily accessible if you need to leave quickly. Keep your car in good repair, with a full gas tank. Use a bathroom in a public place like a gas station, diner, or community center before going out on a home visit.

Park your car so you can head out easily and quickly if necessary. For example, back into a driveway instead of planning to back out at the end of your visit. Lock your car door before going into a home to visit. This step is especially important if you carry confidential records in your car. Older children or neighbors may be curious (or in some neighborhoods, drug addicts or other people looking for something to sell may break in). If you feel embarrassed about locking your car door, thinking it sends a message of distrust, you can mention that it is agency policy.

Checking in with others

Many agencies ask home visitors to provide a designated person in the agency office with a detailed itinerary for each day when home visits will be made, including:

- planned departure times
- planned arrival times at each family's home
- address (and phone, if available) for each destination

Home visitors are asked to check in with their office by phone after visits, either routinely after each visit, or after visits they designate as potentially risky. If the office staff doesn't receive each check-in call, they alert another staff person or the police, who then search for the home visitor. Other agencies feel that such a stringent system is not necessary in the areas where they work, but they do supply home visitors with a car phone to increase safety and let home visitors know of canceled appointments called in by family members. Still other agencies pair up workers making home visits to risky neighborhoods or homes, so that home visitors don't have to go into potentially dangerous situations alone.

Once you and your program become accepted in a neighborhood, you might find that people you used to worry about can become your allies. Once the guys hanging out on the street get to know you and your work, they may help you out. "Hey! Monique's not home. She started having pains this morning, and went to the doctor."

Defusing "hot" situations

The skills learned in Chapter 2 can help you de-escalate situations that are beginning to feel "hot." It is a good idea for agencies to provide extra training for home visitors that is specific to nonviolent conflict resolution, so they will be skilled in defusing (instead of escalating) potentially violent situations. In many communities, dispute resolution or mediation programs can provide such training; in other communities, Quakers, the Alternatives to Violence Project, or other like-minded groups provide nonviolence training.

Using your intuition

While it is important for agencies to have safety policies to help protect home visitors, your most important safety resource is your own intuition. If you have a "funny feeling" when you are approaching a family's home, stop and listen to your own inner voice. Too often, people ignore these warnings because they are supposed to be at a certain place at a certain time and just keep going. Pay attention. Put your own safety first, even if it means canceling an appointment for what seems like "no good reason." You can always reschedule at a time when you can take someone else with you. If you are worried about a particular family (for example, if you see a weapon or drugs in their home), ask them to meet you in your office or at a community center, where there will be other people around.

If you begin to feel uneasy as you enter the home, sit between the door and the family so you can exit quickly if you need to. If you feel you need to leave quickly, you can ask the family member you trust most to walk with you to your car to get something you want to give her (it could just be a brochure from your agency). If you have to, just look at your watch, say, "I have to go now," and leave, even if you're in the middle of a sentence or activity.

Putting yourself first

If someone in a home you visit acts in inappropriate ways (for example, if a woman's male friend puts his arm around you or asks you for a date), use skillful speaking to let him know that you don't want to get involved in that way: "I'm here to work with Sandra and the children. If you'd like to join in our story reading, you're welcome to. But I can't get personally involved with you." These kinds of advances are usually a demonstration of power rather than a true misunderstanding of appropriate roles. He may be uncomfortable with the changes Sandra is making as a result of your home visits (like going back to school or getting out of the house more) and wants to demonstrate that he is still in charge. If he answers the door but there is no sign of Sandra, don't go in. Ask him to have her call you to reschedule the appointment. If he threatens you or says something like, "I raped two of

Sandra's friends," get out! Always keep in mind that your own safety is more important than whatever you're doing with a family.

F. TV, dogs, another cup of coffee: Handling the practical matters of home visiting

Experienced home visitors have developed many sensible strategies for handling the practical challenges of home visiting. In most of the homes you visit, there will be a TV on when you arrive (although the family won't necessarily be actively watching a program). TV is a distraction on many home visits. Don't hesitate to ask them to turn it down or off. Describe this as your need, not something wrong with them. Say, "I wonder if you'd be willing to turn the TV off (or down). I'm not as good as you are at concentrating when it's on." If they're actively watching the TV each time you come, say, "I've noticed there's a program you seem to like on TV each Thursday when I come at two o'clock. Is there a better time for me to come? I'm also available Mondays at one, or Fridays at ten thirty." A family member may like to watch her "program" every day at 2:00 p.m. but be too embarrassed to tell you. Or, she may be used to keeping up with the lives of the TV characters while carrying on other conversations.

Other family members

Interruptions from other family members, visitors, and phone calls can make it hard to keep your focus. Remember that what seem like intrusions from your point of view are part of the family's daily life. Try to look at them as potential opportunities to get to know other family members, and to build on family strengths. When the family member you're working with comes back from answering the phone complaining about her nosy sister, you could say, "We were talking about your plans to try to get a job. Do you think your sister would help in any way?" If a woman's husband or male friend hangs around the edges of your meeting (or stays in the next room, listening), ask her permission to invite him in. Say, "Frank is usually here when I come. Shall we include him in our conversation? I think he might have some good ideas about how you could get down to the job training center." If she agrees, you could say,

> Frank, it seems like you really care about Joyce and the kids. It's hard for most families to make ends meet these days, so a lot of families are trying to get as many of the family members as possible to have good jobs. Joyce said she's willing to take the job training program for computer operators down at the job training center on Peach Street. Right now, we're talking about how she'll get there, and we thought you might have some good ideas.

Dynamics often change depending on who is home. You might be working successfully with a teen mom and her baby or toddler, when the teen's mother arrives home. When you explain the program to her, she may voice (or silently convey) her concerns, causing the teen to withdraw or become defensive. Try to support the teen mom's choices, while conveying respect for her mother's home and opinions.

> I respect your goal of staying in school, Monique. You'll be able to provide better for your baby and yourself in the future, if you finish school now. You also want your baby to have a relationship with his father, so you want to keep seeing Fred. He says he's willing to help support you and the baby is he can have visitation rights.

> I also understand your viewpoint, Mrs. Martin. Monique is a big help with the younger children in the family, so it's nice to have her at home. You also resent the fact that Fred got her pregnant, so you don't want him around. And you haven't seen him follow through on any promise he's made so far.

> Monique, you have some important decisions to make, which will have a long-term effect on you and your baby. Mrs. Martin, your support is so important to Monique right now. It's obvious that you love her and your other children, and that you'll love this new baby, too. I'll be happy to try to help you find solutions that make sense to all of you.

Often when you're trying to work with an adult, children become very curious, and find ways to shift the attention to themselves. Consider carrying a small "goody bag" containing crayons, educational coloring books (for example on good foods to eat), puzzles, and other inexpensive but safe toys to offer to the children.

Animals

Dogs and other pets can present a major hurdle to home visitors. Some families keep guard dogs who are encouraged to bark furiously at strangers, or even to bite if not called off by their owners. Many other families keep dogs that they don't perceive as threatening ("Oh, don't mind him," they'll say about the dog snarling around your feet). Don't hesitate to ask a family member to call the dog off, or even put him in another room or tie up outside. Put your request in a positive light, as a way the family member can help you (instead of implying there is something wrong with the family for keeping such a dog). "Your dog does a great job of guarding your family! I'm not as used to dogs as you are. Would you mind putting him in another room, or tying him outside while I'm here? I would appreciate it so much!" Some home visitors carry dog biscuits in their pockets to offer to the dogs they encounter.

Other pets can interfere with home visits, too. If you're allergic to cats or dogs, you'll need to work out an arrangement with your agency (and the families who keep cats or dogs) so another home visitor can work with these families. In rural areas, roosters, goats, and other farm animals can be aggressive as you make your way to the house or trailer.

Food

Families often offer home visitors something to eat or drink. Sometimes what is offered is not what you would normally eat (for example, highly sugared donuts) or doesn't seem clean. Sometimes you are simply "coffeed out." Other times you worry that you may be taking food the family desperately needs.

Do you accept every offer in order to build a rapport with the family? Do you establish a policy of never accepting refreshments? Most experienced home visitors find a balance between these two extremes. You may want to accept food or drink offered by a family on the first home visit, saying, "Oh, thank you, that would be nice. I don't usually eat anything at home visits because if I did it all the time, I'd weigh five hundred pounds!" (Or, in the case of coffee, "My nerves would get so jittery, I'd fly away!"). "But, since this is my first visit in your home, I'd love to." Particularly if the family has prepared a cultural specialty, it may be worth it to accept "just a taste" and then rave about the food's and the cook's positive qualities (without overeating).

Or you might reply, when offered a cola or coffee, "Thanks so much, but what I'd really like is just a glass of plain water. I get thirsty from so much driving." Be practical: If you accept this offer, you'll soon have to find a bathroom, and the family might be ashamed of the cleanliness of their bathroom, or (in a rural area) might not have indoor plumbing or running water.

There are other ways to establish rapport besides sharing food. You can comment positively on children, photos, crafts, trophies, or any effort the family member has put into making a good life:

> "Your children are so lively and sociable."

> "I enjoy seeing the children's art work up on your fridge. You obviously have some artistic talent in your family!"

> "It's not easy for seven people to live in a two-bedroom apartment. I'm very impressed by the way you have things organized."

> "Look at those beautiful geraniums. Did you grow them yourself?"

It is often your "vibes" and body language that tell families whether you can be trusted and whether they should open up to you. Showing genuine interest in what they are sharing can go a long way. As a program supervisor said at a focus group:

> I find one of the most important things when I go visit a family is to sit there and listen. You have to be able to listen and to speak the language; even when some young people are speaking, I have to work to understand the words they use. But it helps to not be just pushing your agenda but to sit and listen.

It is a skill to be able to take some time to listen yet also be efficient, not taking up too much of your time or the family's.

Another supervisor said:

> I think there's a real skill to conducting an effective home visit. The workers that are best are those who are comfortable doing home visits—aren't frightened or intimidated, but who can also maintain boundaries. They can be open and listen, and speak in the client's language, but they are also there for a purpose and not to have a coffee klatch with the clients. And that's a skill.

Phone, e-mail, or texting contact

Communicating with families who don't have a phone presents another hurdle for many home visitors. Even when families give you a phone number (or a referral source provides one), the phone may have since been disconnected for a variety of reasons: not enough money to pay the bill, a move, or an attempt to avoid contact with bill collectors or an estranged partner. When you first make contact with a family (at a clinic, for example), ask if they have a phone, note the number if they do, and then also ask if there is a friend or relative you may call if you have trouble reaching them on this number. Each time you visit, ask, "Is [phone number] still your phone number?" Since this has become a routine practice in doctor's offices and other places families visit, they will probably take your question in stride.

If a family member tells you they don't have a phone, ask for the number of a friend, neighbor, or relative at which you can leave messages. Be very clear about the dates and times of your appointments, and emphasize that you will appreciate it very much if they will call your office when they need to change an appointment for a home visit. Tell them that they might not reach you directly when they call; they might have to leave a message with another person. If the agency phone is often busy, let them know good times to get through.

Setting up a regular weekly time to visit helps families remember when you're coming. You could say:

> It looks like Wednesday at ten thirty is a good time for both of us. I'll come every week at that time so we can work together on the goals we agreed upon. If you ever know you aren't going to be here at that time, or it's not a good time for me to come, please call my office to let me know. The number is here on this card. Please call by the day before, if you can; it will save me a lot of time. When you call, Li will answer the phone. If I'm there, she'll call me to talk with you. If I'm not there, or I'm with another family, please tell Li your name and the message you want her to give me.

At a focus group, a family member talked about prioritizing the family's schedule when workers plan times for home visiting:

> I think [it's important to take] that into consideration when they're scheduling programs, and even when they're scheduling their home visits, in terms of meeting the parent's needs, rather than their own needs.

G. Home visits in child protection or other domestic violence situations

Calling on a family that has been reported for possible child abuse or other domestic violence is among the most challenging home visiting situations. Your own safety may be in question. You have to determine whether it is safe to allow the child(ren) or adult to remain in the home, and if not, to withdraw them (and yourself) in the face of distrustful, potentially angry or violent family members.

Whether or not you remove someone from the home, you need to try to begin the process of opening the door to future positive contacts.

Your safety comes first

Your safety—and the safety of the child or adult you have been called in to help—is most important. You'll need to pay careful attention to the safety guidelines listed above for all home visitors, plus you may need some extra protection. Child protective caseworkers and domestic violence workers can usually rely on agency agreements with law enforcement officers to accompany them or at least back them up. If you do this kind of work and your agency has not yet established working relationships with law enforcement agencies in your community, ask your agency director to initiate such an arrangement. Where possible, participate in family development cross-agency training with law enforcement officers and other agencies who also serve the families you work with, so you'll all have a similar approach.

Using the Family Development approach

Although it is difficult to establish a mutually respectful relationship with a family when you've been sent to their home to investigate reports of abuse (and possibly to leave with their children), it is not impossible with the family development approach backing you up. The skills you learned in previous chapters will help you convey respect (even if there are certain behaviors—like child abuse—that you cannot allow to continue). For example, if a family member starts shouting and cursing about no-good social workers as soon as you explain the purpose of your visit, you can say, "I've met some social workers who take a hard line approach, too. I have a different approach than most social workers. I want to work with you to figure out how to keep your children safe and healthy."

It's always important to avoid bureaucratic jargon in your work with families, but especially so when emotions are running high and someone's safety is at stake. Don't say, "I'm here from the Department of Social Services Child Protective Service Unit to investigate a report of alleged child abuse." Instead, say "I am Rhonda Brown from the County Child Protection office. I was asked to come here to see if there are troubles keeping the children safe. I imagine you want to keep your children safe and healthy, and I want to find ways to work with you to do that."

This approach doesn't mean that you neglect your responsibility to vigorously and skillfully investigate a report of child abuse. When a child is obviously in danger, your job is to get that child to safety as quickly as possible, without risking your own safety any more than is necessary. That is still your first responsibility.

Looking beneath the surface

Most reports of child abuse and neglect are not that clear-cut. Some families are repeatedly reported for abuse or neglect, investigated, and their cases closed, when in fact their major problem is poverty. They can't afford good childcare, so they leave their children unattended at too young an age, or they leave the children in the care of slightly older siblings or other inappropriate caregivers. They can't afford medical care, and so may avoid taking children to the doctor until a serious illness develops. They often live in crowded, inadequate housing lacking safe, pleasant play areas. The parents often lack good education, and have a hard time getting or keeping jobs. The stress of raising children with little support often results in children who appear to be or who are neglected, and it sometimes leads to abuse.

These are the families you are most likely to be able to help create more positive environments for themselves and their children. But it is hard to do once they've pegged you as an enemy trying to take away their children and cause the family trouble. That is why it is often worthwhile to use the family development approach, especially when investigating a child abuse report in which you find a situation that is not clearly unsafe. This approach encourages rapport between you and the family, built on the presumption that you share a common goal, which builds trust.

H. Ongoing visits

In some home visiting situations, you'll only make one or two visits, but most home visitors establish a rapport and then work with a family for several months. The Family Development Plan you learned about in Chapter 1 is an important tool for keeping ongoing visits productive and focused on the family's goals. If you have not introduced the Family Development Plan during the first visit, be sure to make it the focus of your second visit. Establish a pattern of reviewing and updating the plan at the beginning of each visit (or at every second or third visit, if your visits are devoted to specific tasks like physical therapy or parent-child activities). For example, you could say,

> Your goal was to keep your children out of foster care. I'm impressed with the way you use the skills you're learning in your parenting classes to change Antoine's behavior when he starts to hit or yell. I noticed you've made a "time out" spot over there by the chair, and that you send him there for three minutes when he starts to throw things or biting his sisters. I really like the way you tell him what he can do, instead of telling him what he shouldn't do. And you said that his new childcare program is going pretty well. This is real progress toward meeting your goal. Congratulations on all your hard work! Now that you're going to parenting group on Wednesdays, maybe I could start coming every other week. Shall we try that for a month and see how it goes? How does that sound to you?

The goal of home visiting is to help families develop the skills they need to take good care of themselves and move toward their goals. In a sense, our goal is to work our way out of the job of home visiting. It is a real success when families don't need us anymore. For more information on ending relationships respectfully, see Chapter 7.

Activities to Extend Learning

Chapter 9
Home Visiting

A. Home visiting: A unique relationship

1. List some home visitors that a family working with your agency might have visiting their home. Describe the services each home visitor might offer them and how family members might feel about that relationship. What are some advantages of home visiting for families? What might be some disadvantages?

2. If you are a home visitor, how do you feel about working with families in places other than your agency office? What are some benefits you gain from working with families through home visiting? What are some challenges you've encountered? How do you help families feel comfortable to allow you into their homes?

3. Think of another home visitor that meets with families your agency works with (family worker from another agency, repair person, member of a religious or spiritual group). Imagine and describe the similarities and differences between a home visit you might have with the family, and a visit they might have with the other home visitor. How might the visits be similar and different in tone, purpose, and approach?

4. Describe some differences between a home visiting relationship and a personal friendship. How do you go about establishing a professional relationship while home visiting?

B. A family development approach to home visiting

1. Describe at least two features of a family development-oriented home visiting approach. Give a specific example for each of how you have implemented these.

2. With a new family you are home visiting, describe the family development approach to home visiting. Explain the difference between using a family development approach and the traditional model of home visiting based on the deficit model, they may have experienced in the past. Describe how you feel this approach to home visiting will help them set and reach their goals. How did they respond?

C. How to enter a family's home respectfully the first time and on future visits

1. Describe how you would prepare and present yourself for a home visit in the following situations: your first visit with a family who wants enrollment information in a new program your agency is offering, and an unannounced visit to tell a family about a new service.

2. List three ways of establishing a respectful relationship and building rapport on a home visit. What are steps you can take to encourage families to be at home and ready to work with you when you arrive?

3. Think about your clothes. What do you think would be appropriate to wear on home visits? Do you think deciding on what clothing, jewelry, or other accessories to wear are important considerations when planning a home visit? Why or why not?

4. How can you protect confidentiality while home visiting when neighbors, friends and extended family members are often in the home or in the same building.

D. How to establish the purpose of the home visit

1. How do you decide whom to include in the home visit?

2. What can you do or say to help a family who gets distracted from the purpose of a home visit? Share an example of how you handled this situation from your own experience.

3. What is the main reason or purpose that you make home visits with families involved with your agency? Write a short script as if you were talking with a family member for the first time to describe the purpose of home visits with families working with your agency or program. If their expectations are different from yours, how do you address that? Give a specific example.

E. Safety issues

1. List five ways you can keep yourself safe on home visits. Describe why each is important.

2. Have you ever listened to your inner voice and decided to reschedule or cancel a home visit based on your intuition? Briefly describe the situation and, if you know, what factors affected your decision. Why is it important not to ignore these warnings even if it means canceling an appointment for what seems like "no good reason"?

3. What is your agency's policy or procedure regarding home visits (scheduling, check-in, safety practices, visits alone or in pairs)? What personal safety measures have you practiced on your own to use on home visits? What community resources could provide helpful information about keeping yourself safe on home visits?

F. TV, dogs, and another cup of coffee: Handling the practical matters of home visiting

1. If you are a home visitor, describe ways you have handled the following situations that arise during home visits: small children who want your undivided attention, and asking a family member to relocate a pet that is either too friendly or distracting. How did the family respond? Is there anything you could have done differently?

2. List three ways besides sharing food that you can establish rapport with a family whose home you are visiting. Elaborate on how you have used these strategies and how effective they were in establishing a positive relationship.

3. Describe how you can communicate with a family that doesn't have a working phone or who doesn't respond to your phone messages or texts.

G. Home visits in child protection or other domestic violence situations

1. Describe your agency's protocol to keep yourself safe as a home visitor when there is suspected domestic violence. If there is no agency protocol, what steps would you take?

2. How could you use the family development approach to work with families you've been sent to investigate due to reports of abuse? What are some reasons "beneath the surface" that families may be repeatedly reported for abuse or neglect?

3. Write a short script describing what you might say to a family member you visit to investigate a report of abuse. What communication skills can you use to gain cooperation?

H. Ongoing visits

1. Describe how the Family Development Plan can help you focus your ongoing visits with a family.

2. If you are a home visitor who works with families over a period of several months, how do you help families stay focused and encouraged to reach their goals? How do you help families continue to recognize their strengths and complete steps when the goal is a complex one (such as paying off overdue bills or finishing a job training program)?

3. In this chapter it states: "Our goal is to work our way out of the job of home visiting. It is a real success when families don't need us anymore." How can you use ongoing visits to help families prepare for the time when your home visiting relationship will end? How do you help families appreciate their "success" when they become distressed that "succeeding" means that your relationship as a home visitor will come to an end?

Skills Practices

These skills practices are a suggested list. You may also develop your own skills practice or make modifications to the ones listed below to help you create a meaningful and manageable plan.

1. Review your agency's home visiting safety policy. Determine whether you would suggest any changes. Meet with your supervisor to discuss your suggestions and how you might assist her to implement the changes.

2. Prepare for a first home visit with a family. Refer to FDC skills you have learned about identifying strengths, building mutual respect, helping families set their own goals, confidentiality, and communicating with skill and heart. Write a plan for how you will try to incorporate these skills on a first home visit. Then, make the first home visit. After the visit, write a reflection on the skills you were able to incorporate. Did planning to incorporate these skills make your first visit with the family go more smoothly? If so, how?

3. Discuss with a co-worker who is also home visitor the meaning behind "putting yourself first" and using your intuition as important safety issues on home visits. Together, brainstorm ways to be respectful to families while taking care of yourself. Identify and develop a list of ways you and your co-worker can support one another when difficult situations arise. In addition, how can your agency better support workers who do home visiting?

4. Role-play the following situation with a co-worker: You have scheduled appointments to make a home visit to the Smith family on two occasions and each time you arrived they were not at home. Ask your co-worker to play the role of the Smith family member, and practice what you might say on a third visit about the importance of keeping the appointment or contacting you to reschedule the visit if their plan changes. Practice using techniques you learned in Chapter 2 to express yourself and to listen to the family. After the role-play, ask your co-worker for her/his feedback about what you did well and what you might do differently. As an alternative, address this situation with an actual family with whom you are having a problem being at home for their visits. How did they respond? Is there anything you would do differently?

5. Practice skills to establish the purpose of a home visit and communicate with a family who doesn't have a telephone. Write a letter to a family that has been referred to your agency for services but doesn't have a telephone for you to contact to schedule a home visit. In the letter, introduce yourself and briefly describe your agency and the services it offers to families. Explain the purpose of home visits, whom the family might decide to include, and the family information you will need. Provide information about how the family can reach you at the office or leave a message with another person to confirm the visit. Write a reflection about how you think a family member without a telephone feels and how a family worker can offer support.

Chapter 10
Collaboration and Community Support

Objectives

A. Learn skills that family workers use to foster supportive communities.

B. Help families identify and strengthen their informal helping networks.

C. Understand the purpose and benefits of support and advocacy groups.

D. Use the Family Group Conference model to help families make important decisions in their lives.

E. Teach leadership skills to family members so they can facilitate their own meetings.

F. Understand why collaboration is often one of the most challenging aspects of family development work.

G. Discuss ways to build respectful relationships with community service partners.

H. Explain the differences between coordination, cooperation, and collaboration in family development work.

I. Describe the different levels of collaboration most often used in family development work.

J. Use the "keys to successful collaboration" to build successful interagency partnerships.

K. Recognize common pitfalls of collaboration and know how to turn them into advantages.

L. Understand how agency, state, and national policies affect families and your ability to help them.

M. Learn how interagency training can promote interagency collaboration.

A. The importance of community

Communities have a profound effect on a family's ability to create and sustain a healthy interdependence with family members and others. Most families are members of several communities: their city, village, or rural area; cultural communities; and communities revolving around work, school, sports, music or other creative pursuit; church or spiritual group; other important interests in their lives. When communities break down, it becomes much harder for families to flourish.

At a focus group, a family member said:

> Communities have to realize that children are all of our responsibilities. I can't see your son doing something down the block and say, "Oh, that's not my son, my son would never do that," and turn my face and look the other way. Because, it could be my son. That is my son. We are all each other's children and brothers and sisters and mother and father. We all need to take care of all of our children.

A city or town that lacks safe neighborhoods, good jobs, or effective schools and other services is a hard place for families. Strong families face many extra problems when violence, lack of jobs and other social problems take over their community; for fragile families, living in a troubled community can be overwhelming. A supportive personal community of friends and relatives can strengthen a family's ability to become and remain healthy, but it cannot be expected to overcome the problems of a deeply troubled larger community or society.

One woman spoke about her toxic neighborhood:

> My daughter was molested by the neighbor. I wanted to move, so my daughter doesn't have to go outside and worry about the man next door. But, my husband says no, there's no possible way to do that except to create more stress; we just need to deal with it. The man next door is being prosecuted.

Knowing how to foster supportive communities is an important skill for family development workers. You need to know how to:

- promote the vitality and family-supportiveness of the city, village, or rural area where you work
- help families develop their own informal support networks
- help families conduct their own family conferences
- support family members in facilitating community meetings, and support and advocacy groups

At a focus group, a worker spoke about efforts to build a sense of community in neighborhood programs:

> What we try to do is try to get the different groups, their opinions on what they want to do in the neighborhood. Do you want a garden? Do you want a recreation program? Do you want a GED program? And, then try to go towards writing proposals, which we submit to different agencies. And, so far, little by little, they trickle in. At the time, what we're doing is, we're taking that group and, what do you want? Recreation, okay, fine. Now we set up that group and help them choose a leader, and then sit them down and then we continually work with them, help oversee them. At the same time, let them see it's coming from them, their input is important. And if you have your input in something, you're going to be more focused towards that, you're going to give more energy towards it, and then the fruit of everything is when you see it develop into a reality.

You also need to know how to facilitate family conferences, support groups, and community meetings, and to teach family members how to facilitate meetings so they will be able to work constructively with others toward reaching their mutual goals.

B. Helping families identify and strengthen their informal helping networks

Everyone needs to have a feeling of "belonging," whether to a couple, a family, a network of friends, a culture, or a voluntary group. Being at home within a community—knowing how to act, feeling accepted, making a contribution—is important to everyone's well-being. A supportive community can moderate the stresses of a troubled family life or a harsh work situation, and can offer the information and encouragement needed to make positive changes. Helping families build strong, supportive communities is a good investment of your time as a family worker, because it means families will be able to handle future problems with less agency intervention.

Using the Family Circles Assessment

Some people have the kinds of personalities that easily gather a community around them, but many others have a hard time creating or sustaining a supportive community, especially in hard times. The Family Circles Assessment, which you learned about in Chapter 4, is a good way to help families chart the networks they are part of and identify places where they could find more support from their informal networks.

A person whose Family Circles diagram shows many agency people but few personal friends is probably too dependent on agencies. Once this person has set a goal for himself (for example, finding a new job since he was just laid off), you can ask him who might be able to help him. Support him in making a list of these potential helpers, and ways they might assist him. For example, let's say a veteran formerly active in the VFW is looking for a job. His list might look like this:

1. Jason Andrews—works at store that has "Help Wanted" sign
2. My cousin Amy—started upholstering business that's making money
3. Other veterans—might know of job leads
4. Pastor Johnson—cares about us; knows lots of people
5. Neighbor Al—commutes to nearby city each day; car pool?
6. My mother—believes in me; will encourage me to job-hunt

Family and friends are often willing to help out if they know there's a need (especially when they see the person trying to help himself). Yet many people find it hard to talk with their friends, extended family, neighbors, and fellow group members about their troubles. You can help a person identify a goal and then practice describing it in positive ways that will invite people to help. For example:

> I just got laid off from the furniture plant. I worked there for nine years, driving a forklift, working as a security guard, and doing other jobs. I'm eager to get a new job, and am willing to do any of those things or try something new. My son is just starting his freshman year at the high school, so we'd like to stay around here. Would you be willing to help us out by thinking about who might be hiring, and telling me when you hear about job openings? Thanks! I really appreciate it. Here's a card with my name and phone number on it. I'll write "looking for a job" on it so you'll remember what it's for. Call me any time if you have a lead.

You can also help family members you're working with identify voluntary groups or organizations that might help them. The man in this example, you'll recall, is a veteran who in the past was active in the local VFW post, but lately has been too busy at work to go to meetings or volunteer. Asking him, "Are there organizations you're a member of, or used to enjoy being part of?" can help remind him of potential allies in his job search.

Linking with community groups

Informal networks are a mixed bag of stress and support for many people. Family members have their own problems, or are sometimes bent on giving unhelpful advice. Spending time with friends or participating in sports, clubs, or service organizations can take so much time that it angers other family members, or keeps a person from focusing on necessary goals. Your job is not to tell people what groups they should or shouldn't be part of, or how much time to spend in them. Your role is to encourage people to keep up the supportive relationships they have within their communities, to identify ways to let go of or change relationships that they think are interfering with their goals, and to forge new, supportive relationships that broaden their community.

At a focus group, a worker spoke about the goal of helping families feel more connected with their children's school:

> Our goal is to get parents involved with school and schoolwork, to show the parents that they are part of the community and that you keep your family together by involving them with the students in the schools.

Another worker talked about connecting a program participant to a play group:

> One of the goals we have begun work on is asking for help. Dorothy's cousin is a really good support for her and together we finally now got Dorothy to come to paly groups. I do two play groups a month. So she's built relationships with other families now where she just did not have that support, except her husband.

Although helping people strengthen their informal helping networks is an important aspect of family development, keep in mind that it takes time and other resources to build and maintain these relationships, resources that people living with poverty or other major stress may not have. That's one of the reasons why agencies will always play an important role in supporting families. We are not suggesting that all families should end all dependence on agencies, but that many families can become more independent.

A worker at a focus group explained the way that agencies can provide a helping hand when needed:

> While they're in the shelter or at our program, we hope that we can give them enough support in a way that empowers them, but which does not enable; which allows them to feel that when they're out in the community, either they can stand on their own, or they know how to access the supports that they need to get assistance when they need it.

C. Support and advocacy groups

Support groups can become an important aspect of a family's community, and can advocate for individual family members or for all people in a particular set of circumstances. Support groups are made up of people who share a common situation, such as being nursing mothers, parents of children with a specific kind of disability, or caregivers of Alzheimer's patients. Group members listen to each other's experiences, and share information that has proven useful to them. Often, support group members with more experience teach others how to advocate effectively for themselves and their family members, and raise awareness about their situation.

At a focus group, a worker said:

> One of the barriers that I see in our community is that many of our families live in isolation. Once they come to the center and are involved in parenting groups, a lot of support starts occurring. ... Also, a lot of learning that some of the things that they're going through are normal things that everyone goes through. There's nothing wrong with them. It's just part of being a parent.

Support groups may be sponsored by a voluntary organization and facilitated by a volunteer member, or sponsored by an agency and led by a professional. Learning to effectively lead group meetings, either of a support group or a community organization, can be a significant step in a family's (and their community's) empowerment. You will learn how to teach leadership skills in this chapter.

D. Family Conferences

In Chapter 7, you learned how to help family members set their own goals. Family conferences take this process a step further by supporting family members to make decisions together. A family conference is an informal meeting of all the members of a family who have a stake in the decision they're discussing (and are capable of helping to make the decision). Sometimes one or a few resource people (such as yourself) are also present.

Family conferences differ from other types of decision-making meetings, in that the family facilitates the meetings themselves, instead of relying on an outsider (such as a family development worker, or social worker, or probation officer). A family conference belongs to the family! When members of a family feel invested in making a decision, they are much more likely to support it afterward.

The New Zealand model: Family group conferences[43]

New Zealand has established itself as a world leader in helping families make decisions in high-stakes situations using a particular model of family conference called the Family Group Conference (FGC). New Zealand legislation enacted in 1989, the "Children, Young Persons and their Families Act," mandated that Family Group Conferences be used in all cases involving child protection and youth probation. It established a new and exciting balance between the various rights and responsibilities of families, agencies with concerns for the well-being of children, the state, and the children and young people themselves.

The power of a legal mandate

Conventional intervention for child protective and youth probation cases in New Zealand, as well as in the United States, resulted in children being taken away, parents left feeling like failures, families labeled dysfunctional, communities divided, and caseworkers left feeling frustrated and stretched. The goal of mandating Family Group Conferences in New Zealand was to legitimize families' roles in making important decisions for themselves; and to help to build strong, supportive, nurturing families who were able to function as independently as possible from the state.

Without a similar national law, the United States lacks legislative power to mandate a national system similar to New Zealand's. In the United States, family services are left to the states which often rely on counties or cities. For this reason, family policies and services vary greatly across the country. We can learn from New Zealand's successes as we help our agencies craft conferences with families.

This system is founded not only on the expectation that plans made by families are most likely to be successful, but also on a belief in the right of family members, and in the family as a whole, to have the opportunity as far as possible to determine family matters.

The New Zealand Family Group Conference model has two unique features:

1. The conference is organized by a Family Group Coordinator, who operates independently of the state.

---

[43] Extensive contributions by Aroha Wainui are gratefully acknowledged.

2. All professionals attending the conference must leave the room during the decision-making phase of the meeting, leaving that task entirely to the family.

The role of the Family Group Coordinator

In New Zealand, the 1989 law created a new position of FGC Family Group Coordinators are hired by the New Zealand Department of Social Welfare, but are independent agents whose sole task is to help families hold an FGC and create their own plan.

The FGC Coordinator carries the major responsibility for helping the family prepare for and hold a conference, and create a plan to resolve the situation. On a case-by-case basis, the preparation may be shared between the Coordinator and the family's caseworker, depending on the relationship between the caseworker and the family.

Preparation and planning

Preparation for the Family Group Conference is essential if the family is to have the best chance to create a successful plan for their children. First, the Coordinator meets with the family to enlist their support for having a conference, then they plan together about who will attend, where it will be held, and refreshments to be served.

The Coordinator meets with all family members who will attend to ensure that they understand the importance of this meeting in the life of their child(ren), and their role at the conference. Preparation also includes meeting with information providers to explain their role, help them understand the importance of their participation, and explain what they will be asked to share with the family. A checklist in the appendix outlines steps in each of these areas.

Who attends a Family Group Conference?

In the New Zealand model, all members of the child's family (defined by law as blood relatives) who can be located are invited to attend the FGC. The state pays for transportation and lodging for family members if needed. The child also attends unless it is determined that attendance would not be in the best interest of the child. A child might be exempted from participating if there is fear of a perpetrator, or if a child's age or level of maturity makes it too difficult to understand the proceedings. In such cases, an attorney is appointed to represent the child. (Since there is no law in New York State mandating which family members have a right to participate in these conferences, attendance at meetings of the Family Resolutions Project depended on decision making that occurred between the family and the Family Group Conference Coordinator.)

In addition to family members and friends chosen by the family, "information providers" are invited as guests for the first part of the conference. These are people who can share with the family information about the child's safety and the family's strengths, and include child protection investigators, medical professionals, police, therapists, teachers, clergy, and others.

Three stages of a Family Group Conference

After the groundwork is laid with careful preparation, there are three stages to the actual conference:

1. Welcome, introduction and information sharing

During the first stage, a family member and the FGC Coordinator extend welcomes to all present. If possible, the family conducts a ceremonial opening to indicate that this is a significant family gathering (a greeting by an elder, prayer, song, poem by a child). After participants introduce themselves, the Coordinator explains the process and purpose of the conference. ground rules are set, and answers any questions.

Then, both family and non-family guests provide information about the child's safety and well-being, as well as child and family strengths. Family members can ask questions. The "information providers" describe services they can offer, and explain any "bottom lines" (stated as behavioral outcomes) that must be part of the family's plan.

2. Private family meeting

Next, all who are not family members leave the room, and the family holds private family meeting where decisions are made. And a plan created to protect the child. This plan may include keeping the child at home while providing extra support for the parent(s), or sending the child to live with another family member for a period of time. Ways to monitor the plan to assure child safety are also discussed and written down.

It is critical that professionals/non-family members leave the room at this stage. If professionals attend or even observe the family deliberations, family members may not reveal their true feelings and important information. For example, the child welfare agency might see an aunt and uncle as good potential care-providers, but family members may know that the uncle has a history of child molestation. Yet they might never share that information in pub. In addition, if professionals do not leave the room, the family gets the message that they cannot manage their own affairs without professional help

3. Negotiating and finalizing the plan

During the final stage, the family's plan is shared with the Coordinator, child welfare worker and information providers still present. The details of the plan are negotiated and agreed to by the child welfare worker. The more specific the plan the greater the likelihood that everyone will follow through successfully. If, after the initial plan is implemented, the child protective worker has cause for concern about child safety, the Coordinator may be asked to call another conference. New Zealand law requires the family and the referral agency to agree on the plan and specifically outlines who has veto power over the plan. However, agreement is reached in most (90–95%) of these cases.

Monitoring the plan

Families need to identify individuals responsible for monitoring various aspects of the plan, when this process will take place, and how it will occur. These individuals will need to check in and make any necessary adjustments to the plan with the child welfare worker, not the Coordinator, whose job with this family will be over once the conference is finished.

Helping families facilitate their own family conferences

Family conferences can be useful in many situations other than those involving abuse or neglect. Parents may go back to school or change jobs; the family may need to organize support for a family member who is ill, aging, or a new parent. As a worker, you may help plan and even attend a family conference, but you will not run the meeting. Instead, you can play the role of coach, helping family members learn to run their own conference.

The first time a family member presents the idea of a conference to the rest of the family, he or she might be met with blank stares, lots of questions, or disbelief. "Are you kidding?" or "No way!" might well be the replies. But if a family member willing to serve as conference "leader" can explain how it can benefit each member, many families will try it out.

Usually the first family conference on a topic is spent laying out the situation, hearing everyone's thoughts, and deciding what information is needed before making a decision. (Sometimes a decision can be made in one conference, especially once the family is used to the process, and if they are careful to include the right people.) Many family conferences take place in the family home, but some happen in other places such as an agency or clergyperson's office. Your job is to help them have some success during that first meeting, so the family is willing to try it again. Once a family establishes the habit of holding a family conference when they need to make a decision, it gets much easier.

What can a family conference do?

Family conferences can change the balance of power in a family in ways that may be uncomfortable to some family members. For example, if parents are used to making all the important decisions for the family, they might not like having their teenagers hear about the rent increase, and express their opinions about where they'd like to live. They might find that the younger family members are willing to read the "For Rent" ads each day, help with packing and moving, or offer creative solutions like, "Our cousin Cori is going to computer school here in town starting next fall, and will need a place to live. Maybe Aunt Mable would pay the extra $100 a month so Cori could live here with us, and then we could stay. One hundred dollars is a lot cheaper than the dorm, and Aunt Mable is worried about Cori living away from home. Cori is crazy about babies so maybe she could share Julie's room." When family members are involved in a decision, they feel invested in the solution and are much more likely to support it afterward.

Teaching facilitation skills to families

Few family members have the skills needed to facilitate a family conference, but most can readily learn the basics. Similar to Family Group Conferences, the success of less formal family conferences requires attention to:

1. Getting the right people there
2. Setting the agenda
3. Agreeing on some basic ground rules, and then sticking with them
4. Reaching a decision everyone can agree with
5. Agreeing on a trial period to see how the decision works, and setting up a future family conference to see how the new plan is working

You can tell the family you will be happy to facilitate the first meeting, and will then help them plan and lead the next several. If the family wants to go ahead, facilitate the first meeting. At the end, help the family summarize its progress and next steps, and ask who would be willing to facilitate the next conference. Assure them that you will be there as a resource person if they want you to be. Offer to teach them some basic facilitation skills before the next conference. You'll probably need to schedule a session just for this purpose.

Suggested Guidelines for Family Conferences

1. *Keep the focus on the issues to be discussed.*

2. *Really listen to each other—no interrupting!* In some traditions, a "talking stick" is used. When someone wants to speak he or she picks up the stick or some other object, and puts it down when finished.

3. *Each person who wants to speak gets one turn before anyone else speaks again.* If any one person starts to dominate the discussion, others should notice and make sure everyone has equal opportunity to share their thoughts.

4. *Confidentiality.* Ask people not to share what is said at the meeting outside of this group.

5. *No blaming, put-downs, or physical assault.*

6. *Discuss the hard stuff.* Take risks to say what needs to be said, in order to resolve the issues.

7. *No one will drink alcohol during the meeting.*

8. *Stay in the conference for the whole time* (except for breaks, as needed).

9. *Say what you really feel.* It helps to say "I feel" or "I think" so that it is clear this is how you feel, while others may have differing views.

10. *Smoking.* State the agreements on smoking that the group wants to make. If you are meeting in a family's home, it may be up to them to choose if they will allow smoking, unless a participant expresses a strong request that no one smoke. If there is a "no smoking" agreement, be sensitive for the need for having at least a 10-minute break every few hours.

E. Teaching leadership skills to family members

A major goal of family development is to empower families to develop healthy relationships within their own communities, and to solve their own problems. The ability to effectively facilitate their own family conferences, support groups and community meetings is an important skill for family members to develop. You might feel that it is more efficient to facilitate these meetings yourself. Keep in mind that time invested in teaching families the process and coaching them through facilitating several of their own meetings is an investment in their future, when you (hopefully) will not be as involved in their lives.

Family members who have successfully worked with you to reach their goals, and learned how to use planning and communication skills are often interested in assisting other families. A sure sign of success in teaching facilitation and leadership skills to family members is their ability to supply this kind of support to other families. These basic skills learned during family conferences can help family members to get more involved in their communities, through support and advocacy groups or community meetings.

F. Collaboration

The word "collaboration" comes from the roots "co-" ("together") and "labor" (work). Family development workers need to know how to work together effectively with families, with others in your own agency, and with other agencies and organizations in your community. It sounds simple, doesn't it? Yet collaboration is seldom simple, and is often one of the most challenging aspects of being a family development worker.

How does collaboration work—and not work?

At its best, *collaboration* means different people or groups working together toward a goal they all agree on, with everyone doing what they do best. Collaboration often breaks down when one or two people or agencies set the goals and then expect the other "collaborators" to support these goals (without any power to make decisions). This does not mean that everyone needs to make every decision together. It does mean that the collaborators need to decide in the beginning who will be in on what kinds of decisions.

Sometimes collaboration breaks down because people grow frustrated with being assigned tasks that don't interest them or use their strengths. In other situations, a family's needs are not within the realm of what an agency can offer, so the agency just passes them along to someone else without any real help to the family, instead of getting back to the referring agency to explain that they need to find a more suitable referral.

Why collaborate?

There are many benefits to collaboration. Working collaboratively with families is an empowering way to assist them in reaching their goals. Collaboration with other agency workers can make it possible to work much more effectively with families than one agency operating alone. As workers from various agencies come together to engage with families, they get to know each other and understand each other's services and approaches. Collaboration can make better use of resources and can save agencies money. It can bring more creative energy and resources to a situation or problem. Collaboration can promote the family development approach because workers learn from each other new ways of working with families.

G. Building respectful relationships with community service partners

How do you network and build respectful relationships with other family-serving agencies that may lead to interagency collaborations? Both you as an individual worker and your agency need to know how to reach out in creative and effective ways to government agencies, businesses, and faith communities who may want to collaborate with you through family development opportunities. You can increase your agency's ability to collaborate effectively in three ways:

1. Be accessible and responsive through networking and learning about the needs and interests of potential community service partners.
2. Make sure community partners and service providers who could refer families to your agency understand and support what you offer.
3. Help service providers that show interest to learn about your agency's services. Build and maintain mutually respectful relationships with them.

Being accessible and responsive to your community service partners' needs and interests

Most agencies think they offer what families want and need, and establish interagency relationships with other services providers to bridge gaps in supporting the specialized needs of their families. When a worker from another agency calls to ask for information or to refer a family to your agency's programs or services, you have an opportunity to develop a respectful relationship. Also, it helps to meet with workers from other service providers that you refer families to from time to time, introducing them initially to family development and what your agency has to offer, and then keeping them up-to-date.

Helping community service partners learn about your agency's services

If your agency wants to reach a particular community service provider, you need to get to know people in that agency. As a front-line worker, you probably have good ideas about who these people are and could pass this information along to your supervisors, offering to help with outreach if needed. Make sure community service partners that could refer families to your agency are aware of, understand, and support what you offer. You also need to know the "gatekeepers" in your community, the people whose support will help your agency do its work, and whose negative impressions will hinder you. Gatekeepers are different in each community, but should not be overlooked. They are people who refer families to you: people in official and unofficial positions of respect such as other agency workers, religious leaders, leaders of civic groups, school principals, the director of the local Youth Bureau or Office for the Aging.

Informal gatekeepers are also very important: for example, a seasoned, respected mother of two grown children with development disabilities, who for years has functioned as an informal "information and referral" service for other families. Another example of an informal gatekeeper is the former welfare recipient who has "made it" into a good job, remained in the community, and is dedicated to helping other families move out of poverty.

Anyone people talk to, for example, a beautician or bartender, can be a gatekeeper. They can keep people out of your program or encourage other agencies to work with you. To meet the specialized needs of families in your programs that your agency doesn't currently offer, you need to have up-to-date knowledge and positive relationships with other service providers in your community.

H. Coordination and cooperation: The first steps toward collaboration

Coordination is a first step to collaboration. Sharing information with families about another agency and making referrals is an example of coordination. Checking with other organizations about their hours when planning your services, or listing another group's events in your newsletter, are other examples of coordination. Coordinating schedules or the use of rooms, vans, or equipment requires more effort, and may involve some compromises, but still no fundamental change in the way you each work. You've helped each other out, but no one has changed the way they do business.

When people or groups *cooperate*, they agree to help each other out in specific ways. Cooperation often leads informally to bigger changes, because people begin to trust each other, and see better ways of doing things. For example, several agencies can provide different services to the same family (and sometimes meet together with the family). The agencies may change the ways they work because they see other agencies working very effectively, but there is no agreement among them to work in a certain way.

In a collaboration, partners agree on common goals that are beyond what any one person or group can accomplish alone. They all work toward those goals and the effort does not "belong" to any one of the partners more than any others. Collaboration involves joint planning, pooling resources, and evaluating the outcomes together. Partners in a collaboration usually need to make some changes in the way they each work. For example, a Neighborhood Watch association teams up with a local Office for Aging, youth organizations, and police to collaborate because they all want to prevent crime. They establish a youth escort service for elders, learn new ways of protecting themselves and their homes, and agree on how police officers will handle reports from neighborhood residents. No one person, family, agency, or organization could accomplish these goals alone.

Effective family development work is a collaboration between a family development worker and a family. It begins with building a mutually respectful relationship, and moves on to joint agreement about goals. You and the family plan together. You combine resources the family can provide with those you can bring from your agency and others. You continually reassess progress toward the goals they have agreed on. The outcomes of this collaboration cannot occur without the resources and contributions of both.

I. Different levels of collaboration: Individuals, front-line workers, and systems

Coordination, cooperation, and collaboration can take place at several levels.

Individuals

Individuals (friends, family members, or people who work together) can decide quite easily to coordinate or cooperate. Two workers in the same office *coordinate* by agreeing to take their lunch breaks at different times so the phone is always covered. Family members *cooperate* by pitching in to get the apartment cleaned up. Individuals *collaborate*, too. A couple talks over how they will care for their toddler and new baby. After weighing their options, they decide the mother will quit her job to stay home and care for both children. Her partner will work overtime to replace the lost income. After six months they evaluate how their plan is working and realize the overtime is becoming too stressful. Yet they do need the extra money. They decide the mother will begin doing family day care for two other children and the father will go back to regular hours.

These two individuals agreed on a common goal that neither could accomplish alone (raising a family together). They planned together. They pooled their resources. They evaluated how it was going and readjusted. They *collaborated*.

Front-line workers

As a front-line family worker, you collaborate with families, with your co-workers, and with other agencies. The collaborative approach with families was stated clearly by a worker at a focus group:

> My primary goal is to create an atmosphere where there's a sense of partnership and mutual discovery about what the partnership can hold and what this family believes will be best for them.

There are many ways to collaborate with other agencies. The primary type of interagency collaboration between front-line workers is collaborating around the needs of a particular family. Few agencies can meet all the service needs of the families they work with, so they have to collaborate. This is your main opportunity to find out what you can realistically expect from workers in other agencies, and to earn your agency a reputation for being reliable, skillful, and collaborative.

When families are ready and workers in other agencies are willing, you can suggest a meeting between you, a family you work with, and other agencies who also work with that family. The purpose of such a meeting is to review the family's goals, and decide what each person or agency can contribute. Because family members may be intimidated by such a meeting, preparing them and the other agency workers is crucial. If the family can take an active role in this "case conference," and the other agencies are willing to work with the family members as equals, the family can emerge with an updated plan in which all the necessary agencies have agreed to their specific parts.

Often there is a gap between the goals a family has worked out with you in the family development process, and other agencies' perceptions of the family's goals and progress. Supporting the family in preparing for and taking an active role in their own "case conference" can open other agency workers' eyes to the family's strengths and motivation, as well as the reality of their need for services.

Many frustrations can arise in collaborating with front-line workers in other agencies. Some workers may be less skilled or committed to their work than you, or so steeped in the deficit model that they regard themselves more as vigilant gatekeepers of their agency's services than as collaborators with families. This is especially frustrating when you understand the eligibility requirements of their agency, and know that the family you are both working with is eligible for and badly needs their services. There are six steps to take in this situation:

- Briefly listen to the family members' complaints and needs, using the communication skills you learned in Chapter 2. (Don't get caught in their drama. You need to maintain a good relationship with the other agency if you are ever to influence their ways of working with families.)

- Help the family members decide what they want to do. Be careful not to steer them in a direction you think is best. Deciding for themselves is a crucial step.

- Help them get accurate information.

- Help them learn and practice skills needed to get the necessary services. This could include role-playing a conversation with a worker from another agency.

- If their efforts don't work, advocate for the family with the agency worker. Make sure you allow the family to try first before stepping in.

- Educate front-line workers from other agencies about family development.

These same steps work equally well if a family attempts to play one agency against the other. Family members you are working with may complain bitterly about all the workers who have mistreated them, praising you as the only one who really helps. They may even use what you have told them about family development and empowerment to illustrate their problems with other agencies, attributing their problems to the deficit model! This situation is especially risky when you know that some of their complaints are probably well founded.

While it is nice to be appreciated, don't let people put you up on a pedestal; if you do, you will inevitably be knocked down. You may be the "bad guy" next week or next month. You will help families best if you stick to the actions listed above, which empower families to help themselves.

Front-line workers collaborate with each other across agencies in other ways as well. You may decide to be part of a group dedicated to finding better ways to inform families about needed resources: for example, a computerized human services directory in libraries throughout a rural area, or a group working on an issue facing your community.

The nature of collaboration groups varies from a short-term project such as co-sponsoring a training workshop, to a longer-term interagency effort such as a task force working on services particularly needed in your community. They might study the issues, set goals, and even apply for funding for new services.

In a focus group, we heard about a successful collaboration that led to a sustained community program:

> A few years ago the Mental Health Association had a Community Trust Fund Grant, and we pulled together in a very short period of time a number of different agencies that were really dedicated to trying to pull together services in the area of family violence. And out of that came the Family Resource Center and the Violence Intervention Program for batterers of women. Other liaisons are now being formed with Urban New York Center Outpatient Treatment Facility, free investment money to maintain a parent aid program. ...

> So a lot of really wonderful things happen when you start working with each other, in different ways, through grants, or community planning or whatever. And often times, it's something that continues to benefit the community after the initial money is gone. Once the community realizes it's an important piece of keeping families together, no matter what, they're willing to work on it at whatever level.

262

Systems

Sometimes agency workers feel limited in the amount of collaboration they can do because the funding source may not value collaborative efforts as much as they do an agency's individual efforts. Another major frustration arises when families encounter conflicting requirements from the various agencies whose services they are trying to obtain.

The ability of individual workers or even of agencies to work together is limited unless the *systems* they are each part of begin to recognize the value of collaboration. Most local agencies are part of state (and often federal) systems. For example, a local agency that counsels people who are recovering from alcohol addiction is usually regulated by a state agency. This state agency might license alcoholism counselors, provide funds for local agencies, and review their progress on stated goals and objectives. If the state agency does not value collaboration, the local agency's ability to devote resources to collaborative projects will be limited.

When state agencies do support collaboration, services can be delivered more effectively to families. A very broad example of collaboration is several community agencies working together to create a "seamless" transition between their services for families, so that once a family is working with one agency in the coalition, they can receive services from another without a whole new intake process.

A worker in a focus group shared this example:

> You know on a small scale that was attempted here. We had a Coalition on Adolescence Pregnancy Prevention. Rather than one agency trying to solve each individual's problem, we had core agencies that we worked with and one intake form was developed.
>
> An individual would come to me with a certain problem, and I would fill out the information with her. If I could not handle that problem I would refer that to program B, not guessing that program B could do it, but knowing that program B can do it. When Jane Doe goes to program B, they are already expecting her. Jane Doe walks in the door, "How are you doing, Jane? I talked to Mr. _____, come in." Now Jane is already feeling relaxed.
>
> Now this person at program B may be able to help Jane's family with part of their problem. When needed they'll refer them on to the next agency, with another very personal referral. In other words, the whole person could be served within three or four agencies. It worked fine for a while, but I think everybody started going their own way; directors changed, personnel changed, so nobody really followed up on that good model.
>
> So, I think that if the state agencies [in Family Development] can come up with a general approach, if that indeed can happen, that's good! In terms of meeting the needs of your funding source, every agency would be able to count Jane Doe as a client because it did perform a service. You could count how many times you dealt with the person.

"Seamless" family services, in which one worker works consistently with a family to make sure they don't fall through the cracks and then end up, more troubled, back in the "system," require collaboration at each stage of planning and service delivery.

The most effective systems-level collaboration begins with needs assessment. Too often, systems only begin to collaborate because someone has an idea for a program that requires several partners, or because funders require interagency collaboration. While worthwhile initiatives for families can emerge from these types of collaborations, it is even more effective to begin with collaborative assessment of the community, and use this assessment (and the partnerships developed through the process) as the springboard to offering a service that the community needs.

J. Keys to successful collaboration

As a front-line family worker, you will sometimes have opportunities to work with interagency groups to fill some of the gaps families encounter in your community. The skills you have already learned in collaborating with families are readily transferable to working with interagency groups. The seven steps of Family Development will also work in interagency collaborations:

1. *Develop a partnership with the people or agencies* you want to collaborate with.

2. *The collaborators assess their reasons for collaborating and their strengths.* This is an ongoing process.

3. *The collaboration group sets its own major goal,* and smaller goals working toward the major goal. They identify action steps for reaching these goals.

4. *The collaborators make a simple written plan for pursuing these goals,* having made decisions about who will be responsible for which tasks, including the tasks of convening group meetings, setting agendas, and following up (leadership tasks). This plan must be straightforward and doable enough to actually be pursued. Accomplishments are celebrated, and the plan is continually updated.

5. *The collaboration group learns and practices skills needed to accomplish its goals* (for example, group process and decision making or publicity). This is an ongoing process.

6. *The collaboration group uses members' skills and contacts as stepping-stones to reach its goals.* They may also decide to ask for assistance from others outside their group when needed, for example, to accomplish specific tasks or to improve the way their group is functioning or making decisions.

7. *The group's ability to work together to accomplish a goal is developed.* Each member's skills and abilities are strengthened through this process, so they are better able to handle future challenges and collaborations.

Developing a partnership

Collaborations usually begin because someone has an inspiration that they need help to accomplish. Before any real progress can be made, the people involved need to figure out how they are going to work together. First, the people or agencies in a collaboration need to develop mutually respectful relationships. Once these connections have developed, and the group has done some successful work together (even small tasks), people will start to trust each other more.

Doing this in a group is similar to the process you go through with families, only it is complicated by all of the different personalities, agency issues, and goals in the group. Sometimes groups lose their focus before they are able to build trust or figure out how they are going to work together.

It helps for one person or group to suggest some simple ground rules (see section on ground rules, below), and then ask if all others can agree to them. If anyone has a problem with some of the ground rules, ask for an alternative, and then ask the group if they can agree to the suggestion. If you think a group you are part of is getting stuck, politely help the facilitator move the meeting along:

> My agency asked me to attend this meeting because we are concerned about the lack of housing for people with low incomes in this community. We want to be helpful. Those ground rules sound good to me. I need to leave by 10:30 to meet with a family. Are there other things on the agenda I can be helpful with while I'm here?

You can support the group's productivity by helping to keep the focus on the reason you all came. The skills you learned in Chapters 2 and 6 will be very helpful in establishing collaborative relationships with families and other agencies.

Assessing reasons for collaborating

The next step is to help the collaborators clarify their reasons for working together, and identify contributions each can offer the project. This is an ongoing process. Only after this foundation is solidly in place can the group set its major goal, and define the smaller steps that will lead to achieving that goal. Unfortunately, many groups jump in with a goal set by one person or agency, without going through the crucial first steps as a group.

A group that doesn't take the time to clarify its goals together, and consider what each person or group brings to it, will often break down in the middle of an important project. The vision will not stay in focus when times get tough if it was never jointly developed. The preliminary steps of setting ground rules and setting a goal don't need to take a lot of time, and they can be changed later if the group wants.

Setting goals and making a written plan

It is valuable for a collaboration group to *write down* its goals, and the steps needed to reach these goals, indicating who will be responsible for which tasks. Even if you are not the group's leader, you can help by offering to bring newsprint (big paper), markers, and tape, and to write down possible goals as your group discusses them. Don't change what other people say, just write their words on the newsprint and ask if you got it right.

Then the meeting facilitator can help your group decide which goal to pursue first, and what steps to take. If the facilitator doesn't take this step, you can suggest it, because you are a member of the group. When the group is discussing goals and action steps, you can offer to take notes on newsprint. Most facilitators will be grateful to a group member who is willing to help in this way, and you will have the satisfaction of helping your group make progress.

The step of dividing up tasks can be delicate. The facilitator will probably ask who is interested, and who has the time and resources to accomplish particular tasks. Once each person's desires are on the table, the group will need to negotiate responsibilities. To create a structure of accountability, it is important to write down these commitments. These decisions will need to be reviewed as the group progresses toward its goals, because some people may need to reevaluate where they can make their best contribution after they have thought more about it and, possibly, talked with their supervisor and/or co-workers.

Learning and practicing skills

Your group members may need to learn some new skills in order to reach your goals. One of the advantages of group collaboration is that it increases the range of available skills and contacts. You will teach each other and you can invite additional assistance as needed. As your group meets its goals, the confidence and ability of group members will grow. You will each know better which people and agencies you can work easily with on future collaborations. For example, your group may decide it wants to make a video about low-income people's struggles to find decent housing, and show it to local organizations. People in the group might need to learn how to interview people, make and edit videos, set up and run video players, make presentations, and meet with the press (or find people who have these skills and are willing to work with your group).

Celebrating accomplishments

Celebrating accomplishments together is too often overlooked because each agency is on to another project, or another crisis. Be sure to take the time to celebrate your joint accomplishments with the families, workers, funders and others who have supported the collaboration. You will also need to check back with each other periodically, to continually update the plan.

K. Practical pitfalls of collaboration—And how to turn them into advantages

Knowing what can happen to disrupt a collaboration before you begin working can help you to plan a more successful working relationship.

Collaborating on tasks that really don't require collaboration

If you are looking for the fastest way to get a simple task done, don't collaborate on it. Do it yourself, or delegate it to someone else. If, on the other hand, you want to accomplish something that one person or agency can't do alone, or will have much more impact if done with others, that is the time to consider collaboration.

Maybe you want to encourage another person or agency to grow in their ability to do something you are good at (or you want to learn from them). Maybe you want another person to understand better what your agency does. These are also worthwhile times to collaborate.

Carefully consider what you or your agency wants to accomplish, and which would benefit from collaboration. Choose only one or two to work on, so you can invest the time needed to build reliable partnerships.

Underestimating how much time it takes to collaborate

People and agencies do not just magically collaborate. It takes time to do the following:

1. Build mutually respectful relationships.
2. Talk over goals, and define goals you can all agree on.
3. Discuss individuals' responsibility for tasks.
4. Work out the leadership.
5. Negotiate about money and other resources.
6. Schedule and attend meetings. Make phone calls. Write follow-up letters and agreements.
7. Get support within your agencies or families.
8. Clear up misunderstandings.
9. Get back to each other.

Ironically, many potential collaborations have been damaged by hurrying to create a "collaboration" to meet a deadline for a grant proposal that required interagency collaboration! Agencies get overlooked in the hustle, or are offended by being asked only for a letter of support (when they wanted a bigger role and/or a share of the grant money!). Rushing may undermine your collaboration, making it less effective and your goals more difficult to accomplish, or causing the intended effort to fail.

When you begin collaborating (whether it's with a family, a co-worker, or with another agency), first talk over your goals. If you agree on goals, then talk over who will do what, and when. Draft a simple work plan for the length of time you think you'll work together on your joint project. List the tasks. Note how long you think each will take. Put initials next to each task to show who will do it. Then talk over this draft work plan with all of the collaborators on your joint project, and revise it where needed. Be sure to build in time for meetings and phone calls with each other.

Drafting a simple work plan and talking it over will give you all a realistic picture of how much time each of you will need to put into your joint project. Then you can each decide if it is realistic to collaborate on this project. If your agency has assigned you to collaborate on a project, try writing out a work plan for your part of the project. This will help you talk over with your supervisor any changes you might need to make in the rest of your job to assure success with new collaboration responsibilities.

Lack of clarity in leadership

The way leadership is carried out in collaborations can vary a great deal. Sometimes a lead agency reaches out to other organizations. The group makes decisions but the lead agency retains central leadership functions such as convening and facilitating meetings, keeping minutes, and following up to ensure that tasks are getting done.

If it is a short-term group and the issues are not too complex or controversial for any of the agencies, this can be an effective way to work. Be aware, however, that there is great power in setting agendas and leading meetings. If the group is to be truly collaborative, it may be better for the group to share leadership.

Leadership does not have to be traditionally hierarchical, where the "chair" or "president" is responsible for the group's progress and outcomes. The group can appoint one person to assemble the agenda and another person to chair or facilitate the meetings, or these roles can be rotated between members. Because few of us are experienced with such a process, it may flounder a bit initially. As the group becomes comfortable sharing power, individual members are empowered by the process and the group can begin to take real ownership of the collaboration. If you represent your agency in a collaborative group, remember to check in with your supervisor and/or co-workers when key decisions are being made.

The way leadership is handled will make the difference between success and failure for a collaboration. No matter how relevant the goal, how carefully the collaborators are selected, or how much money is available, every group of interagency collaborators needs to figure out how they will make decisions, and who will take responsibility for each task. As a front-line family worker, you can urge any interagency group you are part of to clarify leadership responsibilities.

"Turf" issues

Within families, individuals occupy roles or "turf" that give them a sense of identity; they can experience others' interest in those roles as unwanted interference. For example, in some families the children's health care is the mother's turf. She may feel defensive if someone else (like a family development worker) asks whether the children's immunizations are up-to-date.

Agencies often have similar turf issues. An agency that has been providing the same service for many years may feel threatened if another agency begins offering a similar service, or doing things in a new way. In most communities, each agency has its turf staked out.

Anything that jeopardizes this informal, often unnamed arrangement—like a large new grant, or several agencies agreeing to shift to the family development approach—can upset this balance. Agency administrators want to make sure they will still receive funds to operate their agencies. Workers begin to worry whether they will have jobs if another agency begins offering a service like "theirs."

These turf issues can be very frustrating to front-line family workers. You understand the urgency of families' needs within the community, and want to spend your time doing things that make a real difference to families. Even after agencies have agreed to collaborate, turf issues can disrupt the collaboration. For example:

- Too much time is taken up deciding which agency's name is listed first in publicity (it helps to do it alphabetically).
- A few people dominate the collaboration meetings.
- In a public meeting, one organization announces major decisions that affect the rest, yet their "collaborators" weren't consulted on these decisions.

Understanding why people and agencies are often so touchy about their turf can help you know how to handle turf issues. Every person has an "identity," the part of ourselves that says, "I am this, I do that." Work is a big part of many people's identity. Many agency workers' identities are intertwined with the services their agencies provide. Collaborations offer endless opportunities for identities to be shaken. When identities are threatened, it becomes very difficult to collaborate.

What can you do about turf issues? First, be generous with genuine appreciation for your collaborators (and potential collaborators). Tell others (in public, if possible) about the good things your collaborators do. If you have concerns, raise them privately, using the communication skills you learned in Chapter 2. Earn yourself and your agency a reputation for reliable good work. Take on only what you know you can follow through with. Be trustworthy.

When you or your collaborators seem to be getting caught up in turf issues, bring yourself (and your collaborators) back to the reason you are collaborating: to help families become more empowered and self-reliant. You may want to tape this question on the front of your calendar, and ask it in a respectful tone during meetings with your collaborators:

How will this action help families become more empowered and self-reliant?

If you are not satisfied with an answer, it would probably be best not to do what is being proposed.

Leaving out key people or agencies

If you are beginning a collaboration either with a family or with another agency, be careful not to leave out important people or agencies accidentally. In some families, a religious leader is consulted before a big decision is made. While it is probably not appropriate for you to contact that person when you are working with a family, failing to leave time for the family to talk things over with this person can mean that any decision you think has been made is actually tentative until that person is consulted by the family. It also helps to include religious leaders in your agency's general outreach efforts, so they'll know what your agency's purposes are, and how you work.

There are people and agencies in every community who must be included if a collaboration is going to succeed. Ask collaborators you trust who the key players are. Someone in your group should call these key players to explain the need for the proposed project, and then invite all of the potential collaborators to meet to discuss the need for your project, whatever it is.

Your group could agree that for the next three months (or some other specified time), new collaborators are welcome to participate. That way, if you have left anyone out, they have a chance to join in. As a member of an interagency group, you can welcome newcomers warmly when they do come. You don't have to be the group's official leader to graciously greet newcomers.

Help your group to remember that some people with important viewpoints or information may not choose to take an official advisory role, but would still be willing to share their thoughts with a group member by phone or in person.

When you begin to think about a collaboration, or at a first meeting of a collaboration group, consider together whether you have all the "players" at the table, or whether you want to suggest inviting other key people or agencies to join the group. Think about diversity: are groups you work with represented appropriately? For example, if you want to look at social activities for young people in your community, do you have young people in your group?

You may feel that the collaboration will be most effective if you invite the families who are most affected by the problem to join in the collaboration. Some other agencies might balk at this idea. It is worthwhile to bring families into the decision-making process, even if your collaborators think this is a lot of trouble.

Lack of a common vision

Lack of a goal you all agree on, and differences in your ideas about how best to reach that goal, are the most frequent collaboration pitfalls, whether you are working with an individual family or with an interagency group. You might agree on a very big goal, like "increase the family income" (for a family) or "do something about homelessness" (for a community). But in order to make a real difference, all of the collaborators must agree on smaller, more specific steps, measurable objectives, and strategies. This process of reaching agreement is an essential stage in the collaboration. It is here that you all learn how to work with each other most effectively.

For example, a family that wants to increase its income will, with your help, explore various possibilities. Maybe one family member who retired two years ago is willing to start working again part time. Another family member who is still working would like to switch jobs but wonders if she could get a job that would pay more than her current one. She is also thinking of taking on a second job, part-time.

You help the family explore what is behind their desire for more income. Are their housing costs too high? Do they need money for their daughter's college costs? Will a higher family income reduce the scholarships they will be eligible for? Has the daughter applied to a state university, where tuition will be lower? Can the daughter work part time while in college?

Although this family stated that their goal was to increase their income, once you help them clarify their goals, it becomes clearer that the common vision they all share is to see the daughter graduate from college. Once all the collaborators agree on this common vision, they can begin to work on the smaller, more specific steps needed to reach those goals.

Your experience as a family development worker can help you with interagency collaborations, too. Perhaps your agency and several others are concerned about the families you work with who are homeless (or close to becoming homeless). Someone thinks the city should open more shelters. Someone else thinks their agency should apply for a big "homelessness prevention" grant. The police department wants money to hire more officers to patrol the streets at night, taking people to shelters when needed. A housing agency wants funds to repair old apartment buildings, so they can increase the supply of low-rent housing. A young mother currently living in a city shelter with her two children says she just needs "decent housing" for her family.

Homelessness is obviously too big a problem for any one person or agency to solve. Many people and agencies have ideas and potential solutions. This situation is ripe for collaboration, but first someone will have to bring all these people and agencies (and probably several others) together to find a common vision. One strong personality or agency may already have a vision that they want others to "buy into." That may work if there are enough incentives, or if that vision is close enough to others' ideas that they can readily join in. But it can backfire too, if there is not true consensus or "buy-in" on each person or agency's part. Taking the time to explore the vision and develop goals everyone supports will pay off in the long run.

Lack of agreed-upon ground rules

Many potential collaborations fail because they don't take the time to establish agreement on ground rules. Here is an example of a ground rule that can avoid misunderstandings in an interagency group: Any major changes in direction or hiring must be agreed on by the Collaboration Committee, but decisions about scheduling and carrying out projects already agreed upon can be made by staff.

Specific ground rules for meetings are also helpful. The following "Quality Meeting Guidelines" are used by the New York State Developmental Disabilities Planning Council:

1. The agenda is published in advance of the meeting.
2. Participants are punctual.
3. Meetings start at the specified time.
4. Meetings are uninterrupted.
5. Participants listen actively.
6. There are no one-to-one or side meetings.
7. There is active participation.

8. Participants are willing to reach a kind of consensus: "Although I may not agree with the team's decision, I can support it because it has been reached through a fair and open process that has considered my point of view."

9. Participants share responsibility for the team's progress.

10. There is freedom to check process and ground rules.

11. Participants respect the agenda.

12. Timekeeping is observed.

These ground rules are offered as guidelines; your group will need to develop its own. The process of agreeing on ground rules is as important as the list you come up with.

Lack of skill in working constructively with conflict

Conflict is inevitable in collaborations. It can even be a benefit, because it can deepen the group's understanding of each person or agency's point of view. Sometimes conflict is as simple as a family worker and a family member disagreeing politely. Sometimes it can grow into hurt feelings or open anger, in which people start to take sides. Frustration is a common feeling in collaborations. If conflict is not handled skillfully, it can easily break down a collaborative project.

Sometimes people gain power and control in a group by not moving forward on agreed upon goals, or by passively blocking actions. For example, a family member may never say she disagrees with the family's plan or state her concerns, but she may not help a project move forward either. Such behaviors need to be named and discussed. By dealing early with these behaviors, silent concerns can be shared and addressed.

You may find that there are reasons why a person is behaving this way, reasons related to unspoken fears about the direction the family is taking, or resentment about a past incident. If nobody deals with these behaviors, they can begin to spread, eventually undermining the group's effectiveness.

The same thing can happen in an interagency group. Maybe a group member is afraid he'll lose his job, or is remembering a time when he felt left out of your project. The group's leader or another designated person may want to bring these concerns up individually with this person outside of a meeting.

Using the communication and goal-setting skills learned earlier, you or another skilled group member may be able to help this person decide how he wants to handle feelings about the group: whether to resign, or whether he could openly state his concerns and then recommit to the collaboration group as a positive team member. If conflict is significantly slowing progress, the group may want to call in a skilled mediator to facilitate a few meetings.

The communication skills you learned in Chapter 2 will help you handle conflict well before it blows up. Listening well, reflecting what another person tells you to make sure you understand, and expressing your own thoughts and feelings respectfully will go a long way toward resolving conflict.

Lack of appropriate incentives

In the best situations, people want to collaborate on a project just because they see a need and want to help. In reality, it is often unrealistic to expect the families you work with, your co-workers, or other agencies to put much time into collaborating unless they can benefit in some way. This is not because everyone is selfish; it is because people and agencies already have much to do without taking on your projects.

What are some appropriate incentives?

- For the families you work with:
    - being able to meet their own goal
    - learning a teamwork process they can use with other people in their lives

- For your co-workers, incentives could include:
  - meeting a need or solving a problem that also affects people they work with
  - streamlining a procedure, so their job is easier
  - trust that you will help them out in return
  - an opportunity to learn new skills or grow professionally
  - looking good to their supervisor or co-workers
  - time away from an unpleasant task or place
  - higher pay
  - job security
- For other agencies, incentives can include all of those listed above for families and co-workers, plus:
  - the ability to offer a much-needed service for families (or a more effective way of working with families)
  - new grant money
  - an opportunity to learn more about other agencies and have your agency be better understood
  - an opportunity to get to know other people who work with the same families
  - a chance to increase their own visibility in the community, or to "make a name" for themselves
  - a feeling that what you are proposing will be "big," and they don't want to be left out

Incentives can help the collaboration process by encouraging people to join and stay with the effort. Incentives become a problem if people or agencies agree to something they don't believe in or don't really want to do, for hidden motives. For example, it can undermine any potential collaboration if a family agrees to enter your agency's family development program because it is the only way they can get subsidized housing. Interagency collaboration will be undermined if an agency joins a collaborative project in the hopes of winning grant money, even though they don't have a real commitment to the proposed work.

If you are the one calling people together to discuss a possible collaboration, you can begin by briefly explaining what you are concerned about, what you want to do about it, and why you need their help. Then you can ask for their ideas and reasons for joining in (and what would keep them away from the collaboration). This same first step works with families, co-workers, and other agencies.

L. The bigger picture: How agency, state, and national policies affect your work

As a family development worker, you work with people and their hopes and problems. When they describe their goals and problems to you, it is usually in very personal terms. They say things like:

> I couldn't afford not to go right back to work when my second baby was born, even though the WIC nurse said it would be good to breastfeed as long as I could. I tried breastfeeding and working, but the babysitter would always give my baby a bottle, so pretty soon my baby didn't want to breastfeed any more.

People seldom relate their problems to state or national policies. It would be rare for a mother describing her problems to you to say:

> In other countries, mothers are paid an allowance for several months or years to stay home with their babies. If the United States had family policies like that, I could have gotten my baby off to a better start.

Yet state and national policies (or the lack of policies) have a profound impact on the daily lives and decisions of families, and on your ability to help them. Funding availability and funding cuts have an obvious effect on families and the agencies that work with them. Yet funding is not the only way that state and national policies affect families and agencies. When research shows that a certain way of working with families is highly effective (for example, home visiting), the people making funding decisions often make more money available for programs using that method. When an influential agency or group adopts policies promoting a certain approach (for example, the family development and empowerment approach), more and more agencies begin to use that approach.

Communicating with elected officials

An important aspect of collaboration is to let your elected officials know what helps families to develop healthy self-reliance. You can also teach families how to become good citizens in the same way, by providing opportunities for them to meet with elected officials and government staff who create the policies that affect families. Most elected officials want to do what is best for families, and need your help (and that of the families you work with) to know what really works.

In a focus group, workers talked about how much it matters that politicians understand and can advocate for your work:

> If the Commissioner's mother has Alzheimer's disease, you know, we all celebrate. Or we hear the rumor that a politician's mother is in a nursing home. I'm counting on that. What about former presidents with Alzheimer's?

> But the problem is that for other agencies, such as the preventive programs, politicians are not going to know somebody using those type of programs. So you really can't count on these folks understanding.

In an interview, one worker said:

> When you work for the government, you have rules and regulations. No worker can change the rules immediately. You can try to work within the rules and when you have chance, you can meet with the decision makers, you can express what you think.

How can you and the families you work with help politicians understand and have the information they need?

- State and federal representatives often have hearings in their districts where they want to hear from local people. Discuss with your supervisor whether it is appropriate for you to attend these hearings and encourage family members you are working with to go, too. Although it may seem intimidating to speak at such a meeting, once there, you and the family members may find that your practical knowledge of what families need is just what politicians want and need to hear. Think of the examples you can give as stories they can take back and use when they are debating in the legislature.

- If your agency guidelines permit, call, fax, e-mail, or write your elected officials and express your opinion. They usually have offices in their home district as well as in the state capital or Washington, so it doesn't have to be a long distance call. If you've heard or read something that you need more information about, call your legislator's office. Their staff want to help voters make their opinions heard and are happy to help.

- Make sure you vote in every election (local, school board, state, and national) and encourage the families you work with to register and vote. Voting is one way of showing a healthy interdependence with our communities. While it may not be appropriate for you, as an employee of your agency, to advocate for a particular position or piece of legislation, it is an important part of the empowerment process to encourage the families you work with to understand and participate in the democratic process.

When one state legislator at a lobbying workshop was asked what workers could do to be most effective in communicating with politicians, he said that so often they see angry people who may have a right to be angry. But what really helps, he said, is when people see that he is a human being too, and relate to him as if they believed that he really was a good person, trying to do his best for the people he serves. He asked human service workers to bring him information and stories about the real lives of people in his community. Using your family development skills, you can see your politicians' strengths, identify shared goals, and reflect them back to him or her.

Collaborating with community leaders

Politicians are not the only people with influence who need to understand your work and the needs of families. It's important to collaborate with business people and community leaders as well.

In a focus group, a worker said:

> I'm really concerned with the fact that all of our efforts are geared to those that we already stigmatize and label as the people who need assistance. I would love to see family development also offered to and spoken about with people that have everything and where things seem to be working well. Because what the empowerment model is encouraging within a community is for the community to assume more responsibility for itself, and this can only happen if people who are regarded as having what they need, understand how the approaches used with families affect them.
>
> In most communities, there is tremendous difference between the upper middle class and people that are struggling economically and otherwise. You often hear, "I paid my taxes, I don't need to spend time or do other things to help," or, "Why do we need a sliding fee scale? I put myself through school and I'm not going to support Joe Blow over there in the apartments."
>
> Many people in the human service sector have already been trying for many years to use an empowerment model. It's something we are all committed to even if it wasn't in a curriculum. Now we need to reach the masses.

Another worker affirmed this view:

> All families have needs, they're just different kinds of needs. And all families (and individuals, too) feel unempowered to a large extent. We all deal with bureaucracies, we all have to deal with schools, so it really does cut across, and I think probably you guys are right, we need to look at everybody as a stakeholder. The middle and upper classes are as much stakeholders in this.

In many communities, workers have joined or offered to speak about family development at local civic groups or service organizations, such as Kiwanis or Rotary, so that they will get to know people from the business sector. These organizations are often concerned about the same issues that you are—education, employment, job training—and they have the resources to make things happen.

In summary, remember that funders, whether they are local, state, or federal agencies, or foundations, recognize how important it is for agencies to collaborate with each other and with families. Many funders know that collaboration is important at the level of service delivery and at the level of policy-making. As a front-line worker, your ability to collaborate effectively with families, and with front-line workers from other agencies, is vital to your work.

It is just as important to learn how to represent your agency skillfully, because the way front-line workers do their jobs has a big impact on interagency collaborations. If you do your job well, your agency is more likely to be asked to collaborate with others in your community.

M. Interagency training: A key to interagency collaboration

Interagency training such as the Family Development Training and Credential program is a powerful tool for promoting interagency collaborations. When staff from several different agencies participate in the same training, they get to know each other and the services other agencies offer. They also begin to speak the same language, and use the same approach to working with families.

A worker in a focus group was enthusiastic about the potential for interagency training based on her experience:

> One of the great things that comes out of it is then the people that you're working with have the same philosophy. They're striving for the same goals. We're all working with families with the same mindset. And that's going to be just nothing but wonderful for the families. And if the workers can get the same philosophy going, then, you know, we'll really be able to pull as a team.

Another worker said:

> The networking is good, sitting down on a staff level with people from DSS and other agencies, getting to know people and resources. We can hear each other's perspectives. It would personalize it a lot too. Sometimes we're on the phone and we don't have a clue who we're talking to. Even though we're involved with the same families, it can be a nightmare if the philosophies don't match. I live with that. It can be a power struggle, but if you can get all these people in a room . . .

When families who have received services are included in this training (for example, as potential peer counselors), it can also help collaborations grow between agencies and the families they serve.

Collaboration between families and workers, and across agencies, is essential to families becoming self-reliant. Yet collaborations are not always easy. Fortunately, the same skills you use to help families meet their goals also work well in helping agencies collaborate with each other.

Reference

Merkel-Holquin, L. A. (1997). *Innovations for children's services for the 21st century: Family group decision making and patch*. Englewood, CO: American Humane Association.

Activities to Extend Learning

Chapter 10
Collaboration and Community Support

A. The importance of community

1. Write a reflection on how supportive overall you feel your community is to the families you work with, why and/or why not?

2. Describe the aspects of your community that make it a good place for families, and aspects that make it hard for families to live there.

3. As a family worker, what does the statement "We are all each other's children and brothers and sisters and mother and father" mean to you? How do you help foster a supportive community where you live?

B. Helping families identify and strengthen their informal support network

1. Describe some community groups available where you live that help support individuals and families. What are some reasons people belong to these groups? Choose one community group and describe how you think that group fills its members' need to belong?

2. Some families consistently use helping agencies as their primary source of informal support. How does this affect a worker-family relationship when the family has few friends and informal supports to turn to? How can a worker help a family that seems to rely mostly on workers or agencies for their informal support?

C. Support and advocacy groups

1. Choose a support or advocacy group in your community that you are not familiar with and arrange to speak with its leader or facilitator. Learn why and how it was started, reasons why people become involved, and the purpose of the group. Read their brochure or other promotional materials. Write a reflection on what you learned and how you feel the group fulfills the need they serve in your community.

2. Choose a statewide or nationally-based support or advocacy group that you are not familiar with. Consult their website or contact a regional office to gather information. Describe how the state or national organization supports local chapters in helping individuals and families. How does this organization advocate for individuals and families at the state or national level?

3. Talk with someone who has participated in a support or advocacy group in your community. Why did he/she get involved and how was it helpful to them? What did he/she learn from the experience?

D. Family Conferences

1. Propose a family conference to your own family. Arrange to talk with your family members when they are relaxed and receptive. To begin, ask "What important goal can our family work on together?" in your own words. Listen to their ideas and come up with a goal everyone is willing to work on. Then, briefly describe to them the steps of a family conference. Note their reactions. If they resist, explain the benefits and how it can help your family. After the discussion, write a reflection on the experience.

2. The chapter states, "Family conferences can change the balance of power in a family in ways that may be uncomfortable to some family members. Think of a time in your life when your views or concerns were not included in the process of making an important family decision.

How did you feel? How does giving each family member a "voice" affect a family's decision making process?

E. Teaching leadership skills to families

1. How might a family member feel about facilitating a family conference for the first time? What steps might be easiest? What steps might be more difficult? What could you do to help a family member with the more difficult steps?

2. How could you help a family member who wants to facilitate a family conference with the rest of his/her family, but is facing resistance from them when introducing the topic?

F. Collaboration

1. Define collaboration with examples from your own work situation.

2. Describe two experiences you have had with collaboration: one positive, one you wish had gone differently.

G. Building respectful relationships with community service partners

1. How do you, as a family worker, network and build relationships with other family-serving agencies that might lead to interagency collaborations?

2. In your opinion, who are your agency's "gatekeepers" (people in your community whose support will help your agency do its work and whose negative impressions will hinder it)? How does your program/agency keep these people informed about your agency's services? How do these people, in turn, support your agency in the community?

H. Coordination and cooperation: The first steps toward collaboration

1. Describe the differences between coordination, cooperation, and collaboration. Give two examples of each from your work or personal life.

2. Sometimes agencies decide to collaborate when it is really more appropriate to coordinate or cooperate in offering services together. Describe one situation when the most appropriate way to offer an interagency service is through coordination; one, through cooperation; and one, through collaboration.

3. Why is effective family development work between a worker and family a good example of collaboration? Describe a situation to illustrate how the process of collaboration works between a worker and family.

I. Different levels of collaboration: Individuals, front-line workers, and systems

1. Describe an individual-level collaboration.

2. List three reasons why collaboration is often needed at the systems level for services to be delivered more effectively to families.

J. Keys to successful collaboration

1. Describe a successful interagency collaboration in which you took part or are doing so now. Using the seven steps, explain how the group applied the keys to successful collaboration to make the partnership work and achieve their goals.

2. Think of an interagency collaboration your agency is involved with right now. Answer the following questions or talk with an agency colleague to find out the answers: What was the inspiration for creating an interagency collaboration? How were partners' tasks and responsibilities assigned? How do the partners keep each other informed? What new skills has your agency learned as a result of the collaboration?

K. Practical pitfalls of collaboration (and how to turn them into advantages)

1. Describe examples of some of the pitfalls of collaboration that have occurred in your community or that you think could happen. For each, describe one way the pitfall could be turned into an advantage.

2. How can the pitfalls of collaboration influence effective working relationships between family workers of partnering agencies? What can family workers do to help their agencies turn the practical pitfalls of collaboration into advantages?

3. The chapter states, "Conflict is inevitable in collaboration. It can even be a benefit, because it can deepen the group's understanding of each person or agency's point of view." What do you think about this? Describe an experience when a conflict within an interagency collaboration helped deepen each partner's understanding of the goal or of each other.

L. The bigger picture: How agency, state, and national policies affect your work

1. Describe in some detail, three examples of state or national policies affecting the families you work with.

2. How can you encourage families to take an active role in influencing policies that affect their ability to become self-reliant? Think of examples from your experience when you have or might have taken this action.

M. Interagency training: A key to interagency collaboration

1. Describe how interagency training can promote interagency collaboration. Give a specific example.

2. How has your participation in FDC training helped you recognize ways that interagency training can promote interagency collaboration?

Skills Practices

These skills practices are a suggested list. You may also develop your own skills practice or make modifications to the ones listed below to help you create a meaningful and manageable plan.

1. Review the sections in this chapter on Family Group Conferences. Talk with a co-worker or supervisor about how you might use this process with families you serve. Try it out with a family you are working with, who is receptive to the idea, and write a reflection on the experience. What are the benefits and challenges?

2. Attend a support group meeting in your area to learn how communities support individuals and families who share a common situation. In advance, contact the group's leader and explain your purpose for attending. At the meeting, use skillful listening to learn how members relate to and support each other. Write a reflection on the experience and describe ways you feel support groups help families feel connected and supported in their community. (Note: Choose a different Skills Practice if you attended a support group meeting for your Chapter 8 Skills Practice or an Activity to Extend Learning.)

3. Arrange to talk with an informal "gatekeeper" in your community (a person in an official or unofficial position of respect who refers families to your agency and whose negative impressions will hinder your agency's efforts). Provide up-to-date information about your agency's services and ask for her/his ideas and suggestions about ways to build positive relationships with families and other service providers in your community. Ask about areas of need in the community that she/he feels are not being met. Describe how interagency collaborations your agency is involved with help bridge gaps in support or services. Write a reflection summarizing this gatekeeper's impression of your agency's strengths, challenges, and recommendations for increasing your agency's ability to collaborate effectively.

4. Arrange to talk with a family worker from another service provider in your community to network and build a respectful relationship with her/his agency. Choose a family worker who you know from working together on an interagency committee or who has referred families to your agency. Ask if she/he would like to meet for coffee or lunch to talk about ways the agencies can work together more effectively. At the meeting, use techniques for "communicating with skill and heart" to develop a mutually respectful relationship and share helpful information about ways the agencies can cooperate or coordinate services. Write a reflection describing the skills you used to develop a respectful relationship and how you think the meeting will help families involved with both of your agencies.

5. Before the next agency staff meeting or in-service, talk with your supervisor and offer to share a brief explanation of the differences between interagency coordination, cooperation, and collaboration to other family workers and staff. If your supervisor agrees, prepare notes to explain the differences using examples from your own agency's services and programs. At the meeting, share the information, present the examples, and facilitate a short discussion to respond to questions and comments. Write a reflection on how you prepared for the meeting, how it went, and how the group responded to the information you presented.

6. Arrange to talk with a colleague (co-worker, supervisor, or leader) who coordinates a program or service of a successful interagency collaboration. Ask her/him to describe how the collaboration progressed through the following steps: developing a partnership; assessing reasons for collaborating; setting goals and making a plan; learning and practicing skills of collaboration, and celebrating accomplishments. Write a reflection describing what you learned, the strengths of each partner, and how the collaboration help bridge any gaps in support or services to families.

Conclusion

I once asked a family worker, "Why did you go into family development work?" She thought for a moment and then replied, "I don't think I chose to go into family development work; I think it chose me." You may have chosen to work as a family development professional for a variety of reasons: to help families you work with, to feel good about the work you do, to support your own family financially, or to make an important contribution to your community and the world. Whatever the reason, you make a difference in the lives of children and families every day, in a way that no one else can.

I am deeply grateful to the families, workers, colleagues, and leaders who shared their knowledge and wisdom to nurture the collaboration that has brought this Handbook to its third edition. I hope this book has provided useful tools that will continue to support and guide you in family development and in the hopes, dreams, and goals you have for your own life.

I wish you peace, happiness, and success, whether family development is the profession you have chosen, or the family development profession has chosen you. May you touch others' lives as they touch yours in ways that fill your own bone-deep longing for freedom, safety, self-respect, and hope as you make unique and important contributions to your family, community, and the world.

Be well,

Claire Forest

Comments and feedback

Please send feedback about your use of *Empowerment Skills for Family Workers: A Worker Handbook*, including:

- its readability
- information that you feel should be added or updated, on any of the topics
- suggested changes (with reasons)
- suggested refinements in the Activities to Extend Learning sections
- success stories

Feedback from family members, workers, program directors, college instructors, or others using the handbook (or affected by its recommendations) will be greatly appreciated, and will be used to update future editions.

Please include your name, position, address, and phone number. Send your feedback via e-mail to Claire Forest at cnd3@cornell.edu.

General Appendix

Studies that Shaped the FDC—And Results of New Ones

The Family Development Credential program was initially built upon the theories of human ecology and parental empowerment, as well as years of professional practice by the author and others in testing and applying these theories. When the first edition of *Empowerment Skills for Family Workers* was written, these concepts were relatively new. Now that the FDC has helped these ideas to become more widely known to family practitioners, many front-line workers and their supervisors have wanted to know the basis of the research behind FDC and are also interested in newer research. This 2015 edition provides an overview of the research underlying the FDC as well as the results of more recent FDC program studies.

Bronfenbrenner's *The Ecology of Human Development*

Cornell University's Urie Bronfenbrenner described his work *The Ecology of Human Development* as an "interface between developmental psychology and public policy" (1979, p. xiv). He believed that research could—and should—help improve human lives but criticized prevailing methods of psychological research and questioned the resulting conclusions. He commented that "much of contemporary developmental psychology is the science of the strange behavior of children in strange situations with strange adults for the briefest possible periods of time" (p. 19).

In this influential book, Bronfenbrenner introduced his ecology of human development theory. He understood that repeated, enduring interactions, such as feeding or playing with a child, form the foundation of human development. He called these "proximal processes" and knew that for these processes to be effective, they must be consistent and positive. He recognized that poverty interferes with healthy proximal processes because of factors such as crowding, instability, poverty, and time limitations. To help counteract the growing chaos of US family life, Bronfenbrenner designed and championed social programs, including Head Start.

He knew that although families are affected by relatives, neighborhoods, schools, jobs (or their lack), laws, and social policies, the process also works in reverse: individuals and families likewise have an impact on these other factors. Sometimes this impact is profound, especially over time. For example, as more mothers entered the workforce, lawmakers and employers (at the later urging of Bronfenbrenner and others) began offering child care subsidies, and schools and day-care centers responded by offering after-school child care. Many scholars, including Bronfenbrenner's Cornell University colleagues and graduate students, critiqued and refined his initial theory, sometimes with his collaboration.

In his book, Bronfenbrenner also suggested that researchers not study children in university laboratories, but in the *environments* in which they develop: families, neighborhoods, schools, and day-care centers. He understood that although much of children's growth occurs within these close settings, development is also indirectly yet profoundly affected by more distant environments and influences, such as a parent's workplace or public policy.

Using everyday words, Forest (2003) adapted Bronfenbrenner's (1979) ecological model into a "Family Circles Model" for the FDC text *Empowerment Skills for Family Workers* and in 2003, with Bronfenbrenner's approval, added an outer circle ("Nature") to recognize that the natural environment contains and interacts with all the other circles. Credentialed workers use the Family Circles Model to help families identify stressors and supports in their lives, along with ways they can reduce their stressors and strengthen their supports.

Parental Empowerment

Cornell's Moncrieff Cochran, through his observations within the ecology of human development (Family Matters) study, which he codirected with Bronfenbrenner and William Cross, Jr., described the developmental stages of a parental empowerment process. Cochran recognized that as people change how they look at themselves, their relationships with family and friends also change. They gather information about how they might improve their own situation as well as that of their community, and often become involved in making a difference.

Cochran and Henderson's (1986) definition of parental empowerment was informed by the work of earlier researchers and community leaders, especially Brazilian community activist Paulo Freire and German sociologist Jürgen Habermas. Freire taught poor farmers to read, encouraged them to talk with each other about issues that affected their lives, and to write and speak up to those in power. In *Pedagogy of the Oppressed* (1970/2007), Freire introduced the concept of *conscientização*—consciousness-raising about injustice. He worked *with*, not *for*, people. In his next book, *Education for Critical Consciousness* (1973/2003), Freire suggested that "the democratization of culture has to start from what we are and what we do as a people, not from what some people think and want for us" (p. 81). This concept forms a cornerstone of the Family Development program: through the Family Development Plan, workers help families voice their own goals and ideas for reaching them. The pen needs to be in the family's hands, not the family worker's.

Parental empowerment is also built on the theory of "communicative action" described by Habermas (1984). This involves a process through which critical discourse regarding societal problems can lead to taking action to remedy them. According to Habermas, the ability to look critically at one's circumstances is key to being able to foster change in society and in one's own life. Critical discourse—talking with another about personal or societal issues and deciding whether and how to take action—is key. The term "critical" does not refer to criticism, but to the ability to look deeply at one's own life, with fresh eyes and no assumptions. "Discourse" refers to conversation or writing between two or more people, for the purpose of considering anew something previously taken for granted.

Cochran and Henderson (1986) combined Freire's notion of working with, not for, economically disadvantaged people with Habermas' ideas on the role of critical discourse about social problems into an approach they called "parental empowerment." They described parental empowerment as a "power with" relationship, in contrast to the "power over" approach more common in social services. The term "power with" was first used by organizational consultant Mary Follett (1924), who used it to describe more equal relationships in business settings. A key component of the parental empowerment approach is understanding that empowerment is not something a person can do for someone else through compassion or force. Empowerment happens when people set their own goals for change. The role of helping systems, whether family, friends, or agencies, is to *support*—not to set—the goals of those they serve.

Together, the concepts of ecology of human development and parental empowerment guide FDC workers in helping families and communities. FDC workers are taught to coach and share power with families as they reflect on experiences in the context of their own culture and community. The families then set and pursue *their own* goals for improving their lives in that context.

Transformative Learning

My own recent research showed that critical discourse between credentialed workers and the families they coached led to "transformative learning." Before describing that study, however, some background on transformative learning is necessary. Jack Mezirow used the myth of Sisyphus to introduce the theory of transformative learning and illustrate the need for "perspective transformation" (Mezirow, 1978b): Sisyphus was doomed to push a boulder up a mountain, and then, with the end of his heavy labor in sight, watch it crash down. Sisyphus would then once again attempt to push the boulder back up the mountain, and was thus forever doomed to repeat this ineffective cycle (Camus, 1955). Mezirow (1978b) suggested that perspective transformation could have freed Sisyphus from his futile labor:

> This involves learning how we are caught in our own history and are reliving it. We learn to become critically aware of the cultural and psychological assumptions that have influenced the way we see ourselves and our relationships and the way we pattern our lives. [This] ... refers to the structure of cultural assumptions within which new experience is assimilated to—and transformed by—one's past experience. It is a personal paradigm for understanding ourselves and our relationships. (p. 101)

Mezirow and colleagues (1990) suggested that a "disorienting dilemma" (p. xvi) such as a divorce, job loss, or health crisis, often sparked a perspective transformation, which he considered a first step to transformative learning (p. 101). When something happens that no longer fits a person's way of understanding, a transformation can occur. Adding knowledge, skills, or increasing competencies within the present perspective no longer works; integrating new experience within the same way of looking at things no longer solves the conflict. The person must critically reflect upon his or her own reactions (p. 104).

Mezirow (1978b) outlined a three-phase cycle of transformation:

1. *alienation* (from prescribed social roles)
2. *reframing* (restructuring one's conception of reality and one's place in it)
3. *effecting change* (through one's own initiative) (p. 105)

Mezirow (1978a) developed the theory of transformative learning, drawing on his research with middle-class white women returning to college. Over the past three decades, hundreds of scholars (Cranton, 2002; Merriam, Caffarella, & Baumgartner, 2007; Taylor, 1997, 2000, 2007; Tennant, 1993) have studied transformative learning, but few have studied this concept with people living in poverty, despite its inherent pattern of relentless labor with little hope of escape to a better life (as in Mezirow's example of Sisyphus)—an all-too-familiar circumstance for families living on low incomes.

I wondered, "What about transformative learning in factory workers, fast-food servers, hotel chamber maids—the kind of workers welfare reform assumes parents living in poverty will become? Do they feel doomed to a Sisyphus-like struggle? Can transformative learning free their lives from drudgery and limited prospects? Do credentialed family workers adequately foster the transformative learning process?

The study *Mothers overcoming barriers of poverty: The significance of a relationship with a credentialed coach* (Forest, 2009) examined how 25 randomly selected rural and urban mothers living in poverty in the United States and their 10 FDC-credentialed workers (coaches) used healthy mother-coach relationships grounded in the FDC process to help families identify and overcome barriers to self-reliance. The study looked at (1) barriers mothers encountered and the methods used to overcome them, (2) how mothers and workers perceived their relationship, and (3) aspects of this relationship that empowered mothers to pursue goals for a better life.

Before working with a credentialed coach, these mothers' ability to set and pursue goals was limited by personal, family, and economic factors, including chaos. The study found that mother-coach relationships reduced these barriers. Supportive, critically reflective conversations between mothers and coaches resulted in mothers' transformative learning. In other words, FDC-credentialed coaches formed mutually respectful relationships with families, using the skills learned in the *Empowerment Skills for Family Workers* course, to help the families reflect critically on their situations and then take action. Many of the families in this study experienced transformative learning, which appears to have been a significant factor in their empowerment.

The updated Family Development Plan (see Chapter 1) guides families and their credentialed workers through transformative conversations in which families set their own major goals and identify the steps to lead them there. They subsequently revisit the Family Development Plan at least three times, critically reflecting on their continuing development, so they are less likely to repeat ineffective patterns from their past.

References

Bronfenbrenner, U. (1979). The ecology of human development: Experiments by nature and design. Cambridge, MA: Harvard University Press.

Camus, A. (1955). *The myth of* Sisyphus. New York: Random Vintage.

Cochran, M., & Henderson, C. R., Jr. (1986). *Family matters: Evaluation of the Parental Empowerment Program: Summary of a final report to the National Institute of Education*. Ithaca, NY: Cornell University Department of Human Development.

Cranton, P. (2002). Teaching for transformation. *New Directions for Adult and Continuing Education, 2002*(93), 63–72.

Follett, M. P. (1924/1951/2013). *The creative experience*. Eastford, CT: Martino.

Forest, C. (2003). *Empowerment skills for family workers*. Ithaca, NY: Family Development Press.

Freire, P. (1970/2007). *Pedagogy of the oppressed* (trans. Myra Ramos). New York: Continuum/Bloomsbury.

Freire, P. (1973/2003). *Education for critical consciousness*. New York: Continuum/Bloomsbury.

Habermas, J. (1984). *The Theory of Communicative Action, vol. 1: The theory and rationalization of society*. Boston: Beacon.

Merriam, S. B., Caffarella, R. S., & Baumgartner, L. M. (2007). *Learning in adulthood: A comprehensive guide*. San Francisco: Jossey-Bass.

Mezirow, J. (1978a). *Education for perspective transformation: Women's re-entry programs in community colleges*. New York: Center for Adult Education, Teachers' College, Columbia University.

Mezirow, J. (1978b). Perspective transformation. *Adult Education Quarterly, 28*, 100–110.

Mezirow, J. & Associates. (1990). *Fostering critical reflection in adulthood: A guide to transformative and emancipatory learning*. San Francisco: Jossey-Bass.

Taylor, E. W. (1997). Building upon the theoretical debate: A critical review of the empirical studies of Mezirow's Transformative Learning Theory. *Adult Education Quarterly, 48*, 34–59.

Taylor, E. W. (2000). Fostering Mezirow's Transformative Learning Theory in the adult education classroom: A critical review. *Canadian Journal for the Study of Adult Education, 14*(2), 1–28.

Taylor, E. W. (2007). An update of transformative learning theory: A critical review of the empirical research (1999–2005). *International Journal of Lifelong Education, 26*, 173–191.

Tennant, M. C. (1993). Perspective transformation and adult development. *Adult Education Quarterly, 4*, 34–42.

The FDC Code of Ethics

The FDC Code of Ethics was developed by Wojciech Konopka, MSW, in collaboration with the Cornell Empowering Families Project and statewide FDC instructors, portfolio advisors and supporters. We encourage you to share and discuss the FDC Code of Ethics, which follows, with everyone in your organization and to refer to it whenever your agency develops and implements agency-wide staff policies. Using the Code as a guide will help you and other workers in your agency respect the individuality and value the collective contributions of all staff members as well as the family members you serve and support.

Introduction by Wojciech Konopka, MSW [44]

Ethics is defined as the systematic exploration of questions about how we should act in relation to others.

Ethical dilemmas come in all shapes and sizes. Our task is to prevent and deal appropriately with ethical problems. The thoughtful study of ethics and FDC Code of Ethics can not only benefit one's professional interactions, but also all areas of one's life.

Why do we do, or not do, the "right thing"? Often it is because of an established rule or law, but without thoughtful reflection, our ethical decisions are too often based on our own moral judgments and standards, as well as our personal needs. As we study ethics we touch on conscience, our basic inner guidance system, and the consequences of our actions. Discussion of ethics is vital and can motivate us to reach for a higher standard of integrity in all areas of our life.

The development of our moral judgment is an ongoing and continuous process. Practical tools such as the FDC Code of Ethics can help us make the right ethical decisions. Following rules, laws, codes of conduct are all a part of living an ethical life, but the real strength comes in the principles that we internalize and integrate into our lives. When we do this, behaving in an ethical manner becomes automatic.

A well-rounded life-long education in ethics considers character, conscience, courage, and other principles and traits that play a part in our decision-making process. Rules do not cover every situation. Life is full of gray areas. The FDC Code of Ethics provides a reference for developing skills of ethical conduct.

These principles can help us find direction in murky situations. As ethical people, what can we do when we find ourselves in a situation that presents an ethical dilemma? Often the "right thing" is obvious, but sometimes it is not easy to know if you have made the right choice or chosen the higher principle. The Code helps us consider our options, and refine our responses.

---

[44] Our thanks to Wojciech Konopka, MSW, for his leadership role in the development of the FDC Code of Ethics, and to the FDC facilitators, field advisors, and supporters who collaborated with him.

THE FDC CODE OF ETHICS

FDC recognizes that many decisions required of those who work with families are of a moral and ethical nature. The FDC Code of Ethics gives guidelines for responsible behavior for resolving ethical dilemmas encountered by FDC workers, field advisors, and trainers. The Code also establishes shared professional ideals and principles that affirm our commitment to strengthening families. The guidelines and principles are intended to provide a basis for conscientious decision-making.

Section A: Families and Ethics

Principle: The goal of family development is best accomplished by ethical care and concern in helping families identify, set and achieve goals of healthy self-reliance and interdependence with their communities.

Family development professionals can support families in identifying, setting and achieving goals in the family development process by:

- Developing strengths through collaboration and promotion of self-esteem

- Supporting family empowerment by helping families build upon their strengths and competencies

- Safeguarding confidentiality in working with families and treating all information with care

- Maintaining safe, healthy, nurturing, and mutually respectful relationships and refraining from inappropriate physical, verbal, or sexual conduct with family members and co-workers

- Establishing relationships based on mutual trust and respect

- Respecting the dignity and valuing individual differences of all families and cultures as well as their customs, and beliefs

- Respectfully interrupting and handling oppressive behavior that is disrespectful, degrading, dangerous, exploitative, intimidating, psychologically damaging, or physically harmful toward others

- Recognizing and striving to eliminate practices that discriminate based on race, ethnicity, gender, class, family form, religion, physical and mental ability, age, and sexual orientation

- Reporting suspected abuse and neglect of children and adults to appropriate authorities

- Enhancing their knowledge base, skills, and competencies to work effectively with others through continuing education and training.

Section B. Ethics in the Workplace

Principle: All individuals and families have the right to privacy and confidentiality.

Family development professionals protect the right to privacy and confidentiality by:

- Obtaining written permission to provide information to others and knowing the legal guidelines and procedures for sharing information based on situations of abuse, neglect, or in life-threatening situations

- Developing relationships that strictly avoid potential exploitation of others or using relationships for private advantage or personal gain

- Maintaining confidentiality regarding information shared in meetings regarding individuals, problematic work situations and personal information

- Respecting a family's right to have access to records and receive assistance in interpreting them.

Section C. Workplace and Community Ethics

Principle: Family development professionals and their organizations coordinate, cooperate, and collaborate with families, agencies and other helping systems to develop and offer services and support to families.

Family development professionals and their organizations can establish and maintain relationships with families, agencies and other helping systems based on developing trust and mutual respect by:

- Sharing resources and information with families, colleagues and other agencies as appropriate

- Reporting unethical or incompetent behavior only after direct informal efforts to resolve conflicts have failed

- Providing the community with high-quality, culturally sensitive programs

- Recognizing the strengths and needs of families and communities and empowering them through research, education and advocacy

- Supporting policies that promote the empowerment of families and cooperating with other individuals and groups in these efforts.